Land and

Land and Revolution

*Nationalist Politics
in the West of Ireland
1891–1921*

FERGUS CAMPBELL

OXFORD
UNIVERSITY PRESS

OXFORD
UNIVERSITY PRESS

Great Clarendon Street, Oxford, OX2 6DP,
United Kingdom

Oxford University Press is a department of the University of Oxford.
It furthers the University's objective of excellence in research, scholarship,
and education by publishing worldwide. Oxford is a registered trade mark of
Oxford University Press in the UK and in certain other countries

First Edition published in 2005

Published in the United States of America by Oxford University Press
198 Madison Avenue, New York, NY 10016, United States of America

British Library Cataloguing in Publication Data
Data available

Library of Congress Cataloging in Publication Data
Data available

ISBN 978-0-19-954150-8

For my mother,
and in memory of my father

Acknowledgements

I first had the idea for this book when I was an undergraduate student at the University of Oxford in the early 1990s, but my interest in the west of Ireland was sparked much earlier by childhood visits to my grandfather's farm in county Galway. As I read about the Easter Rising, I wondered how people like the farmers whom I had met in Galway would have responded to Patrick Pearse's ideas about nationality, and why so many small farmers voted for Sinn Féin in the aftermath of the Easter Rising. That question provided the starting point for this book and although I have since turned my attention to broader questions, I have remained committed to writing the history of the ordinary people who lived in the west of Ireland at the end of the nineteenth and the beginning of the twentieth century.

In the course of my research, I have received help and support from many people. This book began as a Ph.D. thesis at the University of Bristol where I was privileged to work with three great historians: John Vincent, who provided inspiration and encouragement in the early stages of research; William Beinart, who brought a comparative perspective to bear on Irish agrarian history, and Roy Foster, who was an unfailing source of advice, criticism, and encouragement. At NUI Maynooth, I have learned a great deal from Vincent Comerford about the Irish land question, and I am most grateful to him for his exceptional generosity and continued support. Paul Bew, the Irish historian whose work has influenced me the most, provided invaluable support and criticism. Not only did Peter Hart suggest the title of the book, he also read and commented on the entire text, thereby improving each chapter. Tony Varley discussed many aspects of this book with me, helped in innumerable ways, and read and commented on the later chapters. Patrick Maume generously shared his encyclopedic knowledge of modern Irish history with me, and provided valuable criticism of several chapters. Paul Dillon discussed this book with me probably more often than he would have liked, and his often brilliant insights clarified a great deal about rural Irish society. My greatest intellectual debt, however, is to my friend and fellow historian Andrew Shields, who patiently read drafts of every chapter, discussed popular politics in the west of Ireland with me in endless detail, and continued to believe in the importance of the project even when my resolve wavered. His tactful comments have improved every page, and I could not have written this book without him. I completed this book as a Government of Ireland post-doctoral research fellow in the Department of Modern History, NUI Maynooth, and I am grateful to the Irish Research Council for the Humanities and Social Sciences for their support, and to all my colleagues and friends in Maynooth for making my years there such happy ones.

In Galway, I have benefited greatly from discussions with Gerry Cloonan, who generously provided a wealth of information, and helped me to unravel the intricacies of local politics in east Galway. I have also been fortunate enough to meet and interview some of the children (and grandchildren) of political and agrarian activists, who have shared both family lore and family papers with me. In particular, I owe a special debt to the late Mattie Finnerty who taught me so much about his native east Galway, and a great deal else.

My colleagues and friends at a number of institutions have made the study of history both stimulating and enjoyable, and it is a pleasure to thank Joost Augusteijn, Stephen Ball, Colin Barr, Gerry Bowe, Inga Brandes, James Brennan, Damien Carbery, Jim Cassin, Paul Clear, Colin Coulter, Tom Crean, Ken Crotty, John Cunningham, Cliff Davies, Enda Delaney, Anne Dolan, Terry Dooley, Martin Crossley Evans, Jane Garnett, Evi Gkotzaridis, Katrina Goldstone, Mick Gordon, Brian Hanley, Jim Herlihy, Mark Humphries, the late Dave Johnson, Eamon Kane, Mark Kendall, Liam Kennedy, Ben Levitas, Georgina Laragy, Tom Kenny (of Kenny's bookshop, Galway), Sean Lucey, Deirdre McAllister, Jim McAllister, Conor McCabe, Sinead McEneaney, Fearghal McGarry, Tim McMahon, Mairead MacQuaid, Ann Marie Mealey, Carmel O'Doherty, Sean and Claire O'Doherty, Ciarán Ó Duibhir, Gearóid Ó Tuathaigh, Chris Reid, Philip Sheppard, William Smyth, Jean Walker, Mike Wheatley, and Fergus White. My students at NUI Maynooth, and especially those at the Kilkenny campus, have been a joy to teach, and have often forced me to sharpen and clarify my ideas. I am grateful to all of them. I owe a special debt of gratitude to the Corcorans of London, and especially to Stephen, whose brilliant mind and loyal friendship were a great source of support until his death in 1996. To everyone else who has helped and supported me over the years (you know who you are), my thanks to all of you.

The staffs of the following libraries and archives were extremely helpful, and I am grateful for their patience, and for their permission to quote from documents in their care: the James Hardiman Library, NUI Galway; the John Paul II Library, NUI Maynooth; the National Library of Ireland;

the National Archives, Dublin; the Military Archives, Dublin; the University College Dublin Department of Irish Folklore; the Irish Valuation Office; the Trinity College, Dublin, archives; Special Collections, the Boole Library, University College, Cork; John Rylands Library at the University of Manchester; the University of Bristol library; the British Library; and the Public Record Office, London. Thanks also to Anthony Coughlan for permission to quote from documents in the C. D. Greaves archive. Patrick Kavanagh's 'Epic' is reprinted by kind permission of the Trustees of the Estate of the late Katherine B. Kavanagh, through the Jonathan Williams Literary Agency. I am grateful to James Keenan of NUI Maynooth for making the maps, and to Helen Litton for compiling the index.

At Oxford University Press, Ruth Parr has been unfailingly patient and supportive, Jackie Pritchard's excellent copy editing saved me from many errors and inconsistencies, and Kay Rogers, Anne Gelling and Louisa Lapworth brought the book successfully to completion.

My family have been a constant source of love, support, and friendship. Beedie and Tom Carroll (and family), Anne and Steve Fisher (and family), the Gilligans of Eyrecourt, Bee and John Hughes, Christine Jordan (and family), Johnny and Eleanor Jordan, Tony and Ita Jordan, and the Campbells of Naas and Thurles have all provided essential assistance over the years. I reserve special thanks for Padraic and Catherine Jordan, who helped me through the final stages of completing this book: Padraic's motivational speeches were (and continue to be) an inspiration! Annie and Michael Jordan, my late grandparents, were greatly loved and are greatly missed. My sister-in-law, Leah, and the Loughnanes of Chicago and Indiana, have been extremely supportive of me, and their generosity is warmly appreciated. My brother Sean has done more than he knows to keep this book (and me) on track. For his endless encouragement, patience, and advice, I will always be grateful. Finally, without my parents' belief in the importance of history, this project would never have got off the ground. I am indebted to my mother Margaret for countless acts of kindness and encouragement. My late father Sean was my first and best teacher. This book is dedicated to both of them.

F.C.

Colmanstown,
County Galway,
March 2004

Contents

List of Tables   xiii

Abbreviations   xv

Maps   xvii

Introduction   1

1. The 'Western Problem': Land and Politics in
   Connacht, 1891–1899   8

2. Popular Politics and the Making of the
   Wyndham Land Act, 1900–1903   42

3. The Ranch War and Irish Nationalist Politics, 1904–1910   85

4. The 'Law of the League': United Irish League Justice,
   1898–1910   124

5. The Evolution of Sinn Féin: Separatist Politics in County
   Galway, 1905–1918   166

6. Land and Revolution in the West of Ireland, 1918–1921   226

Conclusion   286

*Appendix I: Methodology and Sources Used to Identify
the Social Background of Nationalist Activists in
Galway, 1899–1921*   305

*Appendix II. Chronology of the War of Independence in
Galway, 1919–1921*   312

Bibliography   316

Index   333

List of Tables

1. Acreage and use of untenanted land in Connacht in 1907 — 15

2. The membership of the United Irish League, 1898–1901 — 30

3. Estimated annual land purchase figures in Ireland, 1881–1920 — 91

4. Number of combinations against the payment of rent identified in the Inspector General's monthly reports, January 1907–June 1908 — 98

5. Number of unlet grazing farms by county, 1905–1910 — 101

6. United Irish League membership and agitation, 1902–1908 — 105

7. The result of 100 cases heard at 36 United Irish League courts held in Ireland, 1900–1901 — 133

8. The frequency of penalties imposed by agrarian agitators in Ireland, 1902–1908 — 140

9. The occupations of the Kennyite and Hallinanite factions at Craughwell in 1911 — 163

10. The acreage occupied by Kennyites and Hallinanites who were farmers or eldest farmers' sons — 163

11. The ages of Kennyites and Hallinanites in 1911 — 163

12. Agrarian agitation in Ireland, 1907–1914 — 186

13. The occupations of the Galway secret society and the 1916 insurgents — 186

14. The valuation of the family farm of farmers and farmers' sons involved in the secret society and the Galway Rising — 187

15. The ages of the members of the Galway secret society and the 1916 rebels (in 1916) — 187

16. Previous political and social involvements of Sinn Féin officers in Galway in 1917–1918 — 223

17. The occupations of United Irish League and Sinn Féin officials in east Galway, 1899–1918 — 228

18. The valuation of the farms occupied by the farmers, farmers' sons, and shopkeeper-graziers who were members of the United Irish League and Sinn Féin, 1899–1918   228

19. The ages of officials of the United Irish League and Sinn Féin in 1918, and the United Irish League in 1899   229

20. Other affiliations of United Irish League and Sinn Féin officers   229

21. Agrarian agitation in Ireland, 1914–1918   239

22. The social composition of the south Galway IRA, 1917–1921   260

23. The valuation of farms of south Galway IRA members who were farmers or farmers' sons   260

24. Other political affiliations of the south Galway IRA, 1917–1921   260

25. Rurality of south Galway IRA members, 1917–1921   261

26. The age of members of the south Galway IRA (in 1918)   261

27. The occupations of the officers and the rank and file of the south Galway IRA, 1917–1921   261

28. The valuation of farms occupied by farmers and farmer's sons who were officers and rank and file members of the south Galway IRA, 1917–1921   262

29. Number of incidents and number of persons killed or seriously wounded during the War of Independence in Galway, 1919–1921   274

Abbreviations

AOH	Ancient Order of Hibernians
CD	contemporary documents
CDB	Congested Districts Board
CI	County Inspector
GAA	Gaelic Athletic Association
IFU	Irish Farmers' Union
IG	Inspector General
IGCI	Inspector General and County Inspector's monthly reports
IML	imleabhar [volume]
INF	Irish National Federation
IRA	Irish Republican Army
IRB	Irish Republican Brotherhood
ITGWU	Irish Transport and General Workers' Union
PLU	Poor Law Union
RIC	Royal Irish Constabulary
TTL	Town Tenants' League
UCG	University College, Galway
UEC	United Estates Committee
UIL	United Irish League
UVF	Ulster Volunteer Force
WS	witness statement

Archives

BM	British Museum
DGAD	Desmond Greaves Archive, Dublin
DIFUCD	Department of Irish Folklore, University College, Dublin
GCCO	Galway county council offices
JRLM	John Rylands Library, Manchester
MA	Military Archives of Ireland
NA	National Archives of Ireland
NLI	National Library of Ireland
PRO	Public Record Office, London
TCD	Trinity College, Dublin
UCC	University College, Cork
UCD	University College, Dublin

RECORDS

ABP	Arthur Balfour Papers
BMH	Bureau of Military History
CAB	cabinet papers
CBS	Crime Branch Special
CO	Colonial Office
CSB	Crime Special Branch
CSORP	Chief Secretary's Office Registered Papers
DE	Dáil Éireann
GPB	General Prisons Board
HO	Home Office
WO	War Office

0   50 miles
0   40   80 km

DONEGAL   LONDONDERRY
               (DERRY)   ANTRIM
       U L S T E R
                                Belfast
       T Y R O N E

SLIGO   FERMANAGH   MONAGHAN   DOWN
                                ARMAGH
MAYO   LEITRIM   CAVAN
C O N N A C H T   LOUTH

       ROSCOMMON   LONGFORD   MEATH

                  WESTMEATH   DUBLIN
GALWAY   Dublin
               OFFALY
               (KING'S COUNTY)   KILDARE

               LAOIS   L E I N S T E R
               (QUEEN'S
CLARE   COUNTY)   WICKLOW

       TIPPERARY   CARLOW
                       KILKENNY
LIMERICK   WEXFORD
M U N S T E R

                       WATERFORD
KERRY   CORK

Map 1. Ireland

Map 2. Poor Law Unions in County Galway

Map 3. Location Map of County Galway

Epic

I have lived in important places, times
When great events were decided, who owned
That half a rood of rock, a no-man's land
Surrounded by our pitchfork-armed claims.
I heard the Duffys shouting 'Damn your soul'
And old McCabe stripped to the waist, seen
Step the plot defying blue cast-steel —
'Here is the march along these iron stones'
That was the year of the Munich bother. Which
Was more important? I inclined
To lose my faith in Ballyrush and Gortin
Till Homer's ghost came whispering to my mind
He said: I made the Iliad from such
A local row. Gods make their own importance.

(Patrick Kavanagh, *Collected poems* (London, 1964), 136)

Introduction

In May 1905, C. P. Scott, the editor of the *Manchester Guardian*, asked the playwright John Millington Synge to write a series of articles about the west of Ireland that would 'give the reader a sympathetic understanding of the people and the way their life is lived'.[1] Synge set out for Galway at the beginning of June and, over the following two months, found that 'most [people in the west of Ireland] are in want one time or another, when the potatoes are bad or few, and their whole store is eaten; and there are some who are near starving at all times'.[2] Indeed, the Government estimated that almost all the farms in the region were too small to support a family.[3] Consequently, the occupiers of these farms and their families experienced severe hardship. Their diet was confined to potatoes, they were often obliged to share their living quarters with their animals, and their subsistence depended on back-breaking work.[4] The artist Jack Butler Yeats, who accompanied Synge on his tour, told Scott that he hoped 'Mr Synge's articles and my drawings may do some good, for the people of the West of Ireland are a great people'.[5]

The poverty of the western smallholders attracted a great deal of public attention in the last decades of the nineteenth century. Many journalists and political commentators visited the region to examine the condition of the people.[6] Royal Commissions were held to investigate the economic problems of the west, and land legislation was passed in an attempt to resolve these problems.[7] By the end of the nineteenth century, however, there was widespread agreement that the only real solution to western poverty was a policy of land redistribution. The vast majority of the inhabitants of the region rented landholdings that were simply too small,

---

[1] Scott to Synge, 26 May 1905, John Rylands Library Manchester (JRLM) Scott papers 126/66.

[2] *J.M. Synge collected works*, ii: *Prose*, ed. Alan Price (Oxford, 1966), 292.

[3] *Royal Commission on Congestion: final report*, HC (1908), [Cd. 4097], xlii. 744; George Wyndham, 'The Irish land question and the need for legislation', PRO CAB 37/59/147.

[4] See Ch. 1 and J. M. Synge's twelve articles published in the *Manchester Guardian* between 10 June and 26 July 1905, reprinted in *J. M. Synge collected works*, ii. 283–343.

[5] Yeats to Scott, 27 May 1905, JRLM Scott papers 126/68.

[6] See, for instance, B. H. Becker, *Disturbed Ireland: being the letters written during the winter of 1880–81* (London, 1881).   [7] See Ch. 1.

and too poor in quality, to provide their occupiers with 'a decent standard of comfort'; and these holdings could best be improved by the addition of extra acres.[8] There was a large amount of untenanted land in the region,[9] occupied by large farmers or 'graziers', and, increasingly, the redistribution of this 'grazing' land was viewed as the solution to the small farmer's economic ills.

While Royal Commissions played an important role in publicizing the problems of the west, they did not improve the living conditions of the smallholders. As this book suggests, the most powerful force for change in the west of Ireland was provided by the people themselves. Through their activism, the small farmers and labourers of the west of Ireland were able to transform their own lives by pressurizing successive governments into introducing revolutionary land legislation.[10] Between 1891 and 1921, their agitation for land reform was largely channelled through two popular nationalist movements—the United Irish League (1898–1919) and Sinn Féin (1905–21)—and this book is primarily a study of these political organizations.

Rather than concentrating on the leadership of the United Irish League or Sinn Féin, the book will instead focus on the rank and file membership. I will describe the kinds of people who joined the nationalist movement in rural Ireland, and explore their motivations, their ideas, and their activities. Because most accounts of nationalist politics in Ireland discuss the 'great' leaders, this book is a deliberate attempt to record the experiences of the thousands of local political and military activists without whom there would have been no revolution in Ireland.[11] This is not to deny the importance of 'national' political leaders, but to recognize that the Irish revolution was driven by a series of great upsurges of popular political activity, which transformed Irish society and shaped political developments in independent Ireland. In this respect, I have been influenced by the historiographical movement to write the history of ordinary men and women, pioneered by E. P. Thompson and Eric Hobsbawm, that has transformed the writing of history in Britain (and Europe), but has—as yet—had only limited impact in Ireland.[12]

---

[8] *Royal Commission on Congestion: final report*, HC (1908), [Cd. 4097], xlii. 744.

[9] Untenanted land is land held directly by the landlord on which no formal tenancy is created. See Ch. 1.   10 See Chs. 2 and 3.

[11] Throughout this book, I use Peter Hart's definition of the Irish revolution as beginning with the Easter Rising (1916) and concluding with the end of the Civil War (1923). For further discussion, see Ch. 6 and the Conclusion.

[12] See Eric Hobsbawm, *Primitive rebels: studies in archaic forms of social movement in the 19th and 20th centuries* (Manchester, 1959); E. P. Thompson, *The making of the English working class* (London, 1963). For further discussion, see the Conclusion.

The approach adopted in this book is rather different from that usually favoured by Irish historians. I do not attempt to describe local life in all of its quotidian detail in a single county study, as others have done.[13] Instead, I explore a single theme—the relationship between agrarian conflict and nationalist politics—over a thirty-year period through a series of interlocking studies of 'national', provincial, county, and village politics. The examination of popular political activity necessitates in-depth local studies, and in this book I have carried out a regional study of the west of Ireland, defined as the five counties of Connacht. This was the most politically active province in Ireland between 1879 and 1918, and the birthplace of the Land League (in 1879), and the United Irish League (in 1898),[14] and it is, therefore, the obvious starting point for a study of the relationship between 'land and revolution'.[15]

However, I do not confine my study to the west. As local historians have pointed out, it is essential that local studies are located in the wider context of both national and international events.[16] Throughout the book, I locate local events in their broader national context. The three country-wide agrarian agitations during this period (the compulsory land purchase agitation of 1901–2; the Ranch War, 1904–8; and the outbreak of agrarian conflict in 1920) are described in detail in Chapters 2, 3, and 6; while the British Government's policies on the land question are considered in detail in Chapters 2 and 3. In Chapter 6, I also consider the contribution of the IRA in Connacht to the War of Independence (1919–21). To understand the dynamics of popular political activity, however, it is necessary to examine a particular locality in detail; and underpinning this book is a detailed exploration of nationalist politics and agrarian conflict in the eastern part of county Galway.

Galway is the second largest county in Ireland (after Cork), and the largest in Connacht, encompassing 1,519,699 statute acres or 7 per cent of the total area of Ireland.[17] It is bordered on the north and east by Mayo, Roscommon, King's county and Tipperary; on the south by the Slieve Aughty mountains and Clare; and on the west by the Atlantic ocean. At the beginning of the twentieth century, there were 192,549 people living

---

[13] See, for instance, David Fitzpatrick, *Politics and Irish life, 1913–1921: provincial experience of war and revolution* (Dublin, 1977).   [14] See Ch. 1.

[15] See the Conclusion.

[16] H. P. R. Finberg, 'Local history', in H.P.R. Finberg, *Approaches to history: a symposium* (London, 1962), 123.

[17] William Nolan, 'Introduction', in G. Moran and R. Gillespie (eds.), *Galway: history and society* (Dublin, 1996), p. xviii; *Census of Ireland, 1901 . . . vol. iv: province of Connaught. No. 1. County of Galway*, HC (1902), [Cd. 1059], cxxviii. 7.

in the county, but the population was steadily declining due to high rates of emigration. The majority of the population made their living from agriculture: of 54,302 adult males, 40,464 (75 per cent) worked on the land. Most of the people (97 per cent) were Roman Catholic, but there were a small number of Episcopalians (2 per cent) and dissenters (0.5 per cent). A small minority spoke only Irish (5 per cent) but a much larger number were bilingual (52 per cent).[18] The county is divided into two halves by Lough Corrib, stretching 30 miles or so from the Mayo border to Galway city. To the west, the peninsular uplands of Connemara were sparsely populated and the land there is rough, barren, and unproductive.[19] In the eastern lowlands, on the other hand, the limestone plain provides rich, fertile grazing land, and there was a much larger urban population in the towns of Galway, Tuam, Ballinasloe, and Loughrea.[20] In the 1870s, the land of Galway was owned by about 200 landlords, some of whom owned extensive estates. Lords Ashtown (37,257 acres), Clanricarde (52,601 acres), Clonbrock (28,246 acres), and Dunsandle (37,057 acres) owned much of east Galway, while the Berridge estate in Connemara encompassed 171,117 acres.[21] The landlords with the largest estates tended to be Protestant, although there were many smaller landlords in the county (the Joyces of Corgary, for instance) who were Catholic.[22] The vast majority of the tenant farmers in Galway were Catholics, and occupied small farms of 30 acres or less.[23] In Galway, there was also a small class of large tenant

[18] *Census of Ireland, 1901 . . . vol. iv: province of Connaught. No. 1. County of Galway*, HC (1902), [Cd. 1059], cxxviii. 7, 144, 253.

[19] In 1901 in the parliamentary division of Connemara, there were ten people for every 100 acres, while the comparable figures for east and north Galway were thirteen and seventeen respectively. *Census of Ireland, 1901 . . . vol. iv: province of Connaught. No. 1. County of Galway*, HC (1902), [Cd. 1059], cxxviii. 10. On the physical characteristics of county Galway, see T. W. Freeman, *Ireland: a general and regional geography* (4th edn., London, 1969), 391–6, 405–24.

[20] The distinction between west Galway and east Galway (or 'the Plain') is brilliantly evoked in Máirtín Ó Cadhain's short story 'The hare-lip', in *The road to bright city* (Dublin, 1981), 85–93. In 1901, these were the only four towns in the county with a population in excess of 2,000. *Census of Ireland, 1901 . . . vol. iv: province of Connaught. No. 1. County of Galway*, HC (1902), [Cd. 1059], cxxviii. 7.

[21] See Patrick Melvin, 'The landed gentry of Galway, 1820–80' (Trinity College, Dublin, Ph.D., 1991), 506–512.

[22] Fergus Campbell, 'Elites, power and society in Ireland, 1879–1914', unpublished paper delivered to the American Conference of Irish Studies, New York, June 2001. The Joyce estate consisted of 4,185 acres, valued at £1,951 in the late 1870s. Melvin, 'The landed gentry of Galway', 510.

[23] In Galway, 76 % of farmers occupied farms of between 1 and 30 acres. This is similar to the figure for Connacht more generally (80 %) but higher than that for Ireland as a whole (67 %). *Agricultural Statistics of Ireland . . . for the year 1901*, HC (1902), [Cd. 1170], cxvi, part one, 364.

farmers or graziers (both Catholic and Protestant), who occupied much of the good grazing land in the county.[24] Although there were grazing farms in west Galway, they were much more profitable on the fertile plains of east Galway.[25] In this respect, my study of east Galway probably illuminates more general trends in east Connacht—where land was more fertile— than west Connacht. Having said that, the dominant concern among smallholders throughout Connacht, from the 1890s onwards, was with the question of land redistribution.[26] In order to further examine the causes of conflict within communities, a study of Craughwell in south-east Galway was undertaken. With a population of 641, most of whom were engaged in small farming, and surrounded by grazing farms, Craughwell was arguably the quintessential east Galway village.[27] This study of the evolution of nationalist politics in the village of Craughwell illustrates the broader county and 'national' developments described in the various chapters.[28] The book, therefore, adopts a concertina motion: shifting from the wide-angle shot to the close-up, and then back again (sometimes within a single chapter).[29]

The book also discusses a much longer period than is usually attempted in a monograph. This study begins in 1891, when the revelation of Parnell's affair with Katherine O'Shea split the Irish Parliamentary Party, and also disrupted agrarian agitation in Ireland, which had been more or less continuous since the formation of the Land League in 1879.[30] After 1891, both nationalist politics and agrarian agitation began to fade, and were only revived by the formation of the United Irish League in 1898. The book concludes in 1921 when Ireland achieved political independence

[24] In Galway, 14 % of farmers occupied farms of more than 50 acres. The comparable figures for Connacht and Ireland are 10% and 18%. *Agricultural Statistics of Ireland... for the year 1901*, HC (1902), [Cd. 1170], cxvi, part one, 364.

[25] More than one-fifth (22 %) of the land of Galway was untenanted. *Agricultural Statistics of Ireland... for the year 1901*, HC (1902), [Cd. 1170], cxvi, part one, pp. 368–9; *Royal Commission on Congestion in Ireland: appendix to the third report*, HC (1907), [Cd. 3414], xxxv. 665.

[26] See Ch. 1.

[27] *Census of Ireland, 1901 . . . vol. iv: province of Connaught. No. 1. County of Galway*, HC (1902), [Cd. 1059], cxxviii. 232. Almost two-thirds of holdings in Craughwell electoral division were between 1 and 30 acres while 13 % of holdings were of more than 50 acres. *Royal Commission on Congestion in Ireland: appendix to the Tenth Report*, HC (1908), [Cd. 4007], xlii. 437.

[28] See Chs. 2, 4, 5, and 6.

[29] See Ch. 2.

[30] Recent studies have viewed the period between the formation of the Land League (in 1879) and the collapse of the National League (in 1891) as constituting a distinct historical era, see Stephen Andrew Ball, 'Policing the land war: official responses to political protest and agrarian crime in Ireland, 1879–91' (University of London, Ph.D., 2000).

under the terms of the Anglo-Irish Treaty (signed in December 1921 and ratified by the Dáil in January 1922). After this date, agrarian conflict in Ireland was a problem for the Provisional Government (later the Irish Free State), rather than the British Government.

I have used a wide range of sources, some of which have not been used by previous historians. The most important and useful sources for this book were those compiled by the representatives of the British government in Ireland. In particular, the monthly reports compiled by the Royal Irish Constabulary on the state of the country (and of each county) between 1898 and 1921 provided the basic narrative of political and agrarian events in Ireland during this period. Although this collection is well known, the monthly police reports for the period between January 1903 and December 1908, which are missing from the series of police reports held at the Public Record Office in London, have only recently come to light.[31] These reports have provided the basis for a new interpretation of the first decade of the twentieth century, presented in Chapters 3 and 4. They are complemented by the more detailed intelligence notes contained in the 'confidential print', which was compiled in the Judicial Division of the Chief Secretary's Office from the late 1880s onwards. The intelligence notes were collated from police reports and newspaper reports, and intended to enable the Chief Secretary to answer questions from the Irish MPs about specific incidents. For this reason, they contain detailed investigations of particular episodes, and also much useful statistical material on agrarian agitation.[32]

A different perspective on agrarian protest is provided by the private papers of nationalist political leaders (particularly those of John Dillon, John Redmond, and William O'Brien), and also of local political activists. In the course of researching this book, I located six collections of letters and diaries, held privately, in the west of Ireland.[33] These letters provide valuable information on the internal workings of the nationalist movement, and facilitate the reconstruction of grass-roots political organization. The provincial press also provided the material with which a narrative of local political life could be constructed, as well as providing the names of local political officers. These names were then traced in the land valuation books and the 1901 and 1911 manuscript census returns, thereby

[31] These reports are missing from the full run of monthly police reports between 1898 and 1921, contained in the CO 904 series in the Public Record Office London (PRO). The missing reports were found by the author in the National Archives, Dublin (NA). See NA IGCI/1–15.

[32] The confidential print, 1898–1919 PRO CO 903/8–19.

[33] See Bibliography.

facilitating the analysis of the social composition of the United Irish League, the Irish Volunteers, Sinn Féin, and the Irish Republican Army.[34] Interviews, often with the children of United Irish Leaguers and Sinn Feiners, also provided useful insights into the *mentalité* of provincial nationalists. The testimonies of witnesses to Royal Commissions (and particularly the Royal Commission on Congestion) provided a vital source on the nature of the agrarian economy, and other parliamentary papers included useful statistics on population, land distribution, and agricultural production. Finally, I have made use of the recently opened Bureau of Military History archives.[35] The Bureau was established in 1947 to 'assemble and co-ordinate material to form the basis for the compilation of the history of the movement for independence' between 1913 and 1921.[36] As a result of its endeavours, 1,770 statements by participants in the Irish revolution were collected,[37] and these provide a most valuable insight into the working of the popular republican mind during this period.[38] Rather than relying only on police descriptions of 'suspects', these statements enable United Irish Leaguers, Sinn Féiners, Irish Volunteers, and even agrarian agitators to speak for themselves.

The book is arranged chronologically, but each chapter engages with specific historiographical debates, thereby providing a thematic dimension. Chapter 1 describes the social and economic circumstances in which the people of the west of Ireland lived in the 1890s; Chapters 2, 3, and 4 examine the activities of the United Irish League between 1900 and 1910; Chapter 5 analyses the development of Sinn Féin between 1905 and 1918; and the sixth chapter explores the broader dynamics of the Irish revolution. The aim of the book is to write the history of Irish agrarian and nationalist movements from below, to reconstruct events on the ground, and to provide an account of the lives of the thousands of ordinary people who, collectively, made the Irish revolution.

---

[34] See Appendix I.

[35] On the Bureau of Military History, see Diarmaid Ferriter, 'In such deadly earnest', *Dublin Review*, 12 (Autumn 2003).

[36] Ibid. 38–9.

[37] Although these statements were collected between 1947 and 1957, they were not opened to the public until March 2003.

[38] Ferriter, 'In such deadly earnest', 45.

1

The 'Western Problem':
Land and Politics in Connacht,
1891–1899

It is sad to learn how many people have a kind word for the grazier, while at the same time, they haven't a single word of sympathy for the wretched people who are squatted in abject poverty on cut away bogs or worn out patches. They speak as if it were an outrage to ask the man who holds anything from 1,000 to 5,000 acres of the peoples' heritage, to stand aside and allow justice to be done to the poor, while they never give a thought to the unfortunate creatures who have, in many cases, not a single acre at all . . . [S]ome people, who should know better, say it is wrong to speak of making the grazier retire. Decent people and nice families are all very well, but what about giving the poor a chance of becoming decent and nice too? Is Ireland to be for the Irish or for the favoured few?

('Graziers versus the People', *Connaught Leader*, 4 Mar. 1905)

I

Louis Paul-Dubois devoted a chapter of his *Contemporary Ireland*, published in 1908, to the 'western problem':

The first point that strikes one throughout the West of Ireland, is the twofold characteristic of a general depopulation combined here and there with a sporadic overpopulation. Whenever the soil permits of it, there you can see vast grazing lands, empty and bare, carved out into quadrilaterals and enclosed within great dry walls through whose interstices the daylight penetrates as through a piece of lace-work. Nowhere is there a living person or a house to be seen. Small black Kerry cows, and Roscommon sheep, — these are the sole inhabitants of this deserted prairie. But then, pass on from the beaten track to the waste lands by the coast or to the rocky parts of the mountain or to the peat bogs on the plain. Here at long intervals you will see masses of hovels glued tightly against each other, very low and, as it were, half sunk into the ground, with thatched roofs of a rounded shape like the outline of an over-turned boat . . . It is here that the peasants are penned together, miserable and unoccupied, possessing nothing of their own, as one of them said to us 'except the good God, the rain from the sky, and the light of day.'[1]

As Dubois goes on to explain, the essence of the western problem was the juxtaposition of vast tracts of untenanted grazing land, occupied by land-lords and graziers, next to the plots of impoverished small farmers, with insufficient land to provide them with a reasonable standard of living. For Dubois, there was only one solution to the poverty of the west: 'Some of the owners of these waste *latifundia* must be expropriated, and the territories cut up into farms of moderate size for the peasants to buy back.'[2]

This view of the causes of poverty in the west of Ireland is borne out by contemporary statistics. In the Westport Poor Law Union in county Mayo, there were over 4,000 families living on holdings valued at £8 and under,[3] while there were 66 graziers occupying almost 100,000 acres and 13 landlords who grazed a further 52,000 acres.[4] The social structure of the townland of Island, near Claremorris, suggests the inequitable distribu-tion of land in the west of Ireland at the turn of the century. The town-land encompassed 846 acres, 126 of which were under water with a further hundred acres of bog. There was one grazing farm in the townland— the Island farm—consisting of 306 acres of good grazing land; and adjacent to this grass farm were twenty-two smallholdings of between 2 and 16 acres of poor, boggy land. One grazing tenant occupied almost half (49 per cent) of the acreage (and most of the productive land) in the townland, while twenty-two small farmers and their families subsisted on the scrub surrounding the rich pasture of the Island farm.[5] This social structure was not confined to west Mayo. In the 'congested districts' as a

---

[1] Louis Paul-Dubois, *Contemporary Ireland* (Dublin, 1908), 298–9.

[2] Ibid. 309.

[3] According to the Congested Districts Board, 'whilst it is uniformly admitted that there must be variation, a holding of which the valuation is £10 has been generally regarded by witnesses as the minimum desirable' that would be 'capable of supporting a man and his family according to any decent standard of comfort'. *Royal Commission on Congestion in Ireland: final report*, HC (1908), [Cd. 4097], xlii. 744.

[4] M. E. Daly, *Social and economic history of Ireland since 1800* (Dublin, 1981), 55; Paul Bew, *Conflict and conciliation in Ireland, 1890–1910: Parnellites and radical agrarians* (Oxford, 1987), 9.

[5] On the Island grazing farm, see PRO CO 904/20.

whole,[6] there were 84,954 holdings, 74,413 of which were valued at £10 or under (88 per cent of the total number of landholdings in the region), and 45,138 of these holdings were valued at below £4.[7] And yet, there were large amounts of untenanted grazing land—in Connacht there were 391,323 acres—which could be used to increase the size of these smallholdings, and thereby provide the occupiers with a reasonable standard of living.[8]

A number of reports on the quality of life of congested tenants in the west of Ireland survive from the 1890s.[9] They were compiled by the Congested Districts Board (CDB) between 1892 and 1898, and enable us to examine the annual income and expenditure of a congested smallholder occupying a holding valued at £10 or under. To take one example, that of Woodford in south-east Galway, the estimated annual income of a family 'in ordinary circumstances' was £38 17s. 6d., and the estimated expenditure, £37 19s. 5d. The bulk of the farmer's income came from the sale of two in-calf heifers, one 2-year-old colt or filly, four sheep, and two pigs which provided the farmer with about £29 5s. annually. This income was supplemented by the sale of eggs (2,000 of which were sold for £6), butter (75 pounds were sold for £2 10s.), and poultry (20 fowls and 5 geese gained £1 2s.). Turf was also sold (40 loads for £7) and some straw and oats, providing an additional £4. As elsewhere in Connacht, remittances from relations who had emigrated, most often to the United States or Australia, constituted an important component of the smallholder's income (£3 annually).[10] In coastal areas, the sale of kelp and lobsters also supplemented the annual income (providing £12 and £3 8s. respectively in the district of Letterfrack).[11] And a number of the reports also indicate that migratory labour was an important source of additional income.

    6 In 1891, 429 electoral divisions in counties Galway, Mayo, Leitrim, Roscommon, Sligo, Donegal, Kerry, and the west riding of Cork were scheduled as the 'congested districts' — those parts of western Ireland where poverty was most acute – and the Congested Districts Board was established to address the problem of poverty in these counties. Under the 1909 Land Act, the extent of the area of the congested districts was greatly increased (by about 500,000 acres). Chris Day, 'Problems of poverty in the Congested Districts, 1890–1914' (University College, Galway, MA, 1986), 8; W. L. Micks, *An account of the constitution, administration and dissolution of the Congested Districts Board for Ireland from 1891 to 1923* (Dublin, 1925), 123–4.

    7 Day, 'Problems of poverty', 8.

    8 See Table 1.

    9 Congested Districts Board, *Baseline reports* (Dublin, 1892–8). TCD Old Library, Microfilm 395.

    10 'Congested Districts Board for Ireland: county of Galway – unions of Loughrea, Portumna, and Scariff. Report of Major Gaskell, Inspector: district of Woodford (26 Aug. 1893)', ibid. 580.

    11 'Congested Districts Board for Ireland: county of Galway – union of Clifden. Report of Major Ruttledge-Fair, Inspector: district of Letterfrack (19 May 1892)', ibid. 449.

At Partry, for instance, 'more than 550 labourers in the district migrate annually to England and Scotland, leaving home in May and June, and returning in October, November and December. They earn on an average about £10 each.'[12] It is noteworthy also that, according to the Woodford report, 'the women assist in all kinds of field work'.[13]

The Woodford congested tenant spent £3 (8 per cent of his annual expenditure) on the rent and rates for a stone-built thatched cabin with a mortar floor, and a landholding valued at £2 15s. (between 20 and 30 acres of poor-quality land).[14] He usually cultivated about 5.5 acres to grow crops for both sale and home consumption, and kept the rest as meadow.[15] Annually, he spent about £10 14s. (28 per cent of annual expenditure) on necessary foodstuffs for home consumption (flour, Indian meal, tea, sugar) and £2 7s. 6d. (six per cent of annual expenditure) on stone seed oats and stone seed potatoes. A further £4 (11 per cent of annual expenditure) was spent on young pigs and lambs which were usually purchased in March and resold in September or October. School and church fees, the cost of a blacksmith, the interest for the shopkeeper, and the service of mare and cows accounted for 8 per cent of annual expenditure. Other necessities—bran, lamp oil, lime, Lewes' manure, and clothes—cost £10 10s. (28 per cent of expenditure) and tobacco and 'refreshment at markets' cost an additional £4 6s. (11 per cent of expenditure).[16] Most food for home consumption was home grown and the congested tenants' usual diet consisted of bread and tea for breakfast and 'chiefly . . . potatoes' for the other two meals. If the annual supply of potatoes was exhausted in March, potatoes were then replaced with a porridge made of oatmeal and a mixture of flour and Indian meal. According to the report, eggs, milk, butter, and herrings were occasionally added to this diet, but bacon and meat were luxury items, only very rarely consumed by the smallholders and their families.[17]

Housing conditions were also very poor. In most parts of the congested districts, houses were built from stone and held together by a mixture of lime and mortar.[18] Usually, these single-storey thatched cottages consisted of one or two rooms, and were approximately 25 feet long by 12 feet wide.[19] Animals were often kept in the house: of eighty-four reports

---

[12] 'Congested Districts Board for Ireland: counties of Galway and Mayo – unions of Ballinrobe and Castlebar. Report of Major Ruttledge-Fair, Inspector: district of Partry (5 Mar. 1893)', ibid., 387.   [13] CDB report on Woodford, ibid. 581.

[14] Ibid. 580, 581, 577.   [15] Ibid. 577.   [16] Ibid. 580.   [17] Ibid. 581.

[18] There were some parts of the west of Ireland, however, where congested tenants still lived in huts made from clay or turf in the 1890s. Day, 'Problems of poverty', 13.

[19] Ibid.

compiled by the CDB Inspectors, thirty-six record that it was customary for animals to share human living quarters.[20] The cattle were tethered
to the wall furthest from the fire, and a drain ran across the house from
the front to the back door, dividing the living quarters from the animal
quarters.[21] According to the Jesuit T. A. Finlay, most congested tenants
did not have beds: 'beds are a rare luxury; a truss of straw or dried sedge
on the earthen floor, usually takes the place of a bed, and the clothes worn
during the day, supplemented in some cases by disused guano sacks, form
a substitute for bed covering.'[22] Not surprisingly, disease and illness were
common in these circumstances. One witness told the Royal Commission on Congestion that the damp conditions gave rise to 'typhus fever,
pulmonary and other forms of tuberculosis, infantile diarrhoea, occasionally diptheria . . . and often times severe forms of influenza, pneumonia
and scarlatina'.[23] Other commentators doubted that 'the social condition
of the people can really improve so long as they live in the same room as
the beasts of the field'.[24] Yet these were the conditions in which the majority of people in the west of Ireland lived.

These smallholders were the 'breeders' who reared the young calves and
bullocks that were the basis of the Irish cattle industry. They then sold their
cattle (typically when aged between one and two years) to the 'grazier',
who kept them for a further period of between six months and two years.
He then sold them as 2- or 3-year-olds to the 'fattener', who grazed them
on the rich grazing lands of counties Kildare, Meath, and Westmeath.[25]
Most of the land of Connacht was insufficiently rich to 'fatten' cattle and
usually this part of the process took place on the large grazing farms of
Leinster.[26] Finally, the 'fattener' sold the finished cattle to the 'shipper' who
exported the cattle to the fairs and markets of England and Scotland.[27] The
smallholders had insufficient land to raise themselves above the role of
'breeders' in the Irish cattle industry. If they were to improve their standard
of living, they would have to rear a larger number of cattle for sale at a

[20] Ibid. 14.
[21] A supply of milk during the winter could only be ensured if the cattle were kept in the
house. Ibid. 16, 14.   [22] Ibid. 20.   [23] Ibid. 11.   [24] Ibid. 11–12..
[25] J. P. Gibbons, 'Local politics and power in county Mayo, 1895–1900' (University
College, Galway, MA, 1980), 18–19.
[26] See Frank Shawe-Taylor's testimony to the Royal Commission on Congestion, *Royal
Commission on Congestion in Ireland: appendix to the tenth report*, HC (1908), [Cd. 4007], xlii.
251. Shawe-Taylor was nominated by the Irish Landowners' Convention to give evidence to
the Royal Commission.
[27] David S. Jones, 'The cleavage between graziers and peasants in the land struggle, 1890–
1910', in Samuel Clark and James S. Donnelly, Jr. (eds.) *Irish peasants: violence and political
unrest, 1780–1914* (Manchester, 1983), 380.

more advanced stage of development. This would require capital, better-quality land, and a certain amount of expertise. The least available of these commodities was grazing land: the primary source of income in an agrarian economy devoted to the sale of cattle.

The transformation of the agricultural economy in the decades following the Great Famine (1845–9) created the circumstances in which small-holders lived in the 1890s. After the Famine, Irish agriculture shifted away from tillage and towards pasture. Between 1841 and 1871, the total number of cattle in Ireland doubled, with the ratio of cattle to people increasing from 22 for every 100 persons, to 74 per 100 persons.[28] This transformation was largely a response to changes in the international economy, and particularly the increased demand for cattle in Britain. Indeed, such was the demand for Irish cattle on the British markets that the price of store cattle almost trebled between 1855 and 1905.[29] Whereas before 1870 the small and large farmer could be distinguished according to the type of farming in which they were engaged, this distinction became less pronounced as the century progressed. Even the very smallest farmers recognized that greater profits could be gained from pasture farming and so converted their land from tillage to pasture to benefit from the changes in the international economy. At the sitting of the Royal Commission on Congestion at Loughrea on 27 September 1907, both Lord Ashtown, one of the largest landowners in the county, and Martin Finnerty, a tenant farmer from Gurteen, told the Commissioners that the bulk of their respective lands was under pasture.[30] As Lord Ashtown stated, 'land pays better in grass than in tillage'.[31]

In the immediate aftermath of the Famine, there was a large quantity of untenanted land available to the investor or the farmer with capital. An estimated 70,000 evictions took place between 1846 and 1853, many of which were part of more general 'clearances', where forty or more families were evicted at the same time from the same estate.[32] Many of these evictions took place because tenants could not afford to pay their

[28] The number of cattle increased from 1.8 million to 4 million between 1841 and 1871. Paul Bew, *Land and the national question in Ireland 1858–82* (Dublin, 1978), 8.

[29] Jones, 'The cleavage between graziers and peasants', 375.

[30] *Royal Commission on Congestion in Ireland: appendix to the tenth report,* HC (1908), [Cd. 4007], xlii. 300. Finnerty was speaking on behalf of the east Galway United Irish League executive.

[31] Ibid. 275. Lord Ashtown was nominated by the Irish Landlords' Convention to give evidence to the Commission. The Ashtown estate consisted of 37,257 acres valued at £15,918 in the late 1870s. Patrick Melvin, 'The landed gentry of Galway, 1820–80', (Trinity College, Dublin, Ph.D., 1991), 506.

[32] W. E. Vaughan, *Landlords and tenants in mid-Victorian Ireland* (Oxford, 1994), 24–6.

rent during the Famine years, but some were also evicted by the new investors who purchased Irish estates under the terms of the Encumbered Estates Act (1849). The Act facilitated the sale of heavily indebted estates to new investors, many of whom tended to view their estates as commodities that could be bought and sold at will, with little regard for the 'rights' of their tenants.[33] One of these new investors, Alan Pollock, a Glasgow shipbuilder, purchased two estates in Galway, one at Lismanny near Ballinasloe and another at Dunmore, consisting of 29,577 acres and valued (in the late 1870s) at £13,313.[34] His first step was to evict all of the tenants and to re-employ them as labourers.[35] According to the Reverend Joseph Alfred Pelly, a curate in the parish of Kilclooney, near Ballinasloe:

No sooner did Mr. Pollock acquire the ownership of the land than he inaugurated the most sweeping and heartless campaign of eviction that ever swept a country-side bare. With the exception of one small village in the parish of Clontuckert [*sic*], where leases existed, and which defied his power . . . not one solitary tenant was allowed to remain, and they were all turned out without one penny compensation . . . Against their will.[36]

Pollock then let this untenanted land to a small number of graziers, there-by making his rent collection simpler, more reliable, and (presumably) more profitable.[37] Elsewhere in Ireland, the amount of untenanted land also increased significantly after the Famine.

David Jones has undertaken a study of the increase of untenanted land in four Poor Law Unions between the Famine and the formation of the United Irish League (in 1898). His findings indicate that in the Kells Poor Law Union (PLU) of county Meath, the amount of untenanted land increased by 109 per cent; in the Athlone PLU of county Roscommon, there was an increase of 32 per cent; in the Tulla PLU of county Clare, an increase of 49 per cent, and in the Belmullet PLU of county Mayo, an increase of 377 per cent.[38] In 1906, 13 per cent of the total area of Ireland was

---

[33] On the Encumbered Estates Act, see Oliver MacDonagh, *States of mind: a study of Anglo-Irish conflict, 1780–1980* (London, 1983), 36. On the effect of the Act in the west of Ireland, see P. G. Lane, 'The impact of the Encumbered Estates Court upon the landlords of Galway and Mayo', *Journal of the Galway Archaeological and Historical Society*, 38 (1981–2), 45–58.

[34] Melvin, 'The landed gentry of Galway, 1820–80', 512.

[35] Vaughan, *Landlords and tenants in mid-victorian Ireland*, 27.

[36] The Reverend Joseph Alfred Pelly's testimony to the Royal Commission on Congestion, *Royal Commission on Congestion in Ireland: appendix to the tenth report*, HC (1908), [Cd. 4007], xlii. 264. Pelly was nominated by the Bishop of Clonfert to give evidence to the Royal Commission.

[37] On the advantages to landlords of letting grazing land to one large tenant rather than to a multitude of smaller ones, see Gibbons, 'Local politics and power', 116

[38] Jones, 'The cleavage between graziers and peasants', 398–9.

TABLE 1. Acreage and use of untenanted land in Connacht in 1907

County	Acreage of grazing farms	Acreage of farms on which grazing cattle are taken	Area of untenanted land valued at 2s. 6d. per acre and above	Area of untenanted land valued below 2s. 6d. per acre
Galway	145,055	12,867	186,036	134,428
Leitrim	646	4,841	12,622	27,938
Mayo	177,659	22,036	95,913	109,633
Roscommon	26,578	22,123	64,138	55,268
Sligo	10,095	15,974	32,614	36,847
Total	360,033	77,841	391,323	364,114

Sources: The confidential print, 1907–8, PRO CO 903/14/69; D. S. Jones, *Graziers, land reform and political conflict in Ireland* (Washington, 1995), 113–14.

untenanted, while in Connacht, 18 per cent of the land was untenanted.[39] The untenanted land in Connacht (excluding Mayo) was owned by landlords who, in 1907, let 62 per cent to graziers, allowed 19 per cent of it to be stocked by small farmers, and grazed 19 per cent of it themselves (see Table 1).[40] Bernard Becker, the Special Commissioner of the *Daily News* who toured the west of Ireland in the winter of 1880–1, explained the view of 'the peasants of Mayo' that after the Famine the population had been 'swept away and the country reduced to a desert in order that it might be let in blocks of several square miles each to Englishmen and Scotchmen, who employ the land for grazing purposes only, and perhaps a score or two of people where once a thousand lived—after a fashion'.[41]

Grazing tenants were imported from Scotland and England to graze landholdings of up to a thousand acres where, before the Famine, there

[39] *Agricultural statistics of Ireland . . . for the year 1901*, HC (1902), [Cd. 1170], cxvi 1. 368–9; *Royal Commission on Congestion in Ireland: appendix to the third report*, HC (1907), [Cd. 3414], xxxv. 665.

[40] Mayo has been excluded as it was the only county in Connacht in which poor grazing land (valued at less than 2s. 6d. per acre) appears to have been let to graziers and stocked by small farmers. Elsewhere in Connacht, the total acreage of grazing farms and of farms on which grazing cattle were taken broadly corresponds with the amount of good grazing land (valued at and above 2s. 6d. per acre) in the counties. These figures present the proportion of untenanted land valued at and above 2s. 6d. per acre let to graziers and stocked by small farmers. See Table 1.

[41] Becker, *Disturbed Ireland*, 37.

had often been several hundred tenants. Mr T. Hegarty told the Royal Commission on Congestion sitting at Ballinrobe that

Within the last twenty years, I believe and previous to that, these lands in my district a good many of them had been in the hands of those Scotchmen and Englishmen. They came over when the people were cleared off and driven off by the landlords of their day. And then when the agricultural prices went down these industrious Englishmen and Scotchmen had to leave the country and these lands that they held in those days are now let as auction lands for grazing farms and on many of these there are poor people congested. Some of these people have to join—two or three of them to take a field and there are big graziers who take the majority of fields.[42]

The agricultural depressions of the late 1870s and the mid-1880s caused many of these graziers to lose substantial portions of their investment so that some of them gave up their grazing tenancies.[43]

In response to the Irish Land War (1879–81), the Government introduced the 1881 Land Act.[44] Under this Act, the landlord's absolute ownership of his (or her) land was replaced by a system of dual ownership.[45] The tenant gained a legal right to his tenancy and could claim a fair rent, security of tenure, and compensation for improvements, should he or she vacate the tenancy for any reason. These rights dramatically reduced the landlords' control over their estates. Their power to evict tenants was qualified, and their control of rent levels was replaced by new land courts that were authorized to fix 'judicial' or 'fair' rents.[46] Under the terms of the Act, tenants could apply for judicial revisions of their rent every fifteen years. The first wave of judicial revisions in 1881–2 reduced rents by about 21 per cent and the second wave, in 1896–7, reduced first-term judicial rents by a further 18 per cent.[47] The Act also had an important impact on the grazing system. In order to supplement their diminishing incomes,

---

[42] Quoted in Gibbons, 'Local politics and power', 15.

[43] On the impact of agricultural depressions on graziers, see Father Alfred Joseph Pelly's testimony to the Royal Commission on Congestion. *Royal Commission on Congestion in Ireland: appendix to the tenth report*, HC (1908), [Cd. 4007], xlii. 267.

[44] R. F. Foster, *Modern Ireland, 1600–1972* (London, 1988), 405, 412. The Land War was a conflict between landlord and tenant over the question of rent levels beginning in 1879 (after the depression in agricultural prices of the late 1870s) and ending in 1881 with the introduction of Gladstone's second Land Act.

[45] On the land legislation of the 1880s, see K. T. Hoppen, *Ireland since 1800: conflict and conformity* (London, 1989), 83–109; and C. F. Kolbert and T. O'Brien, *Land reform in Ireland: a legal history of the Irish land problem and its settlement* (Cambridge, 1975), 34–7.

[46] Under the terms of the Arrears Act (1882), the state paid off £2 million of arrears accumulated by Irish tenants. See MacDonagh, *States of mind*, 48–9; and Kolbert and O'Brien, *Land reform in Ireland*, 35–7.

[47] Kolbert and O'Brien, *Land reform in Ireland*, 36.

landlords began letting their untenanted land on an eleven-month lease that was not subject to the rent-fixing mechanisms of the land courts.[48] The land courts were authorized to fix fair rents on permanent tenancies, that is, tenancies of twelve months or more; tenancies of less than twelve months were outside the operation of the Act. In the aftermath of the 1881 Act, much of the untenanted land in Ireland was let on eleven-month lettings, for rents determined by market demand rather than by the land courts. Indeed, eleven-month lettings became so common at the end of the nineteenth century that contemporaries began to refer to the eleven-months system.

After 1881, a new type of native grazier began to emerge. Increasingly, the majority of tenants who let eleven-month land were large tenant farmers and shopkeepers. The number of shopkeepers who also occupied land increased from 55 to 105 between 1881 and 1901 in Galway (an increase of 91 per cent).[49] Lord Ashtown told the Royal Commission on Congestion that most of the land which he let (in 1907) on the eleven-months system was to shopkeepers,[50] while the Reverend Joseph Alfred Pelly testified that by the late 1890s 'nine tenths of the grazing ranches in this part of the country [east Galway] were occupied by . . . shopkeeper-graziers'.[51]

Not all graziers in the west of Ireland, however, were shopkeeper-graziers. Indeed, there is some confusion as to what exactly constituted a grazier in Ireland in the late nineteenth century. William Feingold argued that a grazier was a tenant who occupied a holding of 50 acres or more. However, his argument is based on evidence from the 1871 census, which suggested that larger tenants grazed more land than they tilled, while small tenants tilled more land than they grazed.[52] This may have been the case before 1871, but the distinction became redundant in the last quarter of the nineteenth century when the smallholder and landlord were both engaged in pasture farming. Paul Bew suggests that a grazier was defined in terms of his acreage: 'To be considered a grazier a man had usually to hold over 200 acres . . . More typically, a grazier's holding was probably

---

[48] George Wyndham, 'The Irish land question and the need for legislation', PRO CAB 37/59/147.

[49] *Census of Ireland, 1881 . . . vol. iv: province of Connaught. No. 1. County of Galway*, HC (1882), [C. 3268–1], lxxix. 159; *Census of Ireland, 1901 . . . vol. iv: province of Connaught. No. 1. County of Galway*, HC (1902), [Cd. 1059], cxxxviii. 179.

[50] *Royal Commission on Congestion in Ireland: appendix to the tenth report*, HC (1908), [Cd. 4007], xlii. 278.

[51] Ibid. 268.

[52] W. L. Feingold, 'The Irish boards of poor law guardians, 1872–86: a revolution in local government' (University of Chicago, Ph.D., 1974), 78–99.

between 400 and 600 acres; though there was an elite grouping which held much more.'[53] There are also problems with this definition because acreage often bears little relation to the actual value of an agricultural holding. In Galway, for instance, the value of a single acre varied from 1s. 10d. to 9s. 8d. between the rough, barren land of Connemara (in Clifden PLU) and the more fertile grazing plains of east Galway (in Ballinasloe PLU).[54] Thus, 100 acres in Connemara would be valued at £9, while in the Ballinasloe district it would have a much higher valuation of £48. Acreage, therefore, is not a useful tool in determining different social groups within the farming class.

Contemporaries defined graziers in terms of the role that they played in the Irish cattle industry. Frank Shawe-Taylor, a Galway landlord and grazier, described the graziers of Connacht as 'the backbone of the West', because they purchased the calves of the small farmers at local fairs and then resold them to east coast graziers or 'fatteners'. Shawe-Taylor argued that, without the graziers of Connacht and Leinster, the small farmers of Connacht would have had to deal directly with cattle exporters, who would not have purchased their small lots of young cattle. In Shawe-Taylor's view, the Irish small farmer was dependent on the grazier, who was effectively a middleman in the Irish cattle industry.[55] The grazier was thus a large farmer with sufficient land to purchase small lots of cattle at village fairs, and to fatten them for resale to the cattle exporter about two years later. Shawe-Taylor's definition of a grazier is similar to that of other contemporaries. Matthew Harris, the Ballinasloe Chartist, Young Irelander, Fenian, Land Leaguer, and MP, described the grazier in 1880 as a tenant in occupation of a farm valued at over £50.[56] And the west Mayo United Irish League in its campaign against the grazing system in 1899 defined a grazier as a non-residential tenant farmer whose holding was valued at £50 or over.[57] A holding valued at £50 or over would have been of sufficient size and quality to enable the occupier to graze cattle to the level of maturity

[53] Bew, *Conflict and conciliation*, 8–9.

[54] *Royal Commission on Congestion in Ireland: appendix to the tenth report*, HC (1908), [Cd. 4007], xlii. 403.

[55] Ibid. 251. Shawe-Taylor was born into a landed family that owned 7,605 acres valued at £3,016 in the late 1870s. Melvin, 'The landed gentry of Galway, 1820–80' 512. On 2 December 1905, a party of men ambushed him and his wife as they returned to their residence at Castle Taylor. Although shots were fired, they were not injured. IG monthly report, Dec. 1905, NA IGCI/8. He was, however, shot dead in March 1920 as a result of an agrarian dispute. See Ch. 6.

[56] Bew, *Land and the national question*, 103–4. On Harris, see P. K. Egan, *The parish of Ballinasloe: its history from the earliest times to the present century* (2nd edn., Galway, 1994), 267.   [57] CI monthly report, Mayo, Jan. 1899, NA IGCI/1.

required by the east coast cattle exporters. Shawe-Taylor's definition of a grazier was thus broadly similar to that of the United Irish League: a grazier was a farmer with sufficient land to raise yearlings to maturity, so that they could be sold for export. The United Irish League's insistence that a grazier was a farmer who occupied a non-residential holding also suggests the contemporary view of a grazier as a farmer whose land was used primarily for business purposes, rather than to support a family.

In the late nineteenth century, graziers were by no means always Catholics or shopkeepers. The graziers on the Clanricarde estate near Portumna and Woodford were Protestants, many of whom had come 'from other counties'.[58] Similarly, Frank Shawe-Taylor, a member of a prominent Galway landlord family, was also identified as a grazier as he let a number of grazing farms.[59] Indeed, graziers were perceived to be the allies of the landlord class. During the second half of the nineteenth century, the market in untenanted land was restricted. Evictions on the scale of the Famine period were not repeated: the total number of families evicted between 1857 and 1880 was about one-third (31 per cent) of that between 1849 and 1856.[60] If an ambitious tenant farmer wanted to benefit from the boom in cattle prices in the post-Famine era, then, he or she was obliged to let some of the landlord's untenanted land.

Graziers were involved in a close economic relationship with landlords. The alliance was advantageous to both parties. From the landlord's point of view, it was easier to collect rent from one large tenant than from a number of smaller tenants; and the landlord could also charge a higher rent for eleven-month land than he could for land let on longer leases. For the grazier, profits from the lucrative cattle trade could be increased by letting a larger amount of grazing land. The graziers' dependence on the landlord posed fewer problems for the Scottish and English investors who let untenanted land immediately after the Famine than it did for the new breed of Irish graziers who emerged after the Land War (1879–81). During the last two decades of the nineteenth century, graziers were increasingly viewed by nationalist commentators as propping up land-lordism. Haviland Burke, MP, stated that the eleven-month grazier was 'the landlord's right-hand man. It was on the ranching system that the landlord fell back against the people of the country; it was the landlord's

[58] CI monthly report, east Galway, Nov. 1902, PRO CO 904/76.

[59] Shawe-Taylor told the Royal Commission that he had 'farmed grazing lands' in Galway for twenty years. *Royal Commission on Congestion in Ireland: appendix to the tenth report*, HC (1908), [Cd. 4007], xlii. 251.

[60] Jones, 'The cleavage between graziers and peasants', 392–3.

last line of defence.'[61] And William Lundon, MP, made a similar point at Labasheeda, county Clare, on 24 November 1901:

Now, what is it that has unfortunately kept the landlord with his iron heel on our necks? (Voices—'the grabber')[62] Yes; the grabber, the grabber, the grabber, and I say this, that the grabber is worse than the man who would put his hand down and take the money out of your pocket . . . You must use all your endeavours inside the law—and may be if you put a leg outside it now and again—to prevent the grabber perpetuating landlordism.[63]

The variety of grazier that aroused the most opposition from nationalists after 1881 was the shopkeeper-grazier. Although some anthropologists have identified the relationship between Irish shopkeepers and their clients as governed by the 'doctrine of mutual dependence', contemporaries tended to view shopkeepers in a more barbed light.[64] George Birmingham,[65] in a letter to the editor of the *Spectator* in 1908, commented that

The shopkeeper occupies a peculiar position in the economic life of the country. He supplies the farmer with flour, American bacon, tea, artificial manure—all on credit. He purchases the farmer's eggs, butter and potatoes and the prices of these are entered in his book against the farmer's debt. He lends the farmer money at unknown rates of interest. He supplies the farmer with the drink in which each bargain in buying and selling is sealed and when the time comes sells tickets to America to the farmer's sons and daughters. As trader, usurer, publican and emigration agent he makes a fourfold profit. His customers are tied to him by their debts. He crowns his life of usefulness by posing as a public benefactor, the man who keeps the farmers going and occupies his leisure hours in nominating M.P.s to fight Ireland's battle on the floor of the House.[66]

Similarly, the Reverend John Flatley, the parish priest on Clare Island, told the Royal Commission on Congestion that the chief cause of poverty in Connemara was:

---

[61] Ibid. 401.

[62] While a 'grabber' usually referred to a tenant who rented a farm from which another tenant had been evicted, after 1898 the term was also applied to graziers, because tenants had often been evicted from untenanted land.

[63] There is a full report of Lundon's speech in PRO CO 904/20.

[64] C. M. Arensberg and S. T. Kimball, *Family and community in Ireland* (3rd edn., Ennis, 2001), 300. For a critique of Arensberg and Kimball, see Peter Gibbon, 'Arensberg and Kimball revisited', *Economy and Society*, 2 (1973), 479–98. Anne Byrne, Ricca Edmondson, and Tony Varley provide an extensive new introduction to the third edition, and respond to some of Gibbon's criticisms.

[65] George Birmingham [pseudonym for James Owen Hannay] (1865–1950), a Church of Ireland clergyman and novelist.

[66] J. Hannay, 'The future of the Irish farmer', letter to the editor of the *Spectator*, 4 Jan. 1908, quoted in Gibbons, 'Local politics and power', 65.

the habit which the people have acquired of living on credit and paying exorbitant prices for the goods that are supplied to them. The consequences are not merely economic consequences . . . to the man who is in debt to the shopkeeper and who is his actual slave. Practically he must elect the shopkeeper or his nominee to the District Council or to the County Council, and every other position that is going, with the most frightful results to the district.[67]

Flatley continued by saying that shopkeepers occasionally seized the cattle and pigs of their clients in lieu of payment and even, in extreme cases, their clients' landholdings.[68]

To assess the nature of the economic relationship between the shopkeeper and his (or her) customers, the account books of John Durkan's general provisions store at Turlough, near Castlebar, county Mayo, were examined by John Patrick Gibbons for the years 1892–5.[69] The account books indicate that the credit price for one bag of flour ranged between 6*d.* and 1*s.* more than the actual price of the flour if paid for in cash at the time of purchase. This was an increase of between 5.5 per cent and 13.3 per cent, with the different credit price being applied arbitrarily by the shopkeeper to customers at around the same time who were from the same townland (Cloonturbrit).[70] Because the credit price for goods was not agreed upon when the customers made their purchases, the shopkeeper could calculate the credit price at a later point. Usually, daily purchases were recorded in a day-book, a light cardboard journal which was kept on the counter of the shop. These were added to the 'debtors' ledger', a much larger leather-bound volume, at the end of the week. It was at this point—long after the customer had actually purchased their goods—that the shopkeeper decided the credit price to charge. Any number of considerations may have informed the shopkeeper's decision as to how much credit the customer should pay: the size of the customer's debt, the value of their custom, or the overall resources of the shopkeeper at that particular time.[71] The shopkeeper's decision as to the amount of credit to charge was, therefore, arbitrarily reached without negotiation with the client, and the customer could only hope that he or she would not be charged too much.

It may be suggested that shopkeepers could not charge whatever credit price they wanted, given that this might alienate their customers. However, this was complicated by the fact that the customer was kept permanently in the shopkeeper's debt. While the shopkeeper was often credited with never pushing for a final settlement of the account, this was calculated to

[67] *Royal Commission on Congestion in Ireland: appendix to the tenth report,* HC (1908), [Cd. 4007], xlii. 114.   [68] Ibid. 115.
[69] Gibbons, 'Local politics and power', 69–70.   [70] Ibid.   [71] Ibid. 67–9.

maintain his power. In a farming economy, this was virtually inevitable: small farmers only obtained a cash income when they sold their cattle, once or twice a year. As long as each customer made at least one payment per year, the shopkeeper did not take any coercive action. But if an annual payment was not made, the shopkeeper could take the case to court, and issue a decree against the customer (the cost of which would be added to the customer's account). For instance, Ned Bradley's account at Durkan's provision store stood at £2 14s. 4d. for over one year without any payment, after which 13s. 6d. was added to pay for the cost of a decree.[72] Alternatively, the customer could pay his debts by asking the shopkeeper to take out a loan from a joint stock bank. The shopkeeper would pay the interest to the joint stock bank, and charge a much higher rate of interest to the customer. This course of action was described by one witness to the Departmental Committee on Moneylending as 'not . . . for the benefit directly of the farmers [but] . . . for the shopkeeper' who 'gives security for a loan to pay himself'.[73] Another witness testified that this practice, which was known as the 'discount system', amounted to a form of 'servitude'.[74] The shopkeeper was the only person in the locality with sufficient security to take out a bank loan and he or she controlled the access of the entire village to any form of credit.[75] In these ways, indebted farmers were forced to 'go on adding to the [shopkeeper's] wealth which is invested in land grabbing or be overwhelmed with a demand for the immediate discharge of their indebtedness'.[76]

The shopkeepers' economic power was enhanced by their involvement in local politics. In 1898, for example, P. J. Kelly, a Westport shopkeeper, began advertising his business with the slogan: 'Who fears to speak of '98, the United Irish League: Tea 2/6'.[77] In November of the same year, John O'Donnell, a UIL organizer in Mayo, wrote to William O'Brien that 'there is more shop than patriotism about some of those who have spouted most around here'.[78] Identification with the political cause of the United Irish League gave the shopkeeper an influence in the local UIL branch, which was often the only local forum where his practices might have been criticized.

    [72] Ibid. 54.
    [73] Ibid. 63–4.
    [74] Ibid. 64.
    [75] Ibid.
    [76] Speech by William O'Brien reported in the *Mayo News*, 4 July 1898, quoted in Gibbons, 'Local politics and power', 94.
    [77] Gibbons, 'Local politics and power', 100.
    [78] John O'Donnell to William O'Brien, 7 Nov. 1898, University College, Cork (UCC) William O'Brien papers AIB/81.

Again, George Birmingham observed the shopkeeper's manipulation of politics for his own ends. The 'politician' in *Irishmen all* is a cutting satirical characterization of the shopkeeper's political opportunism:

What is the good of placarding the county with statements that your seeds and manure are better than any others, when the man next door is saying exactly the same thing about his seeds and manure? Timothy's plan was to become a champion of the people's rights, and to rely on the men whose battles he fought to reward him by dealing at his shop. He took up politics.[79]

The smallholders of the west of Ireland were thus economically dependent on the shopkeeper. Peter O'Malley, a shopkeeper and chairman of the Oughterard district council, told the Royal Commission on Congestion that the smallholder 'invariably lives on the shopkeeper to pay the landlord', thus indicating that the small farmer was caught between two sets of obligations. Indeed, the Reverend Kelly of Clifden described the shopkeeper-grazier as 'acting like double pneumonia on the congestion of the country, because he grinds the people between the shop and the land itself'.[80] The shopkeeper-grazier's role in the grazing system also prevented smallholders from gaining access to untenanted land. For this reason, the shopkeeper-grazier was particularly resented: he used the profits that he made from charging high interest rates to let grazing land.

In April 1895, the *Mayo News* drew attention to the case of the Houston ranch, when a number of shopkeeper-graziers effectively prevented the Congested Districts Board from redistributing a large grazing farm in west Mayo among local smallholders. Lord Sligo and the Earl of Lucan had cleared 48,555 acres of their estates near Westport in the mid-nineteenth century, in order to let the land as a single tenancy to Captain Houston, a Scottish grazier. Houston paid rent of £2,100 per annum for the ranch which he grazed profitably for about twenty years. By 1893, however, he was feeling the effects of economic depression. His 500 cattle were selling for £3–£4 less per head than they had done in 1890, while his 12,000 sheep were selling for 10s. less per head less than in 1888. The Congested Districts Board believed that Houston would give up the ranch due to his financial difficulties, and speculated in 1893 that the land could profitably be used by local congests. They were even more optimistic in this regard because the landlord, the Earl of Lucan, had already divided up two grass ranches, one

---

[79] George Birmingham, *Irishmen all* (New York, 1913), 83.
[80] *Royal Commission on Congestion in Ireland: appendix to the tenth report*, HC (1908), [Cd. 4007], xlii. 104; Gibbons, 'Local politics and power', 21. O'Malley, whose position as chairman of the Oughterard district council made him an *ex officio* member of the county council, gave evidence to the Royal Commission on behalf of the Galway county council.

at Drummin, near Westport, and another near Castlebar.[81] In April 1895, Houston gave up the ranch and the CDB began purchase negotiations with the Earl of Lucan. However, on 6 April, the *Mayo News* reported:

The hopes of the landless villagers, [and] the intentions of the C.D.B. are foiled. The Houston Ranch is once more taken from the people. It has been once more swallowed up by new tenants who are neither genuine farmers nor lacklands— not only by big graziers whose acres are counted by the hundred if not by the thousand—but by successful gombeenmen who having amassed wealth by the custom of the poorest class of farmer turn that wealth against their customers and bid up to the famine prices every scrap of land that falls into the market. The reaction against the big grazing system is thus being steadily counteracted by the uprise of the gombeenmen as landed men and there is no longer any force of local opinion to restrain for their customers are always deeply in their debt and now must either go on adding to the wealth which is invested in land grabbing or be overwhelmed with a demand for the immediate discharge of their indebtedness . . . Given a vigorous and united and popular organisation it is as certain as anything human can be that these 48,000 acres would have lain untenanted until they were partitioned among the congested villagers.[82]

According to Father Joseph Alfred Pelly, the shopkeeper-graziers 'made their money out of the poor, and with the money they made out of the poor they barred the access of the poor to the land'.[83]

II

The Land League was the first organization to draw attention to the western problem and particularly to the need for land redistribution in Connacht.[84] At a Land League meeting held near Claremorris in May 1879, local Fenians called for the redistribution of large grazing farms.[85] Matthew Harris also called for the redistribution of grazing land,[86] and famously

[81] Gibbons, 'Local politics and power', 116–17.

[82] Ibid. 118. 'Gombeenman' was a pejorative term used to denote a usurer, and, after 1881, the term was often applied to shopkeeper-graziers.

[83] *Royal Commission on Congestion in Ireland: appendix to the tenth report,* HC (1908), [Cd. 4007], xlii. 268.

[84] The Irish National Land League (Land League) was established in October 1879 with the aim of reducing rents, in response to the agricultural depression of the late 1870s. It developed into a mass movement to bring about land reform and was suppressed in October 1881.

[85] D. E. Jordan, *Land and popular politics in Ireland: county Mayo from the Plantation to the Land War* (Cambridge, 1994), 223–4.

[86] See NA CSORP 41968/1882. I am grateful to Stephen Ball for this reference.

described the alliance of the large and small farmer in the Land League as 'the union of the shark and the prey'.[87] In a letter to the *Freeman's Journal* in February 1879, he stated that the small farmers objected to the leading role being taken by graziers in the tenants' movement.[88] The demand for land redistribution was confined to Connacht, where there were a larger number of small farmers than in the rest of the country. To unite the large and small farmers, the national leadership avoided the divisive question of land redistribution when the official Land League programme was adopted in 1880. The Land Conference of April 1880 decided that the Land League should focus on achieving fair rents, an issue equally relevant to both the large and the small tenant farmer.[89]

After the suppression of the Land League on 20 October 1881, a new nationalist organization—the Irish National League—was established almost exactly one year later (on 21 October 1882).[90] The police regarded it as a continuation of the Land League: branches were formed in parishes where there had been Land League branches, and National League officials were often former Land League officials. Although some rural branches called for land redistribution, the National League constitution (like that of the Land League) avoided advocating an agrarian policy that might alienate grazier support.[91] Thus, although the early Land League movement in the west of Ireland had advocated land redistribution, the Land League and Irish National League effectively passed over the demands of the congested western tenants.[92]

This was, in part, because the living conditions of the western small-holders were not as well known in the 1880s as they were after 1898. In his *Recollections* and his reports for the *Freeman's Journal* during the Land War, William O'Brien drew attention to the fact that land purchase would not improve the living standards of the western smallholder.[93] Only 'the restoration to the people's use of the enormous tracts of rich grazing lands from which their fathers had been extirpated in the … Great Famine' would achieve this.[94] But, O'Brien continued: 'of this special problem there was

[87] Bew, *Land and the national question*, 102.
[88] Jordan, *Land and popular politics*, 224–5.
[89] See Bew, *Land and the national question*, Ch. 5.
[90] The Irish National League (National League) was established in October 1882. While it inherited aspects of the land reform programme of its predecessor, its primary function was to act as the constituency organization of the Irish Parliamentary Party. It became defunct after the Parnell split in 1891.
[91] Ball, 'Policing the Land War', 236–8.
[92] Bew, *Land and the national question*, 224.   [93] Ibid. 87.
[94] Quoted in Bew, *Land and the national question*, 87.

no particular mention in the original programme of the Land League, nor was it, indeed, understood... for many years afterwards outside the cabins of the congested districts'.[95] That the problems of the west were better understood outside the congested districts after 1900 was largely due to the formation of two organizations in the 1890s, both of which had their attention firmly fixed on the west: the Congested Districts Board and the United Irish League (UIL).

Arthur Balfour, the Irish Chief Secretary between 1887 and 1891, introduced a new Land Act in 1891 that increased the funds available for land purchase and also attempted to relieve the problem of poverty in the west by setting up a new administrative agency, the Congested Districts Board. The CDB consisted of two Land Commissioners, five experts appointed by the Government, and the Chief Secretary (as an *ex officio* member). The Board's objectives were to increase the acreage of congested landholdings so as to make them economically viable; to improve agricultural techniques; to encourage native industries; and to migrate congested tenants from their uneconomic holdings to newly purchased land elsewhere in the region.[96] Underlying the Board's policy was the aim to provide a 'decent standard of comfort' for each smallholder in the west. The Board considered that such a standard could be provided by a 'holding of which the valuation is £10... as the minimum desirable'.[97] However, only 16,000 tenants (less than one-tenth of the total number in the congested districts) had the value of their holdings substantially increased as a result of the Board's activities.[98] This was not a particularly impressive record, as the Board recognized in 1920: 'It will take some years before the resettlement of the land of the west is completed, and before the tenantry are, as far as possible, fixed in farms that will enable them to live decent, self-supporting lives in healthy homes.'[99]

The Congested Districts Board was not adequately funded. Between 1891 and 1903, the Board was granted £41,000 per annum,[100] which was increased to £250,000 under the terms of the 1903 Land Act.[101] These funds were insufficient for the CDB to deal effectively with the social and economic problems of the west. As George Wyndham, the Chief Secretary

---

[95] Quoted ibid.

[96] F. S. L. Lyons, *Ireland since the Famine* (London, 1971), 205.

[97] *Royal Commission on Congestion in Ireland: final report*, HC (1908), [Cd. 4097], xlii. 744.

[98] Day, 'Problems of poverty', 165.

[99] Ibid.

[100] Micks, *Account of the ... Congested Districts Board*, 123.

[101] Ibid.

between 1900 and 1905, commented in 1902: 'large tracts of the country, chiefly in Mayo and Galway, remain in the deplorable condition which induced Parliament to pass the Congested Districts Part . . . of the original Act.'[102] However, the reluctance of landowners to sell their grazing land for redistribution was the most serious obstacle encountered by the Board in its attempt to improve living standards in Connacht. The compilers of the *Baseline reports* identified land redistribution as the solution to congestion, but they were incapable of implementing this reform in congested areas. At Woodford in south Galway, for example, Major W. P. Gaskell, a CDB Inspector, observed that 'much of the best land between Woodford and Loughrea, and between Derrylaur Electoral Division and Gort, is let on grazing arrangements: but none is offered for sale'.[103] Like the congested tenants and small farmers of the congested districts, the CDB were forced to observe as graziers monopolized the untenanted land in the region.

Where the purchase of grazing land was impossible, the Board also looked to various techniques of agricultural improvement in order to improve the quality of life of the congested smallholder. Between 1891 and 1903, £140,000 was spent on improvements ranging from potato spraying to the creation of agricultural banks, all of which altered the way of life in the west and introduced the Congested Districts Board into the everyday lives of the people.[104] The *Baseline reports* recommended the use of different breeds of cattle or better manures to improve agricultural production at the most basic level. They also supported road-building initiatives which might, in south-east Galway, reduce the distance which some tenants had to walk to Loughrea market from 15 to 10 miles.[105] In coastal areas, the Board was aware that the encouragement of alternative industries was as important as migration and land redistribution. New boats and equipment were provided for fishermen; bee-keeping was encouraged; and roads were built to improve communications and to encourage tourist traffic.[106] At Letterfrack, a tradition of

---

[102] George Wyndham, cabinet memorandum on the Irish land question, 8 Oct. 1902, PRO CAB 37/62/139.

[103] CDB report on Woodford, *Baseline reports* (Dublin, 1892–8), 577. TCD Old Library, Microfilm 395.

[104] Lyons, *Ireland since the Famine*, 205–6.

[105] CDB report on Woodford, *Baseline reports* (Dublin, 1892–8), 582. TCD Old Library, Microfilm 395.

[106] Philip James Bull, 'The reconstruction of the Irish parliamentary movement, 1895–1903: an analysis with special reference to William O'Brien' (University of Cambridge, Ph.D., 1972), 110–11; Micks, *Account of the . . . Congested Districts Board*, 32.

basket-weaving which had died out was revived,[107] and at Carna a lace school was founded.[108]

Relatively small-scale investments by the Board could make a significant difference to the lives of people in a congested locality. As the Chief Secretary, Augustine Birrell, told the cabinet in June 1908: 'It [the Congested Districts Board] has found its way into the national life, and is frequently mentioned both in novels and plays; in fact, undoubtedly it has become in its way, a real national institution, unlike any of the other Boards in Ireland.'[109] This achievement had as much to do with the agricultural improvements that the Board fostered, and the consciousness-raising function which it provided in bringing the living conditions of western smallholders to the attention of the rest of Ireland, as it was to do with land redistribution. Nevertheless, the Board's advancement of the principle of land redistribution encouraged nationalist leaders to take up this issue as the basis for a new national movement: the United Irish League.

III

William O'Brien, a journalist from Mallow, county Cork, settled near Westport in 1891, and resigned his Cork city parliamentary seat (which he had held since 1892) in 1895.[110] The Parnell split had caused him to become disillusioned with the Irish Parliamentary Party and his intention, on arriving in Westport, was simply to become better acquainted with Clew Bay, the setting for his novel *A queen of men*.[111] The Parnell split, which resulted from the exposure of Parnell's affair with Katherine O'Shea, caused the Irish Parliamentary Party to split into three factions (Parnellite, anti-Parnellite, and Healyite), and created a hiatus in Irish nationalist politics.[112] Perhaps most importantly, the sustained country-

---

[107] Revd B. McAndrew's testimony to the Royal Commission on Congestion. *Royal Commission on Congestion in Ireland: appendix to the tenth report*, HC (1908), [Cd. 4007], xlii. 140. Sophia Sturge had started a basket-works at Letterfrack in 1888, with the assistance of local priests. This appears to have died out in the 1890s, and to have subsequently been revived by the Congested Disticts Board. See R. F. Foster, *Paddy and Mr. Punch: connections in English and Irish history* (London, 1993), 294.

[108] Revd Michael McHugh's testimony to the Royal Commission on Congestion. *Royal Commission on Congestion in Ireland: appendix to the tenth report*, HC (1908), [Cd. 4007], xlii. 147. [109] Bew, *Conflict and conciliation*, 175.

[110] Bull, 'Reconstruction', 108; Patrick Maume, 'Aspects of Irish nationalist political culture, c.1900–18' (Queen's University, Belfast, Ph.D., 1993), 96.

[111] William O'Brien, *An olive branch in Ireland and its history* (London, 1910), 79; Patrick Maume, *The long gestation: Insh nationalist life, 1891–1918* (Dublin, 1999), 237–8.

[112] Frank Callanan, *The Parnell split, 1890–91* (Cork, 1992).

wide agrarian agitation on behalf of Irish tenant farmers (initiated in 1879) was disrupted by the division in the parliamentary movement. As a result, during the 1890s, landlords were able to force exploitative rent settlements on their tenants, and there was no effective opposition to the letting of untenanted land to graziers, over the heads of small tenant farmers.[113] In these circumstances, O'Brien's interest in the topography of west Mayo was soon replaced by a more pressing concern with the economy. He had written some articles on the west for the *Freeman's Journal* in 1879 but the actual crisis conditions which he observed in west Mayo in the mid-1890s provided the spur for him to end his retirement, and to take up the cause of the smallholder. He wrote in his political memoirs of the sense of outrage that he had felt in the early months of his stay:

It would take a hard crust of selfishness, indeed, to enable a man to settle down in the Mayo of that day without being shocked by its sorrows and incited to redress them. Every other year the turf harvest was ruined in June or the potato harvest in August, and wan faces presented themselves at the windows, and humiliating begging appeals had to be set going to prevent semi-starvation from going the whole length of its ravages amidst the swarming villages. It was impossible to live long in Mayo without seeing that the remedy was as luminously self-evident as the disease: that while the overcrowded villagers . . . lived on patches of heather hills . . . these scenes of wretchedness were surrounded by wide-ranging pastures from which the villagers or their fathers had been evicted in the clearances following the Great Famine of 1847 in the interest of a Big Grazing Plantation.[114]

The sufferings of the Mayo peasantry filled O'Brien with a 'sacred rage' and he committed himself to 'undoing the unnatural divorce between the people and the land'.[115]

He became involved in the Irish National Federation (INF), the political organization of anti-Parnellites that had replaced the Irish National League in 1892.[116] In west Mayo, the INF aimed to redistribute local grazing land and thereby to relieve the poverty in the region.[117] It was, however, incapable of pressing its objectives to a successful result. For instance, the INF-led agitation to redistribute the Houston ranch ended with the Board being outbid by the shopkeeper-graziers of the nearby towns. The *Mayo News*—as we have seen—reported that there was no longer any force of 'local opinion' capable of restraining 'the gombeenmen'.[118] O'Brien recognized that what was required to transplant 'the people from their

---

[113] Bull, 'Reconstruction', 106–7.
[114] O'Brien, *An olive branch in Ireland*, 85–6.   [115] Ibid. 86.
[116] Sally Warwick-Haller, *William O'Brien and the Irish Land War* (Dublin, 1990), 161–2.
[117] Bull, 'Reconstruction', 115–16.   [118] Gibbons, 'Local politics and power', 118.

TABLE 2. The membership of the United Irish League, 1898–1901

County	1898		1899		1900		1901	
	Branches	Members	Branches	Members	Branches	Members	Branches	Members
East Galway	4	310	40	3,866	43	4,757	37	3,000
West Galway	9	755	24	4,246	31	5,954	42	6,733
Leitrim	2	100	31	4,395	31	6,726	31	5,446
Mayo	66	6,915	79	14,260	82	10,615	84	16,200
Roscommon	6	500	43	2,792	53	5,448	61	7,440
Sligo	15	1,288	36	5,040	41	5,500	46	6,100
Connacht	102	9,868	253	34,599	281	39,000	301	44,919
Ireland	121	10,844	408	46,378	892	88,293	1,150	121,443

Source: UIL membership figures, PRO CO 904/20/2.

starvation plots to the abundant green patrimony around them' was 'a great accumulation of national strength'.[119] The INF had proved itself incapable of mobilizing such an accumulation and O'Brien founded the United Irish League with the intention of creating a national political movement capable of simultaneously resolving the problem of poverty in the west of Ireland, and reuniting the Irish Parliamentary Party. O'Brien was also concerned that the new organization should lend its support to the popular movement to commemorate the centenary of the 1798 rebellion. And, as Philip Bull points out, the name of O'Brien's new organization 'revealed its three-fold purpose; it was to commemorate the United Irishmen of 1798; it was to be a new Land League; and it was to be the means of bringing unity to Irish politics'.[120]

The objectives of the west Mayo United Irish League were first adopted at the founding meeting of the League at Westport on 23 January 1898, which was attended by 4,000 people.[121] West Mayo provided the local context and inspiration for these objectives. A partial famine in the west of the county in 1897–8 had created much distress in the region, and caused a dramatic increase in the numbers of people requiring Poor Law Relief. During the week ending 9 July 1898, for instance, 1,372 households required 'outdoor relief' in Westport Poor Law Union, and there was 'acute distress' in the district surrounding Castlebar.[122] The most important resolution adopted at the meeting was:

119 O'Brien, *An olive branch in Ireland*, 89.
120 Bull, 'Reconstruction', 139; on the 1798 centenary movement, see ibid. 91–105.
121 *Mayo News*, 29 Jan. 1898; Bull, 'Reconstruction', 147.
122 Gibbons, 'Local politics and power', 17, 18.

That the most effective means of preventing the frequent cries of distress and famine in this so-called congested district would be the breaking up of the large grazing ranches with which the district is cursed, and the partition of them amongst the small land-holders, who were driven into the bogs and mountains to make room for the sheep and bullocks of English and Scotch adventurers and Irish grabbers.[123]

Although the demand for Home Rule was also expressed at the meeting, most of the speakers called for the redistribution of grazing land.[124] Significantly, Dillon criticized the Government's failure to purchase and redistribute land, and stated that 'the time may come when the people, in their extremity, will be driven to take the ranches, or know the reason why'.[125] The League was, in other words, calling on the Government to legislate more effectively for the improvement of the living conditions of the western smallholders. This represented a sea-change in the agrarian politics of the period. While the Irish National Federation had in some localities adopted this policy and unsuccessfully attempted to implement it, the Federation was by the late 1890s a localized organization with little influence.[126] The United Irish League, on the other hand, fashioned itself as a nationwide organization capable of electing a reunited Irish Party; and it was the first major Irish nationalist organization to adopt land redistribution as its most fundamental and defining policy.

In pursuit of this objective, the United Irish League aimed to complement rather than supersede the work of the Congested Districts Board. O'Brien had welcomed the formation of the CDB, and assisted the new Board in its endeavours to improve the material conditions of the western peasantry. In particular, O'Brien had proposed the setting up of a loan fund for the fishermen at Murrisk to purchase new boats and equipment, and he invested £350 of his own money in the scheme.[127] The construction of a new road (by the CDB) through the Dhulock pass (intended to encourage tourist traffic), and the introduction of spraying machines in the Westport area, were also both attributed to O'Brien.[128] The CDB and O'Brien shared the same diagnosis of western poverty: that land redistribution was the best way to improve the living standards of smallholders. However, as we have seen, the Board was limited in its operations primarily because it did not have the power to compel landowners to sell their land for the relief of congestion. The United Irish League, in order to facilitate

---

[123] The confidential print, 1898–1901, PRO CO 903/8/29–30.
[124] Bull, 'Reconstruction', 147–8.
[125] F. S. L. Lyons, *John Dillon: a biography* (London, 1968), 183–4.
[126] O'Brien, *An olive branch in Ireland*, 103.
[127] Bull, 'Reconstruction', 110.   [128] Ibid. 111.

the work of the Congested Districts Board, introduced an unofficial element of compulsion into the Board's negotiations with landlords and graziers. As William O'Brien stated in a speech at Westport in February 1898, the United Irish League aimed to

assist the Congested Districts Board in . . . [its] efforts to obtain grazing lands for division amongst the people, which efforts had been baulked by the action of landlords in demanding monstrous prices for their lands, and above all by the selfishness and greed of land-grabbers who had stepped in and taken land which the Congested Districts Board would otherwise have purchased.[129]

Those graziers who prevented the CDB from redistributing land were intimidated by the United Irish League to dissuade them from leasing grazing lands. In the autumn of 1898, the newly established United Irish League organized deputations to be sent to every grazier in Mayo asking them to sign the following printed 'form of consent': 'We, the undersigned, holding grazing farms in the parish of——hereby express our readiness to enter into negotiations for the surrender of our non-residential pastoral holdings on moderate terms of compensation, if the Congested Districts Board will purchase them for distribution among the small land owners.'[130] Those graziers who did not sign the declaration were condemned by the League and subsequently suffered, in the words of the Inspector General, 'if not in person certainly in . . . general comfort and in . . . pocket.'[131] This strategy was adopted by the executive of the League but also carried into effect by the numerous presidents of local UIL branches. Father Brett, the president of the Errismore branch, for example, petitioned his fellow Leaguers 'to leave all grazing farms lying idle for a year, when the tenants could memorialise the Congested Districts Board to buy the farms'.[132] The United Irish League orchestrated a dual attack on the grazing system: first, the intimidation of graziers, in order to force them to surrender their grass farms, and second, the petitioning of the CDB to purchase those farms that had been surrendered.

During the first half of 1899, the UIL used a variety of strategies to achieve its objectives. In January the United Irish League branches organized deputations to be sent to every grazier in the county requesting them to sell their grass lands to the Congested Districts Board.[133] In February

---

129 The confidential print, 1898–1901, PRO CO 903/8/31.

130 Graziers were defined as 'all persons holding Grazing farms of a valuation of 50 *l*. and upwards'. The confidential print, 1898–1901, PRO Co 903/8/93.

131 IG monthly report, Sept. 1899, NA IGCI/2.

132 D. W. Miller, *Church, state and nation in Ireland, 1898–1921* (Dublin, 1973), 24.

133 IG monthly report, Jan. 1899, and CI monthly report, Mayo, Jan. 1899, NA IGCI/1.

and March, public auctions of eleven-month land were boycotted by the League.[134] Between March and September, the busiest months in the agricultural calendar, labourers who worked for graziers were boycotted.[135] From April onwards, smallholders who had formerly stocked the grass lands let by graziers were boycotted if they continued to do so.[136] In June, League branches declared their intention to prevent graziers from saving their crops over the summer months; and in the same month, shopkeepers who refused to display a United Irish League membership card in their window suffered serious loss in trade.[137] In July, the League agitated against herds who continued to work for graziers.[138] Each of these strategies constituted an attempt to compel graziers to sell their land to the CDB.

Who joined the United Irish League? Given the social structure of west Mayo—where 98 per cent of landholdings were congested—there was no shortage of smallholders to whom the League might appeal.[139] According to the police, the Mayo UIL was supported by the 'poor struggling tenantry' whose 'natural cupidity' allowed them to be 'taken by the cry of "more land and better land for the people"'.[140] Regarding the specific social background of Leaguers, the police further observed that: 'The prime movers of it [the United Irish League] are "the dissolute ruffians and village tyrants" who have nothing to lose and everything to gain by any social revolution that may be effected.'[141] A study of the social background of nine officers of UIL branches in the Kilmaclasser electoral division of west Mayo suggests the limitations of the Constabulary's observations.[142] To be sure, most of the Leaguers were poor tenant farmers. Of the nine, six were congested tenants, with holdings valued at £10 or under; one was a small farmer and another a publican with holdings valued at between £10 and £20; and there was no information available as to the valuation of one of the officers' holdings.[143] However, the characterization of the local leaders as 'dissolute ruffians' requires some qualification. The officers of UIL branches appear to have constituted an elite group within the

---

[134] IG monthly report and CI monthly report, Mayo, Feb 1899; IG monthly report and CI monthly report, Mayo, Mar. 1899, NA IGCI/1.

[135] CI monthly reports, Mayo, Mar.–Aug. 1899, NA IGCI/1; CI monthly report, Mayo, Sept. 1899, NA IGCI/2.

[136] CI monthly report, Mayo, Apr. and May 1899, NA IGCI/1.

[137] CI monthly report, Mayo, June 1899, NA IGCI/1.

[138] CI monthly report, Mayo, July 1899, NA IGCI/1.

[139] Daly, *Social and economic history of Ireland*, 55.

[140] CI monthly report, Mayo, May 1899, NA IGCI/1.

[141] CI monthly report, Mayo, Oct. 1899, NA IGCI/2.

[142] This study was carried out by J. P. Gibbons in 'Local politics and power', 114–15 and 39–42.   [143] Ibid. 115.

congested community. Eight of the nine officers were aged between 50 and 80 years of age; and seven of the nine could read and write.[144] Although these farmers were by no means wealthy, they were better off than most of their neighbours. Most of the landholdings in Kilmaclasser electoral division were valued at less than £4, while the UIL presidents tended to occupy holdings valued at between £4 and £10.[145] The presidents were senior members of their villages, sufficiently educated to read the local newspapers, and sufficiently respected to influence the political decision-making process at local forums. These local leaders provided the link between the 'national' leadership of the United Irish League and the rank and file membership. They presided at the various local meetings, they explained the new League's policies, and they provided the channel through which local economic frustration could be transformed into political activism.

The local UIL presidents were influenced by the efforts of paid UIL organizers to become politically active. According to the police, the United Irish League would not have spread throughout the county without the efforts of the paid UIL organizers.[146] These were directly funded by O'Brien, who had the financial resources of his wife—Sofie Raffalovich—at his disposal. Sofie was the daughter of a Russian Jewish banker and corn merchant from Odessa, who had given her £50,000, which produced an annual income of £2,000.[147] These funds fed directly into the embryonic League organization. By 1900, there were twenty-eight salaried organizers, all under the personal management of O'Brien.[148] Their role was primarily to organize meetings and to establish new branches of the League. A letter from William Doris, joint founder of the *Mayo News* and a UIL organizer, to William O'Brien, on the eve of the first UIL meeting, suggests the role that they played:

The placards will be out first thing tomorrow and will be sent to the various districts tomorrow evening. The deputations will bring placards—that was already arranged. An announcement of the meeting will appear in the *Mayo News* this evening and in the *Freeman* tomorrow. I hope to be able to devote all day tomorrow to the business. I have had such a busy time of it since I saw you . . . you really need not have any fear of failure, so far at all events as the meeting is concerned.[149]

144 Ibid.   145 Ibid. 41, 115.
146 IG monthly report, Feb. 1900, NA IGCI/2.
147 Maume, 'Aspects of Irish nationalist political culture', 97.
148 The confidential print, 1898–1901, PRO CO 903/8/434–5.
149 William Doris to William O'Brien, 7 Jan. 1898, UCC William O'Brien papers AIA/8. See also AIA/11, 29, 32, 38 and 41.

No political organization could hope to succeed without such organizational endeavours.

The appointment of United Irish League organizers was directly overseen by William O'Brien. John O'Donnell, for example, was appointed by him at an Irish National Federation meeting at Kilmeena in 1896, when O'Donnell was 28 years old. O'Brien was impressed by O'Donnell's 'unstudied eloquence and force of character' but also by his popularity among the congested population 'of whose privations as well as sterling qualities he was a sample'.[150] The UIL organizers whom O'Brien appointed tended to have this in common: they were often local men, who knew the ways of the people, and were trusted in a way that outsiders like O'Brien may not have been. O'Donnell became the organizer for west Mayo where he was known, his father was a congested tenant with a landholding valued at £6 6s. in the Kilmaclasser district of west Mayo, and where he was respected as an authority on the ills of the western smallholder.[151]

In Galway, the most influential UIL organizer was James Lynam.[152] Although he had emigrated to the United States in his youth, Lynam returned to Galway in the 1870s and became an IRB organizer in the county. During the Plan of Campaign, which he played a part in organizing, he was evicted from his holding on the Clanricarde estate and took up residence in a nearby 'Land League hut' where he received grants from the Evicted Tenants' Fund.[153] Lynam's involvement in the IRB, together with his position as an evicted tenant, enabled him to win the support of local farmers and secret society men for the United Irish League throughout Galway. In this way, the UIL organizers connected local interest groups with the national programme of the League, thereby facilitating the rapid expansion of the movement. Philip Bull's examination of the social and political background of forty eight UIL organizers indicates that these men tended to be much more integrated into the local communities of the west of Ireland than the nationalist members of Parliament.[154] Farmers accounted for only 11 per cent of nationalist MPs (between 1895 and 1900), whereas 42 per cent of League organizers (1898–1900) were farmers.[155] Similarly, UIL organizers were able to bring the members of pre-existing radical agrarian networks into the new organization, as twenty-nine of

---

[150] O'Brien, *An olive branch in Ireland*, 107. O'Donnell was first appointed an INF organizer and later became a UIL organizer.

[151] Gibbons, 'Local politics and power', 112.

[152] On Lynam's activism in Galway, see Bull, 'Reconstruction', 270–9.

[153] Ibid. 270–1. The Plan of Campaign (1886–91) was an agitation during which tenants withheld payment of their rent to force landlords to concede rent reductions.

[154] See ibid. 281–90.   [155] Ibid. 286.

the forty-eight salaried organizers (60 per cent) were involved in the Irish Republican Brotherhood.[156] The efforts of these UIL organizers between 1898 and 1900 thus played a critical role in the expansion of the League in Connacht.

The support of the local Catholic clergy also ensured that the UIL won the support of the more moderate members of Connacht society. At the outset, most of the Catholic priests (with a few exceptions) were opposed to the new agrarian movement. However, as the new League established itself in Mayo, clerics recognized that only by participating in the UIL could they hope to moderate its more radical policies.[157] Archbishop MacEvilly of Tuam had initially condemned the new agrarian agitation in 1896, but his views of the campaign to redistribute grazing land had changed by the spring of 1898. In a pastoral letter, read in every parish in the diocese of Tuam on 20 February 1898, the Archbishop expressed his support for O'Brien's call to redistribute grazing land among the rural poor in the region. He was careful to emphasize that land redistribution should be carried out in a legal manner 'without trenching on the just and equitable rights of any class of the community', but his letter was widely regarded as an expression of support for the United Irish League.[158] Indeed, by the autumn of 1898, the police reported that the Archbishop had 'thrown himself into the movement and had counselled his clergy, who were against it, not to interfere with the wishes of the people'. As a result, all of the clergy in the diocese of Tuam (with some exceptions in the district of Castlebar) were reported to be supporters of the UIL by the end of 1898.[159] Undoubtedly, such extensive clerical support played a major role in the expansion of the League throughout the west of Ireland.

O'Brien later wrote that the United Irish League was 'wholly the product of one man operating from a rural solitude in the remotest west, without any political party, without a newspaper, and without public funds'.[160] As we have seen, this was not quite the case. Nevertheless, O'Brien's capacity to overcome the opposition of Parnellite and Healyite, the criticism of the *Irish Independent* and the *Daily News*, and the coercionist tendencies of the Government shows, at the very least, a remarkable resilience of spirit. He possessed an incredible personal energy: in 1881, he had single-handedly written and edited six weeks of the Parnellite weekly—the *United Irishman*—before being thrown into Kilmainham jail in a state of nervous exhaustion.[161] A similar level of energy was invested in the United Irish League in terms of both making speeches and the more mundane organi-

---

156 Ibid. 289.   157 Ibid. 183–4.   158 Ibid. 184.   159 Ibid. 186.
160 O'Brien, *An olive branch in Ireland*, 101.
161 Maume, 'Aspects of Irish nationalist political culture', 81.

zational tasks involved in starting a new political movement. He wrote to Dillon in October 1898: 'I have the whole clerical work of the United [Irish] League (including letters to every part of the country) on my hands, besides attending to every detail (including the paying and instructing of lawyers) in at least a dozen local fights and . . . I have practically had to stand alone for the last nine months in keeping the movement going.'[162]

Apart from his energy and organizational skills, O'Brien also brought the wisdom of a seasoned agrarian agitator to bear on the United Irish League. Unlike the Land League, which the UIL self-consciously emulated in a number of fundamental ways, the new League did not commit serious crimes in order to achieve its objectives. At a number of key junctures, the police discussed the likelihood of the UIL resorting to the commission of 'outrages', and concluded that O'Brien was opposed to serious crime but 'whether he will be able to control the people by and bye is another matter'.[163] O'Brien appears to have learned an important lesson from the Land League experience: that the United Irish League would be proclaimed as an illegal organization if it was associated with serious crime, and thereby lose its potential to become an enduring, popular organization. With O'Brien at the helm, the United Irish League devised new means of implementing its economic and political programme.

In January 1899, the police observed that a number of graziers had signed the declaration presented to them by the League, thereby agreeing to give up their grazing tenancies. According to the Inspector General: 'it is certain that the persons so visited would not consent to part with their interests were it not for dread of the consequences to themselves of a refusal to comply with the request of the League.'[164] What were the likely consequences of refusing to comply with the Mayo United Irish League? At the Sligo Assizes in November 1898, Justice Gibson's comments on the nature of the United Irish League in Mayo suggest the paradox of the new League's power. While it was responsible for 'mischief' and 'the replacement of the ordinary law of property'[165] which had necessitated a dramatic increase in the number of persons protected by police patrols,[166] the level of actual crime in Mayo was 'very much the same' as at the winter assizes of the previous year.[167]

---

[162] Warwick-Haller, *William O'Brien*, 177.
[163] CI monthly report, Mayo, July 1899, NA IGCI/1.
[164] IG monthly report, Jan. 1899, NA IGCI/1.
[165] IG monthly report, Nov. 1898, NA IGCI/1.
[166] The number of persons requiring such police protection increased from 13 to 122 in Mayo between February and March 1898. IG monthly report, Mar. 1898, NA IGCI/1.
[167] IG monthly report, Nov. 1898, NA IGCI/1.

This indicates that the graziers and shopkeepers were not dreading the commission of serious crime against their person or their property. Indeed, the evidence of the League's activism in Mayo suggests that boycotting and intimidation were at the heart of the UIL's campaign against the grazing system. As the police observed in June, individual League branches assumed authority over the agrarian affairs of the neighbourhood: 'all agrarian matters are brought up [at United Irish League branch meetings] & discussed & decisions arrived at which are conveyed to the parties concerned by the delegates of the branches & threats of boycotting, and in many instances quasi boycotting leaves persons afraid to act at all contrary to the rules of the League.'[168] These branch meetings constituted 'regular Courts', the County Inspector continued, which 'adjudicate in cases where members or non members break the rules of the League . . . a great number [of whom] . . . are subjected to annoyance & partial boycotting'.[169] Graziers, 'grabbers', their associates, and employees thus found themselves shunned, ostracized, and in extreme cases intimidated as a result of the United Irish League campaign.

The law was inverted by the United Irish League. Business transactions which were legitimate under the law of the Crown (the letting of grazing land, for example) were declared by the United Irish League to be illegal. The 'dread' which consumed the Mayo graziers who received deputations from the UIL in the spring of 1899 arose not simply from a fear of crime or even public denunciation, but from the knowledge that they were viewed by the Leaguers as criminals. This moral threat to the graziers of Mayo was at the heart of the United Irish League's campaign: the letting of grass lands to the prosperous rural bourgeoisie, over the heads of an impoverished smallholding class, was defined as wrong and therefore interference with the 'legal' rights of graziers was perceived to be just. The County Inspector observed in October: 'The people now regard it as a crime for anyone to take, or even hold, a large grazing farm.'[170]

The UIL in Mayo achieved some important victories in the smallholder interest. The Congested Districts Board's policy of land redistribution was greatly accelerated by the United Irish League's agitation. In particular, the purchase of the Dillon estate in May 1899 by the CDB appears to have been the result of the UIL's campaign. Several smaller estates were also purchased in the same month leading the County Inspector to comment: 'they [the smallholders] fully believe that in time the grazing lands

---

[168] CI monthly report, Mayo, June 1899, NA IGCI/1.
[169] Ibid. On UIL courts in Mayo, see Bull, 'Reconstruction', 207–8. For further discussion of UIL courts, see Ch. 4.   [170] CI monthly report, Mayo, Oct. 1899, NA IGCI/2.

will be parcelled out to them and it seems they are not far astray in their expectations.'[171] Similarly, the United Irish League's agitation against the grazing system was often successful. The auctioning of grazing lands was boycotted; local labourers would no longer save graziers' harvests; smallholders refused to stock grazing lands; police patrols protected the houses of graziers; and shopkeepers who traded with graziers were boycotted.[172]

In 1899, the United Irish League's mobilization of popular nationalist support in the local government elections transformed it from an isolated agrarian movement into a national political organization. The formation of the United Irish League coincided with the introduction of a substantial reform of local government in Ireland. The Local Government (Ireland) Act of 1898 dramatically expanded the electorate for local government elections. In particular, multiple votes (according to the individual's rateable property) were abolished which, in effect, removed the landlords from the new local authorities. Before 1898, they had virtually monopolized the Grand Jury system. As the franchise was now extended to include every householder, the local government elections provided an opportunity for the United Irish League to take control of the business of local government in nationalist Ireland.[173]

The public meetings of the United Irish League became an important forum for local candidates to address the electorate. This contributed to the expansion of the UIL in Connacht during the early months of 1899: 'It has spread rapidly throughout the county as it has been used to advance the interests of the Nationalist candidates in canvassing for [the] coming local government elections.'[174] The local elections created some tension between rival candidates within the League, as the police observed: 'the utilization of the League organisation to further the interests of individual candidates has, as might be expected, aroused jealousies and disputes which seriously weaken its power for evil.'[175] But the Mayo County Inspector's prediction that the UIL would collapse after the elections was overly pessimistic. In March 1899, he wrote: 'The Elections have killed it and after the excitement occasioned by them has passed away I expect Mr Wm. O'Brien and co. will have all their work cut out to reorganise

---

[171] The County Inspector also observed that the United Irish League leaders in the county claimed 'the credit altogether of the purchase of the Dillon Estate & a couple of small estates near Castlebar.' CI monthly report, Mayo, May 1899, NA IGCI/1.

[172] See CI monthly reports, Mayo, Jan. 1898–Sept. 1899, NA IGCI/1–2.

[173] For a discussion of the Act, see Desmond Roche, *Local government in Ireland* (Dublin, 1982), 45–8.

[174] CI monthly report, Roscommon, Feb. 1899, NA IGCI/1.

[175] IG monthly report, Mar. 1899, NA IGCI/1.

and reunite their shattered forces. It may drag out a miserable existence for some time longer but on the present lines it is formed to be unworkable.'[176]

In fact, the UIL was about to become one of the most influential and popular political organizations in modern Irish history, as the Inspector General later acknowledged: 'it quite swept the County [Mayo] and its nominees control the local business absolutely.'[177] At a national level, the majority of new councillors were nationalist, with unionists and ex-Grand Jury members under-represented everywhere except in two or three Ulster counties: 'altogether it cannot be denied that the League wherever it was in strength and used its organization to assist candidates, has shown that it possesses power and influence which cannot be dis-regarded.'[178] The elections constituted a critical point in the development of the League: they demonstrated that the UIL was not just an agrarian pressure group but also a political organization that could mobilize a wide cross-section of popular support. From April 1899, the reunification of the Irish Parliamentary Party, on the basis of the United Irish League organization, was inevitable.

In October 1899, T. P. O'Connor, the Home Rule MP for Liverpool (Scotland division), observed that the United Irish League would be 'a very valuable electioneering engine for the next general election'.[179] The election of John O'Donnell at the south Mayo by-election, with a convincing majority—2,401 votes to 427 votes for his opponent John MacBride—provided further evidence that the western movement could win elections.[180] By January 1900, Redmond and Healy had declared for reunion and were, soon afterwards, joined by the anti-Parnellite faction led by Dillon.[181] As Patrick Maume explains: 'They began a process of reunification among MPs, led from above, to counter the UIL threat growing up from below.'[182] At a national convention in June, the reunification of the Irish Parliamentary Party was copper-fastened, and the United Irish League became the 'sole official organization of the nationalist party'.[183] The UIL had gained

---

[176] CI monthly report, Mayo, Mar. 1899, NA IGCI/1.
[177] IG monthly report, Apr. 1899, NA IGCI/1.
[178] Ibid.
[179] IG monthly report, Oct. 1899, NA IGCI/2; Maume, *The long gestation*, 238.
[180] Maume, 'Aspects of Irish nationalist political culture', 33.
[181] Ibid. 98.
[182] Maume, *The long gestation*, 31.
[183] D. G. Boyce, *Nationalism in Ireland* (3rd edn., London, 1995), 267. On the reunification of the Irish Party, see Philip Bull, 'The United Irish League and the reunification of the Irish Parliamentary Party, 1898–1900', *Irish Historical Studies*, 26/1, (May 1988).

parliamentary influence, and the next chapter will examine the way in which the League used both parliamentary and agrarian agitation to campaign for compulsory land purchase between 1901 and 1903.

2

Popular Politics and the Making of the Wyndham Land Act, 1900–1903

> We owe this [Land] Bill, and let no one have any doubt about it—we owe it not to the good will of English Ministers or Irish landlords, but to the agitation of the United Irish League.
>
> (John Dillon at Swinford, county Mayo, *Irish People*, 29 Aug. 1903)

The national convention of the United Irish League held at the Mansion House in Dublin on 19 and 20 June 1900 effectively created and defined the reunited Irish Parliamentary Party. The branches of the United Irish League became the provincial rank and file branches of the Party; the UIL divisional executives were given the authority to select parliamentary candidates; and John Redmond, the chairman of the Party, was elected to the presidency of the national executive of the United Irish League.[1] Ostensibly, the convention precipitated the 'fusion of the League with the Party', but beneath the surface, a number of significant cracks remained.[2] Most fundamentally, there was no attempt to define the precise relationship between O'Brien's United Irish League and the leaders of the reunited Irish Party, John Redmond and John Dillon.

John Redmond was a county Wexford landlord and barrister who, after the split in 1891, became the leader of the Parnellites.[3] At the national convention, he was selected as the leader of the reunited Party as a concession to the Parnellite faction.[4] He did not share William O'Brien's comprehensive understanding of the Irish land question or his concern for the welfare of the western tenant farmers. Redmond was more concerned with the

---

[1] *United Irish League: constitution and rules adopted by the Irish national convention, 19th and 20th June, 1900* (Dublin, 1900), 1–4.

[2] This phrase is used by F. S. L. Lyons in *The Irish Parliamentary Party, 1890–1910* (London, 1951), 98.

[3] See Paul Bew, *John Redmond* (Dundalk, 1996).

[4] Bew, *Conflict and conciliation*, 67–9.

political struggle for Home Rule in the House of Commons than with the agrarian campaign for land redistribution in the west of Ireland. He was happy to rise to power on the back of the League's extraordinary mobiliza- tion of popular support but was concerned that the UIL's *raison d'être*— the redistribution of grazing land in the congested districts—might alienate the support of the wealthy nationalist graziers of east Leinster. Tim Harrington wrote to him in this vein in early 1901, expressing the view that the League's *Constitution and rules* were sufficiently flexible to 'prevent us from antagonizing any section of feeling . . . in Meath, Dublin and Kildare where they look with suspicion upon the grazing agitation conducted by the League'.[5] In his reply, Redmond made his view of the United Irish League very clear, writing: 'As for the League we can make it <u>our</u> organisation'.[6] For Redmond, the League was the junior partner in the new Irish Party-UIL alliance, an organization that was to be tolerated, by virtue of the subscriptions which it fed into the Party machine, rather than allowed to influence the Irish Party's policies.

Dillon shared Redmond's suspicion of the United Irish League, but for very different reasons. He was the son of John Blake Dillon, a barrister and Young Irelander, who believed that the landlords were respon- sible for Ireland's economic and social ills.[7] He shared his father's view of the landlord class and, as a result of his upbringing in the small town of Ballaghaderreen in east Mayo, had first-hand knowledge of the economic problems of the west. He was more inclined to support agrarian agitations than Redmond and had even flirted with Fenianism in the 1870s, being described by the police (in 1880) as a 'cool Fenian',[8] but after fifteen years of representing east Mayo in the House of Commons, he had become more of a parliamentarian than an agrarian agitator.[9] In his view, the politi- cal campaign for Home Rule was of greater importance than the agrar- ian campaign for land legislation. Dillon's suspicion of the United Irish League was based on his belief that once the land question was settled, the Irish tenant farmers—who filled the ranks of the UIL—would no longer support the parliamentary campaign for Home Rule.[10] This view was also held by Matthew Harris, who observed: 'when the farmers would be emancipated and get their lands, such men would look on the boundary of their farms as the boundary of their country, because farmers as a rule

---

[5] J. V. O'Brien, *William O'Brien and the course of Irish politics* (Berkeley, 1976), 119.
[6] Ibid.
[7] On John Dillon's background, see Maume, 'Aspects of Irish nationalist political culture', 166. See also Lyons, *Dillon*, 1–27.   [8] Lyons, *Dillon*, 15.   [9] Ibid.
[10] Ibid. 175; Maume, 'Aspects of Irish nationalist political culture', 109.

are very selfish men.'[11] Dillon's fear that land legislation would undermine the campaign for Home Rule forced him to adopt a cautious attitude to the United Irish League's proposed agrarian campaign for compulsory land purchase. He aimed to manipulate the UIL into supporting the parliamentary campaign for Home Rule, rather than the agrarian struggle for land legislation.[12]

William O'Brien, understandably, believed that the United Irish League should be the dominant partner in the new Irish Party-UIL alliance.[13] The League had grown into a mass movement without the assistance of either Redmond or Dillon, despite continued attempts by O'Brien to persuade them to join the UIL. In late 1898, for example, O'Brien asked Dillon to join the League and was disappointed by Dillon's refusal, writing: 'What I had hoped . . . was that you and all our most influential friends would throw themselves into the movement.'[14] It was only when the League threatened to supersede the Irish Party as the most prominent nationalist organization in Ireland that Redmond and Dillon began to take an interest in the it. Their attempt to take over the League in mid-1900 was a cosmetic coup that had little effect on the individual UIL branches. William O'Brien continued to be regarded as the leader of the UIL, his newspaper, the *Irish People*, remained the official newspaper of the League, and UIL branches maintained their agitation against the grazing system.[15] Even among the elite of the reunited Party, the United Irish League retained an influence which neither Redmond nor Dillon could prevent. This was demonstrated in the national convention's decision to allow League branches to retain 75 per cent of the subscriptions which they collected and to allocate only 25 per cent to the Party fund; in Parnell's time, 75 per cent of subscriptions to the National League had been allocated to the Party with only 25 per cent retained by the branches themselves.[16] Unlike Redmond and Dillon, O'Brien believed that the agrarian struggle was more important than the political campaign for Home Rule. He viewed the reunited Irish Party as the United Irish League's voice in the House of Commons and urged the MPs to use their parliamentary influence to campaign for ameliorative land legislation at Westminster.[17]

This triumvirate of leaders, who took control of the reunited Irish Party

---

11 Quoted in Bew, *Land and the national question*, 229.
12 Lyons, *Dillon*, 179–86.
13 Maume, 'Aspects of Irish nationalist political culture', 99.
14 Quoted in Lyons, *Irish Parliamentary Party*, 77.
15 Maume, 'Aspects of Irish nationalist political culture', 99, 112.
16 O'Brien, *William O'Brien*, 126.
17 Warwick-Haller, *William O'Brien*, 205–6.

in June 1900, shared little common ground. There was no agreement as to the role which the United Irish League should play in the reunited Irish Party and no consensus as to the policies which the Irish Party should pursue. In the event, practical considerations allowed the leaders of the reunited Party to reach a *modus vivendi*. During the nine years of disunity and disorganization following the Parnell split, subscriptions to the three nationalist factions had dramatically decreased. In the aftermath of the October 1900 general election, the Irish Party could boast of financial resources of only £7,000.[18] If the Irish Party was successfully to contest national and local elections, funds were urgently required. Redmond and Dillon recognized that a vociferous agrarian agitation would increase subscriptions to the Party fund, both at home and abroad, and in August 1901 they sanctioned a new United Irish League agitation in favour of compulsory land purchase.[19] The significance of the agitation was not missed by the Inspector General who observed: 'The necessity for keeping up the supply of subscriptions to the Nationalist party renders it certain that the United Irish League will not relax its efforts to keep a general agitation alive.'[20] Although Redmond disapproved of the agitation, he supported O'Brien's new initiative in view of the effect that it would have on a projected fund-raising tour of the United States.[21]

O'Brien ensured that the United Irish League obtained the upper hand in the reunited Party of 1900–1. But, with the League now established as the official organization of the Party in the Irish countryside, it was necessary to redefine the League's objectives in a national as opposed to an exclusively western context. Even after the League's success in the general election of October 1900, Connacht accounted for a disproportionate number of League branches and members: 33 per cent of League branches and 44 per cent of League members lived in the five Connacht counties in December 1900.[22] If the League was to be placed on a secure national footing, a policy that appealed more explicitly to the tenant farmers of Munster, Leinster, and Ulster would have to be adopted. In a speech at Ballylongford in north Kerry, in December 1898, O'Brien acknowledged the limited appeal of the anti-grazier agitation outside Connacht and suggested that UIL branches should participate in whatever social struggles were most relevant in their localities:

Somebody may say the question of breaking up the grass ranches, upon which you

[18] IG monthly report, Oct. 1900, PRO CO 904/71.
[19] O'Brien, *William O'Brien*, 130.
[20] IG monthly report, Aug. 1901, PRO CO 904/73.
[21] O'Brien, *William O'Brien*, 130.   [22] See Table 2.

lay so much emphasis, in the West, has no application in the South. Of course, it has not. It is solely and wholly a question for the congested districts of the West. Nobody dreams of extending it to the South, where the circumstances are totally different . . . [The United Irish League's] constitution goes upon the principle that the people of each Parliamentary division must govern themselves through an executive . . . and that executive must decide for themselves in what way or as to what particular question this organisation may be made most useful for the people's protection or the advancement of the National cause (cheers). For instance, if you had your branches formed in every parish around, and if you had your executive sitting every fortnight at Listowel, it would be wholly for themselves to decide to what particular question they should apply themselves.[23]

This strategy had borne fruit by July 1901 when District Inspector Winder produced a special report on the expansion of the League between June 1900 and June 1901.[24] He found that in different parts of the country, the League had a different purpose and a different *modus operandi.* In Connacht, League branches were preoccupied with the anti-grazier agitation; in Munster, the reinstatement of evicted tenants was the dominant concern; while in Ulster and Leinster, the League had a very different profile indeed. In Ulster, according to Winder, the League was run along 'sectarian rather than agrarian' lines and constituted a 'rallying point of opposition to Orangeism'.[25] In Leinster, however, the League was less successful in adapting itself to the political and economic preoccupations of the people. The eastern counties were dominated by graziers who were naturally opposed to the UIL's attempts to redistribute their land: as Winder surmised, 'We find that in Meath, Westmeath and Kildare, although the two former Counties have a good number of branches, the League is of little importance which we attribute to the preponderance of the grazier class to whose interests the League is avowedly unfriendly.' And in Dublin and Wexford, the people were more sympathetic to what Winder described as 'Revolutionary methods' than the constitutional agitation of the United Irish League.[26] Notwithstanding the expansion of the League in each province, except Leinster, the bulk of United Irish League branches remained in Connacht. In June 1901, the proportion of Connacht branches and members was only slightly reduced from the June

---

[23] Quoted in Bew, *Conflict and conciliation in Ireland*, 54.

[24] District Inspector Winder, memorandum on the progress of the United Irish League, 7 Aug. 1901, NA CBS, 1901, 24995/S box 19. E. H. Winder, a native of Dublin city and a member of the Church of Ireland, joined the RIC in 1880 as a cadet. See RIC officers' register, PRO HO 184/45/305.

[25] Winder, memorandum on the United Irish League, 7 Aug. 1901, NACBS, 1901, 24995/S box 19.   [26] Ibid.

1900 figures: 29 per cent of League branches and 40 per cent of League members were Connacht based.[27] The approach suggested by O'Brien at Ballylongford was successful up to a point; but if the League was to establish itself convincingly as a national movement, a new policy was required.

After the United Irish League's success in the October 1900 general election, the Inspector General speculated as to the policy which William O'Brien might now adopt:

The farmers of today … are too intelligent and too well off to be easily fooled into a new no-rent agitation; but Mr. William O'Brien is sufficiently ingenious to perceive in the question of compulsory sale a cry which would once more appeal to the cupidity of certain farmers; and which might with success be used as the basis for a new land war.[28]

By the following month, O'Brien had incorporated the demand for 'compulsory sale' or compulsory land purchase into the agrarian objectives of the United Irish League, first adopted at Westport in 1898. George Wyndham, who was appointed Chief Secretary of Ireland in November 1900, told Balfour on 26 November: 'The League began by an attack upon "Graziers". Thanks to T. W. Russell they are now doubling this policy with "Compulsory land purchase". All the 103 Irish members (except two) . . . have committed themselves to that policy.'[29]

The architect of the demand for compulsory land purchase was T. W. Russell, the unionist MP for south Tyrone.[30] In a speech at Clogher on 20 September 1900, he explained what compulsory land purchase would involve:

The central proposition is that the fee simple of the agricultural land in the country not in the use and occupation of the landlord himself should as speedily as possible be transferred to the occupier at a fair valuation, the state advancing the purchase money to the purchaser, and, in certain cases, adding a bonus to the agreed sum as a compensation for compulsion.[31]

The state should purchase all agricultural land in Ireland, except that in the occupation of the landlord, and resell it, on reasonable terms, to the tenants. This was a revolutionary proposal which, Russell argued, would resolve the Irish land question to the satisfaction of landlord, tenant, and

---

[27] Ibid.   [28] IG monthly report, Oct. 1900, PRO CO 904/71.
[29] George Wyndham to Arthur Balfour, 26 Nov. 1900, BM Arthur Balfour papers Add MS 49,803/139–144ᵛ.
[30] On Russell, see Maume, *The long gestation*, 242–3.
[31] Quoted in Bew, *Conflict and conciliation*, 88.

the 'general citizen'.[32] Landlords were losing a substantial amount of their income as a result of the operation of the 1881 Land Act. As we have seen, the Act established land courts which allowed tenants to apply for judicial revisions of their rent every fifteen years.[33] In 1900, therefore, landlords had suffered a substantial reduction in their annual incomes (from rent).[34] Russell claimed that it was in the landlords' interest to sell their estates at a fair price in 1900, rather than face the possibility of further reductions in their rentals in 1911–12.

Tenants were also dissatisfied with the operation of the 1881 Land Act. Although many tenants had benefited from reductions in their rents, the land courts were widely perceived as arbitrary in their adjudication of rent levels. Fair rents were determined by two Sub-Commissioners, employed by the Land Commission, who estimated the value of landholdings and then determined the so-called fair rent on the basis of the valuation. Russell claimed that the land courts did not determine fair rents, because, in the majority of cases, the Sub-Commissioners over-valued the landholdings and, therefore, determined rents that were too high.[35] A symptom of this problem was the large number of appeals made by tenants to the land courts, at great legal cost to both the tenant and the Land Commission. By March 1902, for example, 336,000 rents had been brought into the courts, of which 86,756 (26 per cent) had been appealed by the tenant.[36] Despite the advantages which many tenants had gained from the 1881 Land Act, then, there was a distrust of the rent-fixing mechanism and a perception of the land court as a 'hostile tribunal'. On this basis, Russell argued that it was in the tenants' interest to purchase their holdings, rather than to await the unpredictable and arbitrary revisions of the land court.[37]

Finally, Russell claimed that his new scheme would be to the advantage of the 'general citizen'. Compulsory land purchase, by providing the United Irish League with its central objective—land redistribution in the west of Ireland—would dramatically reduce the level of agrarian agitation in the country. Peace and stability would be the fruits of compulsory land purchase in Connacht, where the resolution of the land question

[32] *Irish Times*, 21 Sept. 1900. In Russell's terms, the 'general citizen' was the British and Irish taxpayer.

[33] Kolbert and O'Brien, *Land reform in Ireland*, 36.

[34] Russell, in his speech at Clogher, states that landlords' income from rent had been reduced by 42 % in 1900 as a result of two judicial revisions. *Irish Times*, 21 Sept. 1900.

[35] Ibid.

[36] Wyndham, cabinet memorandum on the land question, 8 Oct. 1902, PRO CAB 37/62/139.

[37] *Irish Times*, 21 Sept. 1900.

would reduce the likelihood of recurring bouts of agrarian agitation. The Clogher speech made this point in a forceful manner:

> For some years, owing to causes which I do not enter upon here, there has been a period of unwonted repose in Ireland. A cloud—no bigger than a man's hand at first—gathers darkly about us. In the West—that fruitful birthplace of Irish tragedies—in that West which is itself a tragedy—trouble is again brewing. Is it to be ever so? I, for one, say no—a thousand times no.[38]

In one sense, Russell's proposal was a direct response to the United Irish League's agitation. The revival of organized agrarian agitation in 1898 had created a level of disturbance that expressed western farmers' dissatisfaction with the present state of the land question. This also had a profound effect on the taxpayer, since the costs of policing the United Irish League's agitation were in excess of £1.8 million and the numerous appeals to the land courts cost the taxpayer over £2 million in legal fees.[39] Compulsory land purchase would bring peace to the disturbed districts and reduce the cost of Irish government, both of which were in the interest of the taxpayer. Thus, Russell argued, the landlords, the tenants—both in Ulster and in Connacht—and the taxpayer would benefit from the enactment of compulsory land purchase legislation.[40]

William O'Brien was convinced by Russell's arguments, and just two months after the Clogher speech, adopted compulsory land purchase as the new policy of the United Irish League. The adoption of compulsory land purchase, which would include the purchase of grazing lands, confirmed the League's commitment to its primary aim: the redistribution of grazing land in the west of Ireland. But Russell's scheme also offered scope for the League to extend its support base outside the congested districts of the west. The adoption of compulsory land purchase would enable the League to appeal to the large tenant farmers of the eastern counties who had, hitherto, remained aloof from it. Both large and small tenants would benefit from Russell's proposed legislation. They would gain the security of becoming landowners rather than landholders, and the annuity which they would pay, for the purchase of their holdings, would be less than their current rentals.[41] Unlike the League's initial policy which was limited in its appeal to the western smallholders, compulsory purchase contained the potential to appeal to all the varieties of tenant farmer in Ireland—large and small, east coast and west coast, Protestant and Catholic. Given the

---

[38] For a full account of Russell's Clogher speech, see ibid.
[39] Wyndham, 'The Irish land question and the need for legislation', 1901, PRO CAB 37/59/147.
[40] Ibid.   [41] *Irish Times*, 21 Sept. 1900.

problems which the League had encountered in its attempts to expand outside the western counties, O'Brien seized upon the new policy as a means of converting the UIL from a mainly western phenomenon into an organization with strong support bases in each province.

I

The nature of landholding in Ireland had been fundamentally transformed by the 1881 Land Act.[42] Yet by 1900, the Act was seen to be disadvantageous to the majority of both landlords and tenants.[43] It is perhaps unnecessary to explain the landlords' dissatisfaction with the Act, given that it dramatically reduced the amount of control that they held over their properties. But during the passage of the 1881 Act they had been assured by the Prime Minister that they would be adequately reimbursed for any reduction in their income caused by the operation of the Act. In July 1901, the Duke of Abercorn told the House of Lords: 'Mr. Gladstone, when he was carrying the Land Bill of 1881 through the House of Commons, expressed the belief that it would not inflict any injury on the landlords, and he also intimated that in his opinion, if it did do so, they would have a just claim to compensation.'[44] In the event, however, Gladstone's assurances had come to nothing. As Abercorn continued: 'We are willing to believe that it was not the intention of the Government of the day . . . to commit a great act of injustice. But no one can deny that injustice has been done to the landlords.'[45] The problem, from the landlords' point of view, was not with the principles underlying the Act, but with the impact that it was having on their annual incomes. Most landlords appear to have accepted, albeit begrudgingly, the principle of dual ownership. The *Irish Times*, for example, commented:

It is impossible to share the expectation of Lord Kilmorey that the Act of 1881 will be repealed. You cannot put back the hands of the clock in a matter of that kind. For good or ill the system of dual ownership has been set up in this country, and there is no possibility of altering it in the direction of re-establishing the landlord in the position of sole possessor.[46]

But, as the *Irish Times* continued, landlords did have the right to 'claim

---

[42] On the impact of the 1881 Land Act, see MacDonagh, *States of mind*, 48–9.

[43] Wyndham, 'The Irish land question and the need for legislation', 1901, PRO CAB 37/59/147.

[44] *Belfast Newsletter*, 12 July 1901, NLI Clonbrock papers MS 19,666, 140–1.

[45] Ibid.,141.   [46] *Irish Times*, 12 July 1901, NLI Clonbrock papers MS 19,666, 138.

that the Acts should be administered fairly'; and in 1901, it claimed that this was patently not the case.

The Act, in effect, presented the Irish landlords with a choice. They could hold on to their estates and suffer the periodical revisions of rent which the Act inaugurated; or they could sell their estates to the Land Commission through the Land Purchase Acts passed in 1885, 1888, 1891, and 1896.[47] By 1900, the first option was becoming more and more unattractive. At the turn of the century, many landlords had already suffered a severe loss of 42 per cent in their rentals and, in the following decade, they could look forward to yet another revision which would diminish their income from rent even further.[48] If the *fin de siècle* landlord did not find this state of affairs to his satisfaction, he could consider option two: selling his estate to the Land Commission. In 1900, this was an equally unsatisfactory proposal. First, it would involve the legal cost of obtaining satisfactory proof of title, which was necessary before purchase arrangements could proceed.[49] Second, the landlord would be paid for his estate in Government land stock, the value of which had depreciated considerably since the outbreak of the South African war (in 1899).[50] And third, estates which contained a significant number of congested holdings would either be disallowed from purchase arrangements by the Land Commission, or sold for a purchase price that the landlord could not 'prudently accept'.[51]

The latter problem was most acute in the so-called 'congested districts', but it was by no means confined to them. Almost one-quarter (127,000) of all the agricultural holdings in Ireland were congested (or valued at £4 and under) in 1901, and a significant number were outside the congested districts. There were, for example, 21,717 congested holdings in Ulster (exclusive of Donegal).[52] Congested estates were inadmissible for sale under the Land Purchase Acts because the congested tenant was not believed to be a secure investment for the British taxpayer. The Land Commission decided which purchase agreements between landlord and tenant should be sanctioned, not according to the merits of the case but 'in respect of its security to the tax-payer under existing conditions'.[53] It

[47] Wyndham, cabinet memorandum on the Irish land question, 8 Oct. 1902, PRO CAB 37/62/139.
[48] *Irish Times*, 21 Sept. 1900.
[49] Wyndham, 'The Irish land question and the need for legislation', 1901, PRO CAB 37/59/147.
[50] Ibid.; Kolbert and O'Brien, *Land reform in Ireland*, 39.
[51] Wyndham, 'The Irish land question and the need for legislation', 1901, PRO CAB 37/59/147.
[52] Ibid.   [53] Ibid.

was assumed that congested tenants would be unable to pay their purchase annuities reliably and, therefore, they were prevented from purchasing their holdings. This created a problem for landlords who had congested tenants on their estates. They could either sell their non-congested tenancies and keep the congested ones, or they could accept a low price for the congested holdings. Both options were unappealing to the landlord, since the former would force him to retain his most unreliable and unprofitable tenants, while the latter would pressurize him into accepting a prohibitively low purchase price.[54]

In 1900, then, the Irish landlord was confronted with two unattractive courses of action: either to hold onto his estate and endure the reductions in his annual income from rent, or to sell the estate, notwithstanding the costs of obtaining legal proof of title, and the depreciated value of the Government land stock in which he would be paid. If there were any congested tenancies on his estate, he was presented with the further problem of either retaining the congested tenancies or selling the whole estate for a dramatically reduced price. In this climate, few landlords decided to sell their estates. As Wyndham observed: 'The landlords who have sold are chiefly those who derive a considerable portion of their income from sources other than their land . . . and those who have been forced to sell by their creditors.'[55] Only those landlords who could afford to accept a reduced income from their land and those who were in a state of serious indebtedness were inclined to sell their estates in 1901. The 'average' landlord, if such a species could be said to exist, was holding onto his land and hoping that new land legislation, in favour of his interests, would be introduced.

In the interim, a number of landlords had discovered a means of supplementing their diminishing incomes by keeping as much of their land as possible outside the operation of the 1881 Act. In particular, as we have seen, it was their untenanted land that they now attempted to let on the eleven-months system for rents that were determined by market demand rather than by the land courts.[56] In Ireland in 1906, there were 2,555,855 acres of untenanted lands, much of which were let by landlords to graziers on eleven-month lettings, for rents that were far higher than those fixed in the land courts.[57] The eleven-months system appeared to be the salvation of the landlords, but it also created the rationale for a further threat to their economic and political well-being: the United Irish League.

[54] Ibid.   [55] Ibid.   [56] Ibid.
[57] *Royal Commission on Congestion in Ireland: appendix to the third report*, HC (1907), [Cd. 3414], xxxv. 665.

The 1881 Land Act created the precise social and economic conditions which enabled the United Irish League to come to prominence in 1898. Congestion was practically copper-fastened by the Act. Landlords could not evict or reform the congested holdings on their estates, because the Act provided congested tenants with the right to 'fixity of tenure'. Congested estates could not be purchased under the Land Purchase Acts, because congested tenants were believed to provide insufficient security for the taxpayer. Surplus or untenanted land could not be redistributed among the congested tenants because landlords were using the land to buttress their incomes through the eleven-months system. Wyndham recognized, in 1901, that the Act had 'stereotyped' the congested 'holdings which are too small to support a family, frequently divided into detached plots, sometimes, though rarely, held in common (Rundale), and of which the occupiers have undefined rights to cutting turf for fuel. They are prevalent in the "congested districts", but in a lesser degree they exist throughout Ireland.'[58] Seventeen years after the passing of the 1881 Act, the new circumstances in the agrarian economy, which it had largely created, provided the basis for an extensive mobilization of tenant resistance to congestion and the eleven-months system. For this reason, Wyndham characterized congestion not as a merely economic problem but as an administrative and political crisis: congested holdings were, in his view, 'seed-plots of agrarian discontent'[59] which 'exert a far-reaching and baneful influence over the whole agrarian question in Ireland'.[60] Indeed, he argued that the land question had 'reached a deadlock which profits no one except the Nationalist agitator, who finds the staple of his argument in a contrast between "residues" [congested holdings] and the 11,500,000 acres of permanent grass'.[61] From the point of view of the Irish landlords, *circa* 1900, the 1881 Land Act had brought about not merely a dramatic reduction in their annual incomes but also, indirectly, the formation of a strong political movement with the intention of abolishing landlordism altogether.

We have already touched on the impact of the 1881 Act on the congested tenants of the west, but what effect did the legislation have on Irish tenants as a whole? To be sure, the Act provided a number of important benefits

[58] Wyndham, 'The Irish land question and the need for legislation', 1901, PRO CAB 37/59/147.

[59] Wyndham, cabinet memorandum on the Irish land question, 8 Oct. 1902, PRO CAB 37/62/139.

[60] Wyndham, 'The Irish land question and the need for legislation', 1901, PRO CAB 37/59/147.

[61] Ibid.

for Irish tenants. They could no longer be evicted at the whim of the landlord, although they could be evicted for non-payment of rent; if they were
evicted or chose to give up their tenancy, the landlord was obliged to pay
them compensation for improvements which they had made to their
holdings; and they could apply to the land courts for a fair rent, which
was usually about 21 per cent less than their rent before 1881.[62] These were
significant reforms which improved both the status and the income of
the Irish tenant farmer. But the effect of these reforms was uneven. Large
tenant farmers benefited considerably, while the congested tenant was
only marginally affected.

The large tenant farmers experienced something of a golden age between
1881 and 1898. Their rents were substantially reduced by the land courts,
providing them with a larger amount of capital for investment. Increasingly, this capital was invested in renting the untenanted land which landlords were so keen to let on the eleven-months system.[63] The boom in
the international cattle trade in the second half of the nineteenth century
enabled them to use these resources of both land and capital to the greatest
advantage.[64] Indeed, after 1881, the large tenants gained a sizeable share of
the profits from the Irish cattle trade, which had formerly been dominated
by landlords and immigrant graziers. Wyndham suggested in 1902 that
the larger farmers should never have been allowed fair rents: 'They have
been given half the landlord's property & are lucky if allowed to go off
"with the swag." '[65] Despite acquiring the swag, the large farmers remained
dissatisfied with the system of dual ownership. They wanted to purchase
their holdings so as to 'secure . . . absolutely the fruits of their industry and
enterprise'.[66] But, by the turn of the century, the machinery of land purchase had virtually ground to a halt. Whereas in 1898 there had been 8,000
voluntary purchase arrangements between landlord and tenant, in 1902,
there were only 1,990, a decrease of 75 per cent.[67] The reduction in purchase
agreements was, primarily, a consequence of the landlords' reluctance to
sell under the conditions pertaining in 1901–2, particularly the deprecia-
tion in value of Government land stock. For this reason, the large tenant
farmers were dissatisfied with the state of land legislation, *circa* 1900, and
keen to consolidate their status as an *arriviste bourgeoisie* by becoming the

---

[62] See MacDonagh, *States of mind*, 48–9; Kolbert and O'Brien, *Land reform in Ireland*, 36.
[63] Jones, 'The cleavage between graziers and peasants', 396.
[64] See Ch. 1.
[65] Wyndham to Balfour, 8 Oct. 1902, BM ABP Add. MS 49,804/73–76ᵛ.
[66] Wyndham, cabinet memorandum on the Irish land question, 8 Oct. 1902, PRO CAB 37/62/139.
[67] Ibid.

owners of their farms. Their concern to become landowners rather than landholders may also have intensified after 1898, when the gains which they had made in terms of both income and land were placed under threat by the United Irish League.

Of all the groups under discussion, the congested tenants were the most severely affected by the 1881 Act. The legislation of the late nineteenth century, far from improving their living conditions, further restricted their ability to change their economic circumstances. They could not purchase their tenancies, as the Land Commission deemed them to be incapable of paying their purchase annuities reliably; and their access to grazing land was dramatically reduced by the rapid growth of the eleven-months system after 1881.[68] Even the formation of the Congested Districts Board in 1891 had very little impact on their lives.[69]

In fact, Wyndham recognized that the inability of the Congested Districts Board to carry out its proposed reforms caused many small farmers to turn instead to the illegal agitation of the United Irish League: 'the agitators said to the miserable people of Mayo "nothing is being done by the C.D. Board and you must act for yourselves."'[70] Indeed, security of tenure and a paltry revision of rent made little difference to a farmer whose land-holding could not sustain a family. Wyndham suggested that improvements in the quality of the land needed to be made if congestion was to be reformed: 'Some provision [needs to be] made so that the tenant may buy a holding on which he can live instead of scattered patches of soppy bog.'[71] The new Chief Secretary also emphasized the need to redistribute grazing land among the congested tenants who had, before 1881, been dependent on 'grazing accommodation' which they stocked on temporary leases: 'If they could not get that their calves would be of no use to them. But the grass lands are held by the landlord or grazier who can charge what he pleases.'[72] In the years following 1881, grazing accommodation became more and more scarce and no systematic attempt was made to improve the quality of congested land. By the turn of the century, the problem of congestion was entrenched in the rural communities of the west. A cabinet

---

[68] Wyndham, 'The Irish land question and the need for legislation', 1901, PRO CAB 37/59/147.

[69] Wyndham, cabinet memorandum on the Irish land question, 8 Oct. 1902, PRO CAB 37/62/139.

[70] Wyndham to Balfour, 13 Jan. 1901, BM ABP Add. MS 49,803/182–90.

[71] Wyndham to Balfour, 26 Nov. 1900, BM ABP Add. MS 49,803/139–144ᵛ.

[72] Wyndham, 'Land legislation for Ireland' (n.d., probably Jan. 1901), BM ABP Add. MS 49,803/165–81. This appears to be a first draft of Wyndham's cabinet memorandum 'The Irish land question and the need for legislation', PRO CAB 37/59/147.

memorandum of 1902 described congestion in precisely the same terms as it had been described in the 1880s: 'Congestion consists at its worst in the congregation of diminutive holdings held in Rundale, in intermixed plots, or scattered patches without grazing accommodation, undrained, unfenced, sometimes without roads, studded with squalid cabins.'[73]

From the vantage point of the 1890s, there were few legal opportunities for congested tenants to enhance the economic viability of their holdings. In this climate, the United Irish League, which was committed to redistributing grazing land and pressurizing the Government into more effective action, gained an extensive amount of support. The land legislation of the late nineteenth century provided the rationale for congested tenants to turn from legal to illegal courses of action, in pursuit of a reasonable standard of living. In the official mind, congestion had become synonymous with agitation: 'The materials for agitation are preserved in the congestion of a large portion of the population on small and impoverished tillage farms.'[74] By the late 1890s, the congested tenants of the west demanded fair treatment from the Government and, in the absence of substantial reforms, switched their allegiance from the law of the land to the law of the League.

At the end of the nineteenth century, the land question was far from resolved: landlords, large tenants, and congested tenants were all dissatisfied, for different reasons, with the legislation of the 1880s and the 1890s. Landlords felt that they were being financially ruined by legislation; large tenants wanted to consolidate their gains with land purchase; and congested tenants were beginning to turn to the United Irish League for the cure of their economic ills. Wyndham was committed to addressing these problems and devising a legislative solution to the land question.[75] Unlike his predecessors, the Balfour brothers, who had dominated the Irish Office since 1887, Wyndham had 'a genuine desire . . . [for the] constructive rejuvenation of Irish society'.[76] He had some Irish blood—he was a great-grandson of Lord Edward Fitzgerald and a relative of the fourth Earl of Dunraven—and he was an admirer of the Irish Literary Revival.[77] In 1890, he had toured the west of Ireland with Arthur Balfour, and he had an extensive knowledge of the Irish land problem. As an imperialist,

---

[73] Wyndham, cabinet memorandum on the land question, 8 Oct. 1902, PRO CAB 37/62/139.

[74] Wyndham, 'The Irish land question and the need for legislation', 1901, PRO CAB 37/59/147.

[75] On Wyndham, see Andrew Gailey, *Ireland and the death of kindness: the experience of constructive unionism, 1890–1905* (Cork, 1987), 161–72.

[76] Ibid. 163.   [77] Ibid. 162–4.

he believed that the Irish would be more inclined and better equipped to defend the empire if they were 'healthy, energetic, hopeful and independent' and he thus recommended large-scale social reforms, particularly in the congested districts.[78]

Although he was genuinely committed to improving living standards in the west, his motivation was political rather than humanitarian. His view of the people of Connacht was Darwinian in inspiration. The congested districts were 'centres of racial deterioration'[79] and he hoped that a combination of natural selection and social reform would transform the 'obscene reptiles' of this 'backwater' into a 'part of the aryan race'.[80] Despite these views, he was firmly committed to solving the apparently unsolvable land question. In November, he wrote:

In spite of . . . some forty Acts of Parliament, the land question is not progressing towards a solution . . .

Landlordism and political economy were banished from Ireland by the Act of 1881. As a consequence, Ireland, in an age of keen international competition and the universal depression of tillage, is fixed for ever in the deplorable conditions of land tenure which obtained there thirty years ago.[81]

As yet, Wyndham had no clear policy with regard to either the land question or the United Irish League, but it was well known in nationalist circles that he intended to introduce a new Land Bill at an early date.[82] The United Irish League's objective, between 1900 and 1903 was to ensure that Wyndham's solution would take due consideration of the tenants' demand by introducing compulsory land purchase.

II

The United Irish League's agitation for compulsory land purchase was launched by William O'Brien and John Redmond at a meeting at Westport on 1 September 1901. At this meeting, William O'Brien explained the objective of the new agitation:

It is my solemn conviction that unless the people take this matter [the proposed land

[78] Micks, *Account of the . . . Congested Districts Board*, 181; Gailey, *Ireland and the death of kindness*, 165–6.

[79] Wyndham, cabinet memorandum on the land question, 8 Oct. 1902, PRO CAB 37/62/139.

[80] Quoted in Gailey, *Ireland and the death of kindness*, 165.

[81] Wyndham, 'The Irish land question and the need for legislation', 1901, PRO CAB 37/59/147.

[82] *Irish People*, 31 Aug. 1901.

legislation] into their own hands this winter and open the eyes of the Government by very vigorous measures; indeed, unless they make the present state of things uncomfortable and intolerable for every rackrenter and big grazier and grabber during the next six months (cheers), the Government will come down next session with a Land Purchase Bill that might as well be drafted in Lord Sligo's rent-office . . . I can see only one remedy, and that is, that every branch of the League in the West should take action in their own parish and treat every obstructing landlord and grabber, and every shopkeeper who takes sides with them (cheers) in exactly the same manner as you would treat . . . the wretched grabber . . . People may say to me that would be to throw half the country into a blaze (loud cheers). My answer is so much the better if the whole country were in a blaze. Will anybody tell me how otherwise anything has ever been won or will ever be won for Ireland?[83]

O'Brien was aware that the new Chief Secretary was in the process of drafting a new Land Bill to resolve the myriad problems generated by the 1881 Act, and he was keen to ensure that the new legislation would favour the tenant rather than the landlord. In the absence of tenant pressure, O'Brien believed that Wyndham and the Government would draft a Land Purchase Bill designed to placate the aggrieved landlords without address-ing the plight of the tenants and, particularly, the small tenant farmers of Connacht. The new agitation marked a turning point for the League. Formerly, the agitation had focused on applying pressure to the graziers, to force them to surrender their eleven-month tenancies. Now, for the first time, the United Irish League defined the landlords as the enemies of the League. Boycotting was to be applied not just to the graziers and the grabbers, as before, but also to those landlords who refused to sell their land to prospective tenant purchasers. William O'Brien's newspaper, the *Irish People*, confirmed the objective of the new campaign in its appeal to the rank and file members of the United Irish League: 'The English Parliament will only listen and yield to their demands when Government from Dublin Castle has been made unpleasant to the point of impossibil-ity, and when the proteges of Dublin Castle—the rackrenters, grabbers, and graziers . . .—have been convinced that the sooner the existing system is ended the better and the more profitable for themselves.'[84]

O'Brien's strategy for the new agitation appears to have been based on the assumption that an increase in the amount of boycotting in Ireland would force the Government to intervene to restore the authority of the law. As a veteran of the Land War and the Plan of Campaign, O'Brien had an intimate knowledge of Government responses to Irish agitations and could therefore guess at the likely response of the Government to a

---

[83] *Irish People*, 7 Sept. 1901.   [84] Ibid.

campaign which systematically encouraged boycotting. The legislative response to the Irish Land War epitomised the attitude of the British to the government of Ireland in the later nineteenth century. A Coercion Act (the Peace Preservation Act of March 1881) was introduced first, followed by a conciliatory measure (Gladstone's second Land Act of August 1881). This combination of coercion and conciliation became the staple British response to Irish disturbances, particularly in the era of the Balfour brothers, who dominated the Irish Office between 1887 and 1900. Andrew Gailey has described the Chief Secretaryships of Arthur and Gerald Balfour as characterized by a 'Balfourian orthodoxy' which 'demanded that coercion ... [be] coupled with conciliation'.[85] Arthur Balfour's career as Chief Secretary encapsulated this orthodoxy. In 1887, he introduced a new coercionist Crimes Act and this was followed by a spate of conciliatory legislation which culminated in the creation of the Congested Districts Board in 1891.[86] A less experienced agitator than O'Brien could have guessed that the likely Government response to the new agitation would be an admixture of coercion and conciliation.

The campaign for compulsory purchase comprised of two interlinked strategies. First, the United Irish League branches were to increase the amount of boycotting in Ireland and thereby undermine the authority of the law in an increasingly larger area. Second, the Irish Party MPs were to articulate the political demand of the agitation in the House of Commons. League branches were not, therefore, called upon to petition the Government for compulsory land purchase; instead, they maintained agitations against graziers, 'grabbers', and landlords.[87] John Redmond and the Irish Party were responsible for articulating the demand of the agitation and, as Parnell had done during the Land War, of threatening the Government with renewed agitation if the tenants' demand was not conceded. After the initiation of the new campaign at Westport in September 1901, Redmond told the Commons: 'This agrarian trouble which has arisen in the West ... could be stopped tomorrow if the Government simply gave a hope to those people that in the near future they would obtain the concession of their demand [compulsory land purchase].'[88] O'Brien calculated that Wyndham's hand would be forced by a joint campaign of civil disturbance and parliamentary agitation. The Government could not ignore what it perceived as 'lawlessness' and would have to introduce new legislation if

[85] Gailey, *Ireland and the death of kindness*, 181.
[86] Lyons, *Ireland since the Famine*, 189, 205.
[87] See Ch. 4.
[88] Hansard, 4th series, 13 Mar. 1902, vol. civ, col. 1305.

the disturbance created by the United Irish League expanded over a substantial portion of the country.

This was the theory of the new United Irish League agitation, but how did the campaign work in practice? After September 1901, the Irish Party MPs, United Irish League organizers, and nationalist press worked together to increase the amount of boycotting in Ireland. At public meetings throughout the country, a number of MPs openly advocated the boycotting of named individuals. Willie Redmond, MP for west Clare (and John's younger brother), presided at an illegal meeting at Kilmaine, county Mayo, called to intimidate a 'grabber' in the locality; the meeting was violently dispersed by a police baton charge.[89] In November, Dillon indulged in violent rhetoric at Roscommon, calling on his audience to 'Band yourselves together in a ... fighting organization. Make it hot for the graziers and grabbers.'[90] Seven of the Irish Party MPs were paid United Irish League organizers and toured the country making speeches in favour of boycotting and intimidation;[91] of these, Conor O'Kelly and John O'Donnell, the two young Mayo O'Brienites, were particularly vociferous.

The nationalist press was equally influential in expanding the area of disturbance in Ireland. Of the national weeklies, the *Irish People* and the *Weekly Freeman* reported the speeches of O'Brien, Dillon, and Redmond, as well as those of junior members of the Party. The press also increased the power of boycotting by publishing the names of boycotted persons in their columns. The provincial press was of great importance in this respect. A boycott could be enforced only within a limited area by a single UIL branch, but with the assistance of the press, a boycott could be rigorously enforced across an entire county. At least fifteen provincial newspapers in nine counties consistently published the names of boycotted persons in the months after September 1901,[92] providing the provincial

---

[89] IG monthly report, Oct. 1901, PRO CO 904/73.

[90] The confidential print, 1898–1901, PRO CO 903/8/762.

[91] Conor O'Kelly had ceased to be a paid UIL organizer, but he continued to agitate on behalf of the UIL in Mayo. The confidential print, 1898–1901, PRO CO 903/8/180–1, 434–5, 650.

[92] The following newspapers published 'intimidatory resolutions': the *Sligo Champion* (Sligo), the *Waterford Star* (Waterford), the *Waterford News* (Waterford), the *Munster Express* (Waterford), the *Kilkenny People* (Kilkenny), the *Roscommon Messenger* (Roscommon), the *Western People* (Ballina), the *Longford Leader* (Longford), the *Mayo News* (Westport), the *Limerick Leader* (Limerick), and the *Cork Examiner* (Cork). Memorandum on 'Disturbed areas', submitted by David Harrel to Chief Secretary, 22 June 1901, NA CBS, 1901, 24930/S box 19. In the course of the agitation, the Inspector General added a number of other newspapers to this list: the *Clareman* (Ennis), the *Tipperary Champion* (Thurles), the *Midland Tribune* (Longford), and the *Western News* (Ballinasloe). IG monthly report, Aug. 1901, PRO CO 904/73; IG monthly report, Nov. 1901, PRO CO 904/74; and IG monthly report, Feb. 1902, PRO CO 904/74.

League branches with an additional power and potency. Even the threat of publishing the names of boycotted persons in the press wielded a powerful influence over the enemies of the League. According to the Inspector General: 'there is nothing the peasantry and small shopkeepers dread so much.'[93] In the autumn of 1901, the power of the press provided the UIL with an authority which had been achieved in Land League times only through the use of *force majeure*:

Were it not for the publication of reports—true or false—of the proceedings at Committee Meetings of the League branches, clearly inciting persons to boycott and intimidate, and even threatening to compel persons to join the League, by announcing that the names of persons who did not join would be published, the organization would be unable to do much mischief, when its mandates are not enforced by outrages. 'The Sligo Champion' alone has done more harm than all the paid agitators have been able to accomplish.[94]

The cumulative effect of the new campaign was a dramatic increase in both the number and the influence of United Irish League branches. The number of UIL branches increased from 989 in July 1901 to 1,211 in March 1902,[95] an increase of 18 per cent, and the total number of boycotted persons increased from 24 to 39 between September 1901 and March 1902, an increase of 38 per cent.[96] There was also a substantial rise in the number of United Irish League meetings being held: the average number of meetings held each month between October 1900 and December 1901 was 28, while the average number of meetings held each month between January and December 1902 was 81.[97] In terms of the anti-grazier agitation, the League became demonstrably more effective in the course of the new agitation: forty-one grazing farms were unlet due to UIL influence in September 1901, and by March 1902 this had increased to seventy-four. Over the same period, the number of new tenants ('grabbers') who paid compensation to former (evicted) tenants rose from sixteen to twenty-nine.[98] At an electoral level, the League won a decisive victory in the 1902 local government elections. In Connacht, 83 per cent of the new county councillors were members of the League; in Munster, 75 per cent; in

[93] IG monthly report, Nov. 1901, PRO CO 904/74.

[94] IG monthly report, Dec. 1901, PRO CO 904/74.

[95] UIL membership figures, PRO CO 904/20/2.

[96] The confidential print, 1898–1901, PRO CO 903/8/734; the confidential print, 1902, PRO CO 903/9/419.

[97] Calculated from the number of UIL meetings recorded in the confidential print, 1898–1901, PRO CO 903/8, and the confidential print, 1902, PRO CO 903/9.

[98] The confidential print, 1898–1901, PRO CO 903/8/734; the confidential print, 1902, PRO CO 903/9/419.

Leinster, 53 per cent; and in Ulster, 43 per cent. (The national average was 57 per cent.)[99]

The new agitation also manifested itself in what the Government feared was a new Plan of Campaign. From November 1901 an agitation against the payment of rent spread through Roscommon, Sligo, and Mayo and 'seriously disturbed a large portion of these counties'.[100] Over the following six months, combinations against the payment of rent were formed on a number of estates in the five Connacht counties and also in Cavan.[101] The Irish Office feared that this was an aspect of the new campaign and the Attorney General charged O'Brien in the House of Commons with responsibility for what looked like an organized attempt to revive the Plan of Campaign. He argued that the new Plan of Campaign was inspired by an article O'Brien had written for the *Freeman's Journal* on 27 September 1901.[102] The article did encourage tenants to bring the 'question of compulsory sale . . . to an issue in the South' by demanding rent reductions equivalent to those obtained by tenant purchasers under the 1885 and 1890 Land Acts, but it did not recommend that they form rent combinations if their request was refused.[103] O'Brien wrote confidentially to Tim McCarthy, the editor of the *Irish People*:

here am I identified with responsibility for a fight which is diametrically the opposite of what I proposed . . . Read my Westport speech, my Bangor speech, and my letter to the Directory and you will see I never for one moment contemplated a no-rent movement. I knew only too well it would only land us in ruinous responsibility for a few bankrupt estates.[104]

O'Brien had encouraged tenants to boycott those landlords who refused to sell their estates or reduce rents, and he did not advise the revival of a 'no rent' campaign along the lines of the Plan of Campaign. O'Brien was still periodically reminded of the fiasco of 'New Tipperary'[105] by unsympathetic audiences and he had no wish to return to the protracted

---

[99] The confidential print, 1902, PRO CO 903/9/421–2.

[100] IG monthly report, Nov. 1901, PRO CO 904/74.

[101] IG monthly reports, Nov. 1901–Apr. 1902, PRO CO 904/74–5.

[102] Quoted in Hansard, 4th series, 28 Feb. 1902, vol. civ, cols. 106–7.

[103] Quoted in ibid., col. 107.

[104] Warwick-Haller, *William O'Brien*, 213.

[105] O'Brien had attempted, during the Plan of Campaign, to strike a blow against Arthur Smith-Barry, a Tipperary landlord, by migrating the Tipperary town tenants on his estate to a 'new Tipperary', and thus reducing Smith-Barry's rent. The plan backfired, however, when it became clear that the site of the new town market was also on the Smith-Barry estate and the landlord demolished the building. Maume, 'Aspects of Irish nationalist political culture', 88.

and expensive legal struggles with landlords which the Plan of Campaign had involved. In fact, the source of this initiative was not William O'Brien or the Irish Party, but a number of local leaders who capitalized on the strength of local feeling on a number of estates in north Connacht.[106] Even so, the Irish Office continued to view the United Irish League's agitation for compulsory land purchase as the source of the new Plan of Campaign. A section of the confidential print for 1902 is devoted to the 'Plan of Campaign, 1901–2' and states that William O'Brien's speech at Westport on 1 September was 'the origin of the present agitation'.[107]

Undoubtedly, the non-payment of rent on a substantial number of estates in north Connacht compounded the level of disturbance in Ireland, even if it was not intended by O'Brien to be an element of the new agitation. By the early months of 1902, Neville Chamberlain, the Inspector General, was in a state of panic regarding the United Irish League. In his estimation, eleven counties were now in a disturbed state and he wrote, with some trepidation:

I am ... satisfied that the influence of the League is steadily covering a large portion of the Country, and that in localities where circumstances favour the development of secret intimidation, the machinery is complete, and there is reason to fear we may drift into greater difficulties than have been encountered of late years.

Our special arrangements in the disturbed areas can and do deal effectually with open crime ...

We are, however, entirely powerless to touch the local gangs of Conspirators who assemble in their rooms with closed doors, and there formulate decrees which are promulgated by a vicious press, and enforced by a steady pressure with which experience clearly demonstrates the ordinary law is absolutely inadequate to cope. This is evidenced by the fact that, notwithstanding all the support we can give them, many attacked persons have yielded, and are yielding to this pressure.

I am informed by the senior officers of the Royal Irish Constabulary who have had experience of a somewhat similar condition of things in former years, that they consider the general peace of the Country is distinctly endangered by these methods of the United Irish League, that they are of opinion that the ordinary law is inoperative against such methods, and that they feel the time has arrived for considering whether other prompt and summary steps should not be adopted to restore order, and to establish confidence in the power of the law. In these opinions I concur.[108]

---

[106] For a discussion of this local initiative, see Fergus Campbell, 'Land and politics in Connacht, 1898–1909' (University of Bristol, Ph.D., 1997), Ch. 3.

[107] The confidential print, 1902, PRO CO 903/9/185–211; the confidential print, 1902, PRO CO 903/9/186.

[108] IG monthly report, Jan. 1902, PRO CO 904/74.

Chamberlain was, however, an inexperienced Inspector General. He had been in office for only eighteen months and prior to that had no experience of Irish affairs.[109] He was bewildered by the United Irish League and unsure how it could be policed effectively. Other officials in the Irish Office felt that he was prone to exaggeration and on one occasion he was told by the Under-Secretary to rewrite his monthly report on the grounds that it was too pessimistic.[110] It is necessary, therefore, to assess the veracity of Chamberlain's description of the state of Ireland in early 1902 by undertaking a case study of one of the disturbed districts, east Galway.

III

The east riding of county Galway, and, in particular, the two police districts of Athenry and Loughrea in the south of the riding, had been disturbed by agrarian agitation throughout the last quarter of the nineteenth century. A special report on the state of the riding in 1905 observed:

During the past twenty-five years the southern portion of the County Galway has been ever prominent in the agrarian agitation and its accompanying disturbances of the public peace. In the days of the old Land League, from 1879 to 1882, it bore an evil reputation for the number of murders committed within its borders; the adoption of the policy known as the 'Plan of Campaign', in the period from 1886 to 1890, was vigorously supported on the Clanricarde and other estates within the Riding; and in few districts of the country did the programme of the United Irish League, founded in the Spring of 1899, receive a warmer reception than in South Galway.

The United Irish League's agrarian programme had a particular relevance to the smallholders of east Galway, as the special report explained:

The circumstances of a large majority of the small landowners [*sic*] have always favoured agrarian agitation. Living, in great part, on uneconomic holdings in the bogs and by the mountains, the smaller tenant-farmers at all times naturally lent a willing ear to anyone promising them a share of the rich grass lands of which its plains are composed, and to them more than to any other class the programme of the United Irish League forcibly appealed, its primary objective being the breaking up of the large grazing tracts, and their division among the small tenant-farmers.[111]

---

[109] Chamberlain was a regular army colonel and a former commandant of the Khyber Pass and military adviser to the Kashmir Government. Charles Townshend, *Political violence in Ireland: government and resistance since 1848* (Oxford, 1983), 230–1.

[110] IG monthly report, Nov. 1903, NA IGCI/4.

[111] The confidential print, 1905, PRO CO 903/12/97.

Between 1899 and 1901, the League firmly established itself in east Galway. By June 1901, there were thirty-four branches of the League with 2,800 members.[112] The branches actively agitated against the grazing system and, in 1901, the police districts of Athenry and Loughrea were defined by the Under-Secretary as two of the most disturbed districts in Ireland.[113] On the eve of the new UIL campaign for compulsory land purchase, the agitation was primarily focused on the Dunsandle estate in the Athenry and Loughrea police districts and on a grazing farm near Newbridge, in the north of the riding.[114]

After the announcement of the new campaign in September, the county MPs, the local UIL organizers, and the regional press began a comprehensive agitation to increase the level of disturbance in the riding. The two MPs in the riding, John Roche, a miller from Woodford and former Plan of Campaign leader,[115] and William Duffy, a Loughrea shopkeeper and officer of the National League,[116] were both prosecuted in the course of 1902 for making public speeches in support of boycotting and intimidation.[117] The United Irish League organizers were even more vocal in their incitements to increased agitation. In particular, James Lynam had a reputation for making 'violent speeches'.[118] As a result of one speech at Ballygar in December 1901, where he recommended that the local Leaguers should 'Beat the big drum opposite his [the grazier's] door and make it [the farm] be gave up',[119] a grazier named Hughes gave up his eleven-month lease.[120] The local press reinforced the power of the League in the riding. The names of boycotted persons were published in the pages of the *Western News* and the *Loughrea and Athenry Guardian*, which carried 'leading articles against landlords and graziers'. William Hastings, district councillor and proprietor, editor, and publisher of the *Western News*, was prosecuted in 1902 for 'publishing a boycotting article against graziers'.[121]

[112] Winder, memorandum on the United Irish League, 7 Aug. 1901, NA CBS, 1901, 24995/S box 19.

[113] Memorandum on 'Disturbed areas', submitted by David Harrel to Chief Secretary, 22 June 1901, NA CBS, 1901, 24930/S box 19.

[114] Ibid.

[115] John Roche's obituary, *Connacht Tribune*, 29 Aug. 1914.

[116] William Duffy's diary in the possession of Mary Duffy, Loughrea.

[117] Michael Davitt, *The fall of feudalism in Ireland* (London, 1904), 699–700.

[118] The confidential print, 1898–1901, PRO CO 903/8/180–4. On Lynam's organizational efforts in Galway, see UCC Willian O'Brien papers AIB/58, 64, 72, 77, 93, 119 and 127.

[119] The confidential print, 1902, PRO CO 903/9/108. On the intimidatory effect of 'drumming', see Ch. 4.

[120] CI monthly report, east Galway, Dec. 1901, PRO CO 904/74.

[121] The confidential print, 1902, PRO CO 903/9/529, 571–3.

As a result of the new agitation, the County Inspector observed in February 1902:

The state of the Riding is satisfactory as far as freedom from outrage & serious crime is concerned. In this respect it compares favourably with the same period in 1900. I cannot say however that men can go about their lawful business without hindrance or interference . . . Men dare not take grass farms, some of which were let in 1900. The absence of boycotting and intimidation is due less to the growth of a law abiding spirit than to the fact that such practices are unnecessary to compel submission to the U.I.L. As a rule people make no effort to resist its influence or ignore its dictates.[122]

The most significant problem, from the County Inspector's point of view, was that the so-called 'law of the League' appeared to be superseding the 'law of the land' in the region. It was virtually impossible to gain information from the community as to who was responsible for the intimidation and boycotting which the United Irish League used to 'enforce its dictates'. As early as August 1900, the County Inspector observed: 'The police labour under the greatest difficulties in obtaining information in agrarian cases in this county. The people including the persons injured have a horror of appearing to assist the Police & much prefer to thwart their efforts. In the few cases where information has been obtainable no person on earth would induce the informants to give evidence.'[123] The problems encountered by the Royal Irish Constabulary in their endeavours to uphold the law are illustrated in the following study of their attempt to prosecute the UIL branch at Craughwell.

The Craughwell branch of the United Irish League initiated a campaign against the local graziers in the spring of 1900: 'During the year 1900 the Craughwell Branch was very active against graziers and a considerable number of outrages were committed, all of which were attributed to the influence of the branch.'[124] In April, the branch posted threatening letters to all the graziers in the locality, demanding that they give up their grazing tenancies,[125] and passed a resolution calling 'on all the graziers holding grass lands in this parish to surrender them on May Day next'.[126] Those graziers who refused to comply with the League's demands were systematically boycotted and intimidated by the League. James Kelly and

---

[122] CI monthly report, east Galway, Feb. 1902, PRO CO 904/74.
[123] CI monthly report, east Galway, Aug. 1900, PRO CO 904/71.
[124] The confidential print, 1898–1901, PRO CO 903/8/585.
[125] 'Statement of Mr. Thomas Ryan of Coscorrig', 7 June 1901, NA CBS, 1901, 24770/S box 19.
[126] Ibid.

Richard Allen, for example, who refused to give in to the League's wishes, had shots fired through their windows; crowds assembled outside their doors who shouted and booed at them; and 'imitation' coffins were dug into the ground outside their houses.[127] Not surprisingly, they gave up their grazing tenancies as a result of this intimidation, and succumbed to the demands of the local UIL.[128]

The success of the UIL in Craughwell created a problem for the local Constabulary, who were unable to protect farmers who exercised their legal right to lease grazing land. In January 1901, the County Inspector expressed his exasperation at the paralysis of the ordinary law in the Craughwell area: 'The sufferers . . . [of] terrorism . . . can't be induced to support the ordinary law, because they have absolutely no faith in its power to protect them.'[129] In this climate, the local police were becoming desperate and, in an attempt to secure a prosecution of the branch, Sergeant Costello entered the League room during a meeting on 28 January 1901 and forcibly seized the books and papers which he found there.[130] The County Inspector hoped that these items of evidence, which he told the Inspector General had been collected '[b]y dint of patience & perseverance', would result in a successful prosecution of the League for criminal conspiracy.[131] However, the Law Officers did not share the County Inspector's optimism. The bulk of the evidence against the Craughwell United Irish League was the book which Sergeant Costello had seized. It contained 'the names of persons who had grass lands and the names of farms—notably Tallaroe and it is at all events a peculiar coincidence that outrages occurred as regards the persons named and the farms'.[132] In the estimation of the Crown Solicitor, a conspiracy 'to compel occupiers to give up grazing farms' undoubtedly existed 'but it is difficult on the evidence available to bring the case home to the Defendants'.[133]

The greatest obstacle confronting the local police was the reluctance of the victims to give evidence against their assailants. This was most apparent at the hearing of the case at Athenry Petty Sessions on 8 March.

[127] Crown Solicitor's report, *R. v. Connolly, Clasby, and others*, submitted to Under-Secretary, 29 May 1901, NA CBS, 1901, 24770/S box 19.

[128] The confidential print, 1898–1901, PRO CO 903/8/585.

[129] CI monthly report, east Galway, Jan. 1901, PRO CO 904/72.

[130] Crown Solicitor's report, *R. v. Connolly, Clasby, and others*, submitted to Under-Secretary, 29 May 1901, NA CBS, 1901, 24770/S box 19.

[131] CI monthly report, east Galway, Jan. 1901, PRO CO 904/72.

[132] Crown Solicitor's report, *R. v. Connolly, Clasby, and others*, submitted to Under-Secretary, 29 May 1901, NA CBS, 1901, 24770/S box 19.

[133] Crown Solicitor's report, *R. v. Connolly, Clasby, and others*, submitted to Under-Secretary, 29 May 1901, NA CBS, 1901, 24770/S box 19.

Richard Allen, who had told the police in November 1900 that he had been 'charged'[134] with grazing the Tallaroe farm at a League meeting to which he had been summoned, 'swore he was never summoned to attend a meeting of the League, that he was never charged before the League with having taken Tallaroe grass farm, and that he did not remove his cattle off this farm owing to the action of the League'.[135] James Kelly 'swore the same' but his earlier statements to the police suggest why he did not assist the Crown prosecution. On 28 November he told the local Constabulary that he had attended a meeting of the local UIL where he had 'heard' some remarks, one of which suggested that 'if I am examined to give evidence against the league, its as well for me to throw myself into the thurlough [sic] or brake [sic] up my house'.[136] By the following January, his memory was fading, as he told the police: 'I attended the League several times. I could not give any date. I dont [sic] know what was said to me in the league room or who was there. My memory sometimes is not very good. I have nothing to say . . . A man has a conscience to save.'[137]

The changes in Kelly's statements indicate that he was pressurized into concealing the identity of those who had intimidated him into giving up his grass land. This is confirmed by Sergeant O'Connor's report of the proceedings at the hearing: 'It was the general opinion in Court that these witnesses were perjuring themselves, and that they were doing so through fear of the League and its agents. When they made replies favourable to the accused, the civilians present smiled and looked at each other.'[138] One grazier who had been intimidated by the Craughwell UIL, Anthony Ryan, was summoned as a Crown witness but did not attend because 'he knew he would have to perjure himself in order to please the Craughwell Leaguers, and, being, as he is, subject to epileptic fits, he was afraid of dying after having perjured himself, before he could repent'.[139] The magistrates returned the defendants for trial to the summer assizes in July, but the Law Officers decided in June that the case was 'not one that could be presented

---

[134] Richard Allen statement, 28 Nov. 1900, NA CBS, 1901, 24770/S box 19.

[135] Sergeant J. O'Connor, report of the Craughwell conspiracy case at Athenry Petty Sessions, 8 Mar. 1901, submitted to the County Inspector on 10 Mar. 1901, NA CBS, 1901, 24770/S box 19.

[136] Ibid.; first statement of James Kelly to Sergeant Costello, 28 Nov. 1900, NA CBS, 1901, 24770/S box 19. There is a turlough or lake at Craughwell.

[137] Second statement of James Kelly to Sergeant Costello, 28 Jan. 1901, NA CBS, 1901, 24770/S box 19.

[138] Sergeant J. O'Connor, report of the Craughwell conspiracy case at Athenry Petty Sessions, 8 Mar. 1901, submitted to the County Inspector on 10 Mar. 1901, NA CBS, 1901, 24770/S box 19.

[139] Ibid.

at Assizes with a reasonable prospect of success' and the prosecution was dropped.[140]

This case illustrates the problems which the police confronted in their attempt to uphold the law in the disturbed districts. By the early months of 1902, it was clear that the law was inoperative in east Galway and that the United Irish League branches, in the words of the County Inspector, 'control the whole affairs of the Riding'.[141] On the evidence of one of the disturbed districts, then, Chamberlain's diagnosis of the state of Ireland in January 1902 was correct. It was now the responsibility of the Government, and particularly the Chief Secretary, to decide on a policy that would restore the authority of the law in the disturbed districts.

IV

Wyndham spent his first two years in office considering the question of land reform. He believed that extensive land purchase would satisfy both landlord and tenant. In two cabinet memorandums, he outlined a scheme whereby the landlord would be paid a sum in cash that he could reinvest, and that would provide him with an income comparable to that which he had gained from his land. The tenant, on the other hand, would pay an annuity which was at least 20 per cent less than his current rent; and the Government would pay the difference between what the tenant paid and what the landlord would accept. In addition, congested holdings would be consolidated and improved at the Government's expense, so that they would provide congested tenants with an adequate living.[142] In this way, both landlords and tenants would be tempted into land purchase agreements, and the present 'deadlock', which Wyndham described as profiting 'no one except the Nationalist agitator', would be overcome.[143]

If Wyndham's proposals were to become law, he required the support of the Irish Party both to assist the passage of a Land Bill in the House of Commons and to gain acceptance for the measure in Ireland. He was obliged, therefore, to court the support of the moderate wing of the Irish

---

[140] Minute on Craughwell conspiracy, submitted by David Harrel, the Under-Secretary, to Inspector General, 3 June 1901, NA CBS, 1901, 24770/S box 19.

[141] CI monthly report, east Galway, Apr. 1902, PRO CO 904/75.

[142] Wyndham, 'The Irish land question and the need for legislation', PRO CAB 37/59/147; Wyndham, cabinet memorandum on the Irish land question, 8 Oct. 1902, PRO CAB 37/62/139.

[143] Wyndham, 'The Irish land question and the need for legislation', PRO CAB 37/59/147.

nationalist movement. Wyndham believed that the Irish nationalist movement was composed of two polarized groups: the moderates, which included many members of the Irish Parliamentary Party, the Catholic bishops, and most priests; and the extremists or members of secret societies who, he believed, constituted 10 per cent of the United Irish League membership.[144] It was well known in Dublin Castle that Redmond, the leader of the moderates, did not want a 'stand-up' fight; but Wyndham feared that if the Government introduced coercive legislation in response to the UIL's campaign, the initiative in the nationalist movement would go to the extremists. In a letter to Hicks Beach, the Chancellor of the Exchequer, in March 1902, Wyndham outlined his views on the question of coercion:

A great bulk of moderate Nationalist opinion in Ireland which includes one-third, perhaps nearly one-half, of the Nationalist Parliamentary Party, wishes to avoid a 'stand-up' fight & is genuinely alarmed at the prospect of the extreme men & secret societies capturing the organization in the disturbed areas.

The R. C. Bishops, without exception, & the great majority of the priests are alarmed at the agitation and opposed to boycotting.

Coming to myself . . . I am strongly opposed to magnifying the Agitation & piling up the cost of coercion by proclaiming the United Irish League.[145]

In his correspondence with the cabinet, Wyndham was careful to play down the extent of the United Irish League's agitation, fearing that if he did not do so, the Government would unhesitatingly re-introduce coercion. Even in March 1902, when eleven counties were described by the Inspector General as in a 'disturbed state',[146] Wyndham was blithely informing the cabinet that

It [the agitation] is partial in its area; being mainly confined to the adjacent portions of 3 counties, Sligo, Mayo, Roscommon; to Clare, to Tipperary, & to a portion of Galway. Its area and virulence have been deliberately exaggerated by a Press Campaign, in the Dublin Unionist papers, some London papers & throughout the Provincial Press by the simultaneous publication of special articles evidently furnished by an agency.[147]

Wyndham's colleagues in the Irish Office and the cabinet did not share his view of the Irish land question. While he endeavoured to find a long-term

---

[144] Wyndham to Hicks Beach, 7 Mar. 1902, NLI Hicks Beach Papers MS 24,948 (1) [copies of originals held in Gloucestershire Records Office]; Wyndham to Balfour, 26 Nov. 1900, BM ABP Add. MS 49,803/139–144ᵛ.

[145] Wyndham to Hicks Beach, 7 Mar. 1902, NLI Hicks Beach Papers MS 24,948 (1).

[146] IG monthly report, Mar. 1902, PRO CO 904/74.

[147] Wyndham to Hicks Beach, 7 Mar. 1902, NLI Hicks Beach Papers MS 24,948 (1).

solution to the problem of Irish land agitation, they were more concerned with maintaining 'law and order' in the short term. By the spring of 1902, the tensions between the two opposing points of view had reached breaking point.

On 10 March 1902, the Viceroy, Lord Cadogan, submitted a memorandum to the cabinet on the state of Ireland.[148] He stated that policing measures taken in the summer of 1901 had failed and that

> The ordinary law is admittedly powerless to supply a remedy . . .
>
> The only further remedy remaining is to be found in the clauses of the Crimes Act, and I am of opinion that the time has now arrived for putting in force by Proclamation the provisions of that Act. The information I have been receiving daily for many weeks strengthens my conviction that it cannot be any longer postponed.
>
> The steps taken by the Irish Government up to the present time, with the hope of avoiding a Proclamation under the Crimes Act, have not been attended with the desired results, and the consequent effect has been to some extent discouraging to the loyal section of the community.[149]

He went on to recommend that seven counties 'where boycotting and intimidation have prevailed for some time, and are steadily growing and strengthening' should be proclaimed under sections 2, 3, and 4 of the Crimes Act.[150] Wyndham was infuriated by the Lord Lieutenant's intervention. He told Balfour that Cadogan knew 'nothing about either the Crimes Act or the law of Conspiracy and [that he] was absent from Ireland during most of the Autumn and Winter'.[151] For eighteen months, Wyndham had worked hard to formulate a considered Irish policy and he resented Cadogan's attempt to seize the initiative: 'I decline to defend a policy improvised to meet Newspaper attacks and gossip, as a substitute for a Policy submitted to the Cabinet in last July and vigorously pursued ever since by the officials in Ireland and myself.'[152] The London press, in particular, *The Times*, the *Globe*, and the *Morning Post*, were demanding that the Lord Lieutenant should restore 'law and order' in Ireland by proclaiming the United Irish League.[153] Their attacks on the Lord Lieutenant had an added sting because they implied that he was restraining Wyndham from 'enforcing the law' when it was, in fact, the other way round.[154]

---

[148] Lord Cadogan, cabinet memorandum on the 'Condition of Ireland', 10 Mar. 1902, PRO CAB 37/61/58.

[149] Ibid.   [150] Ibid.

[151] Wyndham to Balfour, 9 Mar. 1902, BM ABP Add. MS 49,804/8–11.

[152] Wyndham to Balfour, 3 Mar. 1902, BM ABP Add. MS 49,804/5–7.

[153] Gailey, *Ireland and the death of kindness*, 180.   [154] Ibid.

Wyndham was perhaps unfair in his characterization of the Lord Lieutenant's policy as an improvised response to press criticism.[155] The administrators in the Irish Office agreed with the Lord Lieutenant's proposals. Chamberlain described the state of Ireland in the spring of 1902 as 'unparalleled in any civilized country at the present time'.[156] David Harrel who, as Under-Secretary, was primarily responsible for the day-to-day administration of Ireland, 'had become greatly perturbed at the decline in law and order . . . and the chief secretary's reluctance to act decisively'.[157] The Irish Unionist Alliance, a strong extra-parliamentary lobby composed of some of the most prominent Irish landlords, wrote to the Prime Minister in March and asserted that

the first duty of a Government is to maintain order, to secure freedom for every man in all lawful dealings, and to check violence and injustice, and [we] . . . cannot but point out that such ends have not been attained in Ireland . . . [We call on the Government to take measures] vigorous and immediate, which may restore order and freedom of action in this country.[158]

The Irish administration and the Irish landlords, in addition to the London press, called for the Government to intervene to restore law and order, but Wyndham was determined to introduce a Land Bill before the Lord Lieutenant could introduce the Crimes Act.

In the course of March, Wyndham worked tirelessly to introduce a Land Bill which might placate the United Irish League's agitation and render the re-introduction of the Crimes Act unnecessary. On 7 March, he wrote to Michael Hicks Beach recommending 'an early introduction of the Bill, if possible before Easter, in order to give all parties in Ireland something with which they can occupy their minds during the recess more profitably than with the Agitation'.[159] Six days later, he told Balfour: 'I must bring in the Bill before Easter if I am to avoid whole sale [*sic*] coercion & 1/2 a million extra for police.'[160] Eventually, on 25 March, the Bill was introduced for what Wyndham described as 'political reasons'.[161] It did not include a number of the proposals which Wyndham had made in his cabinet memorandums. In particular, the Chancellor of the Exchequer, Hicks Beach,

---

155 Wyndham to Balfour, 3 Mar. 1902, BM ABP Add. MS 49,804/5–7.
156 IG monthly report, Feb. 1902, PRO CO 904/74.
157 Gailey, *Ireland and the death of kindness*, 180.
158 *Irish Times*, 11 Apr. 1902.
159 Wyndham to Hicks Beach, 7 Mar. 1902, NLI Hicks Beach Papers MS 24,948 (1).
160 Wyndham to Balfour, 13 Mar. 1902, BM ABP Add. MS 49,804/14–15.
161 Wyndham, cabinet memorandum on the Irish land question, 8 Oct. 1902, PRO CAB 37/62/139.

refused to allow the purchase instalment to be reduced. As Wyndham had outlined, this was a necessary reform if tenants were to be tempted into purchasing their holdings and, without it, the Bill contained little to recommend it to the Irish tenants.[162] The Bill also attempted to prevent tenants from applying for further revisions of rent in the land court. In the event of a tenant applying for a revision of his rent, the landlord was empowered by the new Bill to have a purchase price fixed on the holding and, if the tenant refused to purchase at that price, he would lose the right to have a fair rent fixed for fifteen years.[163] This compelled the tenant to purchase at a price over which he had no control, and even the pro-landlord *Irish Law Times and Solicitor's Journal* argued that it was an indefensible proposal that should be amended.[164] In every other respect, however, the *Irish Law Times* described the new Bill as 'a felicitously conceived measure'.[165] According to their statistics, the landlords would get an advantage of £232 on each £100 of rental if they sold their estates under the new Bill. A tenant who paid an annuity for twenty-two years, for example, would 'under the new system of finance, secure to the landlord not 22, but 25 years' purchase'.[166] The Bill attempted to accelerate land purchase in Ireland but it did so by making purchase more attractive to the landlords and less attractive to the tenants. For this reason, O'Brien described the Bill as 'not one to abolish Landlordism but to reinforce it'.[167] The Irish Party, despite their feelings of goodwill towards Wyndham, rejected the Bill *tout court* as an inadequate and insubstantial measure.

The advantage now fell to the coercionists in the cabinet and the Irish Office. After the failure of the Bill, the Irish Party 'spurred on by the U.I.L. . . . indulged in obstructive tactics [in the House of Commons] not seen since Parnell's heyday'.[168] This, combined with increased pressure from the London press, the Irish Unionist Alliance and the extensive lawlessness in Ireland, forced the Government to re-introduce the Crimes Act in April. On 16 April, just three weeks after the introduction of Wyndham's Bill and six days after the Prime Minister had received a deputation from the Irish Unionist Alliance,[169] the cabinet ordered Wyndham to proclaim nine counties and two county boroughs under the Criminal Law and

---

[162] Wyndham to Hicks Beach, 7 Mar. 1902, NLI Hicks Beach Papers MS 24,948 (1).
[163] *Irish Law Times and Solicitor's Journal*, 5 Apr. 1902.
[164] Ibid.
[165] *Irish Law Times and Solicitor's Journal*, 12 Apr. 1902.
[166] *Irish Law Times and Solicitor's Journal*, 5 Apr. 1902.
[167] O'Brien to Redmond, 14 May 1902, quoted in Warwick-Haller, *William O'Brien*, 216.
[168] Gailey, *Ireland and the death of kindness*, 177.
[169] *Irish Times*, 11 Apr. 1902; Gailey, *Ireland and the death of kindness*, 181.

Procedure [Crimes] Act.[170] The Act was intended to restore the primacy
of the law in Ireland, primarily by making it easier to prosecute agrarian
offenders successfully. Three major reforms of the criminal justice system
were introduced by the Act. First, serious offences could be tried by two
Crown-appointed Resident Magistrates rather than by a jury. Second, the
venue of a trial could be moved from the county where the offence had
taken place. And third, special jurors could be appointed whose property valuation was £100 higher than that of ordinary jurors. Each of these
reforms was calculated to increase the likelihood of a prosecution resulting in a conviction.[171] In many cases, prosecutions had fallen through due
to 'the reluctance of local Justices or Juries to convict'.[172] The Crimes Act
was designed to prevent this from happening. Resident Magistrates could
try cases of serious agrarian crime and would be more likely to convict
than a jury who might sympathize with, or even know, the defendant. If
trial by jury was availed of by the prosecution, they could move the venue
of the trial so that the jurors would be less likely to know or sympathize
with the defendants. And, if the prosecution wished, they could appoint
special jurors, who were substantial property owners and, therefore, less
likely to be intimidated by the United Irish League into acquitting agrarian offenders. As a result of these provisions, there were a large number of
successful prosecutions of agrarian offenders. Of 186 persons proceeded
against under the Crimes Act from 10 August 1901 to 21 January 1903, 144
(77 per cent) were convicted.[173] Ostensibly, the law was now being upheld
in the disturbed counties, but Wyndham believed that these measures
would advertise rather than demoralize the United Irish League.

At a meeting of the National Directory of the United Irish League
on 27 June, it was decided that a new agitation should be inaugurated,
both to campaign for a more far-reaching Land Bill and to protest at the
prosecutions under the Crimes Act.[174] In an 'Address to League Branches',
the National Directory expressed 'the settled determination of the Irish
people to extort from this or some other British Ministry the great
measure of compulsory land purchase and to get rid once and for ever of
the incubus of landlordism . . . In every part of the country a movement

---

[170] In April 1902, Cavan, Clare, Cork, Leitrim, Mayo, Roscommon, Sligo, Tipperary,
Waterford, and the county boroughs of Cork and Waterford were proclaimed under the
Crimes Act. See the confidential print, 1902, PRO CO 903/9/276–83.

[171] For a summary of the reforms in the criminal justice system which the Crimes Act
introduced, see 'The Crimes Act in relation to cattle driving', PRO CO 904/121/139.

[172] Winder, memorandum on the United Irish League, 7 Aug. 1901, NACBS, 1901, 24995/S
box 19.   [173] The confidential print, 1902, CO 903/9/818–26.

[174] IG monthly report, June 1902, PRO CO 904/75; the confidential print, 1902, PRO CO
903/9/411–12.

against landlordism ought to be made, strong, effective, and fearless.'[175] This policy effectively renewed the agitation initiated in September 1901, which had been held in abeyance while the Land Bill was being discussed in Parliament. The leadership of the Party placed itself behind the renewed campaign. At a United Irish League convention in Limerick on 5 July, both Redmond and O'Brien made 'strong' speeches, with that of O'Brien being viewed by the police as 'a general incentive to rent conspiracies and boycotting'.[176] In the House of Commons, Redmond warned the Government that the agitation would continue until compulsory land purchase was introduced:

[the Chief Secretary] is not prepared, at the present moment, to introduce a compulsory Bill; popular agitation in Ireland is not yet a sufficiently strong power, or perhaps, I might say, not quite menacing and dangerous enough, and therefore there is this pretext that he will introduce a Land Bill; and we may have half a day wasted in a description of the details, and then we shall hear no more of it, and the right hon. Gentleman will go back to Ireland to get another lesson on the land question, and next year we may get compulsory purchase.[177]

And William O'Brien reiterated the objectives of the agitation in a speech at a convention held at Galway Town Hall on 13 August 1902 where he told his audience to 'throw toleration to the winds, and to tackle the evictors and the ranchers and the grabbers parish by parish and to bring it home to them in their daily lives that if they have made things intolerable for the people, the people can make life intolerable for them in return'.[178]

As a result of the renewed agitation, between March and December 1902, the number of unlet grazing farms increased from 74 to 76; the number of instances of 'grabbers' paying compensation to evicted tenants increased from 29 to 36; and the number of UIL branches increased from 1,211 to 1,242.[179] Cumulatively, the renewed agitation created a greater level of disturbance than that which had existed in the spring of 1902. Chamberlain observed in October that there was a significant amount of boycotting in ten counties and that: 'In many parts of Ireland widespread and unconcealed disloyalty exists, and is encouraged by many of those

[175] Memorandum on 'Alleged new plan of campaign', submitted by David Harrel to Lord Lieutenant, 14 July 1902, NA 999/619/4.

[176] 'Police and Crime Division: files recorded for the information of the Lord Lieutenant and Chief Secretary for week ending 12th July 1902.' Submitted by David Harrel to Lord Lieutenant, 12 July 1902, NA 999/619/4.

[177] Hansard, 4th series, 23 Jan. 1902, vol. ci, col. 703.

[178] The confidential print, 1902, PRO CO 903/9/496.

[179] The confidential print, 1902, PRO CO 903/9/419; 791; UIL membership figures, PRO CO 904/20/2.

who are leading the people . . . The agitation for a measure of compulsory purchase continues in an acute form all over Ireland.'[180] The Government responded once again with coercive legislation and, at the end of the summer, six more counties and two county boroughs were proclaimed under the Crimes Act.[181]

The United Irish League's agitation was also taking its toll on the Irish landlords. On 7 April, a number of prominent landlords, including the Duke of Abercorn, the Marquis of Waterford, Lords Ashtown and Clonbrock, and the Right Honourable Smith-Barry, issued a circular on behalf of the Irish Land Trust. The Trust aimed to resist tenant combinations demanding land purchase and to assist landlords in their attempts to stock evicted and boycotted farms: 'The necessity for a new defensive organisation . . . arises from the widespread revival of boycotting, intimidation, refusal to pay rent, and other forms of unfair or illegal pressure at the instigation of the United Irish League.'[182] Wyndham remarked in October that 'landlords desire to "get out" with a capital sum that can be reinvested without seriously diminishing [their] incomes'.[183] By the autumn, a number of moderate landlords were beginning to recognize that this was their best option and they agreed to meet in conference with representatives of the tenants to negotiate a solution to the land question.

The spark for the conference came from a Galway landlord, Captain John Shawe-Taylor, who wrote to *The Times* in September suggesting a conference of landlord and tenant representatives. Shawe-Taylor was from a comparatively small landed family (in Galway terms) at Castle Taylor, near Ardrahan.[184] Like his aunt Lady Augusta Gregory, the playwright and folklorist, he held views which were atypical of the class from which he came.[185] He supported land purchase, believing that once the land question was solved, landlords and tenants could work together in a new Ireland. In August 1904, he outlined his views in a letter to John Dillon:

I had hoped that the Land Act would have gone so far by this time that absolute confidence between man and man would have been restored in Ireland and so self-government would have been demanded by a United Ireland. This will come,

[180] IG monthly report, Oct. 1902, PRO CO 904/76.

[181] In September 1902, Galway, King's, Limerick, Longford, Queen's, Westmeath, and the county boroughs of Dublin and Limerick were proclaimed under the Crimes Act. The confidential print, 1902, PRO CO 903/9/528.

[182] 'Irish Land Trust', NLI Clonbrock papers MS 19,666, 158.

[183] Wyndham, cabinet memorandum on the Irish land question, 8 Oct. 1902, PRO CAB 37/62/139.

[184] The Shawe-Taylor estate consisted of 7,605 acres valued at £3,016 in the late 1870s. Patrick Melvin, 'The landed gentry of Galway, 1820–80', 512.

[185] Lyons, *Ireland since the Famine*, 218.

the only difference is that we cannot go as far at present as we should if this wretched land business were completely out of the way.[186]

After the upheavals of the late nineteenth-century, it was perhaps naive of Shawe-Taylor to believe that an atmosphere of 'absolute confidence between man and man' could emerge overnight; yet his vision of a post-land question 'United Ireland' represents an astute appreciation of the landlords' options in the early years of the new century. The trajectory of nineteenth century legislation suggested that the economic and political power of the landed classes would eventually be lost. If the landlords were to retain a role in Irish public life, therefore, it would have to be on the tenants' terms, and this meant accepting land purchase. Once the 'wretched land business' was out of the way, Shawe-Taylor argued, the landlords could begin to 'take a hand in the social & national uplifting of the Country'.[187] To understand the evolution of Shawe-Taylor's views on the land question, it is necessary to consider the influence of the east Galway locale on his thinking.

As we have seen, the east riding of county Galway was one of the most disturbed parts of Ireland in the course of the new United Irish League agitation. The closest branch of the United Irish League to the Shawe-Taylor residence at Castle Taylor was at Craughwell which was just 3 miles east of Ardrahan. This was one of the most active branches in the county.[188] It is unlikely that John Shawe-Taylor and his brother Frank, who resided with him at Castle Taylor, could have remained unaffected by the agitation in their immediate locality.[189] Indeed, it was believed locally that John Shawe-Taylor had witnessed the murder of Walter Bourke of Rahassane House on Thursday, 6 June 1882. As Gerard Greene, a native of Craughwell, recalled in 1988: 'they [the men responsible for killing Bourke] met Shawe-Taylor [after they had shot Bourke] . . . and they said that Shawe-Taylor . . . knew them and he was able to identify them and he never pretended that he did', presumably fearing that if he did, he would be shot too.[190] This is also confirmed by Martin Newell, who told the Bureau of Military History:

After the attack [on Walter Bourke], the men [who had shot him] crossed the farm

186 John Shawe-Taylor to John Dillon, 18 Aug. 1904, TCDA Dillon papers 6773/728.
187 John Shawe-Taylor to John Dillon, 8 Aug. 1904, TCDA Dillon papers 6773/726.
188 CI monthly report, east Galway, Jan. 1901, PRO CO 904/72.
189 On Frank Shawe-Taylor, see Ch. 1 and Ch. 6.
190 Interview by Jim Fahy with Gerard Greene, broadcast on RTE radio programme, 'Looking west', 18 Feb. 1988. One of the men in the party of five who shot Bourke (William Greene of Rathcosgrave) may have been Gerard Greene's father. Martin Newell witness statement, MA BMH WS 1,562.

of another landlord named Shaw-Taylor [*sic*], and on the way met Shaw-Taylor himself. Some of the men wanted to shoot Shaw-Taylor, but as all five men did not agree to do so, no attempt was made on him. The men got safely away ...

My father was one of the jurymen at the inquest [into the death of Bourke], and Shaw-Taylor, who was summoned to give evidence, never took his eyes off my father during the whole of the proceedings. When questioned if he knew any of the five men whom he met on his farm after the shooting, Shaw-Taylor stated that he knew intimately every man who lived within a six-mile radius of where he himself lived and none of the men he saw on his land lived within that radius. It was believed that Shaw-Taylor had recognised the men but, through fear, gave the evidence he did.[191]

The intensity of the agitation in east Galway (and Shawe-Taylor's previous experience) surely provided a powerful stimulus for him to write his famous letter to *The Times* and it is likely that the other 'moderate' land-lords who attended the Land Conference were similarly influenced by the high level of agitation generated by the United Irish League in 1901–2.

The Land Conference was held, with Wyndham's blessing, in the Mansion House in Dublin in December. In 1903, a report of the Conference was published which stated that:

it is expedient that the Land Question in Ireland be settled ... without delay ... [T]he existing position of the Land Question is adverse to the improvement of the soil of Ireland, leads to unending controversies and lawsuits between owners and occupiers, retards progress in the country, and constitutes a grave danger to the State ... [S]ettlement can only be effected upon a basis mutually satisfactory to the owners and occupiers of the land ... [T]he only satisfactory settlement of the land question is to be effected by the substitution of an occupying proprietary in lieu of the existing system of dual ownership.[192]

The conference report went on to adopt most of the proposals which Wyndham had made in his two cabinet memorandums on the Irish land question. Landlords were to be paid an 'equitable price' for their estates based on their income, which they defined as second-term rents; and tenants were to pay an instalment that was at least 15 per cent less than their second-term rents. In this way, a settlement was reached by the Conference which satisfied 'the just claims of both owners and occupiers'.[193] Wyndham was delighted by the result of the Conference and began preparing a new Land Bill which would adopt its proposals.[194]

[191] Martin Newell witness statement, MA BMH WS 1,562.

[192] *Land Conference: report of a conference held at the Mansion House, Dublin, 1902–1903* (Dublin, 1903), 1.   [193] Ibid. 2–3.

[194] For a discussion of the Conference by one of the participants, see the Earl of Dunraven, *Past times and pastimes*, ii (London, 1922).

In March 1903, Wyndham put his second Land Bill before the House of Commons. It was a very different measure from the Bill which he had introduced in March 1902. The tenant's instalment was reduced so that the purchase annuity would be at least 20 per cent and not more than 40 per cent less than a first-term rent, and at least 10 per cent and not more than 30 per cent less than a second-term rent. Untenanted land was also to be included in the purchase arrangements under the new Bill. To compensate the landlords for the loss which they would incur from the lower instalment, they were to be paid a bonus of 12 per cent on the total purchase price, which would be drawn from a fund of £12 million.[195] Although the Bill attempted to reach a satisfactory solution for both landlord and tenant, the *Irish Law Times* argued that it favoured the tenant at the expense of the landlord. Whereas under Wyndham's first Land Bill, landlords stood to gain £232 from each £100 of rent, under the second Bill, according to the *Irish Law Times*, the landlord would receive only £48 from each £100, on account of the reductions in the tenants' annuity. Neither did the bonus impress the *Irish Law Times*, which argued that under the new Bill landlords stood to lose £50 million while they were compensated to the tune of only £12 million: 'Facts are stubborn things and so are figures, and not even the eloquence of Mr. Wyndham . . . can repair a wrong involving a loss of fifty millions by the magic of a bonus of only twelve.'[196] The difference between the two Bills could not have been more dramatic. In the estimation of the *Irish Law Times*, the first favoured the landlords while the second favoured the tenant.

Even so, the Landowners' Convention, which included Lords Londonderry and Barrymore, believed that the Conference had worked to their advantage and were 'inclined to attribute the result to the folly of the Nationalists rather than to the wits of Dunraven'.[197] In Wyndham's view, most of the landlords were prepared to accept the new Bill, if only because they dreaded a third revision of rent.[198] The cabinet also responded well to Wyndham's second Land Bill, although it made a demand on Government credit of approximately £70 million. Wyndham told the Prime Minister:

It is well worth the State's while to settle the Irish Land Question by using its credit in this way . . . It insures [*sic*] in the near future considerable savings in respect of annual charges amounting to over £1,500,000 for Land Courts and Police. It is, indeed, imperative that the question should now be settled. Otherwise the

---

[195] For a summary of the terms of the Wyndham Land Act, see Kolbert and O'Brien, *Land reform in Ireland*, 39–41.   [196] *Irish Law Times and Solicitor's Journal*, 4 Apr. 1903.

[197] Wyndham to Balfour, 11 Jan. 1903, BM ABP Add. MS 49,804/115–118ᵛ.

[198] Wyndham to Balfour, 30 Apr. 1903, BM ABP Add. MS 49,804/127–130ᵛ.

discrepancy between the position of the 70,000 tenants who have purchased their holdings, and some 400,000 who are debarred from purchasing will precipitate an agitation throughout Ireland of unprecedented magnitude.[199]

If the Land Bill was not passed, Wyndham warned, the United Irish League would initiate yet another agitation of unprecedented magnitude which would create even greater administrative and financial problems than those created by the agitation of 1901–2. The Chancellor of the Exchequer was persuaded by this argument and told Wyndham, 'don't let us have another scheme that fails . . . If there is a really reasonable hope of peace, it will be worth some payment.'[200] Arthur Balfour, who was now Prime Minister, also agreed that the expenditure was justifiable. He told the King in March: 'This is a very far reaching measure; and the Irish government are sanguine that it will settle for all time the Irish Land difficulty! The objections to it . . . arise from the fact that it makes a heavy call on British credit . . . The cabinet . . . were clearly of opinion that in the interests of a great policy minor difficulties must be ignored'.[201]

Although the Bill fell short of compulsory purchase, it proposed a revolutionary reform of the land question and the Irish Party congratulated Wyndham on its introduction in the House. Redmond described it as 'the greatest effort ever yet made to settle the Irish Land Question by purchase. This is a great Bill.'[202] The United Irish League also expressed its approval of the new Bill and the amount of intimidation in Ireland dropped dramatically by 32 per cent.[203] With the support of the Prime Minister, the cabinet, many of the Irish landlords, the Irish Party, and the United Irish League, the Bill became law in August and effected a revolutionary transformation of the Irish land question. Almost 200,000 Irish tenant farmers, like Murtagh Cosgar, the central character of Padraic Colum's play *The land*, became owner-occupiers under the Act:

Ah, but that's the sight to fill one's heart. Lands ploughed and spread. And all our own; all our own . . . Isn't that a great thought . . . and isn't it a great thing that we're able to pass this land onto them [our children], and it redeemed for ever? Ay, and their manhood spared the shame that our manhood knew. Standing in the rain with our hats off to let a landlord—ay, or a landlord's dog boy—pass.[204]

199 Wyndham, 'A policy for Ireland', 14 Nov. 1902, ABP Add. MS 49,804/96–114.
200 Quoted in Gailey, *Ireland and the death of kindness*, 192.
201 Balfour to the King, 10 Mar. 1903, PRO CAB 41/28/5.
202 Hansard, 4th series, 25 Mar. 1903, vol. cxx, col. 216.
203 The number of persons requiring protection by police patrols decreased from 308 to 210 between March and May. IG monthly reports, Mar. and May 1903, NA IGCI/3.
204 Padraic Colum, *The land* (Dublin, 1905), 17–18.

V

After a tour of the west of Ireland in September 1901, Wyndham observed: 'The Irish believe . . . we only spend money on reproductive works under compulsion of lawlessness and agitation.'[205] This 'error' arose, he suggested, from the fact that throughout the nineteenth century, the Government had only spent money on the resolution of Irish social and economic problems after periods of serious civil disobedience: in 1830–2, after the 'emancipation excitement', in 1883, after the '[18]80–[18]81 trouble' and in the 1890s, following the Plan of Campaign.[206] Wyndham believed that these relief works were the results of coherently planned Government policies, and not the short-term responses to social disorder which the Irish apparently believed they were. Yet Wyndham's own great reproductive work, the 1903 Land Act, seems to substantiate the Irish belief that land legislation was only introduced under compulsion of lawlessness and agitation. The United Irish League certainly believed that the Wyndham Land Act was the result of their agitation,[207] but this belief did not give due credit to Wyndham whose researches and convictions decisively influenced the form which the Act took.

Wyndham was firmly committed to introducing a substantial reform of the land question when he became Chief Secretary in November 1900.[208] He was informed, from the outset, by a belief that a 'peasant proprietorship . . . was the indispensable condition of national peace'[209] and his two cabinet memorandums on the land question, drafted in 1901 and October 1902, reveal a comprehensive and detailed understanding of the land problem.[210] But Wyndham's colleagues in the Irish Office and the cabinet did not share his views. In January 1901, Wyndham told Balfour that Cadogan 'dreads' any proposal that would 'make the State . . . buy out the landlord', when this was a pivotal element of Wyndham's proposed legislation.[211] Tensions in the Irish Office reached a climax in March 1902 when Wyndham felt that his carefully considered Irish policy was to be

[205] Wyndham to Balfour, 20 Sept. 1901, BM ABP Add. MS 49,803/211–19.
[206] Ibid.
[207] *Irish People*, 29 Aug. 1903.
[208] Gailey, *Ireland and the death of kindness*, 162–6; J. W. Mackail and Guy Wyndham, *Life and letters of George Wyndham*, i (London, 1925), 77.
[209] Mackail and Wyndham, *Life and letters of George Wyndham*, i, 83.
[210] Wyndham, 'The Irish land question and the need for legislation', 1901, PRO CAB 37/59/147; and Wyndham, cabinet memorandum on the Irish land question, 8 Oct. 1902, PRO CAB 37/62/139.
[211] Wyndham to Balfour, 13 Jan. 1901, BM ABP Add. MS 49,803/182–90.

dropped in favour of a short-term expedient. On 3 March, he told Balfour: 'If it were not against my principles to resign I should have "sent in my papers" a fortnight ago.'[212] Cadogan later informed the cabinet that there was a rift in the Irish Office between himself and Wyndham:

> In our recent correspondence . . . the Chief Secretary did not agree with me in thinking that the time had arrived for Proclamation . . . [but] I am not without hope that, in view of the circumstances and the admitted urgency of the present situation, he will be disposed to acquiesce in the course which I have now felt it my duty to urge upon the Cabinet.[213]

Although Wyndham had, by the spring of 1902, devised a sophisticated Irish policy, the Lord Lieutenant succeeded in implementing a policy in 1902 which was little more than a hand-to-mouth strategy: the proclamation of sixteen Irish counties and four county boroughs under the Crimes Act. Wyndham's failure to introduce a substantial Land Bill during the crisis of March 1902 was a direct result of cabinet opposition, and, particularly, that of the Chancellor of the Exchequer. Hicks Beach refused to accept Wyndham's proposal that the tenant's purchase instalment should be reduced and, without this reform, the Bill was doomed to failure. By the autumn of 1902, all of Wyndham's plans to reconstruct Irish society had come to nothing.

The United Irish League's agitation of 1901–2 played a fundamental role in transforming the views of the cabinet and the Irish Office on Wyndham's proposed land legislation. The renewal of the League's agitation in the summer of 1902 forcefully warned the Government that unless a substantial reform of the land question was introduced, the agitation would continue indefinitely. At the end of August the League's agitation was creating serious administrative problems for the Government, and the 'general state of the country' had 'not improved'.[214] Remedial measures were immediately called for and the Government's decision to implement Wyndham's great scheme of Treasury-funded land purchase was informed by the fear that if it did not do so 'an agitation . . . of unprecedented magnitude' would ensue.[215] In contrast to the opposition which Wyndham had encountered in the spring of 1902, both the Prime Minister and the Chancellor of the Exchequer told Wyndham that Government expenditure of almost £100 million could be justified in the

---

212 Wyndham to Balfour, 9 Mar. 1902, BM ABP Add. MS 49,804/8–11.
213 Cadogan, cabinet memorandum, 10 Mar. 1902, PRO CAB 37/61/58.
214 IG monthly report, Aug. 1902, PRO CO 904/75.
215 Wyndham, 'A policy for Ireland', 14 Nov. 1902, BM ABP Add. MS 49,804/96–114.

interest of a 'great policy', which might solve the Irish land question 'for all time'.[216] Without the United Irish League, Wyndham might have never been able to introduce his famous Land Act.

Historiographically, the 'Wyndham' Land Act has been viewed as the product of the conservative policy of 'constructive unionism'.[217] A number of conservative administrations in the late nineteenth century passed ameliorative Irish legislation with the object of 'killing Home Rule with kindness'; in other words, legislation was passed with the intention of resolving the social and economic problems which were presumed to be the source of nationalist activism. The Wyndham Land Act is correctly understood by this school as the pinnacle of constructive unionism's achievement. There is, however, a tendency in the historiography to overemphasise the importance of developments in the Irish Office at the expense of events taking place on the ground in Ireland. F. S. L. Lyons, for example, presents the classic exposition of this viewpoint in *Ireland since the Famine*:

His [Wyndham's] first attempt [at a Land Bill] in 1902 was an ill-considered measure which was wisely dropped, but before he could gather himself for a much more comprehensive bill in 1903 the entire situation was dramatically changed by another of those independent and unofficial Unionist initiatives . . . This time . . . the credit belonged . . . to . . . Captain John Shawe-Taylor . . . On 2 September 1902 he wrote a short letter to the newspapers inviting certain named representatives of landlords and tenants to meet in conference to bring about a settlement of the long struggle between the two classes . . . This letter, coming as it did from an unknown private individual, might well have been ignored had not Wyndham given it a benediction . . . [I]n December the Land Conference assembled in Dublin . . . After only a fortnight's discussion the Conference produced a unanimous report which, though brief, was comprehensive enough . . .

The report formed the basis of the Land Act Wyndham triumphantly passed through parliament during the session of 1903.[218]

In this version of events, Captain John Shawe-Taylor and George Wyndham are elevated to the status of major actors while the extensive United Irish League agitation, and the coercive response which it elicited, are relegated to a background role. It is as if the Chief Secretary and Shawe-Taylor operated in a vacuum, unaware of the disturbances around them. This interpretation of the origins of the Land Act is discussed in a more subtle and sophisticated manner by Andrew Gailey in his study of

---

[216] Balfour to the King, 10 Mar. 1903, PRO CAB 41/28/5.
[217] On constructive unionism, see Gailey, *Ireland and the death of kindness*.
[218] Lyons, *Ireland since the Famine*, 217–18.

constructive unionism, but the broad contours of his argument are the same: Wyndham presents his second Land Bill to the cabinet in March 1903, for example, not 'as a concession to anarchy but as an act of the highest statesmanship', and the ultimate success of the Bill is described by Gailey as the result of 'Wyndham's opportunistic manipulation of Irish politics'.[219] Neither of these accounts gives sufficient weight to the level of agitation which the United Irish League organized on behalf of the campaign for compulsory land purchase or sufficient consideration to the effect which the agitation had on the Government, the Irish land-lords, or Captain John Shawe-Taylor. The United Irish League's agitation fundamentally influenced both the timing and the substance of the 1903 Land Act; and, in order to understand the origins of this legislation, it is necessary to view it in the context of both popular and 'high' politics; and to take note of T. W. Russell's timely warning to the House of Commons in 1902 that 'it was not in that House that Land Acts were created they were created . . . in the bogs of Connaught'.[220]

219 Gailey, *Ireland and the death of kindness*, 190, 192.
220 Hansard, 4th series, 28 Feb. 1902, vol. civ, col. 95.

3

The Ranch War and
Irish Nationalist Politics, 1904–1910

> A Social Revolution is going on in this part of Ireland [the east riding of county Galway] and it is fortunate that we are keeping it a bloodless one.
>
> (Anthony MacDonnell, the Under-Secretary, 19 Feb. 1907)[1]

In the years between 1904 and 1908, the United Irish League orchestrated the most significant agitation in its twenty-year history. The Ranch War remains the most serious outbreak of agrarian conflict in twentieth-century Ireland and takes its place alongside the Land War and the Plan of Campaign as a major episode in the broader struggle between landlord and tenant. For this reason, the Ranch War has attracted some historical attention.[2] However, the existing accounts are not—by and large—studies of 'popular politics', as they tend to view the agitation from above, from the vantage point of London or Dublin, rather than from the perspective of rank and file activists. This chapter, on the other hand, will examine the Ranch War from below, and provide a new interpretation of the dynamics of the conflict.

The Ranch War has been characterized as an anti-grazier agitation, with combinations against the payment of landlords' rent playing 'an inessential role'.[3] According to Bew, 'Catholic nationalist was set against Catholic nationalist—it was not simply or even, in many places, mainly the landlord stratum who felt the heat.'[4] A study of events on the ground, however,

---

[1] Minute by Anthony MacDonnell, the Under-Secretary, 19 Feb. 1907, IG monthly report, Jan. 1907, NA IGCI/11.

[2] Bew, *Conflict and conciliation*; Philip Bull, *Land, politics and nationalism: a study of the Irish land question* (Dublin, 1996) and David Seth Jones, *Graziers, land reform and political conflict in Ireland* (Washington, 1995).

[3] Bew, *Conflict and conciliation*, 42. Bew suggests: 'The object [of the Ranch War] was to harass and demoralize the graziers.' Bew, *Conflict and conciliation*, 140.

[4] Bew, *Conflict and conciliation*, 206.

suggests the limitations of this analysis. The Ranch War comprised two interlinked agitations, both of which originated in the spring of 1904 and drew to a close in the winter of 1908. In the first instance, the Ranch War was an agitation against the landlords, to force them to sell their estates at prices determined by the tenants. Usually, this agitation took the form of rent combinations. There were an average of thirty-five combinations each month between January 1907 and June 1908, and at the height of the Ranch War (in January 1908) there were sixty-three combinations in ten counties.[5] Second, the Ranch War involved an agitation against the grazing system. This initiative aimed to reduce landlords' profits from their untenanted land—by intimidating grazing tenants into giving up their grazing leases—so that landlords might be induced to sell their grazing land to the Estates Commissioners.[6] Rather than being an anti-grazier agitation, then, the aim of the Ranch War was to pressurize landlords into selling their tenanted and their untenanted land at prices deemed to be fair by the tenants. In this respect, the Ranch War was primarily a conflict between landlord and tenant, and the intra-tenant hostility between smallholder and grazier was a subsidiary aspect of this broader struggle.

I

After the implementation of the Wyndham Land Act, there was uncertainty as to what the future role of the United Irish League would be. The Inspector General speculated that the new Act would mark the end of the UIL and its various agitations, writing: 'It is reasonable to anticipate that if the . . . Land Bill increases very appreciably the number of peasant proprietors, it will become more difficult to collect funds for the purposes of agitation . . . Some considerable portion of those forming the present U.I. League will probably settle down to work their farms.'[7] The leaders of the Irish Parliamentary Party were also keen to ensure that the United Irish League would not return to the militant agrarianism of 1901–2. Instead, the Party leadership advocated a policy of conciliation, and, in September 1903, Redmond stated at Aughrim, county Wicklow:

let the tenantry of Ireland take care that if this Act fails that the failure of it cannot be atttributed to their unreasonableness or irreconcilability. I say to them—Enter

---

[5] See Table 4.

[6] The Estates Commissioners was the new agency set up by the Wyndham Land Act to facilitate the sale of estates from landlord to tenant.

[7] IG monthly report, Dec. 1902, PRO CO 904/76.

into negotiations in a friendly and conciliatory spirit, in a reasonable spirit and a moderate spirit. . . I confess I have very little fear of this Act failing through the unreasonable action of the Irish tenants. I know the consuming passion in the heart of every Irish tenant to become the owner of the soil, and I know that he will make sacrifices, if necessary, to obtain it.[8]

The United Irish League branches appear to have accepted the advice of their leaders. Between 1902 and 1904, agrarian agitation in Ireland markedly decreased, and almost 12,000 members of the UIL (9 per cent of the total) left the organization, presumably because they had purchased their farms.[9] By the spring of 1904, the United Irish League appeared to be a spent force. In the absence of a new agrarian policy, the United Irish League had lost its *raison d'être*, and newly purchased farmers were not renewing their political subscriptions.[10]

It has been suggested that the Wyndham Land Act signalled the beginning of the end of the United Irish League as a popular agrarian movement.[11] Certainly, the Act appeared to address the United Irish League's two most fundamental demands: 'The abolition of landlordism in Ireland by means of a universal and compulsory system of sale . . . [and] [t]he putting an end to periodical distress and famine in the West by abolishing on terms of just compensation to all interests affected the unnatural system by which all the richest areas of that region are monopolised by a small ring of graziers.'[12] However, if land purchase and land redistribution were to be implemented under the Act, both landlord and tenant would have to be prepared to compromise. The Inspector General warned that 'As regards the general peace of the country much will depend on the immediate sequel to the passing into law of the Land Bill. If the one side abstains from illegal pressure, and the other from extravagant demands, the present truce may develop into a real peace.'[13] In the event, however, some of the Irish landlords rejected the conciliatory spirit of the Land Conference, and tended not to compromise during purchase negotiations. Instead, many of them attempted to gain inflated prices for both their tenanted and their untenanted land, and this provided the UIL

[8] *Irish People*, 19 Sept. 1903.

[9] The membership of the UIL decreased by 11,713 between 1902 and 1904. See Table 6.

[10] For example, a report on the Ahascragh UIL branch in Galway retrospectively commented in 1909: 'The tenants now possess the farms and the League room is now practically deserted.' *Connacht Tribune*, 16 Oct. 1909.

[11] Townshend, *Political violence*, 233.

[12] *United Irish League: constitution and rules adopted by the Irish national convention, 19th and 20th June, 1900* (Dublin, 1900), 2.

[13] IG monthly report, July 1903, NA IGCI/4.

with a new *raison d'être*. After 1903, the United Irish League became the organization through which tenants negotiated terms of purchase with their landlords and helped tenants to defend themselves against the often unreasonable demands of the landlords.

The Wyndham Land Act introduced a new 'zones' system which landlords manipulated to gain higher prices for their estates. Under this system, the Estates Commissioners were not allowed to inspect an estate where a purchase agreement had already been reached, as long as the agreed price fell within a zone which secured the tenant's annuity at between 10 and 30 per cent less than his rent. The zones system had been intended by Wyndham to expedite land purchase by reducing the work of the Estates Commissioners, and encouraging amicable voluntary agreements.[14] In practice, however, landlords abused the zones system to inflate the value of their estates. According to the *Freeman's Journal* landlords attempted to raise the price of their land artificially by holding back from sales and allowing the more well-to-do tenants, who were prepared to pay higher prices, to come forward and set the market price of the estate.[15] Once an agreement had been reached with a tenant, the Estates Commissioners were not allowed to assess whether the agreed price corresponded with the real value of the estate or not; and such assessments generally resulted in a lowering in the price of an estate.[16] As tenants were often impatient to purchase their holdings, many of them accepted the terms offered by their landlords. While these terms may have satisfied the rubric of the zones system, the purchase price was actually much higher than it had been under previous land legislation, because the annuity was to be paid over a much greater number of years. The *Weekly Freeman* observed that landlords' demands were 'uniformly exorbitant' but that tenants had 'made an initial mistake in rushing wildly and blindly to the rent offices' when they should 'insist on Ashbourne prices'.[17]

While the zones system did ensure that the tenant's annuity was substantially lower than his former rent, this concealed the fact that the actual price of the land had increased considerably. Before 1903, tenants measured the purchase price of their land according to the number of years' purchase, or as a multiple of their annual rent. Under the Wyndham Land Act, however, a new means of measuring the price of land was devised

---

14 Bew, *Conflict and conciliation*, 99–100.

15 R. G. Mullen, 'The origins and passing of the Irish Land Act of 1909' (Queen's University Belfast, MA, 1978), 19.

16 Bew, *Conflict and conciliation*, 100.

17 *Weekly Freeman*, 7 Nov. 1903. 'Ashbourne prices' refers to the prices tenants paid for their holdings under the Ashbourne Act of 1885.

by the members of the Land Conference. The new method calculated the purchase price in terms of the reduction of rent that the new annuity would reflect, and played down the fact that repayment would take place over a much longer period. Many commentators, including John Dillon, regarded this as a smokescreen designed to mislead tenants into believing that they were purchasing their holdings on equitable terms. In an important speech at Swinford on 20 October, Dillon outlined the problems with the zones system:

I am most deeply convinced that in making their bargains with their landlords the only safe plan for the tenants is to insist on the price to be paid for their farms in terms of the number of years' purchase of the rental, so that the tenants may have an opportunity of comparing easily and simply the price they are called upon to give with the price which their neighbours across the ditch gave under the old Acts. Go to any farmer in Ireland today who has bought under the Ashbourne Act and ask him what did he pay; he would tell you at once in the terms that are most familiar to him, 'I paid so many years' purchase.' Why, then, I ask, should we be called upon today under the new Act to apply a different measure of value unless it be for the purpose of deceiving the people?[18]

In fact, the terms of purchase under the Wyndham Land Act (when measured according to the number of years' purchase) were substantially higher than they had been under the Ashbourne Act. In 1902, for example, the average price of land had been 17.9 years' purchase, whereas under the Wyndham Act the average price of tenanted land sold between 1903 and 1909 was 22.5 years' purchase.[19] This represented an average increase of 4.6 years' purchase (26 per cent). According to the Estates Commissioners, the increase in prices was even higher. In their annual report of 1906, they claimed that there had been an increase of 50 per cent on pre-1903 prices, and that this was because landlords were escaping inspection under the zones system.[20]

This attempt by the Irish landlords to extract the highest possible prices from their tenants seriously disrupted the operation of the Wyndham Land Act.[21] Many tenants could not afford the prohibitive prices demanded by landlords, and were therefore reluctant to purchase their holdings. In November 1904, the Inspector General stated: 'In some Counties . . . and especially in the poorer Districts, there is [an] indication that negotiations

[18] *Weekly Freeman*, 24 Oct. 1903.

[19] R. G. Mullen, 'The origins and passing of the Irish Land Act of 1909', 14–16.

[20] Ibid. 20.

[21] This was the view of a Treasury committee which estimated that the total cost of land purchase had increased from £100 million (in 1903) to £180 million (in 1908) as a result of the exorbitant prices demanded by landlords. Ibid. 48–9.

under the Land Purchase Act may result in increased, but possibly, temporary friction between owners and occupiers. The latter desire to buy their farms, but, apparently, they are not prepared to give prices which will satisfy the owners.'[22] As a result, successful land purchase agreements were unevenly distributed across the country. Between 1903 and 1908, most purchases took place in Ulster (34 per cent of the total) and Leinster (26 per cent) because these regions were populated by large tenant farmers who were prepared to pay higher prices for their holdings. In Munster (22 per cent) and Connacht (18 per cent) where tenants were generally poorer, purchase proceeded more slowly as tenants could not afford landlords' prices.[23]

Overall, the progress of land purchase was much slower than is usually recognized by historians.[24] As Table 3 demonstrates, the Wyndham Land Act did initiate a revolution in landholding, but it was a long-term process that did not immediately transform Irish society. Indeed, land purchase would not be completed until well after the implementation of the first Irish Land Act of 1923. Under the pre-1903 land purchase legislation, 18 per cent of tenanted land had been purchased in Ireland. As a result of the operation of the Wyndham Land Act, this figure rose to 30 per cent by 1908. In other words, only 12 per cent of tenanted land was actually sold under the Wyndham Land Act between 1903 and 1908. Five years after the implementation of the Wyndham Land Act, then, 70 per cent of Irish tenanted land had still not been purchased. In fact, land purchase would have to wait until 1913 before it reached the halfway mark (54 per cent of tenanted land had been purchased in that year), and, as late as 1918, it was still less than two-thirds complete (64 per cent). The Irish landlords' self-interest was a significant factor in slowing down the general pace of land purchase.

The Irish landlords also demanded prohibitively high prices for their untenanted land.[25] As eleven-month leases were outside the jurisdiction of the 1881 Act, the rents for eleven-month lettings were determined by market demand rather than by the land courts. On the Mahon estate in Galway, for example, the ordinary rent declined by 20 per cent between 1889 and 1895, while the rent from untenanted land increased by 500 per cent in the same period. A similar trend can be observed on Captain Henry Hastings Jones's estates in counties Mayo and Sligo. Whereas in

22 IG monthly report, Nov. 1904, NA IGCI/6.
23 Mullen, 'The origins and passing of the Irish Land Act of 1909', 11.
24 See, for instance, Bew, *Conflict and conciliation*, 221.
25 See Ch. 2.

TABLE 3. Estimated annual land purchase figures in Ireland, 1881–1920

Year	Acreage Purchased	Cumulative acreage purchased	Percentage of total amount of land purchased in Ireland up to 1971
1881–1902	2,415,180	2,415,180	18
1903–5	386,793	2,801,973	21
1905–6	422,297	3,224,270	24
1906–7	434,298	3,658,568	27
1907–8	413,801	4,072,369	30
1908–9	502,842	4,575,211	34
1909–10	510,193	5,085,404	38
1910–11	686,860	5,772,264	43
1911–12	768,780	6,541,044	48
1912–13	754,235	7,295,279	54
1913–14	601,374	7,896,653	58
1914–15	390,804	8,287,457	61
1915–16	75,412	8,362,869	62
1916–17	160,602	8,523,471	63
1917–18	138,879	8,662,350	64
1918–19	46,283	8,708,633	64
1919–20	58,360	8,766,993	65
Total (1881–1920)		8,766,993	65
Total (1881–1971)		13,526,078	100

Notes and sources: The land purchase statistics presented here were collated from three sources: the annual reports of the Estates Commissioners, the Land Commission and the Congested Districts Board between 1905 and 1920. For the purposes of this analysis, land purchase was defined as having taken place only when payment was advanced by the purchasing agency to the owner. A figure for the total amount of land purchased in Ireland before 1903 was gained from the annual report of the Irish Land Commission (Dublin, 1928), and a figure for the total amount of tenanted land purchased in Ireland up to 1971 was obtained from the annual report of the Irish Land Commission (Dublin, 1971). In both cases, it was necessary to estimate the total for 32 counties from the figure for the 26 counties by applying a multiplier of 6/5. I am grateful to David Fitzpatrick for discussing the methodology which he used to calculate land purchase figures with me.

1888 eleven-month rents accounted for 6 per cent of Hastings Jones's total income (from rent), between 1911 and 1918, eleven-month leases provided him with 30 per cent of his rental income.[26]

These examples illustrate the growing importance of eleven-month

[26] Jones, *Graziers, land reform and political conflict in Ireland*, 129.

leases to the Irish landlord class in a period when ordinary rents were being substantially reduced by the operation of the 1881 Land Act. As a result, landlords were reluctant to sell their untenanted land, except at extremely high prices. Sir Henry Doran, the Chief Land Inspector of the Congested Districts Board, told Lord Dudley, the Viceroy and the chairman of the Royal Commission on Congestion, that landlords generally refused to sell their untenanted land:

Lord Dudley:	Do you find that you have a great deal of difficulty in getting untenanted land?
Henry Doran:	Yes; especially where we want it most …
Lord Dudley:	And is the reason of that because the landlord will not sell at any price, or because the price is generally more than you can afford?
Henry Doran:	I would say that it was because he would not sell except he got more than the value of it; such a price as the Board would not give.[27]

Laurence Ginnell, the MP for north Westmeath, described the social conditions that were maintained by the landlords' refusal to sell their untenanted land: 'after three years of the "greatest Land Act ever passed", ranchers' cattle [were] still grazing over evicted lands, and young people [were] still emigrating from the neighbouring uneconomic bog holdings for want of land to live upon, while the parts of the Act purporting to have provided for them remained a dead letter.'[28] Despite the existence of widespread congestion throughout Ireland,[29] the redistribution of untenanted land proceeded at an even slower pace than that of tenanted land. As late as 1923, only 750,000 acres of untenanted land had been redistributed, leaving almost two million acres to be re-allocated between 1923 and 1973.[30]

Although the Irish landlords had rejected the spirit of the Land Conference, the leaders of the Irish Parliamentary Party continued to advocate a

---

[27] *Royal Commission on Congestion in Ireland: appendices to the first report*, HC (1906), [Cd. 3267], xxxii. 736.

[28] Laurence Ginnell, *Land and liberty* (Dublin, 1908), 202.

[29] According to the *Agricultural statistics*, 34 % of Irish farmers occupied holdings sized between 1 and 15 acres in 1908. Given that a congested holding was defined as being that under about 10 acres, this indicates that over one-third of Irish farmers still lived either marginally above or below the poverty line in 1908. While the highest density of small farms was in the West of Ireland (45 %), there were also a high proportion of smallholders in Ulster (39 %), Leinster (30 %), and Munster (21 %). The problem of congestion was, therefore, by no means confined to the west of Ireland. *Agricultural statistics of Ireland … for the year 1908*, HC (1909), [Cd. 1940], cii. 401.

[30] Jones, *Graziers, land reform and political conflict in Ireland*, 219.

conciliatory policy. A mass meeting at Cork city, presided over by William O'Brien, resolved:

That we believe, and recommend to the tenantry in this constituency and throughout the country, that the Land Act should have a fair and friendly trial; and while the tenants should, above all things, act unitedly for their mutual protection against improvident bargains ... we further recommend that the tenants so banded together should carry on their negotiations in the spirit of conciliation that has hitherto prevailed where they are met by the landlord in the same spirit.[31]

While O'Brien was careful to emphasize that tenants should avoid 'improvident bargains', the Irish Parliamentary Party's position on the Land Act was clarified by the Party leader, John Redmond: 'Let us, in a spirit of moderation and of conciliation, but of caution and of firmness, do our very best to promote the rapid and successful working of the new Land Act.'[32] Indeed Redmond had been committed to a policy of conciliation between landlord and tenant since the introduction of the 1896 Land Act, which he believed to have substantially solved the Irish land problem.[33]

The ordinary members of the United Irish League, however, refused to accept the exorbitant demands of the landlords. Rather than adopting a 'spirit of the utmost friendliness' in the course of purchase negotiations, they initiated an agitation to force down the price of land. The Ranch War originated on the Wills-Sandford estate in Roscommon where the tenants pressurized the landlord into selling by withholding their rent until purchase terms were agreed. The Inspector General observed developments on the Wills-Sandford estate in Roscommon with some apprehension, noting:

Such tactics would be very dangerous to the public peace if extensively followed. They would in all probability lead to a renewal in a modified form of the No Rent Campaign, wherever there might be a temporary failure to complete the sales ...

The general peace and prosperity of the country are so completely identified with the smooth and efficient working of the Land Act that it would be calamitous if both parties do not approach the subject of sales in a purely business spirit.[34]

Wyndham was also concerned with the precedent set by the Wills-Sandford tenants, writing to the Under-Secretary in September: 'A proposal to "withhold rent" pending an agreement to sell would be most improper, [and] contrary to the spirit in which the Land Bill was accepted by the leaders of the Nationalist Party.'[35]

---

[31] *Irish People*, 26 Sept. 1903.   [32] *Irish People*, 19 Sept. 1903.
[33] Bull, 'Reconstruction', 244.   [34] IG monthly report, Aug. 1903, NA IGCI/4.
[35] George Wyndham to the Under-Secretary, 30 Sept. 1903, IG monthly report, Aug. 1903, NA IGCI/4.

The tactics used by the Wills-Sandford tenants were imitated the following month on the Dunsandle estate in the east riding of county Galway.[36] On Sunday, 18 October, a meeting was held at Laragh Hill in the centre of the property at which the tenants were instructed by local United Irish League leaders to demand a rent reduction to pressurize the landlord, William Daly, to sell his estate.[37] John Roche told the Dunsandle tenants: 'Should your landlord refuse to sell to you on reasonable terms, do everything in your power to cut down the rent of that landlord.' Two months later, on 7 December, a deputation of 300 tenants, accompanied by two priests, waited on Daly but he refused to 'treat with them'. A public meeting was then held at which Father Fallon advised the tenants to form a 'Defence Fund' to defend themselves against any action that Daly might take to recover the rents they had not paid on that day.[38] Daly then served notice on the tenants that he would hold a rent office on 4 and 5 January 1904, to collect the unpaid November rents. A further deputation of 250 men approached Daly on Tuesday, 5 January 1904, during which he refused to give a rent reduction, but agreed to sell at a general reduction of 15 per cent. The deputation then voted on the course of action they would take, and Martin Finnerty 'called upon the people to remain firm, that they had the country at their back; even if Mr. Daly put them out they would have six months to redeem; and that they had Craughwell, &c., at their backs'. A vote was then taken, and tenants decided 'not to pay without an abatement'.[39] A meeting of the Dunsandle Estates Committee was held on 9 January at which it was decided 'that each tenant should be visited and asked if he were willing to pay over to Patrick Carr, as Treasurer, his rent at the rate of 16s. to the £1'.[40] Many tenants did so, and the police were concerned that the dispute 'was likely to lead to evictions and their attendant disturbances'.[41] However, Father Cahalan undertook

---

[36]　The Dunsandle estate consisted of 37,057 acres valued at £17,193 in the late 1870s. Melvin, 'The landed gentry of Galway, 1820–80', 506. A small portion of the estate was located in county Tipperary.

[37]　The confidential print, 1904, PRO CO 903/11/39; CI monthly report, east Galway, Oct. 1903, NA IGCI/4.　　　　　[38]　The confidential print, 1904, PRO CO 903/11/39.

[39]　Martin Finnerty (1882–1959), a tenant farmer from Tample, near Gurteen, county Galway, sworn into the IRB in 1900, a leading member of the 'Major MacBride secret society' (see Ch. 5), secretary of the east Galway UIL executive, founder of the United Estates Committee in 1910, defects to Sinn Féin in 1917, joins the Farmer's Party in the early 1920s and then Fianna Fáil, before founding Clann na Talmhan in 1938. On Finnerty, see the *Connacht Tribune*, 11 Aug. 1917; *Galway Express*, 20 Oct. 1917; obituary in the *Connacht Tribune*, 17 Oct. 1959; and interview with the late Mattie Finnerty at Galway, 30 Jan. 1998; the confidential print, 1904, PRO CO 903/11/39–40.

[40]　The confidential print, 1904, PRO CO 903/11/40–1.

[41]　The confidential print, 1905, PRO CO 903/12/97–8.

independent negotiations with Daly who agreed to settle with the tenants if they paid their rents less 2 shillings in the pound. Although the commitee agreed to these terms,[42] a further rent combination was established in the spring of 1904,[43] resulting in Daly agreeing to sell his estate, including 2,500 acres of untenanted land, to the tenants.[44]

The success of this test case created the precedent for a countrywide no-rent agitation on behalf of land purchase. As Martin Finnerty told the Royal Commission on Congestion, the tenants

know their rights and are prepared to struggle for them . . . They feel that what was possible on the Dunsandle . . . [estate] may be possible on theirs . . . I do say that feeling will run higher and higher until something is done to allay the terrible discontent prevailing at present. No proper settlement of a district can be made where a landlord stands out, here and there.[45]

Between October and November 1904, rent combinations were formed on ten estates in east Galway.[46] In five cases, the combination aimed to force the landlord to sell his estate, and on the other five the object was to force the landlord to include his untenanted land in the sale.[47] The local UIL branches supported these combinations and, in the estimation of the local police, the new campaign originated in the success of the Dunsandle dispute: 'In consequence of the successful issue of the combination among the Dunsandle tenants, efforts were being made by the tenants of other estates to induce graziers to surrender their holdings . . . and to force owners to sell their estates by withholding the rent.'[48] Neither was this campaign confined to the east riding of county Galway. The compilers of the confidential print found that there were at least fifty-nine combinations between November 1904 and April 1905 in ten counties, twenty-seven of which (46 per cent) had had a successful outcome for the tenants.[49] These combinations aimed 'to compel . . . landlords to sell their estates [under the Wyndham Land Act] at prices fixed by the tenants'; and 'to obtain the grass lands held by graziers on the eleven months system' for redistribution among smallholders.[50]

The dispute between the Dunsandle tenants and William Daly provided the model for the ensuing Ranch War agitation and defined a new role for

---

[42] The confidential print, 1904, PRO CO 903/11/41.

[43] IG monthly report, May 1904, NA IGCI/5.

[44] The confidential print, 1905, PRO CO 903/12/98.

[45] *Royal Commission on Congestion in Ireland: appendix to the tenth report*, HC (1908), [Cd. 4007], xlii. 300.

[46] The confidential print, 1905, PRO CO 903/12/98–9.   [47] Ibid.

[48] Ibid., PRO CO 903/12/98.   [49] Ibid., PRO CO 903/12/92–5.

[50] Ibid., PRO CO 903/12/93.

the United Irish League in the new post-Wyndham Act circumstances. After 1903, the rent combination—which had been widely used during previous agrarian agitations—was revived in a new context. Whereas, during the Land War and the Plan of Campaign, combinations had aimed to force landlords to reduce rents, they were now established to pressurize landlords into selling their estates at prices fixed by the tenants. Martin Finnerty, and the other leaders of the Dunsandle tenants, had converted a traditional form of tenant protest into a strategy for negotiating better terms of land purchase.

This agitation provided a new and popular social function for United Irish League branches. Generally, UIL branches (together with parish priests) supported the rent combinations, and were often responsible for communicating tenants' demands to landlords.[51] As the County Inspector for east Galway observed in the spring of 1905: 'The United Irish League is showing renewed signs of activity, numbers of new members are joining it and subscriptions are increasing, the prevailing impression being that to compel landlords to sell and get the grass lands divided it is necessary to work under the banner of the League.'[52] Elsewhere, UIL branches became advisory bodies and forums for discussing the complex procedures of land purchase, which was (arguably) the most important issue in Irish public life at this time: 'In some of the remote districts where the daily papers do not extensively circulate, the farmers at times join the League to discuss the prospects of Land Purchase, and to take counsel on the best methods of striking an advantageous bargain with the landlords.'[53] However, the leaders of the Irish Party kept their distance from this new agitation, and made no public comment whatsoever on what the police were calling 'the movement . . . of with-holding rent'.[54]

In the course of 1904, two United Irish League policies emerged: the official policy of the UIL elite, and the unofficial policy of the League branches. Having initially supported a moderate policy, the Party withdrew its support for conciliation when it became clear that the landlords were demanding unreasonable prices. Even William O'Brien, the main exponent of the conciliatory policy, recognized that the landlords had reneged on the spirit of the Land Conference. In a letter to Lord Dunraven in November 1903, he confided: 'The trouble [with the Wyndham Land Act] has arisen . . . to a shocking extent from the unreasonable demand of the

51   Ibid., PRO CO 903/12/92.
52   CI monthly report, east Galway, Feb. 1905, NA IGCI/7.
53   IG monthly report, Jan. 1904, NA IGCI/5.
54   The confidential print, 1905, PRO CO 903/12/93–4.

landlords... I confess I am no longer sanguine [about the future operation of the Act].'[55] According to the Inspector General, the Party leadership had 'put aside' the policy of conciliation by August 1904, 'but no other policy which commands the united support of the Nationalists has been hitherto found in substitution for it'.[56] The militant activities of UIL branches were privately discouraged by the Party leadership,[57] and, according to the police: 'The League as an organization gave no countenance to those tenants who, when abatements were refused, contemplated the withholding of their rents.'[58] In the absence of an official agrarian policy, the Ranch War was promoted by local members of the United Irish League, as the police acknowledged: 'The people in the affected Districts have got out of hand: they have run ahead of their leaders, who are compelled to follow—in many cases against their better judgment—in order to retain some semblance of influence.'[59]

The Ranch War reached its apogee between the autumn of 1906 and the winter of 1908. In this period, the rent combination on the Dunsandle estate became the model for a new agitation which extended throughout Connacht, and into Munster and the midlands.[60] While there are no precise figures on the number of rent combinations in Ireland between 1907 and 1908, an impression of the extent and the objectives of the new agitation can be gained from the Inspector General's monthly reports between January 1907 and June 1908.[61] There were between seven and sixty-three combinations each month, and over the whole period, there were combinations in fifteen counties (six in Connacht, six in Munster, and three in Leinster).[62] These numbers are impressionistic (see Table 4), as only those rent combinations that the Inspector General mentioned by name were counted, and in his reports he often remarked that there were several combinations that he did not individually name. Overall, these

---

[55] William O'Brien to Lord Dunraven, 12 Nov. 1903, NLI William O'Brien papers MS 8554/2.

[56] IG monthly report, Aug. 1904, NA IGCI/6.

[57] For example, R. A. Corr, a UIL organizer in Galway, was told not to intervene in the Dunsandle rent combination. CI monthly report, east Galway. Jan. 1904, NA IGCI/5.

[58] IG monthly report, Jan. 1904, NA IGCI/5.

[59] IG monthly report, May 1907, NA IGCI/11.

[60] For example, in January 1908, there were rent combinations in ten counties (or ridings): east Galway, west Galway, Sligo, west Cork, east Cork, Leitrim, Roscommon, Westmeath, Meath, and south Tipperary. IG monthly report, Jan. 1908, NA IGCI/13.

[61] IG monthly reports, Jan. 1907–June 1908, NA IGCI/11–13.

[62] These counties (or ridings) were east Galway, west Galway, Sligo, Leitrim, Roscommon, Westmeath, east Cork, west Cork, Mayo, south Tipperary, north Tipperary, Meath, Kildare, Clare, and Limerick. See IG monthly reports, Jan. 1907–June 1908, NA IGCI/11–13.

TABLE 4. Number of combinations against the payment of rent
identified in the Inspector General's monthly reports,
January 1907–June 1908

Month	No. of combinations	No. of counties	No. of sales
January 1907	21	7	
February	29	4	
March	28	4	
April	14	4	
May	7	3	1
June	30	7	15
July	16	4	24
August	28	7	19
September	22	4	7
October	32	6	10
November	57	10	18
December	52	8	19
January 1908	63	10	28
February	44	6	32
March	60	9	30
April	55	8	30
May	43	6	38
June	35	7	34

Notes: The number of sales have been calculated from those described in the Inspector
General's monthly reports, and probably do not reflect the total number of sales throughout
Ireland for each month. In cases where counties were divided into ridings (Galway, Cork
and Tipperary), I have counted the ridings as separate counties.

Source: IG monthly reports, Jan. 1907–June 1908, NA IGCI/11–13.

figures probably underestimate the total number of rent combinations in
this period.

The Inspector General did not explain the objectives of each combination, but he did make observations about the overall aims of the agitation. In February 1907, for instance, there were fourteen combinations
against the payment of rent in west Cork, which aimed 'to bring pressure
to bear on the landlords to sell under the Act of 1903'.[63] Less than a year
later, there were sixty-three combinations in ten counties, primarily in
Galway, Cork, Sligo, Roscommon, and Leitrim, which aimed to influence

[63] IG monthly report, Feb. 1907, NA IGCI/11.

'either . . . [the] breaking up [of] the grass farms, or . . . [the] conditions of purchase. Many of these disputes appear to have been conducted by the tenants on a uniform plan, i.e. they offer to purchase on very low terms, or to pay the rent due less about 30% reduction, and if both alternatives are rejected they decline to pay any rent at all.'[64] The rent combinations had two objectives: first, to pressurize landlords into selling their estates at fair prices, and, second, to force landlords to include their untenanted land in the sale.

This campaign for better terms of land purchase was accompanied by a revival of the agitation against the grazing system. As we have seen, landlords were reluctant to sell their untenanted land primarily because it provided them with a substantial component of their income. Consequently, the new agitation attempted to reduce the income that landlords gained from their untenanted land by intimidating grazing tenants into giving up their leases. The agitators calculated that if the landlords were left with unlet grazing land that no longer generated income, they would be more inclined to sell it to the Estates Commissioners. The Inspector General acknowledged that this was the overarching aim of the Ranch War, writing: 'The objects of the general agitation seem to be to harass owners and occupiers into submission, and to prevent all private competition with the Public Departments formed for the purpose of acquiring land.'[65]

The members of the UIL were, in effect, exerting an illegal pressure on the operation of the land market, so that the Estates Commissioners could acquire untenanted land at a more reasonable price. A senior member of the Land Commission, C. J. Beard, described the sophisticated rationale of the agitation in a letter to James Bryce:

The Land Act of 1903 gave, for the first time, the power to buy grazing lands for distribution among small land-holders. <u>Every</u> small farmer, and for that matter a great many men who had no land at all, expected to get a slice of a grazing ranch, and in that expectation remained quiet for the first two or three years. But landlords who were making good rents out of grazing tenancies naturally declined to sell, and in any case the Land Commission could not get money enough or get through the work fast enough to satisfy all this demand for land. So the people, losing patience . . . started to make the life of graziers unendurable, with the idea of forcing these men to leave grazing lands derelict, and thus of forcing the landlords to sell at any price.[66]

---

[64] IG monthly report, Jan. 1908, NA IGCI/13.
[65] IG monthly report, July 1907, NA IGCI/12.
[66] C. J. Beard (secretary to the Land Commission) to James Bryce (the Irish Chief Secretary, 1905–7), 23 Dec. 1908 NLI Bryce Papers, MS 11,016 (1).

Once grazing tenancies had been given up, landlords were placed under further pressure to sell their untenanted land by the formation of rent combinations on their estates.

The agitation against graziers was initiated by local UIL leaders in east Galway. In December 1904, the police reported: 'The . . . question [of the division of grass lands] appears to be more vigorously taken up in Galway than in other counties.'[67] By the spring of 1905, the agitation had begun to demand the attention of the Inspector General, who observed that in east Galway.

the people generally are more insistent than they are elsewhere in carrying out the land settlement on lines favourable to the small farmers. Unfortunately those who are directing the agitation do not give much attention to the limitations of the law . . . The small farmers desire to have the grazing farms divided amongst themselves. They are advised therefore to adopt a course which will temporarily depreciate the value of the [untenanted] lands the ownership of which they covet.[68]

By May 1905, forty-five tenants in east Galway had given up their grazing leases as a result of the agitation.[69] However, the conflict remained confined to Galway, despite some instances of anti-grazier conflict in other parts of the country in the course of 1905.[70] Table 5 indicates the extent to which the new agitation was almost exclusively confined to this region between 1905 and 1906. Even when the agitation had spread into other counties, particularly in 1907–8, the conflict in Galway remained more intense than elsewhere, because:

Here [in east Galway] landlords in past times were hard on their tenants and conspiracies & combinations against landlordism have been continuous. In this part of the country landlords have not been slow to combine to uphold prices and no wonder that they should be met by efforts to reduce them. It is in this part of the country that the campaign against 'Grass Ranches' is most bitter.

The police have done their best to detect crime & protect unpopular people: but if such people have come to see that they cannot hope to heal popular disapproval, & submit, I do not see that the govt. are to be blamed. A Social Revolution is going on in this part of Ireland and it is fortunate that we are keeping it a bloodless one.[71]

67 IG monthly report, Dec. 1904, NA IGCI/6.

68 IG monthly report, Feb. 1905, NA IGCI/7.

69 The confidential print, 1907–8, PRO CO 903/14/68.

70 In April 1905, for example, the Inspector General reported that there was anti-grazier agitation in Sligo, Roscommon, Mayo, and north Tipperary, while in November, the agitation was reported to have extended into east Cork and south Tipperary. IG monthly reports, Apr. and Nov. 1905, NA IGCI/7–8.

71 Minute by Anthony MacDonnell, the Under-Secretary, 19 Feb. 1907, IG monthly report, Jan. 1907, NA IGCI/11.

Table 5. Number of unlet grazing farms by county, 1905–1910

County	May 1905	May 1906	May 1907	May 1908	May 1909	May 1910
Kildare	0	0	0	2	0	1
King's	0	0	5	17	10	6
Longford	7	7	0	11	3	3
Meath	0	0	0	26	9	0
Queen's	0	0	5	7	3	0
Westmeath	0	0	1	4	2	1
E. Galway	45	36	79	95	27	6
W. Galway	4	4	9	19	2	6
Leitrim	0	0	0	4	3	2
Mayo	3	2	3	5	1	1
Roscommon	1	0	46	23	11	3
Sligo	6	3	4	16	7	3
Clare	5	1	13	39	16	10
E. Cork	2	0	1	0	0	0
W. Cork	0	0	0	1	0	0
Kerry	0	0	0	0	0	1
Limerick	0	0	0	1	0	0
N. Tipperary	14	14	3	14	2	0
S. Tipperary	9	0	2	0	1	1
Waterford	0	0	0	0	1	0
Total	96	67	174	284	98	44

Notes: These figures denote the 'number of grazing farms, including 11 months tenancies, unlet, or surrendered after having been let, owing to U.I. League influence' and the 'number of farms on which grazing cattle are usually taken, unstocked, or only partly stocked owing to U.I. League influence'.

Sources: The confidential print, 1907–8, PRO CO 903/14/67–71; the confidential print, 1909, PRO CO 903/15/114; the confidential print, 1910–11, PRO CO 903/16/141.

With the intervention of two dissident MPs in October 1906, the agitation began to spread rapidly into the rest of the country.

In the autumn of 1906, a new form of protest—cattle driving—was initiated by two MPs, Laurence Ginnell and David Sheehy, the MP for south Meath.[72] Cattle driving involved the dispersal by large crowds of graziers' cattle, up to 20 miles from the grazing farm. This made profitable grazing practices extremely difficult, but it also conveyed to the graziers the

[72] IG monthly report, Oct. 1906, NA IGCI/10.

intensity of popular feeling against them.[73] Both aspects were important in the success of this form of agitation, which became common after 1906. The objective of cattle driving was to force graziers to give up their eleven-months leases, thereby to facilitate the sale of grazing land to the Estates Commissioners (and CDB) for redistribution. This is clear from the first known case of a cattle drive in this period, at Tonlagee in county Roscommon in October 1906. According to the police, Ginnell advised the small farmers:

> that cattle should be driven off grazing farms [and] [t]he dispersal of Beirne's cattle at Tonlagee followed . . . [W]hen it was found that the Estates Commissioners were prepared to consider the question of the purchase and division of the lands involved in these disputes . . . the people . . . [became] imbued with the belief that if they . . . [followed] the example of the 'brave men of Tonlagee' the grazing ranches . . . [would] be purchased and divided amongst them.[74]

As a result of Sheehy and Ginnell's intervention, the agitation began to spread rapidly throughout the country. In the month after Ginnell's speech, the Inspector General noted that there was anti-grazier agitation in east Galway, Leitrim, Sligo, Roscommon, and Clare.[75] By the following May (1907) the agitation had extended into Galway and Roscommon (in Connacht), Clare and Tipperary (in Munster), and two midlands counties (King's and Queen's), where there had been no previous incidence of anti-grazier agitation.[76] Altogether, in the period between the revival of the anti-grazier agitation in east Galway in March 1904 and the spring of 1907, the new campaign extended into ten counties: Galway, Mayo, Roscommon, Leitrim, and Sligo in Connacht; King's and Queen's in Leinster; and Clare, Tipperary, and Cork in Munster.[77] A large number of cattle drives followed: 390 in the course of 1907, resulting in an unprecedented 174 unlet (or unstocked) grazing farms.[78] Generally, the cattle driving took place in counties where there was a high proportion of untenanted land.[79]

The Ranch War was thus characterized by two distinct, yet complementary, agitations. First, an agitation to force landlords to sell their estates; and, second, an agitation to pressurize tenants into giving up their grazing

[73] See Ch. 4.
[74] IG monthly report, May 1907, NA IGCI/11.
[75] IG monthly report, Nov. 1906, NA IGCI/10.
[76] IG monthly report, May 1907, NA IGCI/11.
[77] IG monthly reports, Mar. 1904–May 1907, NA IGCI/5–11.
[78] The confidential print, 1907–8, PRO CO 903/14/69–70; 37–8.
[79] Jones, *Graziers, land reform and political conflict in Ireland*, 195.

leases. Both aimed to implement the United Irish League's two most urgent demands—land purchase and land redistribution—and both were a response to the Irish landlords' attempts to obtain high prices for their land. And, both, it would appear, succeeded in gaining more advantageous terms of purchase for the Irish tenants. While it would require detailed research into the circumstances of individual sales to assess the full impact of the UIL's agitation on the progress of land purchase, it is possible to make some preliminary observations. First, it is clear that over one-third (36 per cent) of the total number of purchase agreements reached between 1903 and 1908 were signed during 1908, when the UIL's agitation was at its peak.[80] It is likely that this was, in part, a consequence of the Ranch War. Second, it is unlikely that combinations would have been adopted on so many estates and across so many counties,[81] if they were not successful. Indeed the agitation appears to have spread because it was successful. In east Galway, for instance, the police reported: 'In this county the progress of purchase does not seem to make any appreciable difference to the public peace at present, for no sooner has agitation resulted in the sale of one Estate, than the same plan is adopted by the tenants on another.'[82] Third, although the contemporary police reports do not provide statistics as to the success or failure of rent combinations, they do provide anecdotal evidence which suggests that the combinations generally achieved their objectives. In the spring of 1908, for instance, the Inspector General observed that in twelve counties, the tenants

have endeavoured by agitation to force landlords to agree to their terms. These were usually lower than the owner was prepared to accept; and almost invariably included a demand for sale of 'untenanted' or grass farms. To enforce these demands, 'no-rent' combinations have been formed, and the grazing system has been attacked. This policy has been successful in many cases, and such a result encourages the discontented to adopt it elsewhere.[83]

The agitation also appears to have helped tenants to gain better terms of purchase for their holdings. Generally, landlords wanted to sell and tenants wanted to buy and the only obstacle to an agreement being reached was the price. As we have seen, the prices that landlords gained for their estates between 1903 and 1908 were higher than they had been in 1902. Clearly, then, the Ranch War did not succeed in keeping prices at the

[80] Between 1903 and 1908, there were 202,906 applications for the purchase of holdings, 72,386 of them in 1908. Mullen, 'The origins and passing of the Irish Land Act of 1909', 7, 9.
[81] See Table 4.
[82] IG monthly report, July 1908, NA IGCI/14.
[83] IG monthly report, Mar. 1908, NA IGCI/13.

desired level of eighteen years' purchase.[84] But the United Irish League was probably responsible for the lower purchase prices in the west and the south-west. In Connacht and Munster, where the UIL agitation was most intense, the average purchase prices agreed by tenants were 22 years' and 21.3 years' respectively, whereas in Leinster and Ulster, where the agitation was at its weakest, purchase prices were higher, at 22.7 years and 23.9 years respectively.[85] While this evidence is impressionistic, it does suggest that the agitation may have enabled the tenants of the west and south-west to obtain better terms of purchase than their contemporaries in Leinster and Ulster.

As a result of the Ranch War, both United Irish League membership and agrarian conflict increased. These changes are depicted in Table 6, which indicates that between 1904 and 1907, the number of UIL branches increased by 11 per cent, while the total membership increased by 12 per cent. In addition, agrarian conflict increased dramatically in this period. According to four different indexes of agrarian agitation—the number of unlet grazing farms, the number of agrarian outrages, the number of persons requiring special police protection, and the number of cases of boycotting—there was a significant increase in the volume of agrarian conflict. Yet, despite the intensification of the Ranch War, the leaders of the Party continued to ignore the new agitation.

After 1904, a split within the leadership of the Irish Parliamentary Party, between the radical agrarians and the conciliationists, appears to have prevented Redmond from adopting a specific agrarian policy. The Inspector General, for example, observed:

The United Irish League is split over the quarrel amongst its leaders, and their attacks on each other have exposed the faults of each, and have shaken the faith of the people in this organization, which, just now, is degenerating into a mere money collecting machine for the Irish Parliamentary Fund. The leaders whole time is taken up in internecine war, and no programme which receives undivided support is laid before the country.[86]

The tensions within the leadership of the Party on the question of agrarian agitation had already caused William O'Brien, a committed conciliationist,

[84] The *Freeman's Journal* estimated that the price of land 'should be calculated by the actual amount of money going to the vendors and on this basis they calculate that eighteen years' purchase of second term rents should be the amount offered by the tenants.' IG monthly report, Oct. 1903, NA IGCI/4.

[85] Mullen, 'The origins and passing of the Irish Land Act of 1909', 16. This may also have been because the land in Leinster and Ulster was generally of better quality than that in Connacht and Munster.

[86] IG monthly report, Oct. 1905, NA IGCI/8.

TABLE 6. United Irish League membership and agitation, 1902–1908

	1902	1904	Percentage difference (1902–4)	1907	Percentage difference (1904–7)	1908	Percentage difference (1907–8)
UIL branches	1,242	1,171	-6	1,297	+11	1,096	-15
UIL members	136,089	124,376	-9	139,283	+12	122,834	-12
Unlet grazing farms	89	42	-53	174	+314	284	+63
Agrarian 'outrages'	253	206	-19	372	+81	576	+55
Persons receiving police protection	401	164	-59	281	+71	344	+22
Cases of boycotting	189	45	-76	125	+178	197	+58
Cattle driving				390		681	+75

Sources: United Irish League membership figures (on 31 Dec. of each year), PRO CO 904/20/2; Breandán Mac Giolla Choille, *Intelligence notes, 1913–16* (Dublin, 1966), 246, 250–2; Jones, *Graziers, land reform and political conflict*, 189.

to resign from political life in November 1903.[87] In order to avoid an open split, the Party leader, John Redmond, remained silent on agrarian matters while an extensive agitation against graziers and landlords swept from west to east across the country.[88] The policy vacuum left by Redmond and his fellow leaders was filled by an agrarian campaign orchestrated from below. Indeed, by the spring of 1907 the new agitation had extended into a large part of the country, and the leaders of the Party could no longer ignore it.

---

[87] Bew, *Conflict and conciliation*, 111. William O'Brien formally returned to the Party in January 1908, see ibid. 168.

[88] 'The ... U.I.L ... .appears to be without a distinct agrarian policy.' IG monthly report, Nov. 1905, NA IGCI/8.

II

In July 1907, John Redmond made a speech at Battersea at which he called for a 'widespread and vigorous agitation in Ireland [and] especially a movement which will force compulsory purchase of the grazing tracts in the West of Ireland'.[89] At the same time, Joseph Devlin issued a confidential circular to all of the branches of the United Irish League in Ireland, outlining a programme for agrarian agitation.[90] The Irish Parliamentary Party's change of policy had an immediate effect on the scale of the agitation. A large number of MPs now openly promoted cattle driving, boycotting, and intimidation. In June 1907, Michael Reddy made 'a violent speech in favour of the anti-grazing movement'[91] at Banagher, while in October, the Inspector General observed: 'In the speeches of Messrs Ginnell, Sheehy, Hayden, and Farrell, M.P.s, and Mr Cogan, U.I.L. organizer the people are plainly advised to break the law, to clear the cattle off the grazing lands, and to boycott those people who resist.'[92] Even Redmond attended a meeting at Portumna in October called to intimidate the 'Planters' on the Clanricarde estate.[93] In addition, the Party now sanctioned the cattle-driving policy of the fomer dissidents Ginnell and Sheehy. In July, the police noted that Ginnell had been 'sent by the National Directory' to make a speech at Elphin where he called for the boycotting of graziers until 'the ranches were purchased by the Estates Commissioners'.[94] The UIL National Directory's position on cattle driving was clarified in November 1907, when the Inspector General reported that: 'Information has been received from a reliable source that Mr Ginnell, M.P. is still detailed to address meetings by the "standing Committee of the U. I. League". This clearly shows, if proof were necessary, that the policy advocated by him is the policy of the U.I.L.'[95]

The Ranch War agitation now intensified and extended into new counties. In July and August, Ginnell attempted to initiate cattle driving

[89] IG monthly report, June 1907, NA IGCI/11.

[90] The confidential circular issued by the UIL National Directory in June outlined a programme for further action regarding evicted tenants, the distribution of untenanted land, the operation of the Labourers' Act, and financial abuses by landlords of the Wyndham Land Act. Ibid.

[91] Ibid.

[92] IG monthly report, Oct. 1907, NA IGCI/12.

[93] CI monthly report, east Galway, Oct. 1907, NA IGCI/12. The 'Planters' were a group of predominantly Protestant graziers on the estate. See CI monthly report, east Galway, Nov. 1902, PRO CO 904/76.

[94] IG monthly report, July 1907, NA IGCI/12.

[95] IG monthly report, Nov. 1907, NA IGCI/12.

in Westmeath and Meath, where there had previously been very little agrarian conflict. According to the police, Ginnell received a 'very cool reception' in Westmeath, where only three of the forty-three UIL branches were 'active',[96] while in Meath he was more successful: 'Strenuous efforts are being made by Mr Ginnell to stir up and organize an active agitation in Meath. Six farms have been cleared of grazing stock during the last few days of August, although local conditions seem opposed to the success of the movement, as the U.I.L. is not active.'[97] By October, the Ranch War had been initiated in several new counties and created extensive disorder, as the Inspector General confirmed:

the area which is disturbed owing to the anti-grazing agitation has increased in size, and the agitation has been carried on with great vigour. The counties of Roscommon, Clare, Longford, Meath and both Ridings of Galway are in a worse condition than in the month of September. Kildare and Westmeath are now affected, and Kings County and the North Riding of Tipperary are very unsettled.[98]

The Party's new policy also caused the pre-existing agitation to intensify, as Table 6 demonstrates.

Joseph Devlin, the MP for west Belfast, explained the rationale for the Irish Parliamentary Party's new policy in a letter to John Dillon in June 1907. As a result of several conferences with Redmond 'in regard to the present situation', he wrote, it had been decided that 'prompt steps should be taken to give the country a lead and to deal with the situation that has arisen in consequence of the rejection of Birrell's [Irish Council] Bill'.[99] The situation to which Devlin referred in this letter was the Liberal Party's failure to honour its pledge to introduce a Home Rule Bill after their electoral victory in 1906. Since 1886, the Irish Party had been committed to an alliance with the Liberal Party, which—in return—pledged itself to introduce a measure of Home Rule. However, when the Liberal Party were re-elected in January 1906, rather than implementing Home Rule, they offered only the Irish Council Bill.

The Irish Council Bill proposed to set up an Irish council consisting of eighty-two elected and twenty-four nominated members, including both the Viceroy and the Under-Secretary for Ireland. To this council, it proposed to transfer the control of eight of the forty-five existing Government departments, most notably, the Education Board, the Local Government Board, the Congested Districts Board, and the Department

---

96 IG monthly report, July 1907, NA IGCI/12.
97 IG monthly report, Aug. 1907, NA IGCI/12.
98 IG monthly report, Oct. 1907, NA IGCI/12.
99 Joseph Devlin to John Dillon, 5 June 1907, TCDA Dillon papers 6729/118.

of Agriculture and Technical Instruction.[100] As Campbell-Bannerman, the Prime Minister, explained, the Bill was a 'little, modest, shy, humble effort to give administrative powers to the Irish people'.[101] Indeed, the proposed Irish council would have been authorized only to administer several minor aspects of British rule in Ireland. The council would have controlled eight Government departments, and the funds necessary to administer them, but the Lord Lieutenant would have retained wide powers of veto and the overriding power of the cabinet would have remained intact.[102] According to Augustine Birrell, the Irish Chief Secretary between 1907 and 1916, the Irish Council Bill 'does not contain a touch or a trace, hint or a suggestion of any legislative power'.[103]

In comparison with the Liberal Party's second Home Rule Bill of 1893, the Irish Council Bill was a huge disappointment to the Irish nationalist community. The second Home Rule Bill would have created a two-tier legislative body with an elected upper house.[104] Although the resulting Irish parliament would not have had control over defence or trade, after a probationary period it would have gained control over critical aspects of Irish life, including landlord–tenant relations, taxation, the judiciary, and the police. In effect, the 1893 Home Rule Bill would have created a fully elected, virtually autonomous Irish parliament with legislative powers, while the Irish Council Bill offered only a semi-elected body, with no legislative power, and administrative responsibilities over a narrow range of issues. As a result, many members of the Irish nationalist movement viewed the bill as an affront to their loyalty to the Liberal Party.

The Irish Council Bill created a serious political crisis for the Irish Parliamentary Party. John Dillon had been optimistic that the Bill would be broadly acceptable to popular nationalist opinion in Ireland. In early May 1907, for example, he told Redmond that: 'I think the *Freeman* will give fair play to the bill—more it would not be reasonable to expect from them . . . I have had very little opportunity so far of gauging feeling here. But I fancy there is a tendency to reaction in favour of giving the bill fair consideration.'[105] Dillon was, however, out of touch with popular nationalist opinion, which was vehemently opposed to the Bill. The *Freeman's Journal* was extremely hostile to the Bill, as were most of the

---

[100] Bew, *Conflict and conciliation*, 130.

[101] Quoted in Lyons, *Ireland since the Famine*, 264.   [102] Ibid. 264–5.

[103] Bew, *Conflict and conciliation*, 130.

[104] For a summary of the clauses of the second Home Rule Bill, see Foster, *Modern Ireland*, 424–5.

[105] Quoted in A. C. Hepburn, 'The Irish Council Bill and the fall of Sir Anthony MacDonnell, 1906–7', *Irish Historical Studies*, 17/68 (Sept. 1971), 488.

provincial nationalist newspapers. In his study of the Irish Council Bill crisis, A. C. Hepburn examined the views of twenty-six provincial newspapers on the Bill. His findings revealed that seventeen were opposed to it, four were prepared to leave the decision to the upcoming convention, and five were in favour of amending it in committee.[106] None of the provincial newspapers (in this sample) supported the Bill as it stood. Locally elected bodies were equally hostile to the Bill. Of thirty-five local bodies whose decisions were reported in the *Freeman's Journal* between 9 and 20 May 1907, sixteen instructed their delegates to vote against the Bill, fourteen expressed hostility to the Bill but instructed their delegates to vote as directed by Redmond, and only five voted in favour of it.[107]

Why were so many Home Rulers opposed to the Irish Council Bill? Sir Thomas Esmonde, MP for north Wexford, who temporarily resigned from the Party over the issue, explained:

For twenty years we have supported the English Liberal Party. All we have obtained—and we have obtained much—has been won from their opponents, whom we have persistently fought. We have supported the English Liberals in the confident expectation that, when their day came, they would concede legislative and administrative autonomy to Ireland. Our hopes have been rudely disappointed. The day of the English Liberal Party came. They got into power—largely through our help—with an unprecedented majority. They have done nothing for us. They will do nothing for us. Their day is already past . . . I do not believe that the English people will ever grant Home Rule, or anything like it, to Ireland, if they can help it. Why, then, degrade ourselves by begging for it?[108]

While Esmonde may have overstated the case against continued parliamentary attendance, it is likely that his reason for rejecting the Bill— because it did not 'concede legislative and administrative autonomy to Ireland'—was widely held by constitutional nationalists more generally. A letter from Denis Johnstone, the secretary of the UIL, to John Dillon suggests that this was the case: 'if the [Irish Council] Bill is accepted it will demoralize the National Organisation and destroy the hopes of the people [for Home Rule].'[109] Evidently, provincial nationalists were seriously committed to the achievement of legislative political independence. And at the national convention held to debate the Irish Parliamentary Party's response to the Bill on 21 May 1907, the delegates (80 per cent of whom were rank and file members of provincial nationalist organizations)

[106] Ibid. 488–9.
[107] Ibid. 491–2.
[108] *Sinn Féin*, 27 July 1907.
[109] Denis Johnstone to John Dillon, 13 May 1907, TCDA Dillon papers 6763/39.

rejected the Bill *tout court* as an inadequate substitute for Home Rule.[110]

Neither was the Bill popular among the members of the Irish Parliamentary Party. Indeed, it threatened to split the Party. Broadly speaking, there were three main responses from the Irish MPs. First, that of the Redmondites in the Party, including Hugh Law, Joseph Nolan, J. J. O'Shee, J. H. McKean, M. J. Flavin, J. J. Clancy, and J. P. Hayden, who supported the Bill and claimed that it could be amended and improved in committee.[111] Second, a group of dissidents and agrarians, including Tim Healy, John O'Donnell, Laurence Ginnell, Michael Meagher, Tom Kettle, John O'Dowd, J. Murphy, William O'Malley, J. P. Farrell, and Michael Joyce, who denounced the Bill as 'an insult to Ireland' and called on the convention to reject it.[112] And third, a group of predominantly younger members, including Edward Barry, Thomas O'Donnell, Sir Thomas Esmonde, Charles Dolan, and James O'Mara, who threatened to resign from the Party if the Bill was not rejected.[113] The latter group constituted the most serious threat to the Party, since they called on the IPP to withdraw from Westminster, and to adopt the abstentionist policy of a rival political party, Sinn Féin.[114] Although the Sinn Féin party advocated a sophisticated political programme, in the popular mind Sinn Féin was identified with two central policies: first, that the Irish MPs should withdraw from Westminster; and, second, that they should establish an assembly which would encourage Irish economic and cultural development.[115]

The Sinn Féin policy acquired a strong contemporary relevance after the Liberal Party's landslide electoral victory in January 1906. Following the general election, popular nationalist opinion expected the Liberal Party to deliver on its Home Rule pledge, and Sinn Féin was quick to cast a cynical eye on the Liberal Party's commitment to Home Rule. In January 1906, for example, an editorial in the Sinn Féin newspaper—the *United Irishman*—explained that Sinn Féin had not contested the election because 'It leaves no shred of excuse to the Irish Parliamentarians to cover their

---

[110] The convention was attended by 4,293 delegates, including 61 MPs, 283 Roman Catholic priests, 571 AOH. delegates, 101 Irish National Foresters, 264 representatives of the United Irish League in Great Britain, 2,133 delegates from Irish United Irish League branches, 726 local councillors, three representatives of the UIL in America, one UIL representative from Australia, and fifteen others described by the police as 'miscellaneous'. IG monthly report, May 1907, NA IGCI/11.

[111] Hepburn, 'The Irish Council Bill', 489.   [112] Ibid. 489–90.

[113] Maume, *The long gestation*, 89; Lyons, *Dillon*, 299; Ciarán Ó Duibhir, *Sinn Féin: the first election, 1908* (Manorhamilton, 1993), 19–20; Hepburn, 'The Irish Council Bill', 494.

[114] Hepburn, 'The Irish Council Bill', 489–90.   [115] See Ch. 5.

political nakedness when they return to Ireland at the close of the forthcoming session of parliament without that Home Rule Bill which three
out of every four of their followers are firmly persuaded will be passed by
the Liberal Government this year.'[116] Indeed, at the local level, nationalists
were aware that the Liberal majority meant that Home Rule was probably
an unlikely prospect. The County Inspector for east Galway reported:

The only thing I can gather from conversation with the people generally is that
they are greatly disappointed that the Liberals should have come in with such a
large majority as to make them independent of the Irish National votes. They had
counted on the Liberals being dependent on this and expected great things from
such a state of the political parties.[117]

The Liberals' watered down attempt to introduce a substitute for
Home Rule played directly into the hands of Sinn Féin. On 25 May 1907
the National Council published a resolution on the Bill in *Sinn Féin*,
stating:

That the Irish Council Bill is an insult to the Irish nation, and this council calls
upon the Irishmen who have attended the British parliament during the last 21
years in support of the British Liberal Party to withdraw from that parliament,
return to Ireland, and, assembling in Dublin, in conjunction with the General
Council of County Councils and authorised representatives of all Irish interests,
devise and direct measures for the material betterment of Ireland, and the securing
of international recognition and support for Ireland's political rights.[118]

Senior members of the Liberal Party had even anticipated that the Irish
Council Bill might strengthen the position of Sinn Féin, as James Bryce
told Anthony MacDonnell (the Under-Secretary, 1902–8) in August
1906:

The exclusion of any legislative function may prove to be a grave disappointment
to all sections of nationalists . . . What one fears is that the ultra party, the fenian
dregs, the Sinn Fein men, etc., etc., will, when our little chicken is hatched, cry
out 'so this is all the result of your parliamentary party and its dealings with the
English government!' J.E.R., who already thinks himself in a tight place, will be in
a tighter one.[119]

And Bryce was proved correct. The Irish Council Bill undermined the
entire rationale for the Irish Parliamentary Party to remain at Westminster.
If Home Rule could not be achieved through an alliance with the Liberal

---

116 IG monthly report, Jan. 1906, NA IGCI/9.
117 CI monthly report, east Galway, Jan. 1906, NA IGCI/9.
118 *Sinn Féin*, 25 May 1907.
119 Hepburn, 'The Irish Council Bill', 475.

Party, then there was no reason for the Party to continue to attend at the House of Commons. As a *Sinn Féin* editorial pithily put it: 'if the Irish Parliamentary Party cannot achieve Home Rule at Westminster, why are they there?'[120] And, in this context, Sinn Féin's policy of abstentionism became an important alternative strategy to that of parliamentary agitation.

At least five members of the IPP recognized this, and called on the Party to adopt the Sinn Féin policy and withdraw from Westminster. At a meeting of the National UIL Directory in June 1907, Thomas O'Donnell, the MP for west Kerry, resolved:

That after the betrayal of Irish hopes and demands by Mr. Birrell's Irish Council Bill, we feel that the Irish Party could do better work for Ireland . . . by devoting their energy and their talents to the work of rebuilding, extending and protecting Ireland's industries, of fostering the National Language, of acting as guides in land sales, of helping the labourer and town tenant; and we call upon them to withdraw from an assembly which neither legally nor morally has a right to make laws for Ireland, and to initiate at home in Ireland an active campaign of constructive work combined with open and defiant hostility to all English interference in our internal affairs.[121]

This resolution was moved by O'Donnell, seconded by Charles Dolan, the MP for north Leitrim, and supported by Dr Mulcahy of Leitrim and William Ganly of Longford.[122] John Redmond, the chairman, refused to allow the meeting to vote on the resolution. According to *Sinn Féin* it was 'declared lost by [Redmond] . . . without calling for a vote against it'.[123] Redmond later told Dillon that a group of MPs had proposed a 'silly resolution' to withdraw from Westminster, and that the dissident group consisted of Thomas O'Donnell, Charles Dolan, James O'Mara, Patrick White, and Edward Barry.[124] Although Redmond played down this resolution, he did take it sufficiently seriously to quash it before it could go to a vote.

In the event, only three members of the Party resigned: James O'Mara, the MP for south Kilkenny, Charles Dolan, and Sir Thomas Esmonde (who later rejoined the Party).[125] But a much larger number of the rank and file members of the United Irish League appear to have defected to Sinn Féin. The number of United Irish League branches declined by 15

---

120 *Sinn Féin*, 1 June 1907.
121 Quoted in Ó Duibhir, *Sinn Féin: the first election*, 20.
122 Ibid.   123 *Sinn Féin*, 22 June 1907.   124 Lyons, *Dillon*, 299.
125 Ó Duibhir, *Sinn Féin: the first election*, 16; Maume, *The long gestation*, 227.

per cent between 1907 and 1908, and almost 17,000 members of the UIL left the organization, while over the same period, the number of Sinn Féin clubs doubled.[126] In part, this was as a result of Charles Dolan's decision to resign from the Party and re-contest his seat on a Sinn Féin ticket, thus initiating Sinn Féin's first electoral challenge to Home Rule hegemony.

On 28 January 1908, Dolan resigned from the Irish Parliamentary Party, and stated his intention to contest the north Leitrim by-election on 21 February.[127] An extensive Sinn Féin campiagn was initiated in the constituency resulting in the formation of eleven Sinn Féin clubs and a local Sinn Féin newspaper, the *Leitrim Guardian*.[128] Despite this electoral campaign, Dolan polled only 1,157 votes, to 3,103 for F. E. Meehan, the Party candidate, or one-quarter of the votes cast.[129] It is likely that most of the Sinn Féin voters were former members of the north Leitrim UIL executive who were opposed to the Irish Council Bill. As *Sinn Féin* reported in June 1907: 'At a meeting of the north Leitrim Executive of the United Irish League a resolution was adopted calling on the Irish Party to withdraw in a body from Westminster as a protest against the betrayal of Ireland by the British Liberals.'[130] Many members of the Leitrim UIL during this period appear to have adopted Sinn Féin views and, when the Party leadership decided to remain at Westminster, a large number of them were forced to leave the United Irish League. At Manorhamiltion, for example, the local UIL branch expelled members of the committee for holding Sinn Féin opinions in October 1907.[131]

Although Sinn Féin was a relatively small and inexperienced political organization, the Irish Parliamentary Party took the Sinn Féin challenge seriously. As the Inspector General observed: 'The strength and importance of this movement [Sinn Féin] is shown by the anxiety of the Irish Parliamentary Party to crush it.'[132] Joseph Devlin, the Party's election campaign organizer, told Redmond:

The case of North Leitrim is . . . serious. Dolan has been here in Dublin for the past few days consulting the leaders of the Sinn Fein Movement. There is a meeting on next saturday in Manorhamilton—his own town—at which McHugh and Sheehy will be present and speak, and my impression is that that Constituency will go all right if the situation is handled with boldness. As far as I can see Dolan is determined to find out what is the real sentiment of the people. If he finds he

---

[126] On UIL membership, see Table 6; on Sinn Féin, see Richard Davis, *Arthur Griffith and non-violent Sinn Fein* (Dublin, 1974), 81–2.

[127] Ó Duibhir, *Sinn Féin: the first election*, 56. [128] Ibid. 23, 102.

[129] Davis, *Arthur Griffith*, 48. [130] *Sinn Féin*, 22 June 1907.

[131] Ó Duibhir, *Sinn Féin: the first election*, 45.

[132] IG monthly report, June 1907, NA IGCI/11.

will be beaten he will not apply for the Chiltern Hundreds, and will not go to the poll unless he sees he has a good chance. If a good fight is carried on against him he will not have a ghost of a chance. I think it very important that if the Convention is held you should attend it yourself . . . and you can then make a speech on the Sinn Fein Policy . . .

David Sheehy proposes to remain in North Leitrim until after the Convention, and I think it would be well that . . . you sent over here about a dozen of the best members who can be relied on to take a thorough interest not only in the immediate situation, but in the future work, so that they might be sent to districts where personal effort is badly needed.[133]

In addition to orthodox electioneering, the Party also used some underhand tactics to maintain their position. On the eve of the largest political meeting of the campaign, held at Drumkeerin in October, Denis Johnstone informed a local organizer: 'I hope our old friends in Drumkeerin will see that any attempt of outsiders to speak at the meeting will be met with determined opposition. You will see Mr. Myles McKenna and say how anxious I am that should Dolan or his crowd put in an appearance the people ought to hunt them out of town.'[134] As a result of Johnstone's intervention, when Dolan stood up to address the meeting three days later, he was jeered with taunts of 'Clear out' and 'traitor'.[135] When he continued to speak, the crowd began throwing mud and stones at him to such an extent that the police were called upon to disperse the crowd. At the same meeting, Anna Parnell, Charles Stewart Parnell's sister and a Sinn Féin supporter, was unceremoniously pelted with eggs and had a bucket of water emptied onto her head by the local Home Rulers.[136] This was not an isolated incident. Indeed, there is evidence that Devlin imported Hibernian thugs from Belfast to attend Dolan's meetings and assault his supporters.[137] Even the tyres of the Sinn Féiners' motor car were cut and damaged (apparently) by a gang of Redmondites.[138] It is clear that the Party identified Sinn Féin as a serious threat in north Leitrim, and as a consequence all of the Party's financial and intellectual muscle was mobilized to crush the Sinn Féin challenge. Indeed, given the combined efforts of MPs attending meetings in the constituency and hired Redmondite mobs intimidating Sinn Féin supporters, it is remarkable that Dolan polled as highly as he did.

---

133 Joseph Devlin to John Redmond, 25 June 1907, NLI Redmond papers MS 15,181 (2).
134 Ó Duibhir, *Sinn Féin: the first election*, 114.
135 Ibid. 46.
136 Ibid. 72; Davis, *Arthur Griffith*, 47.
137 Davis, *Arthur Griffith*, 46–7; Maume, *The long gestation*, 97.
138 Davis, *Arthur Griffith*, 47.

Sinn Féin was also expanding in other parts of the country. Indeed, the movement expanded rapidly outside Dublin between 1907 and 1908.[139] However, the provincial Sinn Féin movement was characterized by a different set of priorities from the Dublin-and-Belfast-based Sinn Féin elite. Whereas the national leaders paid little attention to agrarian issues, these were often vitally important to rural Sinn Féin activists. At Tullamore, in King's county, a Sinn Féin meeting held in December 1907 identified the anti-grazier agitation with the anti-recruitment campaign. A police report on this meeting observed: 'The grazing system was also referred to, and it was resolved to keep a fatherly eye . . . [on] the grabber, grazier, and would-be English soldier.'[140] At Carron, in north Clare, a Sinn Féin meeting held on 25 October 1908, and attended by forty members, resolved 'that all herds in the parish refuse to herd graziers' cattle'. The police further commented that this branch had 'frequently interfered in the grazing question'.[141] A similar tendency was noted by the police in Tipperary in November 1908, where it was reported that: 'The Sinn Fein and I.R.B. men around Thurles and Holycross are taking an active part in the agrarian agitation now being waged in that locality.'[142]

In Galway, the Sinn Féin movement was prominently involved in the agrarian agitation of 1907–8. The Ranch War was vigorously waged in the east riding and organized primarily by the Town Tenants' League (TTL) in Athenry.[143] The TTL was formed in early 1906 by a group of town tenants who were also involved in the Gaelic League and the Gaelic Athletic Association. Stephen Jordan, a bootmaker, and Lawrence Lardner, a publican's assistant, both of whom were members of the IRB, were leading figures in this organization, which was composed of both town tenants and rural tenant farmers.[144] Although the TTL did not formally constitute itself as a Sinn Féin branch until 1914,[145] it did adopt the Sinn Féin policy in 1907 when it called on the Irish MPs to withdraw from Westminster in order

---

[139] See Ch. 5.

[140] Précis of information received in Crime Special Branch, Dec. 1907, PRO CO 904/117.

[141] Ibid., Oct. 1908, PRO CO 904/118.

[142] Ibid., Nov. 1908, PRO CO 904/118.

[143] There is an account of the Town Tenant League's agitation during the Ranch War by the editor of the *Connacht Tribune* (Thomas J. Kenny) in the *Connacht Tribune*, 13, 20, 27 Nov., and 4 Dec. 1909. Kenny refers to the organization as both the Town Tenants' League and the Town Tenants' Association. For the sake of consistency, I refer to it as the Town Tenants' League.

[144] *Connacht Tribune*, 20 Nov. and 27 Nov. 1909; Stephen Jordan witness statement, MA BMH WS 346; see Appendix I. For further discussion of the TTL, see Ch. 5.

[145] In the aftermath of the Irish Council Bill crisis, the Athenry TTL openly advocated the Sinn Féin policy. *Sinn Féin*, 25 May 1907; CI monthly report, east Galway, Nov. 1914, PRO CO 904/95.

to constitute an Irish Assembly which could work for the 'material betterment of Ireland'.[146] According to the editor of the *Connacht Tribune*, Mr
Thomas J. Kenny, who wrote a history of the movement in 1909, the Town
Tenants' League 'superseded the National Organisation' between May
1906 and May 1907.[147] It organized a campaign of cattle driving on all the
large grazing farms surrounding the town, and also a 'no-rent' campaign
on the Lambert estate in an attempt to force the landlord to sell under
the Wyndham Land Act. Kenny wrote that the League 'swept all before it
... In a few days Athenry and its vicinity was a place of agitation, yet the
most perfect unity prevailed amongst the members of this all powerful
League.'[148]

The unity of rural tenants and town tenants was strengthened by the
fact that both were tenants on the Rodney and Lambert estates, which
encompassed the town of Athenry as well as much of the agricultural land
in the hinterland of the town. As a result of the League's agitation the two
estates were sold, the purchase money for the sale of the Ormsby estate
was advanced, and the Caheroyan grazing farm was distributed among
seventy town tenants.[149] According to Kenny, the agitation provided
800 tenants with 'comfortable holdings', for which they paid 'reasonable
rents [annuities]'.[150] Kenny's only reservation about the agitation was
that he 'would rather have seen the success achieved under the banner
of the National organisation, and the same would have been achieved if
that body ... could have been organised as the Town Tenants' League
undoubtedly was'.[151]

But at Athenry, as elsewhere, the agrarian agitation that reached its
peak in 1908 was not initiated by the Irish Parliamentary Party leadership.
Indeed, Sinn Féin's ability to outflank the Irish Parliamentary Party in
terms of agrarian militancy during this period was an important factor
in forcing Redmond to adopt a radical agrarian policy in June 1907. As
Devlin wrote to Redmond on 25 June 1907:

I think too, that as far as possible the representative for each district where cattle
driving is being carried on, should be sent into these places to associate himself
with the people. I was told by [William] Duffy that it is the Sinn Féin Party who
are carrying on the fight in Athenry, and as they are making a great fight there, it is
rather a pity that some of our members should not be associated with it.[152]

---

146 *Sinn Féin*, 25 May 1907.   147 *Connacht Tribune*, 27 Nov. 1909.
148 Ibid., 27 Nov. and 4 Dec. 1909.   149 Ibid.
150 Ibid., 4 Dec. 1909.   151 Ibid., 27 Nov. 1909.
152 Joseph Devlin to John Redmond, 25 June 1907, NLI Redmond papers MS 15,181 (2).

The radical agrarian policy, which underpinned the Ranch War, was traditionally associated with the IRB in the west of Ireland.[153] In this region, the agitation was implemented both by the more extreme UIL branches and by the new Sinn Féin clubs. After June 1907, the leaders of the IPP, by identifying themselves with the Ranch War, succeeded in out-flanking these radical elements and restored the authority of the official UIL leadership.

Perhaps most important of all, Sinn Féin was challenging the IPP in the realm of ideology. In particular, Sinn Féin made a strong case against the continued value of both the Liberal alliance and attendance at Westminster. As the Inspector General recognized in June 1906:

Those who support the National Council and the Sinn Fein policy are not themselves making much progress in the country, but the debates which they organize and the literature which they publish decrying parliamentary agitation and advising people to desist from contributing to parliamentary Funds, appear to have some effect in curtailing the subscriptions received through the U.I. League Branches.[154]

Indeed, Sinn Féin literature was disseminated throughout the country. According to the Inspector General: 'The SINN FEIN party does not command a large following, but the literature explaining its doctrine is widely distributed.'[155] Sinn Féin pamphlets were sold for one penny, particularly at GAA tournaments, while anti-recruiting literature was distributed in every Irish county between 1905 and 1909.[156] The following anti-recruiting poster, for example, was 'extensively circulated' by Sinn Féiners in Wexford during 1908:

JOIN THE ARMY

Sell your soul, your country and your God for the Saxon Shilling. Join England's hireling murderers that pitchcapped and hanged your forefathers in 98' [*sic*] and that would do the same with you tomorrow. Your reward will be a life of immoral-ity and a dog's death in the gaol or by the road side. Go to India to murder women and children and shoot down men who are fighting for liberty.

JOIN THE POLICE

Become one of England's paid spies and murderers, become a Sullivan or a Sheridan, one of the creatures in England's pay who evicted your fathers, and would do the same with their own. One of the men who shot young Stenson,[157]

---

[153] See Ch. 4.   [154] IG monthly report, June 1906, NA IGCI/9.
[155] IG monthly report, Mar. 1907, NA IGCI/11.
[156] Michael Laffan, *The resurrection of Ireland: the Sinn Féin party, 1916–1923* (Cambridge, 1999), 3; IG monthly report, May 1906, NA IGCI/9; IG monthly reports, Jan. 1905–Dec. 1909, NA IGCI/7–14; PRO CO 904/77–9.   [157] On John Stenson, see Ch. 5.

and would shoot you tomorrow. Soldiers and Peelers are alike; don't associate with them; make it impossible for England to get recruits here, and her power is at an end. God Save Ireland and To Hell with England.[158]

Such literature, understandably, concerned the Inspector General, who was anxious that it would 'embolden ... the disaffected' and 'efface the memory of anything good which England has done'.[159]

As a result of the widespread dissemination of this literature, Sinn Féin ideology influenced members of the Home Rule movement. Indeed, the Inspector General recognized in June 1907 that 'In spite, however, of the denunciation of the Sinn Fein movement it is possible that Mr John Redmond and his followers may feel constrained to adopt most of the Sinn Fein programme, excepting, however, the portion which demands abstention from attendance at Westminster.'[160] In August 1907, he was proved correct: 'The struggle between the League and the advocates of the Sinn Fein policy continues. The former recently issued a circular to all Branches calling on them to encourage Irish Industries, one of the leading items in the Sinn Fein programme—and the National Council promptly responded by advising the formation of local committees to deal with agrarian questions.'[161] The increased influence of Sinn Féin ideas, particularly after May 1907, together with Sinn Féin's support for radical agrarianism, and the consequent decline in UIL membership, are the context in which Redmond's changed policy on the Ranch War should be considered. This is made most clear in a letter from Devlin to Dillon on 5 June 1907, where he suggests that they respond immediately to the Irish Council Bill debacle:

It is rather difficult to know what precisely is the best course to adopt but we believe that under the circumstances that a meeting of the Party should be called; that from that meeting a manifesto should be issued ... & that subsequently a meeting of the National Directory in Ireland & the National Council in Gt. Britain should be held to lay down a plan of Campaign for the Irish people & for the British constituencies. We think at the Directory a series of city & county meetings should be organized in Ireland in favour of Home Rule & that later a campaign ought to be commenced in the English constituencies. That the fight in the West should be judiciously encouraged & during the Autumn the country ought to be roused by meetings—Home Rule meetings in every constituency.[162]

---

[158] Précis of information received in Crime Special Branch, Dec. 1908, CO 904/118.
[159] IG monthly report, Sept. 1906, NA IGCI/10.
[160] IG monthly report, June 1907, NA IGCI/11.
[161] IG monthly report, Aug. 1907, NA IGCI/12.
[162] Joseph Devlin to John Dillon, 5 June 1907, TCDA Dillon papers 6729/118.

The Irish Parliamentary Party's new policy had two central aims. First, to win back lost support in the country, especially in areas where Sinn Féin was taking the initiative in the agrarian agitation; and, second, to restore confidence in the power of parliamentary agitation by pressurising the Government into introducing a new Land Bill. In order to achieve these objectives, Redmond presented the pre-existing Ranch War agitation to the Government as a campaign for new land legislation. In July 1907, Redmond told the House of Commons that the Wyndham Land Act had broken down financially, and demanded that the Government introduce a new Land Bill.[163] When the Government did not respond, Redmond threatened that in the absence of new land legislation, 'the results this winter in Ireland cannot fail to be extremely serious ... [and that] it will be impossible for the National Party to hold themselves responsible for the peace of Ireland'.[164]

Redmond explained the new policy in a letter to John O'Callaghan, of the UIL in the United States:

I think it certain that we will have an Autumn and Winter of a most exciting character in Ireland, and that the Irish question will, therefore, be very much to the front indeed. Of course, there are friends of ours who say that any violent action in Ireland will alienate support here. But the sounder view, in existing circumstances, is, in my opinion, that you have got, in some way or other, once more to impress the English mind that the Irish Question is a real, urgent one.

He added, however: 'All this, of course, for your own private eye only ... What I mean is, that you are not to publish anything contained in this letter as coming from me.'[165] Evidently, Redmond was playing a political game: he did not want to be publicly associated with the new agitation, but he did want to manipulate it to his advantage. Redmond's personal views on the Wyndham Land Act had probably not changed since 1903, and his support for the Ranch War was calculated to restore the IPP to pre-eminence and no more. As Redmond told Bryce: 'the question as to whether [the proposed new land legislation] ... should be a compromise or not or whether it should be proceeded with seriously or not could be left over for the present.'[166] In other words, Redmond was not primarily interested in the form that the new Land Bill would take, but with obtaining legislation that might demonstrate the continuing vitality of the Liberal alliance.

---

[163] Mullen, 'The origins and passing of the Irish Land Act of 1909', 74.
[164] Redmond to Birrell, 21 July 1908, TCDA Dillon papers 6747/376.
[165] Redmond to John O'Callaghan, 3 Apr. 1908, TCDA Dillon papers 6747/291.
[166] Redmond to Bryce, 29 Jan. 1906, NLI Bryce papers MS 11,012.

The Government was well aware of the source of Redmond's conversion to agrarian radicalism. In October 1907, Birrell told Campbell-Bannerman:

Redmond's position is a ticklish one . . . He has very little personal control. The next session he will be watched with scrutinizing eyes by the whole country. He can't rest on his oars for a single moment. He must be up and doing from the very first. The impression is general in Ireland that the Irish Parliamentary Party have allowed Home Rule to be snowed under and that it can't emerge for at least a decade. Were this impression to become a belief, Redmond and his whole party would be kicked into space, and their maintenance fund would disappear, and the Sinn Feiners, who are Fenians and Ribbonmen and separatists in new clothes and with some new ideas, would reign in their stead. Redmond who has still got hold of the machine at Westminster must, therefore, make great play, somehow or other, next session. If he can't give us support he must fight us tooth and nail, and at least half his supporters would be just as well pleased if he decided to fight us.[167]

Indeed, it was widely recognized in the Irish Office that the Party was not in control of the agrarian agitation. C. J. Beard told Bryce in December 1908:

So far as the leaders of the Irish Party (Dillon, Redmond & co) are concerned, I think that even crediting them with every desire to keep down agrarian crime, they have no power to do it, and they know it. They might at least try; but their own position is none too secure, & I suppose they are not inclined to risk it.[168]

Even so, Birrell argued that the Ranch War demonstrated the necessity for new land legislation. In a memorandum of June 1908, he informed the cabinet that

I cannot hope to get through the winter in Ireland unless I take a first step of some kind and give Ireland something to talk about. At present, cattle-driving is the sole political movement in the west. Devolution for the moment has disappeared, and as for Home Rule, no one can say where it is . . .

Anyhow, I must in October introduce a Bill amending the Land Purchase Act of 1903 in certain particulars . . . Such a Bill, of course, could not be proceeded with beyond Second Reading, but it would be a subject matter for discussion in Ireland between landlords and tenants, between the followers of Mr. Dillon and the followers of Mr. William O'Brien, and although I am not very sanguine about it I still think it is possible that some agreement might be come to between these parties . . .

I cannot part with the question without reiterating an opinion I have already expressed more than once in the Cabinet that, in my judgment, the present

---

[167] Birrell to Campbell-Bannerman, 30 Oct. 1907, BM Campbell-Bannerman papers, Add. MS 41,240/130–1.

[168] C. J. Beard to James Bryce, 23 Dec. 1908, NLI James Bryce papers MS 11,016 (1).

situation in Ireland is capable of very dangerous development, and that past experience teaches us that we do not in the long run secure economy by simply refusing to listen to Irish demands.[169]

As in 1903, the Government was pressurized into introducing new land legislation by an extensive agitation from below, and a new Land Bill was introduced by the Liberal Government on 23 November 1908. However, due to the lateness of the session, the Bill was held over and reintroduced early in the next session, and eventually became law on 3 December 1909.[170]

The new legislation did little to further the progress of land purchase. Four years later, Birrell even contemplated introducing another Land Bill, such was his dissatisfaction with the 1909 Act. He claimed that one-third of Irish land was still outside land purchase operations in 1913, and that a new Bill was required to solve the Irish land question.[171] Indeed, the terms of the 1909 Land Act made land purchase less attractive to both landlord and tenant than it had been under the Wyndham Act. Under the new Act, landlords were paid in land stock, as opposed to cash, and the tenants' annuity was increased, which recommended the legislation to neither landlord nor tenant.[172] The Act did reduce the block of pending agreements. Even so, in 1916, £26 million worth of pending agreements remained outstanding, including £18 million which had been pending since 1908.[173] The Birrell Land Act, then, did not succeed in accelerating the pace of land purchase.

The Act did, however, introduce some important reforms in the congested districts. Birrell was influenced by the Royal Commission on Congestion[174] to reform the operation of the Congested Districts Board in two important respects. First, the new Act provided the CDB with an additional £250,000 per annum;[175] and, second, the Board was given compulsory powers to purchase untenanted land for the relief of congestion.[176] As a result, the CDB purchased over one million acres of

---

[169] Augustine Birrell, 'The Dudley report on congestion in Ireland', PRO CAB 37/93/71.
[170] Mullen, 'The origins and passing of the Irish Land Act of 1909', 98, 142.
[171] Ibid. 144.   [172] Bew, *Conflict and conciliation*, 182.
[173] Mullen, 'The origins and passing of the Irish Land Act of 1909', 143.
[174] The Royal Commission on Congestion held 116 public meetings, interviewed 570 witnesses, published eleven volumes of evidence, and concluded that untenanted land should be made available, by compulsory acquisition if necessary, to relieve congestion in the congested districts. Bew, *Conflict and conciliation*, 12; Jones, *Graziers, land reform and political conflict in Ireland*, 211.
[175] Micks, *Account of the ... Congested Districts Board*, 123.
[176] Lyons, *Ireland since the Famine*, 206.

untenanted land between 1910 and 1919, while between 1891 and 1910 the CDB had acquired only 380,000 acres of grazing land.[177] While the reforms of the CDB introduced by the 1909 Act did not solve congestion, they greatly enhanced the ability of the Board to improve the living conditions of the western smallholders.

Although the Birrell Land Act did not solve the Irish land question, it did enable the Party to regain the support of the Irish nationalist community. Indeed, the Act demonstrated that both attendance at Westminster and the Liberal alliance were valuable assets that could be enormously beneficial to the nationalist cause. The Birrell Land Act was not introduced primarily to amend the financial provisions of the Wyndham Act. While it is true that the Act introduced some financial amendments to the 1903 Act, the 1909 Act did not appreciably improve the operation of the Wyndham Land Act. It did, however, restore popular nationalist confidence in Redmond and the Irish Parliamentary Party. The number of UIL branches increased from 1,096 to 1,251 (14 per cent) between 1908 and 1910,[178] following the introduction of the new Land Act, and the membership of Sinn Féin declined to a negligible level. According to Bulmer Hobson, in 1910 'there were about 135 branches [of Sinn Féin] in the country; in the following year there were six and a year later there was one'.[179] By September 1911, Sinn Féin had returned to a similar position to that which it had occupied before the 1906 general election: 'The National Council (Sinn Fein) is inactive every where, but it is explained in the Official Organ that this is in accordance with their present policy of giving Mr Redmond a free hand to redeem his promise of obtaining a satisfactory measure of Home Rule, although they are sceptical as to his ability to do so.'[180]

Redmond's response to the Irish Council Bill debacle rescued the Irish Parliamentary Party from the most serious threat to its political existence before the Easter Rising. His manipulation of the pre-existing agrarian agitation enabled the Party to pose as the leaders of the Ranch War, and thereby to pressurize the Government into introducing a new Land Act. Indeed, with the introduction of the Birrell Land Act in 1909, Sinn Féin's claim that attendance at Westminster was futile was rendered irrelevant. The possible benefits of parliamentary agitation were clearly demonstrated by the new Act. Similarly, the adoption of an agrarian policy in June 1907

---

[177] Mullen, 'The origins and passing of the Irish Land Act of 1909', 147.
[178] UIL membership figures, PRO CO 904/20/2.
[179] Davis, *Arthur Griffith*, 81.
[180] IG monthly report, Sept. 1911, PRO CO 904/85.

re-established the Party's radical agrarian credentials, and outflanked the Sinn Féin branches in the west of Ireland, some of which had been in the vanguard of the Ranch War. As a result of Redmond's ability to lead by knowing how to follow, the Irish Parliamentary Party was restored to its position of electoral and ideological dominance.

After 1909, the Irish Parliamentary Party's authority was further strengthened by the two general elections of 1910, and the Parliament Act of 1911. Whereas in 1907, the Party had appeared to be on the brink of dissolution, in 1911 Home Rule seemed to be inevitable. As a result of the two general elections, the Liberal Party were, once again, dependent on the IPP for votes, and therefore re-committed to Home Rule. And, with the removal of the House of Lords' power of veto by the Parliament Act, the unionists in the Upper House could not throw out a Home Rule Bill, as they had done in 1893. In these circumstances, John Redmond could 'sit back and bask in hyperbole'.[181] However, the political crisis of 1907–8 would have important repercussions for the Party a decade later. Sinn Féin, though it had failed to dent the Party's electoral machine, was now established on the Irish political landscape. In the event of the Liberal Party not implementing Home Rule in the future, Sinn Féin's policy of abstention from Westminster was widely understood as a possible alternative to parliamentary agitation. Similarly, there were now a large number of provincial Sinn Féin activists, who had gained important political experience, and who awaited another opportunity to challenge the Irish Party. Most importantly, the events of 1903–10 revealed the precarious coalition of interests that underpinned the apparent unity of the Home Rule movement; a unity that would be tested once again in the second decade of the new century.

[181] Foster, *Modern Ireland*, 462.

4

The 'Law of the League':
United Irish League Justice,
1898–1910

The law of the land has been openly set aside and the unwritten law
of the League is growing supreme.

(The Inspector General, Apr. 1907)[1]

Whereas the previous chapters have examined the evolution of the United
Irish League between 1898 and 1910, this chapter will analyse the activities
of UIL branches at the local level. This aspect of the history of the League
has been neglected in the historiography of this period. While the two
major published studies of the United Irish League discuss the strategies
adopted by League branches to achieve their objectives, they do not place
these strategies in their proper context. Paul Bew, for example, describes
the *modus operandi* of UIL branches in the following terms: 'The typical
UIL branch had a clear cut method of operation. A group of sturdy young
members would form a "deputation" which would visit prominent local
graziers with the suggestion that they might give up their land in order that
it might be divided up for the people.'[2] David Jones, similarly, identifies a
number of tactics employed by the League to bring about the redistribution of grazing land including public rallies, cattle driving, boycotting,
intimidation, and violence.[3] Neither of these studies, however, examines
the role played by the United Irish League courts in the implementation of
the League's objectives.[4]

The United Irish League's agitation was orchestrated by UIL courts that
claimed authority over all matters regarding the land in their parishes. At

[1] IG monthly report, Apr. 1907, NA IGCI/11.
[2] Bew, *Conflict and conciliation*, 43.
[3] Jones, 'The cleavage between graziers and peasants', 381–7.
[4] There is, however, some discussion of UIL courts in Bull, 'Reconstruction', 207–8.

Kilreekle, for example, the United Irish League branch posted letters to all the graziers in the parish in early 1905 requesting them to surrender their grazing tenancies at the end of the current lease. One of the graziers, a Mr J. Manton, attended the next meeting of the committee where his case was discussed

> at considerable length, a large number of documents being produced in support of [his claim].
>
> The Committee were unanimous that the farm was held on the 11 month's system, and should be surrendered by the 1st May next in the interest of the tenants on the Burke estate. To this demand J. Manton willingly consented and stated he was satisfied to leave the matter in the hands of the Committee.

Those graziers who did not respond to the letter, however, were condemned for not doing so.[5] The United Irish League branches constituted themselves as land courts that tried persons who were accused of breaking the 'law of the League', and imposed penalties on those whom they convicted. In this respect, the League courts were at the interface between the ideology and the practice of the United Irish League. League branches did not merely offer their support to the UIL's agrarian programme, they attempted to enforce that programme in the parishes where they existed.

The League courts were not confined to the disturbed regions of the west of Ireland. In March 1902, the Lord Lieutenant told the cabinet that 'The summoning of obnoxious persons to indoor [UIL] meetings acting as "League courts"' was one of the United Irish League's 'chief methods of attack'. A 'large number' of courts had been held in Connacht and Munster, he wrote, but the police could obtain no further information about the proceedings at these indoor tribunals. Apparently, the Constabulary were restricted to recording 'the names of persons whom they see entering the League rooms, and who consist of (1) members of the League, (2) complainants, such as evicted tenants, and (3) defendants, such as those who have taken evicted farms'.[6] The Inspector General also confirmed that United Irish League courts were held regularly over a large area of the country. In May 1908, for instance, he observed that in twelve Connacht, Munster, and midlands counties, the United Irish League was 'the guiding power in agrarian matters... The decisions of the Branch Committees, which act as local Courts in questions relating to the land, are said to have more general effect than those of a Court of law.'[7] According to the police, these courts

---

[5] *Connaught Leader*, 4 Feb. 1905.
[6] Lord Cadogan, cabinet memorandum on the state of Ireland, 10 Mar. 1902, PRO CAB 37/61/58.   [7] IG monthly report, May 1908, NA IGCI/13.

were the source of the United Irish League's country-wide agitation: 'they summon before them persons against whom are complaints, and decide whether men may or may not hold certain farms, their decisions being enforced by boycotting, intimidation, and thinly veiled allusions in the Press.'[8] The League courts decided which persons the United Irish League would agitate against, and the form that the agitation would take. They were central to the operation of the UIL in that they initiated and maintained the various agitations of the League throughout this period and across a large part of the country.

The United Irish League was not the first Irish political organization to establish land courts. Early nineteenth-century protest groups, such as the Whiteboys and the Thrashers, were described by contemporaries as 'redressers of grievances' who took 'the administration of justice into their own hands',[9] even if they did not do so in a systematic manner through the agency of land courts. The mass political movements of the late nineteenth century, the Land League and the Irish National League, appear to have built on this tradition and established formal land courts which tried persons who were accused of breaking the 'law of the League'.[10] In the period after the eclipse of the United Irish League, Sinn Féin constructed a sophisticated alternative legal system that claimed jurisdiction over all aspects of 'crime', and did so according to a written constitution.[11] The League courts were not merely an aspect of the history of the United Irish League, then, but a pivotal element in the broader process whereby an alternative legal system was devised to defy and eventually displace the law of the Crown in Ireland.[12]

I

While League branches exercised a certain amount of autonomy, the activity of UIL courts in a number of different regions suggests that there were some guiding principles that determined the 'law of the League' across a relatively large area. These principles were, in part, informed by

---

[8] IG monthly report, Sept. 1907, NA IGCI/12.

[9] Arthur Young's account of the Whiteboys' agitation, quoted in George Cornewall Lewis, *Local disturbances in Ireland* (London, 1836), 9.

[10] On Land League and National League courts, see Ball, 'Policing the Land War', 228–32, 246–50. See also Donald Jordan, 'The Irish National League and the "unwritten law": rural protest and nation-building in Ireland 1882–1890', *Past and Present*, 158 (Feb. 1998), 146–71.

[11] See Mary Kotsonouris, *Retreat from revolution: the Dáil courts, 1920–24* (Dublin, 1994).

[12] See Ch. 6.

the leadership of the United Irish League and, particularly, by the *Constitution* of 1900.[13] They were also, however, informed by the local branches, which occasionally forced the leadership to include their objectives in the League's national programme. The 'law of the League' was thus a dynamic and fluid concept, influenced by both the leaders and the rank and file of the movement. Between 1898 and 1910, the League's priorities changed as a result of the evolving objectives of both the leaders and the rank and file; and it is necessary to define the 'law of the League' in each of three distinct phases of activism. The first, between 1898 and 1900, was dominated by the agrarian campaign for the redistribution of grazing land in the west of Ireland. In the second phase, between 1900 and 1903, the League's campaign for compulsory land purchase became the central issue at both the local and the national level. And finally, the agitation to force landlords to sell their estates at prices fixed by the tenants dominated the third phase of activism, between 1903 and 1910.[14]

The first statement of the United Irish League's objectives was made at the Westport meeting on 23 January 1898, when the UIL was founded. William O'Brien told his audience that the best way to resolve the problem of poverty in the west of Ireland was by redistributing grazing land among smallholders.[15] The redistribution of untenanted land was thus defined as the UIL's central agrarian objective. This was further amplified in the United Irish League's *Constitution* which was published two years later in June 1900. The *Constitution* asserted that the League had three aims: the abolition of landlordism by means of a compulsory system of sale, the reinstatement of evicted tenants, and the abolition of the grazing system.[16] These objectives became the foundational principles of the 'law of the League' for the whole period, 1898–1910; but in the first phase of United Irish League activism, the UIL courts were primarily preoccupied with the redistribution of grazing land and the reinstatement of evicted tenants.

The Provincial Directory of the United Irish League expressed these objectives as a series of rules that the members of the UIL were instructed to follow. In order to inaugurate the redistribution of grazing land, for example, the Provincial Directory, at its first meeting at Claremorris on 8 March 1899, told its members

not to bid at any auction of grazing lands; not to renew any lettings of grazing lands under the 11 months' system; not to send any stock to graze upon lands held under

---

[13] *United Irish League: constitution and rules*.   [14] See Chs. 1–3.
[15] The confidential print, 1898–1901, PRO CO 903/8/29–30.
[16] *United Irish League: constitution and rules*, 2.

that system, or to hire such lands for con-acre or otherwise; not to herd, mow, or otherwise work for any landlord, grazier or grabber engaged in maintaining a system which is the fruitful parent of poverty and famine in the West.[17]

These directives became the basis of the alternative law which League courts attempted to enforce in their parishes. In Mayo in 1899, for example, the County Inspector reported that 'all agrarian matters are brought up [at United Irish League meetings] and discussed and decisions arrived at which are conveyed to the parties concerned by the delegates of the branches and threats of boycotting, and in many instances quasi boycotting leaves persons afraid to act contrary to the rules of the League'.[18]

An impression of how League branches understood these rules is suggested by the identity of the persons whom they punished. In October 1898, there were twenty-six cases of boycotting due to the UIL in Ireland, and the victims were predominantly 'grabbers' (31 per cent), graziers (19 per cent), and their associates (33 per cent).[19] The victims of serious crime also tended to be persons who either leased grazing land or occupied evicted farms: thirteen of the fourteen (93 per cent) 'outrages' committed by the UIL in Mayo between 8 February and 10 July 1898 were directed against graziers and their associates.[20] The pattern was similar in other parts of Connacht. In east Galway, all of the crimes attributed to the UIL between October 1899 and October 1900 were committed against graziers and their employees.[21] Judging from their behaviour, League branches appear to have upheld two fundamental laws: that it was illegal to lease grazing land or to assist those who did so, and that it was illegal to take an evicted farm. Throughout Connacht and Munster, according to the Lord Lieutenant, these two 'laws' guided the activities of the United Irish League: 'The persons ... attacked [by the United Irish League] may be described in general terms as those who take or care evicted farms, those who hold grazing land on the eleven months system, and those who work for, deal with, or otherwise aid and support such persons.'[22] As early as October 1899, the County Inspector in Mayo observed that the alternative 'law of the League' had

---

[17] According to the compilers of the confidential print, 'The resolutions adopted by the Directory may be regarded as containing an authoritative statement of the claims and policy of the League.' The confidential print, 1898–1901, PRO CO 903/8/100.

[18] CI monthly report, Mayo, June 1899, NA IGCI/2.

[19] The confidential print, 1898–1901, PRO CO 903/8/190.

[20] The confidential print, 1898–1901, PRO CO 903/8/190–8. The other 'outrage' was committed against a Poor Law Guardian (Mr Kirby) who voted against the local nationalists' candidate for the clerkship of the Westport Union in 1897.

[21] The confidential print, 1898–1901, PRO CO 903/8/439–68.

[22] Lord Cadogan, cabinet memorandum on the state of Ireland, 10 Mar. 1902, PRO CAB 37/61/58.

begun to influence the county community so much that those who let grazing land were regarded by 'the people' as committing a 'crime'.[23]

As yet, the 'law of the League' paid little direct attention to the landlords, despite the explicit statement in the League's *Constitution* that landlordism should be abolished. United Irish League branches penalized graziers and grabbers, but not landlords. Nevertheless, the agitation against the grazing system constituted an indirect attack on landlords. Graziers did not own their grazing land: as the authors of the confidential print observed, 'they had no legal interest [in it] outside the current 11 months' tenancy'.[24] Landlords owned all of the untenanted land in Connacht but grazed less than a fifth of it themselves, letting the rest to graziers and smallholders.[25] The United Irish League's agitation aimed to stop graziers from leasing untenanted land, so that the landlords would sell their land to the Congested Districts Board for redistribution among the small farmers of the region. Landlords may not have been boycotted or intimidated by the League between 1898 and 1900, but they were the ultimate objects of the United Irish League's agitation. Underlying that agitation was an antipathy towards landlordism, which the League characterized as 'the curse of the country and [the] cause of every ill that befalls the tenants'. Western landlords were well aware of this, and Lord Clonbrock wrote to the Chief Secretary in 1899 requesting him to guarantee that the CDB would not purchase lands in areas where there had been interference with legal rights.[26] In the second phase of UIL activism, however, the landlords would be more directly targeted by the League's agitation.

The events of 1900 transformed the United Irish League's position. First, the UIL was formally accepted as the provincial organization of the Irish Party, with influence over the selection of parliamentary candidates and, therefore, over the issues which the Party might raise in the House of Commons. O'Brien was determined that the reunited Party would take up the question of land redistribution in the Commons and combine the agrarian agitation with a parliamentary campaign.[27] Second, a new Chief Secretary was appointed, who was known to want to introduce new Irish land legislation at an early date.[28] These two factors led to O'Brien's

[23] CI monthly report, Mayo, Oct. 1899, NA IGCI/2.
[24] The confidential print, 1898–1901, PRO CO 903/8/94.   [25] See Table 1.
[26] CI monthly report, Mayo, Mar. 1899, NA IGCI/1. Letter from Lord Clonbrock to G. W. Balfour (the Chief Secretary), 26 Dec. 1899, published in *Daily Express*, 6 Jan. 1900. NLI Clonbrock papers MS 19,666, 103.
[27] Maume, 'Aspects of Irish nationalist political culture', 99, 101.
[28] Gailey, *Ireland and the death of kindness*, 162–6; Mackail and Wyndham, *Life and letters of George Wyndham*, i, 77–8.

adopting compulsory land purchase as the United Irish League's central objective in the autumn of 1900.[29]

In the second phase of UIL activism, between 1900 and 1903, the campaign for compulsory land purchase added an important new dimension to the 'law of the League'. William O'Brien articulated the League's new objective in an article for the *Freeman's Journal* on 27 September 1901:

> I have already taken the liberty to suggest that the only means of bringing this question of compulsory sale . . . to an issue in the south is that the tenants on each estate should make a combined demand next November for an abatement of rent equivalent to that obtained by the tenant purchasers under the Acts of 1885 and 1890 . . . [E]very landlord who refuses should be taught the urgency, the practicability, and the justice of the demand, by being placed on the same level as the grabber, and subjected to all the inconvenience the people in the lawful right of combination are able to inflict.[30]

The article asserted that it was a crime for a landlord to refuse rent reductions equivalent to those which tenant-purchasers had obtained under the 1885 and 1890 Land Purchase Acts. Landlords who refused to reduce their tenants' rents were to be 'placed on the same level as the grabber', and thereby punished for their offence. O'Brien believed that a widespread campaign for rent reductions would pressurize landlords into supporting compulsory land purchase.[31] UIL branches absorbed this new objective into their activities and, in at least ten counties, demands for rent reductions were made. In most cases, landlords appear to have refused to allow these reductions, and on seventeen estates combinations against the payment of rent were organized.[32] This represented a decisive change in the operation of the United Irish League. For the first time, landlords were directly targeted by the League's agitation, and the UIL courts began to claim authority over the behaviour of landlords, as well as that of graziers, and 'grabbers'.

The campaign for compulsory land purchase was not confined to direct attacks on landlords. O'Brien believed that a 'vigorous campaign' of boycotting against landlords, graziers and 'grabbers' would force the Government to introduce land legislation.[33] The agitation of 1898–1900 against graziers and 'grabbers' continued between 1900 and 1903, but it

---

[29] Wyndham to Balfour, 26 Nov. 1900, BM ABP Add. MS 49,803/139–144ᵛ.

[30] Quoted by Mr Atkinson, the Irish Attorney General, Hansard, 4th series, 28 Feb. 1902, vol. civ, col. 107.   [31] Ibid.

[32] IG monthly reports, Nov. 1901–Dec. 1902, PRO CO 904/74–6. See Ch. 2.

[33] *Irish People*, 7 Sept. 1901.

was now presented to the Government as an aspect of the agitation for compulsory land purchase.[34] At the local level, the remit of the League courts was expanded rather than transformed. In the majority of cases, the victims of UIL 'justice' remained the same. In Galway, for example, graziers were denounced at twenty-nine (52 per cent) of the fifty-six meetings (about which information is available) held between 1902 and 1905; and 'grabbers' were denounced at fifteen of these meetings (27 per cent).[35] Between 1900 and 1903, the 'law of the League' continued to be guided by the same principles as in the earlier period, but with the addition of a new 'law': that landlords should reduce their unpurchased tenants' rents to a level equivalent to the annuity paid by purchased tenants.

The United Irish League's objectives changed dramatically after the introduction of the Wyndham Land Act in 1903. One of the League's central objectives—the abolition of landlordism—had been virtually achieved, and the majority of UIL leaders were satisfied with the new legislation. John Redmond and William O'Brien advocated a policy of moderation, and urged tenants to be 'patient' during purchase negotiations.[36] The agitation against the grazing system, which had been in full swing between 1898 and 1903, was revived after 1903 with the new objective of forcing landlords to include their untenanted land in the sales of their estates under the terms of the Wyndham Act.

The Wyndham Land Act transformed the circumstances in which the United Irish League existed. Many of the larger farmers probably gave up their membership of the League once they had purchased their holdings.[37] At the same time, it is likely that the smaller farmers of the west were dissatisfied with the Act because it did not address the problem of congestion.[38] Gradually, the Party's moderate policy was sidelined, and the small tenant farmers of Connacht and Munster began to redefine the 'law of the League' in their own interests. Broadly speaking, their objective was to force landlords to sell their estates on terms favourable to the tenant, and to include their untenanted land in the sale for the purpose of enlarging smallholdings. As a result, the role of the UIL courts was transformed. The courts now became forums used by Leaguers to pressurize landlords into selling their estates at terms beneficial to the tenant.

[34] Hansard, 4th series, 13 Mar. 1902, vol. civ, col. 1305.

[35] There were 124 UIL meetings held in Galway between 1902 and 1905, but information as to what was discussed is only available for fifty-six meetings. Landlords were denounced at ten meetings, and eight meetings were held to reorganize the branch and to select local officers or candidates for local elections. Register of United Irish League meetings in Ireland, 1902–5, PRO CO 904/22.

[36] IG monthly report, Sept. 1903, NA IGCI/4.   [37] See Ch. 3.   [38] See Ch. 3.

II

League courts were held regularly at indoor committee meetings of UIL branches. The elected committee of the branch acted in a role analagous to that of the magistrates at petty and quarter sessions: they listened to the cases put forward by the defence and the prosecution and then reached a majority decision. As the Inspector General observed in October 1907: 'Branch Committees hear complaints, [and] give their decisions.'[39] Defendants were requested to attend both to hear the charges made against them, and to enable them to defend themselves. According to the Lord Lieutenant, the defendants 'are summoned to attend in various ways, either by written notice from the Secretary, by verbal notice from a member of the League, or by invitation conveyed in the press report of an earlier meeting.'[40] The Land League courts held in the 1880s, which were the precursor of UIL courts, had also set out deliberately to emulate the British judicial system. A newspaper report on the first sitting of the Athenry Land League court in December 1880 observed that 'from the wisdom and good sense that characterised its deliberations it bids fair to rival, aye to eclipse the modern temple of justice next door known as the Athenry petty sessions court'.[41] In this respect, the United Irish League courts were no different.

The plaintiff was usually responsible for making the case for the prosecution, as at Kilbeacanty in February 1905, where a Mr Deely told the committee that 'he had a grievance to bring up for redress'.[42] The members of the branch also attended the League courts, presumably to add an intimidatory air to proceedings. William Duffy's description of a National League court held in Loughrea in 1887 also captures the atmosphere of one of these tribunals at the turn of the century:

His [Joe Fallon's] defence was weak. He was puzzled and over-whelmed at all the strength of public feeling against him. His voice was husk and tremulous and when he essayed to speak nervousness overcame him. I never seen [*sic*] him in such a corner. Not a friend in the Hall and convicted of as dis-graceful an offence as was ever laid to the door of an Irishman. Generally he is of a boasting nature—bragging independence of the League and vowing eternal hostility to the Cause. These imped-ences invariably take place when he is either in bed or talking to Ladies. On last Ev[enin]g he was as mild as a sucking dove and as quiet as a lamp [*sic*].

---

[39] IG monthly report, Oct. 1907, NA IGCI/12.

[40] Lord Cadogan, cabinet memorandum on the state of Ireland, 10 Mar. 1902, PRO CAB 37/61/58.

[41] 'The Athenry Land League in session', *Western News*, 18 Dec. 1880, quoted in Ball, 'Policing the Land War', 230.   [42] *Connaught Leader*, 4 Feb. 1905.

TABLE 7. The result of 100 cases heard at 36 United Irish League courts held in Ireland, 1900–1901

Result	Frequency
Defendant censured	56
Defendant apologized	13
Defendant refused to accept court	10
Defendant ordered to pay compensation	15
Defendant acquitted	1
Case adjourned	7
Case referred to another tribunal	9
No action taken	5
Other	1
Total	117

Source: The confidential print contains an index of 'League courts' held in Ireland between October 1900 and October 1901. In order to assess the working of the 'law of the League', the deliberations of these tribunals (there were 36 sittings of UIL courts held in Clare, Cork, Kerry, Limerick, Longford, Mayo, Tipperary and Waterford) were systematically examined. Index of all UIL courts held in Ireland, Oct. 1900–Oct. 1901, the confidential print, 1898–1901, in PRO Co 903/8/480–1.

Such a pitiable spectacle of what rash impulsive conduct brings people now and again too [*sic*] was never witnessed. His steep [step] on entering the Hall was firm and steady. His mien suggestive of some Hero who would be about vanquishing some terrible opponent in Conflict. On leaving the Assembly . . . he left all these traces behind him.[43]

The courts appear to have adhered to a strict procedural code. Table 7 outlines the decisions reached at thirty-six UIL courts held in Ireland between October 1900 and October 1901. In the majority of cases, there is no information given as to the way in which these courts reached their decisions. However, an impression of the procedures adopted by the courts can be gained from the reasons given for adjournments, and from the responses of defendants ordered by the courts to pay compensation. Of the five adjourned cases (where information is available): two were to enable the secretary of the court to write to the defendant and request his attendance, two were to allow an out of court settlement, and one was to enable the defendant to produce a document. This evidence suggests that the UIL courts were committed to giving defendants notice of their hearings and allowing them time to produce documentation relevant to

[43] William Duffy's diary, 6 June 1887. In the possession of Mary Duffy, Loughrea.

their cases. In one of the eleven cases where information is available, the defendant successfully appealed the amount of compensation he was asked to pay an evicted tenant, suggesting that the courts did not always take the side of the prosecution.[44] And in one of the nine instances where the case was referred to another tribunal this was to enable the defendant to appeal the decision of a UIL branch at an executive meeting.[45] This indicates that defendants who were dissatisfied with the decisions of branch committees had the right to appeal the court's decision to the UIL divisional executive. Overall, the (admittedly limited) evidence presented here does suggest that the League courts operated according to widely accepted procedures. Defendants were notified before their cases could be heard; adjournments were allowed to enable either party to produce documentation relevant to the case; cases were first tried in the parish court where the disputed land was located before being heard by an executive court; and defendants and plaintiffs both had the right to appeal the decisions of the parish courts in an executive court.

The officials of the League courts were keen to ensure that their decisions would be perceived by the wider community as fair. If the courts' judgements were viewed by the public as arbitrary, members of the parish would not bring their grievances to the League tribunals and the whole system of UIL justice would collapse. This concern was expressed by John Power, the president of the League court at Ardagh, county Limerick, and chairman of the Croom Board of Guardians:

They should be careful to observe the greatest possible care and impartiality in regard to the several disputes to be submitted to them, and try to arrive at a fair and just decision such as will meet with the approval of all fair-minded honest men. Decisions in matters of this description require to be such as will find universal approval by the outside public.[46]

As the decisions of the League courts were published in the local nationalist press, the UIL committee-magistrates were made accountable for their judgements. In east Galway, a grazier named Hession wrote to the *Connaught Leader* accusing the secretary of the Clontuskert UIL of not

---

[44] Information is available on the outcome of eleven of the fifteen cases where defendants were ordered to pay compensation to evicted tenants. In three cases the defendant paid the compensation; in two cases the defendant refused to pay the compensation; in three cases the defendant appealed the amount of compensation he was asked to pay (in one case successfully); and in three cases the evicted tenant demanded more compensation.

[45] Of the nine instances where the case was referred to another tribunal: six were referred by an executive to the branch where the disputed land was located; two were referred to executives as the branch was unable to reach a decision; and one was to enable the defendant to appeal the branch decision at the UIL executive.

[46] The confidential print, 1898–1901, PRO CO 903/8/504–6.

giving him adequate notice that his case was to be tried at the court. The secretary, Thomas Stephenson, responded to the accusation in a letter to the paper dated 21 January 1905:

He [Hession] states that I gave him no notice to attend Convention. That is false. I did write to him as directed by the Committee. He also stated that the Committee consisted of my friends. That is a most notorious lie. The Committee was formed in November 1903 and was comprised of 29 men, none of whom I had the appointing or selection of.

Stephenson concluded by stating that twenty-six of the twenty-nine members of the committee had decided against Hession's 'action'.[47]

Public accountability also exerted a pressure on the courts to ensure that persons accused of breaking the 'law of the League' had indeed done so. A court held at Kilreekle in February 1905 was concerned to establish that a Mr Manton, accused of letting land on the eleven-months' system, was guilty of the crime.[48] For this reason, there do not appear to have been any cases of persons being wrongly convicted by the League courts. Indeed the Land League courts, on which the UIL courts were based, appear to have gained such a high level of legitimacy that persons summoned before them spoke freely to the police about their experiences, not realizing that the proceedings were illegal.[49] The Ardagh court in Limerick convicted seven persons of 'grabbing' in October 1900 and the police, in a special report, confirmed that each of them had taken an evicted farm in the county.[50] However, the fairness (or otherwise) of UIL justice can only be assessed on the basis of detailed case studies, like the following examination of the working of the south Galway UIL court at Loughrea in the spring of 1905.

The south Galway United Irish League executive hosted courts and tried land disputes throughout 1904 and 1905. In February 1905, the County Inspector described the executive as 'a most pernicious body being the origin of intimidation and outrage throughout the surrounding country. Sitting with closed doors it holds regular courts trying all the land disputes in the country round Loughrea, giving its judgements and enforcing them by boycotting and crime.'[51] Yet the court appears to have gained a broader legitimacy, not merely among the United Irish Leaguers of south Galway but also among the graziers and some of the landlords of the locality. At a meeting of the court on Sunday, 12 March, a local grazier and landlord, Harry Persse, sent his representative, John Shawe-Taylor, to the

---

[47] *Connaught Leader*, 4 Feb. 1905.   [48] Ibid.
[49] Ball, 'Policing the Land War', n. 1054, p. 232.
[50] The confidential print, 1898–1901, PRO CO 903/8/506–8.
[51] CI monthly report, east Galway, Feb. 1905, NA IGCI/7.

court to discuss the Woodville grazing farm which he leased from Lord Clanricarde.[52] A report in the *Connaught Leader* declared that the meeting was held

> with a view to bringing about a settlement between Harry Persse, and those who are anxious to have the Woodville farm (now in Persse's possession) divided among them . . . The Hall was crowded with [UIL] delegates, and but for the wise action which was taken in refusing to allow anyone but a delegate to be present, the floor would in all probability have given away.[53]

The proceedings were opened by Michael Forde, the secretary of the Kilchreest branch of the UIL, who made the case for the prosecution. In April 1904, the 460-acre grazing farm had been unlet and the Kilchreest UIL organized a deputation to meet Clanricarde's agent, Edward Shaw-Tener, with a view to redistributing the farm 'among the people' under the Wyndham Land Act. Just before the deputation met Shaw-Tener, however, Persse took the lease of the farm. The Kilchreest branch condemned him for 'taking Woodville farm against the wishes of the people, and without the sanction of the local branch of the League'. According to the branch, Persse had sufficient land already, including the 100-acre Millmount farm and a 200-acre estate at Limepark with a mansion. Meanwhile, the 'Nationalists of Kilchreest' continued to live on mountainy smallholdings valued at between 7s. 6d. and £5 15s. Finally, Forde called for the redistribution of the farm among these smallholders.[54]

John Shawe-Taylor was then called upon to make the case for the defence. He began by saying that he had 'come here today . . . to hear both sides, and try if possible to effect a reconciliation between both parties for their common good'. Persse had signed a twenty-nine-year lease for the farm, he said, and 'it was an absolute impossibility for him to surrender the farm'. He then suggested that Persse should be allowed to keep 100 acres of the farm and Woodville house, and that the remaining 360 acres should be redistributed among the smallholders of the parish. The real problem, in Shawe-Taylor's view, was that Persse was only the tenant and that Clanricarde would have to agree to sell the farm to the Estates Commissioners if the farm was to be redistributed between Persse and the smallholders of Kilchreest. He concluded by appealing to Clanricarde to sell the farm.[55]

52 For a full report of the proceedings at this meeting, see the *Connaught Leader*, 18 Mar. 1905. The Persse family owned two estates at Moyode and Roxborough of 9,496 acres (valued at £4,203) and 13,585 acres (valued at £6,002) respectively in the late 1870s. Melvin, 'The landed gentry of Galway, 1820–80', 511. John Shawe-Taylor was Persse's cousin.
53 *Connaught Leader*, 18 Mar. 1905.   54 Ibid.   55 Ibid.

The case was then discussed by the UIL delegates present. Debate focused initially on the question of whether the lease could be terminated and William Duffy, the vice-chairman of the executive, said that he had examined the lease and it could not be broken. The delegates then discussed how much land Persse should be allowed to retain, and after disagreement on this point the secretary suggested that the matter should be adjourned for one month. Shawe-Taylor objected to this because 'Mr. Persse had been undergoing great hardships lately. His workmen had all left him and stones had been fired into his house . . . If the matter was adjourned it would keep up that unpleasant feeling.' To which Michael Forde replied: 'You must understand he took the farm against the wishes of the people.' Finally, it was decided that the case should be settled by arbitration and a committee was appointed to resolve the matter, including two representatives of the executive, two delegates of the Kilchreest branch and the Roman Catholic Bishop of Galway and Kilmacduagh, the Most Reverend Dr Francis J. McCormack.[56]

Unfortunately, it is not known how this case was resolved. There is no further mention of the farm in the *Connaught Leader* in 1905, and, as the Clanricarde estate was not sold until 1915, it is unlikely that the Woodville farm was divided between Persse and the smallholders of Kilchreest until then. Even so, the case illuminates much about the operation of United Irish League courts. The procedures adopted by the court were similar to those used at petty sessions. Both the defence and the prosecution made their statements and then the case was discussed by the delegates, acting in a role analagous to that of magistrates. Questions were then asked of the defendant and the plaintiff, and 'witnesses' were called to verify and check the statements of the two parties, particularly with regard to Shawe-Taylor's assertion that the lease could not be broken. When the delegates could not agree, an adjournment was proposed to allow further discussion of the case; and, finally, an arbitration committee was appointed to reach a decision as to how much of the Woodville farm Persse should be allowed to retain. This indicates that the court attempted to allow both sides of the case to be heard and to ensure that the final decision would be fair to both parties.

The case also reveals much about the background to the League courts. After all, why did Harry Persse—the member of a prominent landlord family—send his representative to an illegally constituted land court? Persse had broken the 'law of the League' in the parish of Kilchreest: he

---

[56] Ibid.

had taken the Woodville grazing farm 'without the sanction of the local Branch of the League'.[57] For his misdemeanour, he was penalized by the Kilchreest League court. He was boycotted and, according to Shawe-Taylor's statement, his employees had left him. The *Connaught Leader* suggested that it was the boycott that had prompted Persse to send his representative to the south Galway executive: 'The press comments and some other incidents . . . had the desired effect, and Mr. Persse has recognised that . . . the attempts of a local branch of the UIL to secure for the people the rights to which they are entitled . . . is a force to be reckoned with, and cannot be treated with impunity.'[58] Persse could not endure the 'great hardships'[59] imposed on him and was forced to attend the League court to resolve the contentious question of the Woodville farm. This case study reveals the United Irish League's national agitation in microcosm: persons were charged by UIL branches with breaking the 'law of the League' and then penalized for doing so until they adjusted their behaviour and accepted the authority of the UIL. The League courts were, in effect, the engine room of the United Irish League's country-wide agitation: they identified the enemies of the League and decided what penalties should be imposed on them to make them accept the UIL's writ.

The publication of the decisions of League courts in the press inaugurated the process by which persons who broke the 'law of the League' were punished. Of the 117 decisions reached by the 36 League courts held between October 1900 and October 1901, almost half (56) involved the public censure of convicted parties.[60] Usually, this was the prelude to the organization of a boycott of the condemned person. In October 1900, for example, the UIL in Limerick printed a 'circular in the form of a leaflet'[61] which condemned six local 'grabbers' in the following terms:

We, the delegates of the several branches in West Limerick, in Convention assembled, having carefully investigated the cases of Martin Hogan *v.* Colberts; John H. Daniher *v.* J. Daniher, Athea; Robert and Jeremiah Dunworth *v.* Rearden and Agent Saunders; Mrs. Carter *v.* Patt Maune, Whisky Hall; John Hartnett *v.* Massy Drew and Son, landlords and grabbers; and Widow Baker *v.* Michael Ryan, Ballingrane, hereby emphatically pronounce all the foregoing to be cases of notorious grabbing, and we call on all true Nationalists to come to the aid of these several evicted tenants, and stamp out this nefarious grabbing, the bane and curse of our struggling country, and we further condemn the action of any person *grazing on grabbed lands* or *aiding the grabbers.*[62]

---

[57] *Connaught Leader*, 18 Mar. 1905.   [58] Ibid.   [59] Ibid.   [60] See Table 7.
[61] The confidential print, 1898–1901, PRO CO 903/8/504.
[62] Ibid., PRO CO 903/8/506.

As a result, two of the 'grabbers' were boycotted and one other 'feared that these proceedings would revive the ill-feeling against him'.[63] Such was the fear of public condemnation that a Waterford merchant threatened to prosecute the president of the Thurles League court with an action of £1,000 if a resolution 'reflecting upon him should appear in the newspapers'.[64] According to the police, there was nothing that farmers and shopkeepers dreaded as much as seeing their names published in the provincial press.[65]

The police observed that the UIL enforced its 'laws' primarily by organizing systematic campaigns of boycotting and intimidation against those persons who refused to accept the authority of the League courts. In June 1899, for example, the County Inspector for Mayo asserted that 'threats of boycotting . . . leaves persons afraid to act at all contrary to the rules of the League'.[66] An impression of the way in which the 'law of the League' was enforced can be gained from an examination of the Government's statistics on the volume of boycotting, intimidation, and agrarian crime in Ireland between 1902 and 1908. Altogether, 2,798 separate cases of boycotting, intimidation and agrarian outrages were reported by the police in this period (see Table 8). The table indicates that agrarian agitators tended to boycott or to intimidate transgressors of the 'law of the League' rather than commit 'offences' against them. Boycotting and intimidation constituted 64 per cent of the total number of incidents, while the proportion of agrarian 'offences' was much less (36 per cent). Of the agrarian crimes, very few were offences against the person (4 per cent of the total number of incidents), while offences against property accounted for 17 per cent (most of which involved 'incendiary fire or arson'), and 15 per cent were offences against the public peace (the majority of which involved 'injury to property'). The UIL thus appears to have enforced its 'rules' through a combination of boycotting, intimidation, and attacks on property.[67] Only rarely were serious crimes against the person committed by agrarian agitators.

The boycott was the central strategy employed by the UIL to enforce the 'law of the League'. It was the first step taken by the League courts against persons who defied the United Irish League. According to the Inspector General, 'where there is resistance [to the decisions of League courts] a

[63] Ibid., PRO CO 903/8/507.   [64] Ibid., PRO CO 903/8/503.
[65] IG monthly report, Nov. 1901, PRO CO 904/74.
[66] CI monthly report, Mayo, June 1899, NA IGCI/1.
[67] It should be emphasized that this data provides only an impression of the way in which the UIL enforced the 'law of the League', as it is unlikely that all of these agrarian incidents were carried out by members of the United Irish League.

TABLE 8. The frequency of penalties imposed by agrarian agitators in Ireland, 1902–1908

Category	Frequency	Percentage of total
No. of boycotted persons	684	24.0
No. of cases of intimidation	1,128	40.0
No. of offences against the person	98	3.8
No. of offences against property	469	17.0
No. of offences against the public peace	414	15.0
No. of 'other' offences	6	0.2
Total	2,799	

Notes: The statistics on boycotted persons include cases where the victims were 'wholly boycotted', 'partially boycotted', and also 'minor cases' of boycotting. The statistics on 'intimidation' were compiled from two sections in the list of 'agrarian offences': 'threatening letters or notices' and 'intimidation otherwise'. The number of offences against the person, against property, and against the public peace are extracted from the list of 'agrarian offences', with the intimidatory outrages extracted from the number of offences against the public peace. Similarly, 'other offences' are as classified in the list of 'agrarian offences'.

Sources: The statistics for this table were compiled from: the 'return of persons boycotted on the 31st Dec. in each of the following years [1902–8]', and a list of 'Indictable offences for the past ten years', compiled in 1908, and including a separate section on 'Agrarian offences', both of which are in the confidential print, 1907–8, PRO CO 903/14/167–8.

rigorous boycott is at once established'.[68] The objective of a boycott was to isolate the victim from both the social and the economic life of the community. It operated according to two basic principles: first, to prevent the victim from making a living; and, second, to prevent the boycotted person from obtaining necessary supplies of food and other provisions. In a sense, boycotting constituted a form of imprisonment for the victim who was isolated and separated from the rest of the community. They could not purchase goods from local shops, blacksmiths refused to shoe their horses, neighbours refused to assist them with their farming activities, and the wider community would not communicate with them.

At both the economic and the social level, this form of ostracism had a paralysing effect. Bernard Spelman, a Roscommon farmer, was boycotted in June 1908 for remaining on 'friendly terms' with the caretaker of a boycotted grazing farm:

When he is seen in public, horns are blown, the local creamery refuses the milk of his 12 cows, his neighbours no longer allow him to cart their milk to and from the

[68] IG monthly report, May 1907, NA IGCI/11.

creamery; the blacksmith refused to shoe his horse. As this means a loss of about £88 a year, he has now made submission to the League, in the hope of getting the boycott removed.[69]

Similarly, Walter Joyce, a Galway landlord and grazier, lost a substantial proportion of his income after he was boycotted in January 1908 for refusing to sell some of the grass lands on his 1,800-acre estate to local small-holders:

All his servants and workmen have left except one maid. Local shops were warned not to supply him, and he has to get provisions by post. He has had to sell his milch cows, as he is obliged to herd his own stock. The smith refused to shoe his horse, and he has had himself to fill and cart coal from the Railway station to supply his house.[70]

Both the prosperous landlord and the small farmer were adversely affected by the boycott. But, as the police observed, the small farmer was not as well equipped to cope with the boycott's deprivations:

This practice [boycotting] is sufficiently serious for the man who is in a position to obtain supplies by post from a distance, and to employ labourers through a Defence Association; but it is not easy to realize what it means to the struggling farmer in a remote locality, who is accustomed to rely on the co-operation of his neighbours in tilling the land, and to get his supplies from the country shop.[71]

The boycott was often sufficient to force a person to accept the authority of the League courts, but in cases where the victim continued to defy the UIL, intimidation was also used against them.

Intimidation was defined by the Government in 1882 as 'any word spoken or act done in order to and calculated to put any person in fear of any injury or danger to himself, or to any member of his family, or to any person in his employment, or in fear of any injury to or loss of his property, business or means of living'.[72] In most cases, individual intimidatory acts were only of minor significance: one threatening letter, for example, would not necessarily intimidate a person into acknowledging the authority of the League.[73] But a series of intimidatory acts committed over a long period might well force a person to submit to the UIL. It was for this reason that the Inspector General characterized intimidation as

---

[69] IG monthly report, June 1908, NA IGCI/13.
[70] IG monthly report, Jan. 1908, NA IGCI/13. The Joyce estate consisted of 4,185 acres, valued at £1,951 in the late 1870s. Melvin, 'The landed gentry of Galway, 1820–80', 510.
[71] IG monthly report, Jan. 1908, NA IGCI/13.
[72] Townshend, *Political violence*, 173.
[73] See the discussion of the cumulative effect of intimidatory acts ibid. 205–6.

a 'steady pressure',[74] which consisted of a number of different strategies: 'The pressure generally takes the form of band promenades to the farms accompanied by disorderly crowds, horn blowing, and groaning, malicious injuries to the fences and gates, driving off the cattle, intimidation of servants, threatening notices etc.'[75] Usually, a number of these strategies were imposed simultaneously and the longer the victim held out against the League, the more threatening the intimidation would become. In April 1907, the police described the *modus operandi* of the United Irish League in the west of Ireland:

A farm is indicated as suitable for division. The people are forbidden to send cattle to graze on it and in-tending occupiers are warned off. If any person has the hardihood to take the land or if it happens to be occupied the herdsman is warned to leave his employment. The local band organizes 'drumming parties' and these people visit the neighbourhood of the farm to intimidate the occupiers. Parties are also organised both by night and day to drive off the cattle. At times shots are fired into or outside the dwelling house of the herds-man or of the occupier of the farm.[76]

Intimidation was thus utilized by the UIL to reinforce the effect of boycotting, but it was also an important element in the mobilization of popular support for the boycott.

For a boycott to be successful, the unanimous support of the community was required. If one shopkeeper continued to supply a boycotted person, for example, the boycott would be ineffective. To a large extent, the United Irish League's attempt to uphold the 'law of the League' depended on the mobilization and the organization of popular support for boycotting. The Inspector General commented in June 1905 that, whereas the Land League had enforced its decrees with murder, the United Irish League maintained its 'authority by organising the neighbourhood'.[77] Intimidation played a fundamental part in the process by which this popular support was organized. The United Irish League used intimidation to enforce its authority on both the transgressors of the League's laws and the wider community. Most of the forms of intimidation used by the United Irish League— hooting, groaning, horn-blowing, and drumming—were intended to humiliate those persons who had broken the 'law of the League'. But these methods also served as a warning to the rest of the community that if they failed to maintain a boycott or to adhere to the 'law of the League', they

---

74 IG monthly report, Jan. 1902, PRO CO 904/74.
75 IG monthly report, Apr. 1907, NA IGCI/11.
76 Ibid.
77 IG monthly report, June 1905, NA IGCI/7.

could expect to be treated in a similar manner. Hooting and drumming were common strategies used by the United Irish League to shame persons into accepting its 'laws'. In Longford, for example, Harris Martin took the lease of a house and a 57-acre grazing farm at Lismore, and a grazing farm of 109 acres at Killeen, both of which were on the Douglas estate, in November 1908.[78] On 23 November, Martin and his two servants began moving furniture from his residence at Knappogue to Lismore house. As they returned to Knappogue that night, 'the Clondra UIL branch shouted and groaned and beat their drum about 40 perches from my house at Knappogue where I was . . . They paraded up and down the road near my house, continuing their noises until the police arrived.'[79] As a result of this 'rough music', one of Martin's servants refused to continue working for him. Throughout the following week, Martin was 'groaned and hooted through the roads when going to and from Lismore', and on each occasion he required police protection. On 30 November, his second servant, Frank Sharkey, also decided to leave his work, 'saying that he could not stay, as everywhere he went he was groaned and hooted, as also were his children'. Finally, Martin decided to initiate a prosecution against the United Irish League's newspaper in the county, the *Longford Leader*, which he believed was responsible for initiating the campaign against him.[80]

This example suggests the power and the potency of intimidation. Both of Martin's servants left him and his life was made unbearable by the combination of social ostracism and humiliation. The rough music operated at two levels: first, it demonstrated the extent of popular feeling against Martin and, second, it suggested that more serious intimidation would be used against him if he did not give up the farm.[81] At the wider social level, however, this public humiliation conveyed a message to the rest of the community that any person who defied the 'law of the League' could be subjected to a similar form of intimidation. As the police surmised in August 1906: 'the victims of these offences are held up as a warning to those who might otherwise be inclined to disregard the wishes of the local combinations.'[82]

The most common form of intimidation used by the United Irish League between 1906 and 1908 was the cattle drive: a strategy that incorporated

---

[78] Martin also farmed about 200 acres at Knappogue and Clondra. The Harris Martin case is discussed in the returns of agrarian outrages, 1903–8, PRO CO 904/121.

[79] The Harris Martin case, PRO CO 904/121.

[80] Ibid.

[81] For a discussion of 'rough music', see E. P. Thompson, *Customs in common* (London, 1991), 467–538.

[82] IG monthly report, Aug. 1906, NA IGCI/10.

popular protest, ritual humiliation, and economic disruption.[83] At one
level, cattle driving made it extremely difficult for a grazier to profit from
his land. Cattle were often injured in the course of a drive, and a great deal
of time might be spent re-gathering the cattle. At another level, the cattle
drive was intended to demonstrate the level of popular feeling against a
grazier and thereby to shame him into giving up land. Most cattle drives
took place during the day, in full view of the RIC, and were carried out by
large crowds of up to 300 people. A cattle drive at Doolin, county Clare,
on the morning of 22 September 1908, for example, was described by the
police in the following terms:

a large crowd . . . had assembled in Doolin [and] was addressed by Dermot O'Brien,
United Irish League Organiser, who advised the people present, numbering about
300, to then and there drive off the stock . . . and deliver them to their owners. This
the crowd proceeded at once to do in four parties. The police force present was
inadequate to cope with the numbers, but two constables followed each crowd,
and noted the names of such as were known to them. The party engaged in driving
Colonel Tottenham's cattle and sheep, and those of a man named Frank Cahir,
brought them to Kilfenora, where they put Colonel Tottenham's stock in a field
belonging to his manager, Mr. Davies. The party delivered Cahir's stock to his
herd some distance away, and then returned to Kilfenora, being met on the way
by torch-bearers, who escorted them up and down the village, which was illuminated. Brakes and cars arrived from Lisdoonvarna to convey back the cattle drivers.
Before returning a meeting was held, at which Dermot O'Brien and others spoke,
advocating cattle driving. Dermot O'Brien, in the course of his speech, applauded
the action of the Doolin people in clearing the ranches that day, and advised the
people of Kilfenora to follow their good example.[84]

The cattle drive was not simply a tactic adopted by the League to undermine the graziers' position, it was a popular event involving a large section
of the community and incorporating elements of political ritual, including the triumphant public meeting, the torch-bearers and the illuminated
village. In essence, the drive was a popular public spectacle intended to
deter any members of the community from either letting grazing farms or
defying the 'law of the League'.

The United Irish League punished persons who had broken the 'law of
the League' by mobilizing popular feeling against them. Agrarian crime
was, for this reason, rarely resorted to by the UIL. Indeed, the police
speculated that where crimes were committed, this was the result of a

---

[83] For statistics on the number of cattle drives in Ireland between 1907 and 1908, see
Table 6.
[84] Returns of agrarian outrages, 1903–8, PRO CO 904/121.

'weakening in the bonds of [UIL] discipline'.[85] In disturbed counties, the Inspector General reported, 'the number of Indictable Offences has not increased . . . in proportion to the intensity of agitation. There has been a genuine effort [by the United Irish League] to avoid murder and similar forms of outrage.'[86] Where there was opposition to the UIL, according to the Inspector General, 'public disapproval is, so to speak, organized and turned on to them [the transgressors of the "law of the League"] for their disobedience'.[87] This mobilization of popular support, articulated and maintained through boycotting and intimidation, was the central weapon used by the UIL to enforce its authority.

III

The United Irish League drew its support in Connacht from two sections of the rural community: the small farmers, who stood to gain most from the redistribution of grazing land; and the shopkeepers and larger farmers, who often joined the League to influence the decisions of the League courts. These two interest groups interpreted the 'law of the League' in different ways, and attempted to manipulate the operation of the League courts to their advantage. In some localities, the two factions disagreed as to how the 'law of the League' should be both interpreted and enforced, and a contest took place between them for the control of the League court.

The small farmer constituency in the United Irish League was closely connected with the Irish Republican Brotherhood.[88] After the failure of the 1867 insurrection, the IRB began to promote agrarian agitation in an attempt to win the support of farmers for republicanism. In the west of Ireland, the IRB absorbed pre-existing agrarian secret societies so that, by the end of the 1870s, it was identified as a radical agrarian organization.[89] After a series of violent attacks on landlords in Galway and Roscommon in 1877, for example, the perpetrators were reported to be 'an off-shoot of the Fenian organisation',[90] and the members of secret societies joined Land League branches.[91] This combination of physical force republicanism with radical agrarian politics was confirmed by the 'New Departure', which in 1879 inaugurated an informal alliance between the extreme nationalist IRB

[85] IG monthly report, Mar. 1907, NA IGCI/11.   [86] Ibid.
[87] IG monthly report, Apr. 1906, NA IGCI/9.   [88] See Ch. 5.
[89] See Bew, *Land and the national question*, 34–45.
[90] Ball, 'Policing the Land War', 144–5.
[91] According to Ball, the members of secret societies joined Land League committees. See ibid. 146.

and the Land League;[92] an alliance that appears to have persisted in the west of Ireland after the formation of the UIL. A number of IRB members, many of whom had been involved in the earlier land agitations, joined the UIL after 1898. In October 1900, for example, the Inspector General observed:

> While it remains true that the recognised leaders of the extreme revolutionary section . . . are opposed to the League as contrary to their policy of physical force, it is yet a fact that in many districts, and in most cases the places where trouble is likely to arise, the local I.R.B. and Secret Society suspects are ardent Leaguers.
> This repeats exactly the history of the Land League, and these Secret Society members of the League branches now are the same class, and in many districts the same men, who organised and carried out intimidation and outrage in other days.[93]

This tendency was perhaps most marked among the paid UIL organizers. In October 1900, there were twenty-eight salaried League organizers, fourteen of whom were members of the IRB.[94] There was also a substantial amount of IRB involvement in the United Irish League throughout the country. In February 1902, the Royal Irish Constabulary compiled statistics on the number of IRB members in the UIL branches in each county. At that juncture, 8,706 Leaguers were members of the IRB, 7 per cent of the total membership of the UIL (121,794).[95] Wyndham estimated that this figure was probably too low. In a letter to Arthur Balfour, he explained that the leaders of the UIL 'neither can, nor care to, control the action of extremists. These however meet in secret conclave & know the Law of Criminal Conspiracy at least as well as our Law Officers, so that whilst nine-tenths of the League's operations are political & legitimate, the remaining tenth is inscrutable.'[96] By 1900, then, a substantial minority of the United Irish League's membership were also members of the Irish Republican Brotherhood.

During the Land War, the IRB had been closely identified with the small farmer interest in the Land League alliance. At Claremorris in 1879, for example, the IRB faction of the Land League had advocated the redistribution of grazing land, an objective that the Land League leadership did not

---

[92] Paul Bew, 'The Land League ideal: achievements and contradictions', in P. J. Drudy (ed.), *Ireland: land, politics and people* (Cambridge, 1982), 78.

[93] IG monthly report, Oct. 1900, PRO CO 904/71.

[94] The confidential print, 1898–1901, PRO CO 903/8/434–5.

[95] Return showing number of members of the United Irish League who were members of the Irish Republican Brotherhood, 12 Feb. 1902, NA Crime Branch Special, 1902, 26256/S box 20.

[96] Wyndham to Balfour, 26 Nov. 1900, BM ABP Add. MS 49,803/139–144^v.

adopt.[97] Moreover, Matthew Harris constantly called for the redistribution of grazing land in his speeches during the 1880s.[98] The IRB had been identified with the campaign to redistribute grazing land since the late 1870s, and this policy constituted the basis for its alliance with the United Irish League after 1898. In Galway, the police at Turloughmore reported that the local leaders of the UIL and the IRB had met in a public house, and that 'The object of the Conference was to devise plans for the coming battle against graziers, landlords and the Government. It was resolved that a subscription of 2d per week should be collected to defray expenses connected with the movement.' A month later, on 30 March 1902, the RIC reported that 'a rumour had been current in the Tuam district that United Irish League night conferences were to be held at which Irish Republican Brotherhood work would be furthered, as well as the agrarian programme of the United Irish League'.[99]

The IRB faction in the United Irish League were prepared to adopt extreme methods to enforce the 'law of the League'. During the Land War, the IRB element had radicalized the operation of the Land League. In south Galway, for instance, the IRB-Land League alliance were probably responsible for eight agrarian murders in the Loughrea area between January 1880 and July 1882.[100] Certainly, the Craughwell IRB were responsible for the killing of Walter Bourke at Castledaly in 1882.[101] When the Government introduced the Protection of Person and Property (Ireland) Act of 1881, to facilitate the arrest of 'dangerous' Land League activists, 96 of the 955 arrests were of persons who resided in the two police districts of Athenry and Loughrea.[102] After 1898, the police feared that the IRB would also radicalize the operation of the UIL. In August 1901, the Inspector General observed: 'The I.R.B. has no organization but the members endeavour, and with considerable success, to obtain official positions in many branches of the United Irish League . . . and there is little doubt that they will enforce the orders of the League by outrage and intimidation.'[103] These fears were well founded. In November 1904, P. J. Kelly of Killeenadeema, the IRB

[97] Jordan, *Land and popular politics*, 223–4.

[98] For Harris's views on land redistribution, see NA CSORP 41968/1882.

[99] The confidential print, 1902, PRO CO 903/9/273.

[100] 'Analysis of the agrarian and political, etc., murders committed from 1st Jan., 1880, to present time—1st June 1885', Carnarvon papers, police and crime, PRO 30/6/64. There were a total of forty-seven agrarian murders committed in Ireland between 1 Jan. 1880 and 14 July 1882, and eight of these occurrred in the Loughrea police district.

[101] Martin Newell witness statement, MA BMH WS 1,562. See Ch. 5.

[102] 'Protection of Person and Property (Ireland) Act, 1881: list of all persons arrested', NA Protection of Person and Property Act, 1881, carton 1.

[103] IG monthly report, Aug. 1901, PRO CO 904/73.

county centre, and the chairman of the south Galway United Irish League executive,[104] told a public League meeting that any tenant who gave an extravagant price for his land should be shot.[105] Three years later, at a public meeting at New Inn, attended by John Roche and William Duffy, he told his audience:

Well, I have to say as far as [Lord] Ashtown is concerned, if he lived in Loughrea or Killeenadeema, it is on a stretcher he would be brought, perhaps, like John Baker [106] was brought (cheers) . . . Now, I say to you, we will leave Ashtown in this little bog hole until a sufficient number of ye goes over and gets ropes to pull him up . . . But now it has nearly come to the time whether we will be constitutional or whether you will go back to the old Fenian days.[107]

As this example suggests, the small farmer-IRB wing of the United Irish League were committed to enforcing the 'law of the League', but through the use of more extreme measures than those recommended by William O'Brien.

The other major social groups to which the United Irish League appealed were the shopkeepers and the large farmers. Shopkeepers were extremely influential in the UIL at the local level. They were often the officers of the League branches, and also the members of district and county councils. In many cases, shopkeepers were elected as the leaders of the United Irish League because of their economic influence and their role in the dissemination of information.[108] A number of witnesses told the Royal Commission on Congestion that the indebtedness of tenant farmers to shopkeepers explained why so many shopkeepers were elected to positions of local power. If the shopkeeper was not elected to the UIL or the district council, the persons who had not voted for him might be requested to pay off their debts immediately.[109]

In addition to their economic influence, shopkeepers were leading

[104] On P. J. Kelly, see CI monthly report, east Galway, Nov. 1904, NA IGCI/6; ibid., Apr. 1908, NA IGCI/13; register of suspects, PRO CO 904/18.

[105] IG monthly report, Nov. 1904, NA IGCI/6.

[106] The compilers of the confidential print point out that: 'Baker was taken down by the shorthand writer in mistake for Blake. The allusion was to Mr. John Blake who was murdered near Loughrea on 29th June, 1882.' The confidential print, 1907–8, CO 903/14/17. John Blake was Lord Clanricarde's agent.

[107] Ibid., PRO CO 903/14/17–18. The Attorney General expressed the opinion that Kelly's language at this meeting 'was a clear incitement to murder'.

[108] On shopkeepers' involvement in politics, see Liam Kennedy, 'Farmers, traders and agricultural politics in pre-independence Ireland', in Samuel Clark and J. S. Donnelly (eds.), *Irish peasants: violence and political unrest, 1780–1914* (Manchester, 1983), 339–73. See also Ch. 1.

[109] *Royal Commission on Congestion in Ireland: appendix to the tenth report*, HC (1908), [Cd. 4007], xlii. 114.

figures in the discussions of political events that took place in both the shop and the public house.[110] Thomas Cawley's novel about life in a fictional Irish parish, Clochfada, describes the role of the local shopkeeper-publican, Tim Brady, in the following terms:

> He was considered a most enlightened man . . . for he got the daily paper, and he knew what they were doing in all the foreign parts. And for the good of the locality, he sold a couple of the Dublin weeklies, as well as the *Ballyoran Watchman*, a great national organ filled with fine speeches, 'demonstrathions', district councils and petty sessions . . . [And] on Saturday evenings the local lights gathered in to get the news and discuss the great questions of the hour . . . On ordinary week nights only the regular customers turned in, and these came as a matter of business, for they imagined nothing could get along . . . unless they examined it from every viewpoint in Tim Brady's public-house, and that to do this properly, matters should be discussed every night to the accompaniment of 'pints' or 'half-wans', according to tastes . . . it was their idea of work for Ireland![111]

In one sense, the shopkeepers naturally assumed a leading role in rural Ireland: they had the time and the money to take up political positions, they were reasonably knowledgeable about current affairs, and their shops and public houses were central to the social and economic life of the community. But their involvement in the United Irish League was also motivated by a fear that more extreme elements were attempting to take control of local politics.

The United Irish League's agrarian objectives constituted a threat to the economic interests of the rural bourgeoisie. Shopkeepers and large farmers had both been prominently involved in the Land League agitation but, between 1881 and 1898, some of them had become more prosperous and the UIL constituted a threat to their newly won prosperity. In the twenty years after the Land War, many shopkeepers became graziers.[112] Similarly, farmers who had been radical agitators during the Land War often became conservative graziers in its aftermath. Thomas George Griffin of Gurteen in east Galway was arrested under the Protection of Person and Property

---

[110] Seán O'Neill describes the political debates that took place in the shop in which he worked (as a shop assistant) in Mount Bellew during the Great War. Seán O'Neill witness statement, MA BMH WS 1,219.

[111] Thomas Cawley, *An Irish parish: its sunshine and shadows* (Boston, 1911), 55–6. The parish of Clochfada was based on Cawley's native Craughwell, and Tim Brady was probably based on the author's brother, Bartholemew Cawley. Interview with the late Father Martin Coen, the former parish priest of Craughwell and a relative of the Cawley family, at Athenry on 15 May 1994.

[112] *Census of Ireland, 1881 . . . vol. iv: province of Connaught. No. 1. County of Galway*, HC (1882), [c. 3268–1], lxxix. 159; *Census of Ireland, 1901 . . . vol. iv: province of Connaught. No. 1. County of Galway*, HC (1902), [Cd. 1059], cxxviii. 179.

Act in 1881 for inciting tenants not to pay their rents,[113] but by 1898 he
had become a shopkeeper-grazier, who leased a 69-acre grazing farm from
William Daly of Dunsandle.[114]

These interest groups were not prepared to allow the UIL to redistribute
their grazing land, and they joined the League to ensure that the agitation
was directed away from their own properties. As a 'Breaffy Voter' wrote
to the *Connaught Telegraph* regarding James Daly, the UIL leader and grazier, in March 1899: 'A wily customer is James. Be he grabber, be he grazier,
be he anything under the sun, that is out of line with the cause he preaches,
all he need do to hide his rottenness, is to stand on some hurriedly-pre-
pared platform, and denounce some other and much more honourable
person than himself.'[115] Daly's brother Charles used a different method
to protect his grazing interests. In February 1899, the County Inspector
for Mayo reported that: 'Charles Daly has succeeded in buying over more
than half the members of the [Belcarra] branch and as a consequence he
keeps the [grazing] farm and is giving his opponents a hot time of it as
far as words go.'[116] These practices were not confined to Mayo. Laurence
Ginnell published an account of the Irish land question, *Land and liberty*,
in which he described the operation of corrupt UIL branches:

> From the time a public organisation is first founded wily persons whose interest it
> may affect are on the alert to keep it off if they can, and failing that, to join it when
> it comes into their parish, [or] to get some creatures of theirs to join it for their
> purposes; and in some cases they introduce it themselves in order that they may
> more effectually neutralize it from within and guard their own interests. By simply
> putting themselves forward as promoters before the branch has taken organic
> form they may get themselves or their creatures appointed as officers or by similar
> contrivances they may capture an existing branch. Their interests are secured. For
> the legitimate purpose of the organisation . . . it were better if that kind of branch
> did not exist.[117]

How did the shopkeeper and large farmer faction of the United Irish
League interpret the 'law of the League'? The rural bourgeoisie recognized
the power of the League courts, and joined the UIL so that they could
influence the implementation of the 'law of the League' in their localities. Their objective in joining the League was twofold: first, to divert the
anti-grazier campaign away from their own grass lands, and, second, to

---

113 'Protection of Person and Property (Ireland) Act, 1881: list of all persons arrested', NA
Protection of Person and Property Act, 1881, carton 1.
114 Cappalusk district electoral division, townland of Creeraun, LVOD.
115 *Connaught Telegraph*, 25 Mar. 1899.
116 CI monthly report, Mayo, Feb. 1899, NA IGCI/1.
117 Ginnell, *Land and liberty*, 187–8.

ensure that the agitation was conducted in a constitutional and peaceful manner. At Gurteen (in east Galway), for example, there was a dispute between the two factions in the UIL branch led by Thomas George Griffin, shopkeeper-grazier and county councillor, and Martin Finnerty.[118] The branch had conducted an agitation against a local grazier, Mr J. V. Smith, who owned two adjoining grass farms of 1,381 acres at Colmanstown and Cloonkeenkerrill.[119] Under the direction of Finnerty, a number of different forms of protest had been adopted by the UIL to force Smith to give up the Colmanstown farm:[120]

On the 6th January 1907 a public U.I. League meeting was held at Coolmanstown [*sic*] with the object of inducing Mr Smith to sell the Coolmanstown [*sic*] farm for division among the people ... Early in March a committee was formed under the leadership of Martin Finnerty to bring pressure to bear on Mr Smith. On 28th March Finnerty, with others, waited on Mr Smith and asked him to sell the land. Mr Smith declined to do so unless he received full compensation.

On 15th March 6 shots were fired through the windows of the house occupied by Thomas Brown who acts as steward and caretaker to Mr Smith.

About 8—. P.M. on 3rd April the police intercepted a drumming party in the vicinity of the farm. It consisted of about 40 persons, who were beating a drum, blowing horns, shouting, groaning and whistling. These men were with difficulty prevailed on to disperse.[121]

This agitation continued into 1908:

On Sunday, 2nd August, 1908, a meeting was got up by Finnerty at Colmanstown to draw attention to W. Dempsey, who had been engaged as herd by Mr. Smith ...

On the 2nd October, 1908, the house of a farmer named John Mahon was fired into because he had recently bought from the herd, Thomas Killeen, his brother-in-law, a ram belonging to the Messrs. Smith. Mahon was treasurer of the local branch of the United Irish League. Finnerty was suspected of having got the outrage committed.[122]

Notwithstanding this agitation, Smith refused to give up the farm. In November 1908, Finnerty was arrested for his alleged involvement in a fracas with some police constables outside his home at Tample, near

---

[118] Thomas George Griffin's obituary, *Connacht Tribune*, 4 Apr. 1914; Martin Finnerty's obituary, *Connacht Tribune*, 17 Oct. 1959. On Finnerty, see Chs. 3 and 5, and on Griffin, see Ch. 6.

[119] The Smiths purchased the grazing farms under the Ashbourne Act, and Mr J. V. Smith, who managed the farms, resided in Cavan. The confidential print, 1907–8, PRO CO 903/14/56–8.

[120] The Inspector General describes Smith's land as 'the Coolmanstown farm'. IG monthly report, Apr. 1907, NA IGCI/11.   [121] Ibid.

[122] The confidential print, 1907–8, PRO CO 903/14/57.

Gurteen,[123] and Griffin reorganized the branch, and was appointed vice-president in his absence.[124] At a meeting of the League on 3 October 1909, Griffin stated that

He had often felt reluctantly compelled to find find fault with the tactics adopted to obtain possession of that farm [owned by Smith at Colmanstown] by those people, and while not approving of those tactics now, he moved: 'that we . . . respectfully request Mr. Smith to take the necessary steps to relieve the undoubted congestion that exists in the Colmanstown electoral division.'—The resolution was passed unanimously.[125]

Notices were posted at Gurteen calling on people not to join Griffin's 'bogus' UIL branch, and stating that he had agreed to leave the parish without a branch until Finnerty was released. Even more damningly, the notices alleged that 'The object of this League branch is to shoulder Martin Finnerty out of politics, and not to secure "the land for the people." The organizers of this League were heretofore the bitter enemies of the people in their fight for the land. Leave it to the grazier and the blackleg, who are seeking vengeance on Martin Finnerty.'[126]

Indeed, the animosity between Finnerty and Griffin's supporters was such that when Tim Silke emigrated to the United States he wrote to Finnerty, 'let ye be shure and keep the blacks down and when ye get one of them alone kill him'.[127] When Finnerty was released in November 1909, he was greeted by a monster meeting of 5,000 people at Athenry, including John Roche and William Duffy,[128] and as he travelled back to his home: 'From Athenry to Gurteen was one continuous line of fires all along the road. Crowds of women and children, and young and old men stood in groups at every crossroad and boreen leading from the different villages, and as the procession came in view loud cheers rent the air.'[129] On arriving at Tample, a crowd had gathered, and Finnerty was celebrated as their

[123] CI monthly report, east Galway, Nov. 1908, NA IGCI/15. Finnerty was subsequently tried and convicted at the Connaught winter assizes held at Limerick in December 1908.

[124] The president of the reorganized UIL branch at Gurteen was Father Joyce and the other vice-president was Father O'Loughlin. *Connacht Tribune*, 9 Oct. 1909.

[125] Ibid.   [126] Ibid.

[127] Tim Silke, New York City, to Martin Finnerty, 9 June 1910. The Martin Finnerty papers, in the possession of Mattie Finnerty, Galway.

[128] *Connacht Tribune*, 27 Nov. 1909; CI monthly report, east Galway, Nov. 1909, PRO CO 904/79. The *Connacht Tribune* estimated that 5,000 people greeted Finnerty at Athenry, while the police stated that it was 2,000. There is a photograph of Martin Finnerty in the *Connacht Tribune*, 27 Nov. 1909.

[129] *Connacht Tribune*, 27 Nov. 1909. Interview with Kevin Rohan, Tiaquin at Colmanstown, 24 Dec. 2003. Rohan's mother recalled the crowds of people and the lighted tar barrels at Tiaquin when Finnerty returned to Tample on 20 November 1909.

'guide, philosopher and friend'.[130] Even so, he was unable to rejoin the local branch of the UIL, as he later told John Dillon:

As regards my withdrawal from the old Party I could not in a letter tell you the half of it. There was an old dispute in this little parish and in the end we had two branches of the UIL. After a long time my affiliation fee was returned to me. Six delegates from the opposite branch & three from the AOH voted against me at the Ballinasloe Convention.[131] I was then told I had no local standing as Sec to the East Galway [UIL] Executive as I was not a member of a branch. In the end this was too much for me.[132]

Finnerty was thus ousted from local political life by his rival, Griffin, who guided the local branch in a more moderate and conservative direction than that advocated by the Fenian element within the League,

This case study symbolizes the different ways in which the two factions interpreted the 'law of the League'. The small farmers wanted the grazing land redistributed so that their impoverished circumstances could be improved,[133] and they were therefore more willing to use extreme methods to achieve this objective. The shopkeepers and large farmers, on the other hand, had little to gain and possibly much to lose from the redistribution of grazing land, and so they attempted to moderate the radical impulses within the movement. At Craughwell in east Galway, disagreement between the two factions over a decision made by the League court split the UIL branch and inaugurated a dramatic dispute for the control of the 'law of the League'.

The dispute originated in a case that came before the Craughwell UIL court in 1906.[134] Mrs Mary Ryan, a native of Craughwell who had emigrated

[130] *Connacht Tribune*, 27 Nov. 1909.

[131] After the death of John Roche, the MP for east Galway, in 1914, Finnerty put himself forward as his successor but was defeated at a convention of 300 east Galway delegates at Ballinasloe on 23 November to select a parliamentary candidate, primarily due to clerical opposition. IG monthly report, Nov. 1914, PRO CO 904/95.

[132] Martin Finnerty to John Dillon, 4 Sept. 1926, TCDA Dillon papers 6772/234 (b).

[133] There were reported to be twenty 'uneconomic' holdings adjacent to the Colmanstown farm. *Connacht Tribune*, 9 Oct. 1909.

[134] The details of the Ryan case were compiled from a variety of sources: the CI monthly reports, east Galway, Feb. 1906–Dec. 1908, NA IGCI/11–15; the CI monthly reports, east Galway, Jan. 1909–June 1912, PRO CO 904/77–87; 'Case of Mrs. Mary Ryan, of Craughwell, and the murder of constable Goldrick', the confidential print, 1907–8, PRO CO 903/14/151–3; précis of information and reports on secret societies, Mar. 1905–Dec. 1908, PRO CO 904/11–12; *Sinn Féin*, 1906–9; *Connacht Tribune*, June 1909–Feb. 1912; *Galway Express*, 1909; *Blazer* [Craughwell parish magazine], 1 (Spring 1975) – 17 (Christmas 1987); Martin Newell witness statement, MA BMH WS 1,562; Patrick Callanan witness statement, MA BMH WS 347; Thomas McInerney witness statement, MA BMH WS 1,150; and interviews with Gerry Cloonan, Craughwell, 25 Apr. 1995; the late Father Martin Coen, Athenry, 15 May 1994; the late Ned Newell, Craughwell, 15 Dec. 1993.

to the United States and returned in 1900, requested the permission of
the court to lease an evicted farm in the parish.[135] The 16-acre farm in the
townland of Templemartin[136] had been kept derelict by the local branch of
the League since 1889, when Patrick Gilligan was evicted for non-payment
of rent by Lord Clanricarde.[137] In 1904, Patrick Fahy, a small farmer in the
townland, had asked the court if he could purchase the goodwill of the
evicted farm, but his request was refused on the grounds that there was no
proof that Gilligan was dead.[138] Two years later, Mrs Ryan raised the case
of the evicted farm again because she had found Patrick Gilligan in Sligo
workhouse and paid him £20 for the goodwill of the farm, in the presence
of two members of the north Sligo UIL executive.[139] Notwithstanding this
transaction, the Craughwell League court maintained that the farm should
remain derelict until the sale of the Clanricarde estate; and, in February
1906, Mrs. Ryan began renting the farm in defiance of the court.[140]

In April 1906, Mrs Ryan took her case to the south Galway United Irish
League executive for an appeal. Her case was adjourned by the executive
for two weeks to allow the court to investigate her claim that she had paid
Gilligan for the goodwill of the farm. Martin Ward, the secretary of the
south Galway executive, wrote to the secretary of the north Sligo executive
requesting verification that the Sligo workhouse transaction had taken
place. On the second Sunday in May, the south Galway executive recon-
vened and Ward placed the replies of the Sligo executive before the court,
which stated that Gilligan had indeed been paid £20 for the goodwill of his
farm by Mrs Ryan. Given that Gilligan had consented to the sale, the court
then declared that Mrs Ryan could become the tenant of the farm.[141]

There were two factions in the Craughwell branch of the United Irish

[135] *Galway Express*, 30 Jan. 1909; Martin Finnerty's speech at a public meeting at Athenry, *Connacht Tribune*, 17 Feb. 1912.

[136] Craughwell district electoral division, townland of Templemartin, LVOD.

[137] *Galway Express*, 30 Jan. 1909; Martin Hallinan's speech at south Galway UIL executive, *Connacht Tribune*, 27 Jan. 1912.

[138] Letter from Martin Ward, the secretary of the south Galway United Irish League executive, to the *Connacht Tribune*, 17 Feb. 1912; Ned Newell, 'The shooting of the peeler', *Blazer*, 17 (Christmas 1987), 108.

[139] *Galway Express*, 30 Jan. 1909; letter from Martin Ward, *Connacht Tribune*, 17 Feb. 1912.

[140] The confidential print, 1907–8, PRO CO 903/14/152; letter from Martin Finnerty, *Connacht Tribune*, 24 Feb. 1912; letter from Martin Ward, *Connacht Tribune*, 17 Feb. 1912. Ward and Finnerty disagree as to the decision of the Craughwell UIL on the Ryan case, but Finnerty more plausibly suggests that the local UIL rejected Ryan's request to rent the farm, thereby necessitating an appeal to the south Galway UIL executive.

[141] Letter from Martin Ward, *Connacht Tribune*, 17 Feb. 1912. Police intelligence states that Gilligan was payed £25 for the goodwill of the farm. The confidential print, 1907–8, PRO CO 903/14/152.

League, the 'Kennyites', who were predominantly small farmers and led by Tom Kenny, the local blacksmith and leader of the Craughwell IRB; and the 'Hallinanites', who were larger farmers, and led by Martin Hallinan, a local shopkeeper-grazier.[142] The Kennyite faction opposed Mrs Ryan's occupancy of the Templemartin farm.[143] In their view, the congested tenants in the townland had prior claim to the Gilligan farm over returned emigrants who were comparatively well-off.[144] While in America, Mrs Ryan had saved several hundred pounds, and she planned to open a shop in the village as well as renting the small farm at Templemartin.[145] The Hallinanites, in opposition to the Kennyites, upheld the decision of the south Galway executive and supported Mrs Ryan's request to rent the farm.[146] In 1906, the Kennyites were the most influential faction in the branch, and they set about overturning the south Galway executive's decision.[147] Technically, the verdict of an executive court could only be challenged by an appeal to the standing committee of the UIL National Directory,[148] but the Kennyite faction of the Craughwell League used rather different methods to achieve their objective.

A vigorous campaign of boycotting and intimidation was organized against Mrs Ryan by the Kennyites, who were determined to enforce their interpretation of the 'law of the League' in Craughwell. On 8 February 1907, a revolver shot was fired into her house, and in March, shots and stones were fired into the houses of two men who worked for her, in an attempt to intimidate them into leaving her employment. Notices were posted up in Athenry, calling on shopkeepers in the town to refuse to supply her with goods. Her hay was burned, and as she returned from Craughwell railway station in November, shots were fired in a field as she passed by.[149] Remarkably, she endured this intimidation and the boycott of

---

[142] On the social composition of the two factions, see Tables 9, 10 and 11 below. The terms 'Kennyite' and 'Hallinanite' were used locally to denote the two groups. Newell, 'The shooting of the peeler', 108. On Kenny, see Ch. 5.

[143] Letter from Martin Ward, *Connacht Tribune*, 17 Feb. 1912; Martin Hallinan's speech at south Galway UIL executive, *Connacht Tribune*, 27 Jan. 1912; the confidential print, 1907–8, PRO CO 903/14/152.

[144] Letter from Martin Hallinan, *Connacht Tribune*, 9 Mar. 1912; and the confidential print, 1907–8, PRO CO 903/14/152. Patrick Fahy, a congested tenant in the townland, was the main rival claimant to the Gilligan farm.

[145] *Galway Express*, 30 Jan. 1909, and letter from Martin Finnerty, *Connacht Tribune*, 24 Feb. 1912.

[146] Letter from Martin Hallinan, *Connacht Tribune*, 9 Mar. 1912.

[147] The confidential print, 1907–8, PRO CO 903/14/152; letter from Martin Hallinan, *Connacht Tribune*, 9 Mar. 1912, and letter from Martin Ward, *Connacht Tribune*, 17 Feb. 1912.   [148] Letter from Martin Ward, *Connacht Tribune*, 2 Mar. 1912.

[149] The confidential print, 1907–8, PRO CO 903/14/152.

her young family. She told an *Irish Times* journalist: 'Nobody will speak to my children except the policemen. Why the very postboy who delivers letters here won't exchange a word with my lad.'[150] But, in June 1907, the Kennyites appeared to have found a means of finally forcing her to give up the farm. The perimeter walls of her farm were knocked down, and no local labourers could be found to rebuild them.[151] It was customary for an unwalled farm to be used as 'commonage' for common grazing, after a certain amount of time had elapsed.[152] By the end of 1908, it looked increasingly as if Mrs Ryan would have to give up her claim to the Templemartin farm.

In January 1909, Mrs Ryan contacted Edward Shaw-Tener, Clanricarde's agent, and requested him to send two labourers to rebuild her walls. On 9 January, two labourers—Patrick Coady and Patrick Malone—came from Loughrea to carry out the work.[153] For twelve days, they worked under the armed police guard of Constable Martin Goldrick until on 21 January at 9.30 a.m., shots were fired from across the railway line adjacent to the farm at the two labourers, hitting and wounding them both.[154] According to the compilers of the confidential print:

Constable Goldrick, who was armed with a revolver, crossed the road, and the attacking party ran away, pursued by the constable, who threw off his belt and great coat. A lad named Michael Ryan, aged fourteen years, heard the shots, and saw three men running into the scrub, pursed by the constable, and heard shots fired in the scrub afterwards. The constable appears to have followed the men for 200 yards, and was emerging through a gap in the scrub when he was fired on from close quarters and killed, his left lung being shattered with shot. The constable's body was found at this place some time afterwards by a search party of police. In addition to the wound on the lung, the constable's left arm was injured, and there were other shot marks about his body. Two shots had been discharged from the constable's revolver, which was found lying under him.[155]

---

[150] *Galway Express*, 30 Jan. 1909.
[151] The Craughwell murder case, *Connacht Tribune*, 7 May 1910; the confidential print, 1907–8, PRO CO 903/14/152.
[152] *Galway Express*, 30 Jan. 1909.
[153] The Craughwell murder case, *Connacht Tribune*, 7 May 1910; *Galway Express*, 30 Jan. 1909; the confidential print, 1907–8, PRO CO 903/14/152.
[154] The Craughwell murder case, *Connacht Tribune*, 7 May 1910; and the confidential print, 1907–8, PRO CO 903/14/152. Patrick Malone had to be treated in hospital in Dublin. CI monthly report, east Galway, Feb. 1909, PRO CO 904/77.
[155] Goldrick (who had been born on 4 October 1884) was 24 years old, and a bachelor. The confidential print, 1907–8, PRO CO 903/14/153. Local accounts refer to Martin Goldrick as Martin McGoldrick, but I have followed the police usage since this probably reflected Goldrick's own wishes.

Martin Newell, a member of the Craughwell IRB, recalled:

In 1909 there was a disputed farm in Craughwell and the walls were broken down twice. Two bailiffs were sent out from Loughrea to build the walls under police protection. A meeting of the Craughwell Circle of the I.R.B. was held to discuss what action should be taken. It was decided to appoint three men to fire at the two bailiffs, not with the intention of killing them, but only to frighten them off. On the appointed day the bailiffs were fired at and both of them were wounded. An R.I.C. man named McGoldrick, who was protecting the bailiffs, fired at the attackers and followed them; the attackers fired back at him so as to stop him from following them. In the end McGoldrick got so close to one of the men that he had no option but to shoot McGoldrick dead.[156]

The young police guard had managed to catch up with the attacking party and, as he did so, they shot him dead, fearing that if they did not do so he would be able to identify them.[157] 'The District Inspector, reporting on the 23rd January, states that not a single civilian attended the constable's funeral, and that the people in and around Craughwell express themselves pleased that a policeman was killed.'[158]

Two members of the Craughwell IRB, Tom Kenny and Michael Dermody, were arrested for the murder of Martin Goldrick.[159] However, they were both released in February when the police acknowledged that they had insufficient evidence against them.[160] Indeed, Kenny is reputed to have walked into the police barracks to ask the time at the precise moment that the shots were being fired at Coady and Malone.[161] On 20 March, five men were arrested for the murder of Goldrick, and two of them were subsequently identified by an eye-witness.[162] Michael Dermody and Thomas Hynes, two small farmers who were also members of the Craughwell IRB, were later charged with the murder of Goldrick, and returned for trial at the summer assizes.[163] It was widely believed in

[156] Martin Newell witness statement, MA BMH WS 1,562.

[157] The confidential print, 1907–8, PRO CO 903/14/153; Newell, 'The shooting of the peeler', 109.

[158] The confidential print, 1907–8, PRO CO 903/14/153.

[159] CI monthly report, east Galway, Jan. 1909, PRO CO 904/77; Patrick Callanan witness statement, MA BMH WS 347; and Gilbert Morrissey witness statement, MA BMH WS 1,138.

[160] *Galway Express*, 27 Feb. 1909; CI monthly report, east Galway, Feb. 1909, PRO CO 904/77.

[161] Interview with Gerry Cloonan, 25 Apr. 1995.

[162] CI monthly report, east Galway, Mar. 1909, PRO CO 904/77; the confidential print, 1910–11, PRO CO 903/16/41–3. The compilers of the confidential print state that the arrests took place on 21 March.

[163] The confidential print, 1910–11, PRO CO 903/16/41–3; Patrick Callanan witness statement, MA BMH WS 347.

Craughwell, however, that neither Hynes nor Dermody had been involved in the murder, and both the Hallinanites and Kennyites devoted their collective energies to the defence of the 'Craughwell prisoners'. A defence fund was established to raise money to pay for Hynes and Dermody's defence, and it was supported by both the Craughwell UIL branch and the south Galway UIL executive.[164] Between 1909 and 1910, £265 was donated by UIL branches, GAA tournaments, and private individuals for the legal defence of Hynes and Dermody.[165] Although Hynes and Dermody were due to be tried at the summer assizes in Galway on 19 July, the Crown applied for a change of venue and the two men were tried at the winter assizes in Limerick, where the jury disagreed. A further change of venue was applied for, and, on 5 May 1910, the two men were brought before Judge Madden in Dublin, where the Attorney General proposed to try Michael Dermody first.[166]

The Crown's case against Dermody was based on the evidence of Bartley Naughton, a spailpín (migrant labourer) from Rosmuc, who claimed to have witnessed the murder take place from a railway bridge 260 yards from the scene of the crime.[167] In his statement, Naughton described his movements on the day of the murder as follows:

Before I left Athenry that morning I tried to get a drink, but I could not, the public-houses were not open. I walked on towards Craughwell taking my time. I did not meet anyone on the road between Athenry and the bridge over the railway, the one nearest Craughwell. As I came up close to the bridge I heard some shots I saw a man running to the bridge from the Craughwell side. I was just then on the bridge. The man went back again towards Craughwell and did not come as far as me. I looked into the crags where the bushes is on my right hand side. I saw a policeman there. He was running after three fellows out before him. I did not see any gun with him. He had no gun when I saw him. The three fellows had guns. When I saw the police-man first he was a good bit from them, but he came up very close to them. When he was very close to them two of the three men turned back; one of them fired a shot and I saw the policeman fall. After the policeman fell I could not see him on the ground. There were bushes between me and him. The third man was walking on at this time. The two men went about three or four yards towards the third man

---

[164] CI monthly report, east Galway, Apr. 1909, PRO CO 904/77.

[165] 'Balance sheet of the accounts of the Craughwell prisoner's defence fund, 7 Oct. 1910', audited by Martin Finnerty. Every United Irish League branch in east Galway subscribed to the defence fund except those at Woodford, Kinvara, and Bullaun. The Martin Finnerty papers, in the possession of Mattie Finnerty, Galway.

[166] The confidential print, 1910–11, PRO CO 903/16/41–3; the Craughwell murder case, *Connacht Tribune*, 7 May 1910.

[167] When asked by the Judge how he pleaded, Dermody is reputed to have said, 'Whatever you think yourself, Sir.' Interview with Gerry Cloonan, 25 Apr. 1995.

after the policeman fell and then turned and shouted at me to wait for them. They were running towards me at the time. I stood on the bridge and they ran up and came on the road to me. One of these men was bigger than the other. The big man pointed the rifle straight into my body and told me he would have my own life if I would say anything about it. I told him that I would not, that I was the same as themselves. They then ran back the way they came until they were about halfway to the place where I saw the policeman fall. They changed guns there and the two of them ran on to the place where I saw the policeman fall, and the big man—the man who challenged me on the bridge—straightened the gun straight down on the spot where I saw the policeman fall and let off another shot, and two of them ran away through the crags.[168]

This was the substance of Naughton's statement which, under cross-examination by the barrister for the defence, A. M. Sullivan, fell apart. Naughton's account was inconsistent and implausible, and contradicted almost everything else that was known about the case, including medical evidence as to how the fatal shot had been fired.[169] According to Sullivan, the judge, Mr Justice Madden, 'became convinced that he [Naughton] was telling a pack of lies';[170] and Sullivan himself observed that Naughton was

extremely uncomfortable in accounting for his convenient presence on the railway bridge at a time which enabled him to supervise the murder taking place a few hundred yards away . . . It was also perfectly clear that the story he had told in his original questioning was not a true account of his wanderings that day, or, if it was true, it omitted so much that what it conveyed was wholly misleading.[171]

Presumably because Naughton appeared to be an unreliable witness, the Dublin jury acquitted Dermody, and the Crown decided not to try Hynes. Even so, the two prisoners were held in Mountjoy jail until 26 May when, after almost fourteen months in custody and two trials at Limerick and Dublin, they were released.[172] At Craughwell, 'the people collected: tar barrels were lighted and an enthusiastic welcome was given them.'[173] After their release, the two men were treated as 'heroes'[174] and a ballad

[168] Bartley Naughton's statement was made at Ballinasloe on 20 Mar. 1909 in presence of A. C. Newell, Resident Magistrate. The confidential print, 1910–11, PRO CO 903/16/41–3. Later, Naughton identified the 'big man' as Michael Dermody.

[169] The Craughwell murder case, *Connacht Tribune*, 14 May 1910.

[170] A. M. Sullivan, *The last serjeant: the memoirs of Serjeant A. M. Sullivan* (London, 1952), 98.   [171] Ibid. 96–7.

[172] The confidential print, 1910–11, PRO CO 903/16/43; Sullivan, *The last serjeant*, 97–9; CI monthly report, east Galway, May 1910, PRO CO 904/81.

[173] CI monthly report, east Galway, May 1910, PRO CO 904/81.

[174] CI monthly report, east Galway, June 1910, PRO CO 904/81.

was composed about them, 'Hynes and Bold Dermody', which stated the popular view that Naughton had perjured himself for a police bribe:

> Bartley Naughton he swore with vengeance galore
> They should swing on the high gallows tree
> Three hundred pounds and his keep and all found
> Against Hynes and the bold Dermody.[175]

Indeed, Patrick Callanan, an agricultural labourer who was a member of the Craughwell IRB, later told the Bureau of Military History that 'Both of the accused were, in fact, innocent.'[176]

Notwithstanding this period of unity between the Hallinanites and Kennyites, however, the dispute between the two factions was resumed six months later. In December 1910, Hallinan reformed the committee of the Craughwell UIL branch with his own supporters, and initiated a campaign to gain control of the 'law of the League'.[177] Kenny had seceded from the branch with his followers and formed a Sinn Féin club in the parish, which had appropriated the functions of the League court.[178] The Hallinanites wanted to gain control over the parish court for three major reasons. First, they viewed Kenny's interpretation of the 'law of the League' as illegitimate. The executive court had decided that Mrs Ryan could legitimately take the farm, and Kenny should, therefore, accept the court's ruling. Second, the Hallinanites were opposed to the extreme methods adopted by Kenny to uphold his version of the 'law of the League'. To a large extent, this was because Kenny's methods resulted in the state imposing punitive extra taxes on the ratepayers of the parish. In July 1909, for example, the Galway Quarter Sessions decided to award £700 to Martin Goldrick's family as compensation for their son's death; and this sum was to be raised from an extra tax on the two district electoral divisions where the murderers were believed to live: Craughwell and Kileelly.[179] This represented a dramatic increase in the rates of the district, and when Hallinan reorganized the UIL in 1910, almost half of the members (47 per cent) were also members of the Craughwell Ratepayers, Association.[180] Third, the Hallinanites

---

[175] Interview with the late Ned Newell of Craughwell conducted by the author, 15 Dec. 1994. There is a full transcript of the ballad in Newell, 'The shooting of the peeler', 110. Bartley Naughton emigrated to California after the conclusion of the trial.

[176] Patrick Callanan witness statement, MA BMH WS 347. Callanan was known as the 'hare' after a legal dispute in which he was identified as the 'heir', mispronounced as 'hare'. His brother Michael was subsequently known as the 'rabbit'.

[177] *Connacht Tribune*, 26 Nov. 1910.

[178] Kenny formed the Craughwell Sinn Féin club in Feb. 1907, with the assistance of Pat Rogers, a mason from Kilreecle, *Sinn Féin*, 16 Feb. 1907. See Ch. 5.

[179] *Connacht Tribune*, 10 July 1909.   [180] *Connacht Tribune*, 26 Nov. 1910.

recognized that the League court was a powerful institution that exerted a great deal of influence over the economic and political life of the community, and they wanted to control it.

But how were the Hallinanites to replace the Kennyites as the most powerful political faction in Craughwell? Serjeant Sullivan, in his memoirs, recalls that two members of the Craughwell UIL visited him in Dublin in 1910 to ask his advice as to how they could defeat the Kennyites:

A simple solution of the situation occurred to me, and I expressed the most unconstitutional opinion that if, on some dark night, they should contrive to meet the bully of the murder-gang and give him a good beating, they would become the heroes of the countryside ... for the whole population, seeing that the tyrants were vulnerable, would all summon up courage to put an end to their domination.[181]

This advice was taken rather too literally by the two United Irish Leaguers, and the following year, according to Sullivan, 'Redmond Barry, the Attorney General, came to my desk in the library and observed, "For heaven's sake, Alex, can you put the brakes on your friends in Croughwell [*sic*] otherwise you soon will have to defend them for murder".'[182] Indeed, between November 1910 and November 1911, there were at least sixty-three violent incidents perpetrated by the Hallinanites on the Kennyites at Craughwell.[183]

The objective of the intimidation was to force the Kennyites to change their allegiance from Tom Kenny to Martin Hallinan. A number of different kinds of intimidation were employed by the Hallinanites to achieve this. The conflict began at a pig fair held in the village in December 1910 at which Kenny and eleven of his supporters attacked a number of Leaguers with their hurleys resulting in 'fierce faction fighting'.[184] Over the next six months, a party of thirty men armed with sticks paraded up and down the main street in the village on most nights, shouting abuse at Kenny and his followers.[185] The houses of fifteen Kennyites were attacked, resulting in the smashing of windows and substantial damage to their interiors.[186] On at least fourteen occasions, Kenny's supporters were physically beaten as they went about their business in the parish, and 'a good number' were

[181] Sullivan, *The last serjeant*, 100–1.
[182] Ibid. 101.
[183] This figure was calculated from three accounts of the conflict in Craughwell between Nov. 1910 and Nov. 1911: Martin Finnerty's account of the Craughwell dispute, *Connacht Tribune*, 13 Jan. 1912; the report of the Lecarrow shooting trial, *Connacht Tribune*, 15 June 1912; and CI monthly reports, east Galway, Nov. 1910–Nov. 1911, PRO CO 904/82–5.
[184] *Connacht Tribune*, 24 Dec. 1910.
[185] Martin Finnerty's account of the Craughwell dispute, *Connacht Tribune*, 13 Jan. 1912.
[186] Ibid.

also assaulted while attending the newly constituted League court.[187] According to Martin Newell, 'The fights broke out every week and . . . [t]he R.I.C. always took the side of the U.I.L.'[188] On 23 April 1911, the predominantly Kennyite hurling team were fired at as they disembarked from a train at Craughwell railway station. Patrick Callanan was injured and ten of the Great Southern and Western's carriages were seriously damaged.[189] By the end of 1911, most of Kenny's supporters had deserted him, and he was reduced to answering the door of his house with two revolvers in his hands.[190] In this way, the Hallinanites became the dominant political faction in Craughwell, a position they would retain until 1918.[191]

The Craughwell dispute was essentially a struggle between two social groups for the control of the local land court.[192] Kenny's party (see Tables 9, 10 and 11) consisted primarily of small farmers and landless men: 67 per cent of the farmers who supported him occupied farms of under 30 acres, and 29 per cent were middle-sized farmers, with between 30 and 50 acres. Twenty-two per cent of the Kennyites were the younger sons of farmers or agricultural labourers, and 19 per cent were drawn from the labouring and artisanate classes. The economic interests of the Kennyites were thus broadly similar: both the small farmers and the landless men would benefit directly from the redistribution of local grazing land. In terms of age, the Kennyites were predominantly aged between 20 and 30, but there were also a few who were aged over 60. The Kennyites were also closely involved with the IRB. Kenny was the head of the IRB at Craughwell, and his supporters Patrick Callanan, Gilbert Morrissey, and Martin Newell were also members of the IRB.[193] In short, Kenny's party were the young rural poor who were associated with the IRB.

Martin Hallinan's party represented a different economic interest group. They were predominantly farmers and elder farmers' sons: 86 per cent of Hallinanites were responsible for the running of the family farm, as opposed to only 58 per cent of Kennyites. Their farms were also generally larger than those of Kenny's supporters: 64 per cent occupied farms of over 30 acres, and 32 per cent rented farms of over 50 acres. Ten per cent of

---

[187] Ibid; report of the Lecarrow shooting trial, *Connacht Tribune*, 15 June 1912.

[188] Martin Newell witness statement, MA BMH WS 1,562.

[189] CI monthly report, east Galway, Apr. 1911, PRO CO 904/83.

[190] Interview with Gerry Cloonan, 25 Apr. 1995.

[191] See Ch. 5.

[192] For a discussion of the methodology used to compile this study of the social composition of the two factions, see Appendix I.

[193] Patrick Callanan witness statement, MA BMH WS 347; Gilbert Morrissey witness statement, MA BMH WS 1,138; and Martin Newell witness statement, MA BMH WS 1,562. It is likely that many other Kennyites were members of the IRB, see Ch. 5.

TABLE 9. The occupations of the Kennyite and Hallinanite factions at Craughwell in 1911

Occupation	Kennyite	Hallinanite
Shopkeeper-grazier	0	3
Farmer	15	13
Eldest farmer's son	6	9
Younger farmer's son	6	3
Labourer	2	0
Blacksmith	3	0
Postman	3	1
Railway porter	1	0
Number	36	29

TABLE 10. The acreage occupied by Kennyites and Hallinanites who were farmers or eldest farmers' sons

Acres (n)	Kennyite	Hallinanite
$n<30$	14	9
$30 \leq n < 50$	6	8
$50 \leq n < 100$	1	6
$n \geq 100$	0	2
Number	21	25

TABLE 11. The ages of Kennyites and Hallinanites in 1911

Age	Kennyite	Hallinanite
10–19	4	1
20–9	12	6
30–9	7	6
40–9	3	11
50–9	2	4
60+	8	1
Number	36	29

Hallinanites were younger farmers' sons, and only 3 per cent of them were labourers or artisans. The leaders of the Hallinanites—Martin Hallinan and his two deputies, Michael Clasby and Bartholemew Cawley—were all shopkeeper-graziers. In addition, Cawley was the sub-postmaster, and Clasby was the local dispensary doctor and hotel owner.

The Hallinanites were thus conservative, respectable nationalists who were relatively prosperous and did not want to see their world turned upside down by the Kennyites. Most of them were middle-aged: 38 per cent of the Hallinanites were aged between 40 and 50. They counselled moderation in agrarian matters, and were of the school that proposed the writing of letters to graziers and landlords, rather than the firing of shots through windows. For this reason, they were favoured by the local clergy. The Hallinanites, then, were prosperous and conservative nationalists, who aimed to moderate the United Irish League's agitation.

The Craughwell dispute suggests the dynamics of conflict within other United Irish League branches in Connacht. A number of United Irish League branches in east Galway split along similar lines. At Caltra in April 1908, a second branch of the United Irish League was formed by those of the old branch who wanted to organize the boycott of a local grazier, Mr Connolly of Tycooley. According to the local police, the clergy supported the old branch.[194] In June 1908, a second UIL branch was also formed at Kiltormer, in opposition to the existing branch, whose president was Patrick Larkin, a prominent IRB member and the president of the GAA county Board. The second branch was supported by the local parish priest, the Reverend Bowes, who had refused to become involved in Larkin's branch, and who accepted the presidency of the new branch only on the condition that it would not commit illegal acts.[195] At Gurteen, as we have seen, the UIL also split into two factions, one led by Martin Finnerty and the other led by Thomas George Griffin. Indeed, such was the ubiquity of conflicts within the UIL that Martin Ward, the secretary of the south Galway executive, lamented:

These disputes by which parishes and districts are divided, are the curse of the country, and in my opinion, not alone is it right, but absolutely essential that the Executive should interfere, find out who is right and who is wrong, and by a vote of the delegates duly appointed for the purpose, enforce discipline, without which no organisation, or even Government, can carry on.[196]

In many cases, however, the radical agrarian members of the United Irish League defected to Sinn Féin after the formation of the new party, and

194 CI monthly report, east Galway, Apr. 1908, NA IGCI/13.
195 CI monthly report, east Galway, June 1908, NA IGCI/13.
196 Letter from Martin Ward to *Connacht Tribune*, 2 Mar. 1912.

the next chapter will explore the evolution of separatist politics in county Galway between 1905 and 1918.

5

The Evolution of Sinn Féin: Separatist Politics in County Galway, 1905–1918

The Galway Secret Society dates back to 1882 when members of the Dublin Invincibles, who were working at Tullyra Castle, formed it in this County. Its headquarters is at Craughwell in the East Riding, but it extends through Gort and Galway Districts and on up to Tuam. It is the source of most of the agrarian crime and unrest in Galway and was at the back of the recent rebellion.

(The County Inspector for the west riding of county Galway, July 1916)[1]

The victory of Sinn Féin in the 1918 general election constituted a critical turning point in the history of the Irish revolution. As the Inspector General observed in January 1919, 'The victory of the Sinn Fein party at the polls . . . was a foregone conclusion . . . In the Nationalist constituencies the Irish Parliamentary Party . . . suffered a complete debacle . . . [and the Sinn Féin party] was able to command nearly half a million voters—one third of the total register.'[2] On the eve of the election, Sinn Féin had held only seven seats, while the Irish Parliamentary Party dominated Irish nationalist politics with sixty-eight.[3] As a result of its dramatic electoral success, however, Sinn Féin won a staggering seventy-three seats, and the Irish Parliamentary Party held only six.[4] The Home Rule party, which had dominated Irish nationalist politics for a generation, was destroyed by the election, and Sinn Féin became the most popular and influential nationalist organization in Ireland. In 1919, the newly elected Sinn Féin representatives established a separatist parliament, Dáil Éireann, and

---

[1] CI monthly report, west Galway, July 1916, PRO CO 904/100.
[2] IG monthly report, Dec. 1918, PRO CO 904/107.
[3] Lyons, *Ireland since the Famine*, 398.
[4] The remaining twenty-six seats were won by the unionists.

during the course of 1920 they took control of local government, and set up their own land purchase agencies and courts. In short, the moderate Home Rule politics of the Irish Parliamentary Party were replaced by the radical republicanism of Sinn Féin.

While there was a decisive political transformation at the national level, it has been argued that in the provinces the victory of Sinn Féin represented little more than 'a terminological revolution'.[5] In an influential study, David Fitzpatrick argues that the provincial members of Sinn Féin were merely 'the old [Home Rule] wine ... decanted into new bottles':[6]

Early Sinn Féin resembled the late United Irish League to a striking degree. In its post-Rising incarnation it was not so much the League's conqueror as its inheritor. My inquiry into Clare politics suggests that the new movement's political style and organizational technique were largely modelled on those of the old Party, and that the early Sinn Féin clubs tended to be led by men with League or Hibernian experience.[7]

In the provinces, there was 'a thick strand of continuity' between the Home Rule and Sinn Féin movements, with 'much of the early organization of Sinn Féin ... [being] undertaken by former Irish Party adherents'.[8] At the local level, then, Home Rulers appear to have changed their political affiliation and become Sinn Féiners. In part, this continuity of personnel is explained by the absence of an influential separatist tradition in early twentieth-century Ireland. While 'the organised remnants of previous separatist movements' did continue to exist, they 'had little to teach the post-Rising generation, either as politicians or fighting-men'. Indeed, Fitzpatrick suggests that 'in provincial Ireland there was only one political school which mattered—and that was the Home Rule movement'.[9] Because 'Ireland was not large enough to contain two competing nationalist creeds claiming the allegiance of different sexes, ages or income groups',[10] Sinn Féin was obliged to absorb both the personnel and the political tradition of the Home Rule movement. The victory of Sinn Féin, therefore, constituted a purely cosmetic transformation: the slogans may have changed, but the underlying realities of Irish political and social life remained the same.

---

[5] Fitzpatrick, *Politics and Irish Life*, 128   [6] Ibid. 127–8.
[7] David Fitzpatrick, 'The geography of Irish nationalism, 1910–1921', *Past and Present*, 78 (Feb. 1978), 135.
[8] Fitzpatrick, *Politics and Irish life*, 138; Fitzpatrick, 'The geography of Irish nationalism, 1910–1921', 125.
[9] Fitzpatrick, *Politics and Irish life*, 137.
[10] Fitzpatrick, 'The geography of Irish nationalism, 1910–1921', 126.

However, *Politics and Irish life* is based primarily on a study of Clare, and it remains to be seen whether conclusions based on evidence from a single county can be applied more generally to 'provincial' Ireland. Indeed, a study of the continuity of personnel between the United Irish League and Sinn Féin in Galway indicates that only 3 per cent of Sinn Féiners (in 1917–18) had been involved in the United Irish League (in 1914), a far lower level of continuity than that claimed by Fitzpatrick in Clare.[11] This evidence alone suggests that Sinn Féin may have developed along rather different lines in other parts of provincial Ireland. In order to examine the origins of Sinn Féin, this chapter will explore the evolution of separatist politics in county Galway, from the formation of Sinn Féin in 1905 to its electoral victory in December 1918, and including the first detailed narrative account of the 1916 Easter Rising in Galway.

I

The Sinn Féin policy was first adopted by the National Council at a convention held in Dublin in November 1905. In the course of a lengthy speech, Arthur Griffith, a Dublin printer and journalist, outlined his political and economic ideas, which the National Council then resolved to promote through a network of provincial branches.[12] Although it would be two years before the Sinn Féin party was officially formed, it was at this meeting that Sinn Féin first entered the Irish political arena. The policy was largely based on a series of articles by Griffith, first published in the *United Irishman* between January and July 1904, and later republished in 1905 as *The Resurrection of Hungary*.[13] In these articles, he suggested that Irish nationalists should imitate the nineteenth century Hungarian revolutionary Ferenc Deák. The Hungarians had refused to recognize or cooperate with the Austrian regime which governed Hungary, thereby forcing Austria to restore the ancient constitution of the dual monarchy in 1866. Under the terms of the dual monarchy, Austria and Hungary agreed to share a monarch but recognized one another as equal and independent nations.[14]

Griffith argued that Irish nationalist MPs should follow the example of Deák by declaring the Act of Union invalid and withdrawing from

11 See Appendix I for a discussion of the methodology used to calculate the continuities between the membership of the UIL and Sinn Féin in Galway.

12 Davis, *Arthur Griffith*, 23–4; Maume, *The long gestation*, 229.

13 Maume, 'Aspects of Irish nationalist political culture', 35.

14 Laffan, *The resurrection of Ireland*, 18.

Westminster.[15] Instead, the Irish MPs should create an Irish Assembly, on the basis of the General Council of County Councils, and thereby force the British Government to repeal the Act of Union.[16] National-ists were also encouraged to withdraw from the whole edifice of British rule in Ireland—the courts, the police and the army—and to adminis-ter themselves through local authorities and an Irish parliament.[17] This Irish Assembly could then devote itself to economic development. Griffith believed that the Irish economy should be balanced between industry and agriculture.[18] In terms of the former, he advocated the raising of tariffs, in order to encourage and protect Irish industries.[19] Regarding agriculture, on the other hand, he envisaged a radical redistribution of grazing land among smallholders and labourers.[20] This would ensure that half of the Irish population would remain engaged in agricultural production so that the country would be safe from the fluctuations of international markets. Griffith distrusted international trade, and envisaged an Irish economy that was self-sufficient and cut off from the world market.[21]

The Sinn Féin party evolved out of three distinct organizations which had existed in various forms since the turn of the century: Cumann na nGaedheal, the National Council, and the Dungannon clubs. Cumann na nGaedheal was formed in September 1900 by William Rooney, a clerk and journalist, and Arthur Griffith with the aim of bringing about 'the total de-Anglicization of Ireland'.[22] It was, however, a front organiza-tion for the Irish Republican Brotherhood, with the presidency and vice-presidency both occupied by prominent Fenians.[23] The National Council was founded in 1903 to coordinate opposition to the visit of King Edward VII to Dublin. Finally, the Dungannon clubs were formed by two IRB activists, Bulmer Hobson and Denis McCullough, in Belfast in 1905.[24] The clubs aimed to establish an Irish Republic and also demanded that young members attend Gaelic League classes and 'be absolute teetotalers'.[25] The three organizations were united at the third annual convention of the

---

[15] Maume, 'Aspects of Irish nationalist political culture', 36.
[16] Ibid.; Laffan, *The resurrection of Ireland*, 18.   [17] Maume, *The long gestation*, 57.
[18] Davis, *Arthur Griffith*, 128.   [19] Maume, *The long gestation*, 57.
[20] Anthony Varley, 'The politics of agrarian reform: the state, nationalists and the agrarian question in the west of Ireland', (Southern Illinois University, Ph.D., 1994), 219; Davis, *Arthur Griffith*, 129.
[21] Maume, 'Aspects of Irish nationalist political culture', 38.
[22] Davis, *Arthur Griffith*, 17; Maume, *The long gestation*, 242.
[23] Davis, *Arthur Griffith*, 17–18. John O'Leary was the president, and John MacBride and Robert Johnston were vice-presidents, all of whom were members of the IRB.
[24] On the formation of Sinn Féin, see Davis, *Arthur Griffith* 17–36.
[25] Laffan, *The resurrection of Ireland*, 21.

National Council, held in Dublin in August 1907. There were ideological differences within the new party, particularly between Arthur Griffith and Bulmer Hobson. While Griffith promoted the 'Hungarian policy', Hobson (and many of the other Fenians involved in Sinn Féin) remained committed to physical force republicanism. However, the official Sinn Féin programme was based on Griffith's ideas.

Popular support for the Sinn Féin movement in the Irish countryside increased dramatically in the aftermath of the general election of January 1906. After the election, Irish nationalists believed that the Liberal Party would deliver on its pledge to introduce Home Rule. However, in the event, the Liberal Party offered the Irish Parliamentary Party only the Irish Council Bill, a pointedly inadequate measure giving Ireland little more than expanded local government. Irish nationalists felt betrayed by the Liberal Party and rejected the bill out of hand at a national convention in May 1907.[26] In this climate, a substantial number of Irish nationalists began to believe that Sinn Féin's abstentionist policy might be more effective in the campaign for political independence than attendance at Westminster. As a result, the number of UIL branches declined by 14 per cent (and 14,000 members) between 1907 and 1908, while the number of Sinn Féin branches doubled over the same period.[27]

Sinn Féin expanded rapidly outside Dublin between 1907 and 1908. In August 1907, there were 57 Sinn Féin clubs, whereas one year later there were 115 branches.[28] A survey of the reports of branch meetings in *Sinn Féin*, and of the police intelligence on provincial Sinn Féin meetings between 1907 and 1909, indicates the location of 85 of these branches (74 per cent of the total number of branches).[29] Of the 85 branches there were 18 in Munster, 29 in Leinster, 15 in Ulster, 19 in Connacht, 3 in Scotland, and 1 in London. While the majority of Irish branches (52 or 64 per cent) were located in urban areas, there were also a substantial number of branches in the countryside (29 or 36 per cent). Indeed, in Connacht and Munster over half of the Sinn Féin branches were in rural locations (53 per cent and 56 per cent respectively); while in Leinster and Ulster, the

[26] See Ch. 3.

[27] On 31 Dec. 1907, there were 139,283 members of the UIL, while on 31 Mar. 1908, UIL membership had declined to 125,135. United Irish League membership figures, PRO CO 904/20/2. Davis, *Arthur Griffith*, 81–2.

[28] Davis, *Arthur Griffith*, 81–2. Many members of Sinn Féin were not affiliated to individual branches. See James Haverty, 'Memoirs of an ordinary republican', MA BMH CD 72.

[29] In order to identify the locations of Sinn Féin branches throughout Ireland, the Crime Branch Special files on Sinn Féin between October 1907 and December 1908, PRO CO 904/117–18, were systematically examined, as was the newspaper *Sinn Féin* between November 1906 and June 1907.

proportion of rural branches were 21 per cent and 20 per cent respectively.[30] Sinn Féin was thus more rural in the west and the south-west than it was in the east and the north-east. Dublin accounted for the largest number of branches in any one area (eleven), but there were nine branches in Leitrim, seven in Galway, six in Louth, five each in Kerry and Tipperary, and four each in Cork, Wexford, and Cavan. This suggests that the centres of Sinn Féin activity in Ireland between 1906 and 1909 were Dublin, Leitrim, east Galway, the south-west (Cork, Kerry, and Tipperary), Wexford, and the north-east midlands (Cavan and Louth). This suggests quite a broad geographical dispersal of Sinn Féin ideas in a variety of both urban and rural communities. Altogether, there was at least one Sinn Féin branch in twenty-six of the thirty-two Irish counties between 1906 and 1909.

In the provinces, Sinn Féin branches were composed primarily of members of the Irish Republican Brotherhood (IRB). As early as September 1905, the Inspector General observed that the provincial members of Cumann na nGaedheal were recruited from the Irish Republican Brotherhood, and that they advocated 'the "Sinn Fein" or "Hungarian policy"'.[31] Indeed, by the spring of 1907, the police believed that provincial Sinn Féiners were, almost exclusively, members of the Brotherhood: 'It is noticeable . . . that the [local] promoters [of Sinn Féin] are in sympathy with the I.R.B.' and that 'the Sinn Fein movement is becoming more and more the policy of the I.R.B.'[32] In Galway, seven Sinn Féin branches were established in the eighteen months following the 1906 general election. The first branch was formed at Kilreekle in March 1906, followed by branches at Loughrea and Tuam in October, at Mullagh in November, at Craughwell in February 1907, at Galway city in March, and at Athenry in May.[33] As in the rest of the country, the members of these branches were republicans and agrarian agitators. At Kilreekle, for example, the police observed: 'The Officers of . . . [the Sinn Féin branch] have been prominent in local agrarian agitation for the past 20 years, and have suffered imprisonment in connection therewith.'[34] Generally, the members of Sinn Féin in the

[30] This reflects the fact that there were fewer urban dwellers in Munster and Connacht than there were in Leinster and Ulster.   [31] IG monthly report, Sept. 1905, NA IGCI/8.
[32] IG monthly report, Feb. 1907 and Mar. 1907, NA IGCI/11.
[33] Precis of information received in Crime Special Branch, Apr. 1906, PRO CO 904/117; IG monthly report, Oct. 1906, NA IGCI/10; *Sinn Féin*, 17 Nov. 1906, 16 Feb., 23 Mar., 25 May 1907. Of the seven, all were formally constituted Sinn Féin branches except that at Athenry which was initially founded as a branch of the Town Tenants' League. In the aftermath of the Irish Council Bill crisis in May 1907, however, the branch openly advocated the Sinn Féin policy, and its members were described by contemporaries as 'Sinn Féiners', *Sinn Fein*, 25 May 1907; CI monthly report, east Galway, May 1907–May 1908, NA IGCI/11–13.
[34] Précis of information received in Crime Special Branch, Apr. 1906, PRO CO 904/117.

county were recruited from the ranks of the Irish Republican Brotherhood, as the County Inspector noted in August 1907: 'There are about 400
I.R.B. men scattered through the [east] Riding [of county Galway]—no
regular meetings are held but the leaders confer and exchange ideas at fairs
and markets . . . They favour the Sinn Fein movement.'[35]

The most prominent leader of Sinn Féin in Galway was Tom Kenny,
the Craughwell blacksmith. Kenny was born in 1878 at Ardrahan, seven
miles south-west of Craughwell, the son of Matthew and Bridget Kenny.
He was educated at Ardrahan National School and then, following his
father and grandfather, he took up the trade of blacksmith, 'working in
the forge across the road from the house in which he was born'.[36] After
his father's death, he migrated to Craughwell where he undertook most of
the smith work for Thomas Concannon of Rockfield, a stockbroker and
the owner of the local kennels. Kenny was a dominant figure, described
by the police as 'too dictatorial to be personally popular',[37] but capable
of inspiring admiration among his supporters.[38] Gilbert Morrissey later
recalled that Kenny 'had a wonderful personality and inspired us by his
addresses'.[39] He possessed great physical strength and 'strong, sinewy
muscles', which he utilized to the full on the hurling field as the captain
of the Craughwell GAA club.[40] Physically, however, he was of a relatively
slight build, as the following police description of his appearance suggests:
'No marked accent, walks with smart gait, short steps, shows a good deal
of the white of his eyes, near sighted, dark eyes, broad nose, dark com-
plexion, ordinary face, slight make, approximate weight 12 st., 5 ft. 10 ins.
high, about 42 years of age, dark hair, not bald; wore a grey tweed cap, coat,
trousers and vest.'[41] Kenny's political involvement began in 1904 when
he reorganized the Craughwell GAA club and 'that work introduced him
to political activities'.[42] As the president of the Craughwell hurling club,
Kenny came to the attention of Dick Murphy, the IRB centre at Athenry
and a member of the GAA. In 1905 he was sworn into the IRB at Loughrea
by John MacBride, a member of the Supreme Council. Between 1904 and

[35] CI monthly report, east Galway, Aug. 1907, NA IGCI/12.

[36] Tom Kenny's obituary, *Connacht Tribune*, 5 Apr. 1947.

[37] CI monthly report, east Galway, Nov. 1910, PRO CO 904/82.

[38] See letter from Martin Newell, a supporter of Kenny, to the *Connacht Tribune*, 15 Feb.
1966.

[39] Gilbert Morrissey, MA BMH WS 1,138.

[40] Tom Kenny's obituary, *Connacht Tribune*, 5 Apr. 1947.

[41] This description of Kenny, which was first published in *Hue and Cry*, 13 June 1916, when
he was on the run after the Galway Rising, is reprinted in a letter from Martin Newell to the
Connacht Tribune, 19 Mar. 1966. In 1916, Kenny was 38, not 42.

[42] Tom Kenny's obituary, *Connacht Tribune*, 5 Apr. 1947.

1906, Kenny was also a member of the United Irish League but, after reading *The Resurrection of Hungary* in December 1906, he defected to Sinn Féin; and, on 3 February 1907, he founded the fourth Sinn Féin club in Galway at Craughwell.[43]

Kenny quickly became prominent in the GAA, the Irish Republican Brotherhood, and Sinn Féin. In 1905 he was selected as a member of the Galway GAA county board, and four years later he was elected as the president of the Connacht GAA council, a position he would hold for the following seven years. After the death of P. J. Kelly at Killeenadeema on 18 April 1908,[44] the police believed that Kenny had succeeded to the position of IRB county centre,[45] and described him as 'one of the most advanced I.R.B. men in the country . . . [He] is in touch with all leaders of that movement'.[46] Indeed, Kenny was reputed to be the Connacht representative on the Supreme Council of the IRB.[47] By December 1908, he had also become the leader of Sinn Féin in south Galway, as the Inspector General reported: 'The Sinn Fein movement in Athenry and Craughwell is managed by Thomas Kenny . . . who is a most dangerous individual.'[48] As Martin Newell told the Bureau of Military History, 'At that time [1905], Tom Kenny of Craughwell, became IRB centre for the county Galway and he was appointed from Dublin to lead Sinn Fein in the county.'[49] At the local elections in June 1908, Kenny was elected at the head of the poll as a Sinn Féin district councillor,[50] and such was his influence in east Galway that the police referred to him as 'a local monarch'.[51] He also became an associate of prominent Sinn Féiners in Dublin and in September 1910 attended a social entertainment in the Sinn Féin rooms in Dublin, at which Arthur Griffith was present.[52] By the age of 30, Kenny had become the most influential separatist in Galway, and a major figure in the IRB and the GAA in Dublin. He was also a well-known figure in Connacht during this period. On his release from prison in February 1909, having been questioned as to his alleged involvement in the murder of Constable

---

[43] *Sinn Féin*, 16 Feb. 1907.
[44] CI monthly report, east Galway, Apr. 1908, NA IGCI/13.
[45] Précis of information received in Crime Special Branch, Mar. 1909, PRO CO 904/118.
[46] Ibid., Jan. 1909, PRO CO 904/118.
[47] Tom Kenny's obituary, *Connacht Tribune*, 5 Apr. 1947.
[48] IG monthly report, Dec. 1908, NA IGCI/15.
[49] Martin Newell witness statement, MA BMH WS 1,562.
[50] CI monthly report, east Galway, Jan. 1909, PRO CO 904/77. When he sought re-election in June 1911, he did not receive a single vote. Précis of information received in the Crime Special Branch, June 1911, PRO CO 904/119.
[51] Précis of information received in Crime Special Branch, June 1911, PRO CO 904/119.
[52] Précis of information and reports on secret societies, Sept. 1910, PRO CO 904/12.

Goldrick at Craughwell, he wore a green and white ribbon, said to have been sent him by Mrs Stenson, Riverstown, with her thanks for avenging the death of her son.[53] John Stenson had been shot dead on 29 October 1908 when the Royal Irish Constabulary opened fire on a crowd of 100 cattle drivers at Ardcumber, county Sligo, making him the only casualty of the Ranch War.[54] This gesture suggests that Kenny was regarded as a symbol of the wider radical agrarian agitation against both the grazier and the state. Such was his influence that the Chief Secretary was reputed to ask: 'Was Ireland to be governed by a water bailiff in Dublin [John MacBride] and a blacksmith in Galway [Tom Kenny]'[55]

Kenny was also the leader of an agrarian secret society. The Galway secret society, as it became known, first came to the attention of the police in August 1907, when the County Inspector reported: 'A secret organisation for the commission of crime unconnected with [the] I.R.B. exists in Craughwell and its neighbourhood. It devotes its attention exclusively to agrarian matters.'[56] The Inspector General identified Kenny as the leader of this secret society, writing: 'He controls . . . [the] Secret organisation which commits crime.'[57] By May 1908, the secret society had 'taken the power out of the hands of the United Irish League' in south Galway.[58] A substantial proportion of Sinn Féiners in Galway were also members of the secret society. At Loughrea, for example, the leaders of Sinn Féin were 'the old Secret Society men who have not taken any part in the United Irish League and are opposed to it'.[59] Martin Dolan,[60] who interviewed a large number of former Sinn Féiners for a series of articles published in the *Connacht Tribune* in 1966, observed that 'when the policy of Sinn Fein began to spread it moved through the old "Secret Society areas" where once had flourished the "Threshers", the "Ribbonmen", and the Terry

53 CI monthly report, east Galway, Feb 1909, PRO CO 904/77.

54 IG monthly report, Oct. 1908, NA IGCI/14. A monument to Stenson was erected at Riverstown on 31 October 1909. IG monthly report, Oct. 1909, PRO CO 904/79.

55 Quoted in a letter from Martin Newell to the *Connacht Tribune*, 19 Feb. 1966.

56 CI monthly report, east Galway, Aug. 1907, IGCI/12.

57 CI monthly report, east Galway, Nov. 1908, IGCI/15.

58 CI monthly report, east Galway, May 1908, IGCI/13.

59 CI monthly report, east Galway, Aug. 1907, IGCI/12.

60 Martin Dolan wrote a series of articles on the Easter Rising in Galway for the *Connacht Tribune* in 1966 (see *Connacht Tribune*, 2, 9, 16, and 23 Apr. 1966). These articles are of particular use because they were 'compiled from interviews with many of the survivors. He [Dolan] spent many an afternoon during the past three months with leaders of the Rising in south and east Galway recording on tape and in notebook, checking stories against each other and dovetailing them into the story that is now running in this paper', *Connacht Tribune*, 9 Apr. 1966. Dolan was the principal of Ardrahan National School, the south Galway correspondent of the *Connacht Tribune*, and the president of the Ardrahan Fianna Fáil cumann (branch).

Alts, that is the country areas of south, middle and north Galway'.[61] And the police commented that 'the leaders of . . . Sinn Fein [in Galway] are all Secret Society men . . . , many of them are moonlighters and all [of them] are disloyal in the extreme'.[62] Indeed, the secret society was described by the police as 'the back bone of the Sinn Fein movement in this county'.[63]

The Galway secret society, under the leadership of Kenny, first came to prominence in 1907, but the police believed that it was 'a revival of the "Invincible" society'. According to the Galway Special Serjeant, who had received information from different sources, a branch of the Invincibles organization had been formed in 1881 by 'Dublin tradesmen who had been working at Tullyra Castle and Tyrone House [at Clarinbridge]'.[64] There is some evidence to suggest that this was the case. George Fleming, a Fenian from Clarinbridge, was a member of the Invincibles who emigrated to the United States to evade arrest after the assassination of Cavendish and Burke in 1882.[65] However, it is impossible to prove or disprove the Government's assumption that a branch of the Invincibles was responsible for a series of agrarian murders committed in south Galway between 1880 and 1882.[66] These murders may have been carried out by the Invincibles, but it is more likely that they were carried out by local members of the IRB. Martin Newell indicates that this was the case in his account of the shooting of Walter Bourke at Castledaly in 1882:

My father, John Newell, was centre of the IRB for the barony of Dunkellin in the 1880s and, during that time, there was considerable agrarian trouble in the area. In 1882, he worked as a ploughman for Dr. Burke [*sic*] of Rahasane, a landlord. About the only good quality Dr. Burke had was that he never interfered with the men who worked on his farm.

Agitation was high against the landlords at this particular time and Dr. Burke left for a holiday in England. On his return from holiday, he had with him for his protection two English soldiers (Redcoats) who were armed with Winchester rifles. In the afternoon of the day of Dr. Burke's return home, he walked to the extreme end of the farm to where my father was ploughing and walked alongside of him, talking to him for a considerable time while he was ploughing. The

---

[61] *Connacht Tribune*, 2 Apr. 1966.

[62] CI monthly report, west Galway, Nov. 1915, PRO CO 904/98.

[63] CI monthly report, west Galway, June 1916, PRO CO 904/100.

[64] Précis of information and reports on secret societies, May 1910, PRO CO 904/12.

[65] Joseph Murphy, *The Redingtons of Clarinbridge: leading Catholic landlords in the nineteenth century* (Dublin, 1999), 245.

[66] P. J. Tynan attributed the murder of Walter Bourke at Castledaly in 1882 to the Invincibles, and John Mallon of the DMP also linked the Invincibles to two 'very dark agrarian murders', one at Loughrea. See Leon Ó Broin, 'The Invincibles', in T. D. Williams (ed.), *Secret societies in Ireland* (Dublin, 1973), 122–3.

following morning, Dr. Burke went to Gort to get ejectment orders against some of his tenants. He travelled in a back-to-back horse trap accompanied by one of the soldiers who, of course, was armed. On his way home from Gort he was ambushed at Castledaly by five IRB men armed with shotguns. Dr. Burke, the soldier and the horse were shot dead. The slugs used in this attack were actually in my father's pocket the afternoon before when Dr. Burke walked alongside him whilst he was ploughing.[67]

Although we do not know whether the other agrarian murders committed in the region were carried out by the Invincibles or the IRB, it is clear that there was a strong tradition of secret society activity in south Galway, and that Kenny was able to revive this tradition in the early years of the twentieth century. Indeed, Newell explicitly points out that, 'the connecting links between that period [the 1880s] and the founding of Sinn Fein in 1905 were certainly the Land League, the IRB movement and the GAA'.[68]

Like its precursor, Kenny's secret society was associated with the Irish Republican Brotherhood. The County Inspector noted, in February 1909, that the secret society which had existed for a number of years had recently become connected with the IRB.[69] This was the source of some confusion for both the police and the Government, as the County Inspector commented: 'It is peculiar however that the members go in for outrage in connection with agrarian disputes as this is not in accordance with the I.R.B. principles.'[70] However, other sources indicate that the secret society was absorbed into the Irish Republican Brotherhood. An article published in *An t-Óglach* in 1936 by 'a Galway man' who had been involved in the Galway Rising claims that 'Acting on the suggestion of Mr. [Martin] Finnerty of Gurteen, the extreme republicans in Galway were permitted [by the leaders of the IRB] to identify themselves with the agrarian agitation.'[71] The regularity with which John MacBride and Sean MacDermott, a member of the IRB and founder of the separatist newspaper *Irish Freedom*, visited Athenry in this period to meet Kenny and the other secret society leaders substantiates this claim. On 26 November 1907, for example, MacBride visited Athenry and Craughwell:

He was in conversation with suspects Laurence Lardner, Richard Murphy, and Thomas Kenny, who are leaders of the G.A.A., Gaelic League, and Sinn Fein movements in their respective localities, and are said to have great influence with the younger generation. It has been ascertained that he was trying to organise

---

67 Martin Newell witness statement, MA BMH WS 1,562.   68 Ibid.
69 CI monthly report, east Galway, Feb. 1909, PRO CO 904/77.
70 Ibid.
71 A Galway man, 'Galway and the 1916 Rising', *An t-Óglach*, Feb. 1936.

the I.R.B. in these places. He stated that he was in sympathy with the Sinn Fein movement.[72]

In July 1909, Sean MacDermott spent nine days in Galway and associated mainly with members of the Galway secret society.[73] It is likely that both MacBride and MacDermott, who were keen to re-establish the IRB in Galway, were prepared to reach a compromise with the secret society; and this suggests the extraordinary influence which the secret society possessed in the county. In the event, MacBride allowed the secret society to retain its radical agrarian policy, and still be subsumed within the IRB organization. And MacBride's personal involvement led to the secret society being renamed the 'Major MacBride I.R.B.'[74]

The secret society shared the broader republican aims of the IRB. A young farmer, sworn into the secret society by Martin Finnerty, told the police that its objectives were: '1. Enmity to England. 2. Hostility & opposition to English law and government. 3. Separation from England. [And] 4. To prevent recruiting.'[75] However, the primary aim of the Galway secret society was to effect the rapid redistribution of grazing land among the rural poor.[76] The Irish land question remained unsolved long after the introduction of the Wyndham Land Act of 1903.[77] In particular, the Act had failed to address the problem of congestion, and the secret society agitated to divide grazing farms. Kenny had been a member of the United Irish League and, even after his conversion to Sinn Féin, he often assisted individual UIL branches in their campaigns against graziers.[78] At a meeting of the Craughwell hurling club in 1910, he stated that he 'was never found wanting in fighting the grazier and grabber, and he challenged any man to point out a single act where he supported any man condemned by the United Irish League'.[79] For members of the secret society, the two struggles for political independence and land redistribution were closely intertwined. Gilbert Morrissey, who was sworn into the IRB by Kenny in 1906, recalled that 'Kenny's main concern was to keep the spark of nationality alive in us until the opportunity came. This was not so difficult in county Galway because, in a sense, arms were never put away. If the people were not fighting against the British forces proper, they were making a fair stand against its henchmen, the tyrant landlord class, their agents and

[72] Précis of information received in Crime Special Branch, Dec. 1907, PRO CO 904/117.
[73] CI monthly report, east Galway, July 1909, PRO CO 904/78.
[74] CI monthly report, east Galway, Oct. 1909, PRO CO 904/79.   [75] Ibid.
[76] IG monthly report, Oct. 1910, PRO CO 904/82.   [77] See Ch. 3.
[78] In February 1908, Kenny assisted the Kilconieron branch of the United Irish League in its agitation against Mr Blake of Hollypark. CI monthly report, east Galway, Feb. 1908, NA IGCI/13.   [79] *Connacht Tribune*, 24 Dec. 1910.

bailiffs, who were backed up and protected by the Royal Irish Constabulary.'[80] Even so, some members of the revived secret society suggest that it was becoming more republican during the early years of the new century. Patrick Callanan witheringly describes the 'older members of the IRB [who] were in the organisation solely for the purpose of obtaining land and had no national outlook'.[81]

The agrarian aims of the secret society, then, were similar to those of the UIL. However, unlike the UIL, the Galway secret society was prepared to use illegal and violent methods to achieve its objectives. As an informer told the police in October 1909, 'The commission of outrages, generally firing at the person, is the principal weapon of attack [used by the secret society] on those whom it is sought to subdue, and if these are not followed by submission, murder is the alternative.'[82] The same informant added that the secret society members were keen 'to avoid the police but that they . . . [were] to be shot if necessary to escape capture'.[83] The killing of Constable Goldrick at Craughwell in January 1909 by members of the secret society indicates that this was not an idle boast. The agitation for the redistribution of the substantial Monatigue grazing farm (valued at £275) owned by Máirtín Mór McDonagh, a prominent Galway city businessman, illustrates the various strategies used by the secret society to achieve its objectives.[84] On 6 June 1907, an attempt was made to burn Monatigue House, resulting in considerable damage; a month later, one of the labourers who worked on the farm (Walter Burke) was 'frightened into leaving Mr. McDonagh's employment by the firing of shots outside his house'; and in August, one of the herds (Patrick Morrissey) received a threatening letter. During the first half of 1907, efforts were made to petition the Estates Commissioners to purchase the farm for division among the tenants, but to no avail. Consequently, on 26 July 1907 'eighteen head of cattle were either driven off the farm, or allowed to stray through the breaking of the fences, the object being to put pressure on the Estates Commissioners to purchase and divide the farm'. The agitation culminated, however, in 'a daring outrage' committed on the night of 28 August:

an armed party fired some twenty gun and revolver shots into Monatigue House, breaking a number of windows, but doing no further damage. The house was

---

[80] Gilbert Morrissey witness statement, MA BMH WS 1,138.

[81] Patrick Callanan witness statement, MA BMH WS 347.

[82] Précis of information received in Crime Special Branch, Oct. 1909, PRO CO 904/118.

[83] CI monthly report, east Galway, Oct. 1909, PRO CO 904/79.

[84] Patrick Callanan confirms the involvement of the IRB in the agitation to redistribute 'the farm of Monatigue owned by Mr. Martin McDonagh of Galway', Patrick Callanan witness statement, MA BMH WS 347. On McDonagh, see Ch. 6.

occupied at the time by six labourers engaged saving hay on the farm. Two police patrols in the vicinity heard the firing, and one of the patrols observed a number of armed men and pursued them, but were unable to overtake them. Some shots were fired by both patrols.[85]

According to the County Inspector, the attacking party numbered ten and they cocked their guns when challenged by the police, who opened fire on the secret society members as they made their escape through nearby bushes.[86] Although this agitation did not succeed in forcing McDonagh to sell his farm to the Estates Commissioners, this case study demonstrates the violent methods that the secret society were prepared to use to promote land redistribution in east Galway.[87]

The local Roman Catholic hierarchy was vehemently opposed to the Galway secret society. In February 1909, in his Lenten pastoral, Bishop Thomas O'Dea 'said that he had reason to believe secret societies existed in certain parishes in his diocese . . . [and that] he condemned them'.[88] The clergy at Ahascragh, Ballinderreen, Craughwell, Cummer, Gurteen, Kinvara, Gurteen, Oranmore, and Turloughmore also warned their parishioners against joining secret societies.[89] Clerical opposition to the secret society was motivated primarily by a concern that the Church was losing its influence over the young men in the region. According to the police, 'The priests . . . are extremely anxious to see Kenny discredited because of the number of young fellows drawn by him into the secret society.'[90] Indeed, Father Quinn, the parish priest at Craughwell, privately informed the police that Tom Kenny 'takes the young fellows of the parish in hands as soon as they leave school, and gets them to join his G.A.A. Club, and they are only a short time members of this Club when they are sworn into this Secret Society'.[91] At Craughwell, Father Davoren even asked Kenny's permission to purchase a garden on which to build a curate's residence for himself, suggesting the extent of Kenny's power in the village.[92] Certainly there is evidence that during the first half of 1909,

[85] The confidential print, 1907–8, PRO CO 903/14/55.
[86] CI monthly report, east Galway, Aug. 1907, NA IGCI/12.
[87] The agitation of 1907–8 was itself a revival of an agitation to divide the farm in 1901–2 carried out by the Craughwell United Irish League branch (see Ch. 2). McDonagh agreed to give up the farm in 1920 following further agitation (see Ch. 6).
[88] Précis of information received in Crime Special Branch, Feb. 1909, PRO CO 904/118.
[89] CI monthly report, east Galway, Feb. 1909, PRO CO 904/77; précis of information and reports on secret societies, Nov. and Dec. 1910, PRO CO 904/12; ibid., Feb. 1911, PRO CO 904/13; précis of information received in Crime Special Branch, Sept. 1909, PRO CO 904/118.   [90] CI monthly report, east Galway, Jan. 1911, PRO CO 904/83.
[91] Précis of information received in Crime Special Branch, Feb. 1909, PRO CO 904/118.
[92] CI monthly report, east Galway, Mar. 1909, PRO CO 904/77.

the secret society had gained a position of influence to rival (and perhaps supersede) that of the Catholic Church among certain sections of east Galway society. The County Inspector, for example, observed in February 1909, 'It will be interesting to see whether the clergy can regain control. I fear however in parts of the Riding matters have gone too far.'[93]

The secret society had a complex relationship with the Catholic Church. All of the members of the society were practising Catholics, who continued to attend mass despite being condemned from the pulpit for their activities.[94] However, the leaders of the secret society appear to have believed that the Church did not have the right to intervene in political or agrarian matters. New recruits to the secret society swore an oath 'that they . . . [would] conceal from the priest in confession the fact of being a member',[95] thereby undermining the power of the confessional; and members of the society suspected that there was collusion between the Royal Irish Constabulary and the Catholic clergy. James Haverty, of Springlawn, near Moylough, who joined the IRB in 1910, told the Bureau of Military History:

Once we were suspected [of membership of the IRB] the R.I.C. adopted two ways of trying to undermine us. One was to warn our parents that we were embarking on dangerous seas and to ask them [to] advise us differently, with of course the usual predictions of what was likely to happen to us if we did continue in our bad ways. The other was to warn the Parish Priest that we were organising secret societies in the Parish. Secret societies are, of course, strictly forbidden by the Catholic Church, but the only way the I.R.B. could be brought into the category of secret societies was by assuming that the British Government was the legally constituted Government of Ireland. In many cases some of the older priests of the country and also the bishops, took the view that Dublin Castle and all it stood for was the legal Government of Ireland. Hence the condemnation of the I.R.B. and also of the Fenians.[96]

Indeed, there is some evidence that Catholic priests passed on information regarding the secret society to the Constabulary, and this probably explains why the police were able to gain such accurate information about the membership of the society.[97] Patrick Callanan, for example, points

[93] CI monthly report, east Galway, Feb. 1909. PRO CO 904/77.
[94] James Haverty, who was sworn into the IRB in 1910, continued to attend mass at Mount Bellew although he had been denounced by the parish priest during a sermon. Haverty, 'Memoirs of an ordinary republican', MA BMH CD 72.
[95] CI monthly report, east Galway, May 1909, PRO CO 904/78.
[96] Haverty, 'Memoirs of an ordinary republican', MA BMH CD 72.
[97] Father Quinn, the parish priest at Craughwell, 'privately' passed on information to the police regarding the secret society in February 1909. Précis of information received in Crime Special Branch, Feb. 1909, PRO CO 904/118.

out that 'The strange thing about it was that immediately after joining the organisation, members were questioned by the police about agrarian incidents, although never questioned before. In fact, the police never questioned anyone except members of the I.R.B.'[98] This is in stark contrast to the earlier agitations orchestrated by the United Irish League, which had clerical support, and during which the police were unable to obtain any information whatsoever.[99]

Tom Kenny's personal relationship with the Catholic Church is of particular interest and probably influenced the views of other members of the secret society. On 12 September 1909, Bishop O'Dea held a visitation in the parish of Craughwell during which he

referred at length to the murder of Constable Goldrick and to the growth of Secret Societies in that neighbourhood. He deplored the death of the Constable and condemned the many outrages on person and property which had occurred in the parish. Alluding to Secret Societies he said: that young men ought not to be gulled into joining them, and asked those who were already members, 'for God's sake to keep away from the meetings and not to obey the orders of the leaders who always took care to keep their own cowardly skins safe while getting their unfortunate dupes to carry out their evil behests.' During His Lordship's address, Suspect Thomas Kenny, Craughwell, head of the local Secret Society, and Suspect Thomas Martin of Crinnage, Kenny's second in command, stood up and left the church. Kenny, when passing Thomas Niland's house, where Constables Moffett and Devine were on protection duty, was heard to say—'It is enough to give one the blues to be in there.'[100]

Kenny's open defiance of the Bishop must have had a powerful impact on the young members of the secret society who remained in the church, and strongly suggested that Kenny's power was comparable to that of the Church in the locality. There is some evidence that Kenny may have personally tended towards atheism, although this appears to have developed later in his life, notably after he embraced socialist ideas in Boston in 1919.[101] Before emigrating, however, he continued attending mass, and was married in the Catholic Church in 1916.[102] Even so, his ambivalence towards clerical power is striking, and his open defiance of

---

[98] Patrick Callanan witness statement, MA BMH WS 347.
[99] See Ch. 2.
[100] Précis of information received in Crime Special Branch, Sept. 1909, PRO CO 904/118.
[101] Interview with Gerry Cloonan, 6 June 1995; Patrick Callanan witness statement, MA BMH WS 405. In Boston, Kenny renewed his friendship with Jim Larkin with whom he had been friendly in Dublin during the 1913 strike. It should also be noted that Kenny received the last rites before he died. See Kenny's obituary, *Connacht Tribune*, 5 Apr. 1947.
[102] Tom Kenny's obituary, *Connacht Tribune*, 5 Apr. 1947.

the Roman Catholic hierarchy was unusual during the first decade of the new century.[103]

The members of the secret society initiated a systematic agitation to force the redistribution of grazing land in county Galway. In an account of his experiences in the secret society, Patrick Callanan writes:

I joined the Clarinbridge circle of the Irish Republican Brotherhood in April 1905 ... Meetings were held regularly every three weeks; occasionally weekly meetings were held. The principal matters discussed at the meetings were, land division, methods to be adopted to compel landlords to sell holdings to the tenant farmers, which included cattle driving, breaking walls and the firing into the houses of landlords and their supporters.[104]

Similarly, Michael Newell, a blacksmith, provides the following account of his involvement in the Castlegar IRB:

I joined the Athenry Circle of the Irish Republican Brotherhood in 1908 ... Sometime later a Circle was started at Castlegar and I was transferred to it ... There were about thirty members in the Circle. Meetings were held regularly every fortnight and sometimes oftener. Members subscribed twopence per week for the purchase of arms and to defray branch expenses. The principal matters discussed at the meetings were, the recruiting of new members and land division.

At this time there was a great deal of agitation for the division of land. The I.R.B. took a leading part in the agitation and carried out numerous cattle drives, also the breaking down of walls on the farms of landlords and land-grabbers, whose houses were also fired into.[105]

Members of the secret society also pursued their agrarian objectives through other organizations. At Athenry, for example, the leaders of the separatist Town Tenants' League were members of the secret society, and associates of Tom Kenny.[106] In the years between 1906 and 1908, the TTL was responsible for orchestrating a comprehensive agrarian agitation against graziers and landlords in the Athenry region. According to the County Inspector,

103 In the 1930s, Kenny is reputed to have generated controversy by refusing to stand for the angelus at a GAA county convention in Galway. Interview with Tom Kelly of Loughrea, 13 Sept. 2003. This incident is also alluded to in a letter from Peter O'Farrell (2 Mar. 1966) published in the *Connacht Tribune*, 2 Apr. 1966.

104 Patrick Callanan witness statement, MA BMH WS 347.

105 Michael Newell witness statement, MA BMH WS 342. Michael Newell was a friend and associate of Tom Kenny, see Martin Newell's letter to the *Connacht Tribune*, 19 Feb. 1966. Brian Molloy, another member of the Castlegar IRB circle, confirms that 'the members took a leading part in the agitation for the division of land in the area'. Brian Molloy witness statement, MA BMH WS 345.

106 The leaders of the Athenry Town Tenants' League were Stephen Jordan, Lawrence Lardner, Dick Murphy, P. J. Holland, and William O'Reilly. For photographs of these men, see *Connacht Tribune*, 27 Nov. 1909.

the TTL 'takes up cases in which the Athenry United Irish League will not interfere and has practically supplanted the latter organisation as a guiding body. A number of town rowdies are members and enforce its wishes with terrorism.'[107] Stephen Jordan, a leading member of the secret society and the TTL, recalled:

> In or about 1908 a strong branch of the Town Tenants' Organisation was formed in Athenry. Although it was against IRB rules to join it, all members did so. This organisation by agitation and agrarian outrages, as the British Authorities called them, succeeded in forcing the sale of the houses to the tenants and also the division of the adjoining lands in what was then called accommodation plots to each tenant purchaser. This led to a series of activities for the division of lands in all areas bordering Athenry.[108]

As a result of a concerted campaign, involving both cattle driving and the non-payment of rent, a number of estates were sold, grazing land was redistributed, and 800 viable small farms were created.[109]

In March 1910, Martin Finnerty formed the United Estates Committee (UEC). This organization, which had branches on at least fifteen east Galway properties, was mainly composed of members of the secret society.[110] The primary aim of the UEC was 'to force the Congested Districts Board to acquire by compulsion or otherwise every acre of grazing land for division amongst the people'.[111] This organization was also involved in the agitation to force landlords to sell their estates on terms dictated by the tenants.[112] In order to achieve this aim, the leadership advocated the use of violent intimidation. At a meeting held in April 1910, for example, the United Estates Committee sanctioned the use of violence in the campaign to redistribute grazing land.[113] As a result of the United Estates Committee's activities, an anti-grazier agitation of 'considerable force' swept across east Galway in the summer of 1910, prompting the police to observe that there was 'a general conspiracy to compel the immediate distribution of [grazing] farms by means of outrage & intimidation'.[114] By September,

---

[107] CI monthly report, east Galway, May 1907, NA IGCI/11.
[108] Stephen Jordan witness statement, MA BMH WS 346.
[109] *Connacht Tribune*, 4 Dec. 1909.
[110] *Connacht Tribune*, 19 Mar. 1910; CI monthly report, east Galway, July 1910, PRO CO 904/81; IG monthly report, Mar. 1910, PRO CO 904/80.
[111] CI monthly report, east Galway, Mar. 1910, PRO CO 904/80.
[112] Ibid.
[113] At this meeting, a resolution passed at a previous UEC conference which had condemned the commission of agrarian crime was rescinded. CI monthly report, east Galway, Apr. 1910, PRO CO 904/80.
[114] CI monthly report, east Galway, July 1910, PRO CO 904/81.

the UEC was 'thoroughly organized' and had become—as far as the police were concerned—'an effective agency for evil'.[115]

Some members of the secret society were also members of the United Irish League.[116] As we have seen, before the formation of Sinn Féin, a number of prominent Galway republicans—including Tom Kenny—had been involved in the United Irish League. Indeed, the Chief Secretary estimated that one-tenth of the membership of the United Irish League in Ireland at the turn of the century were members of the IRB.[117] After the formation of Sinn Féin in 1905, however, many of these republicans withdrew from the League and joined the new party. Even so, a number of republicans retained their membership of the United Irish League. In May 1910, the Galway Special Serjeant observed:

[Some] members [of the Galway secret society] have . . . joined the U. I. League and are known to each other, though not to ordinary members, as the 'Secret League', and where open intimidation of the ordinary character is not successful in compelling persons to obey the League mandates, the 'Secret League' resorts to outrage to bring about the desired effect.[118]

As we have seen, there were two wings of the United Irish League: a radical agrarian section, which was associated with the secret society and the IRB, and a moderate, constitutional group, composed of large farmers and shopkeepers.[119] Both were committed to the redistribution of land, but the radical wing was prepared to use more violent methods to achieve it. Even after the formation of Sinn Féin, some secret society members remained involved in the UIL, and ensured that it contributed to the violent agitation to force the sale of estates and the redistribution of grazing land.[120]

After the introduction of Birrell's Land Bill in parliament in the autumn of 1908, the National Directory of the United Irish League changed its policy on agrarian agitation. Having encouraged an 'active agitation' since June 1907, the leadership now discouraged renewed agitation, believing that it would hinder the progress of the Land Bill in the House of Commons.[121] Although there was some uncertainty as to the policy which the

[115] IG monthly report, Sept. 1910, PRO CO 904/82.
[116] While figures are not available, the County Inspector reported that 'many UIL members belong to the secret society', CI monthly report, east Galway, May 1909, PRO CO 904/78.
[117] Wyndham to Balfour, 26 Nov. 1900, BM ABP Add. MS 49,803/139–144ᵛ.
[118] Précis of information and reports on secret societies, May 1910, PRO CO 904/12.
[119] See Ch. 4.
[120] According to the County Inspector, the IRB, Sinn Féin, the GAA, and the UIL 'work hand in hand', CI monthly report, east Galway, Nov. 1909, PRO CO 904/79.
[121] See IG monthly reports, Oct. and Dec. 1908, NA IGCI/14–15.

Irish Parliamentary Party would adopt towards the new Land Act (which became law in September 1909), by the early months of 1910 it was clear that the leaders of the United Irish League had 'ceased to advocate what is known as "active" agitation'.[122] However, between 1909 and 1914, agrarian conflict remained significant in at least fifteen counties.[123] The agitation aimed to force landlords to sell both their tenanted and untenanted land through the dual strategy of rent combinations and anti-grazier activity,[124] and an impression of the volume of agrarian conflict in Ireland during this period is provided in Table 12. In the post-Ranch War period, these agitations tended to be promoted by local radicals who remained members of the United Irish League (like the so-called 'secret League') and by alternative organizations like the United Estates Committee.

A study of the social background of 211 members of the Galway secret society (see Tables 13, 14 and 15) indicates that 60 per cent of them were farmers and farmers' sons, most of whom occupied small farms.[125] Almost one-fifth (18 per cent) were tradesmen, and 13 per cent were agricultural labourers. Of the remainder, 4 per cent were professionals (solicitors and teachers), 3 per cent were small shopkeepers, and 2 per cent were shop assistants. As we might expect from an organization committed to the redistribution of grazing land, the members of the secret society were the rural poor: small farmers, farmers' sons, and landless agricultural labourers (73 per cent). However, the leaders were often the artisans, small businessmen, and professionals who founded Sinn Féin in the villages and small towns of Galway.[126]

Kenny acted as a bridge between the local politics of the Galway secret society and the 'national' politics of Sinn Féin and the IRB. Between March 1909 and November 1913, he travelled from Craughwell to Dublin on at least sixty-seven occasions, ostensibly on GAA business, but his trips also allowed him to meet with prominent members of both Sinn Féin and the IRB.[127] According to the police, who observed all of Kenny's movements

[122] IG monthly report, Feb. 1910, PRO CO 904/80.

[123] Between 1909 and 1914, there was agrarian agitation in Galway, Sligo, Roscommon, Leitrim, and Mayo (in Connacht), in Clare, Limerick, Tipperary, and Cork (in Munster), in Longford, Westmeath, Meath, King's, Queen's, and Kilkenny (in Leinster), and in Cavan (in Ulster). See IG monthly reports, Jan. 1909; Mar. 1909; Feb. 1910; Aug. 1910; and Feb. 1911, PRO CO 904/77–83.

[124] See IG monthly report, Feb. 1909, PRO CO 904/77; IG monthly report, Aug. 1910, PRO CO 904/81.

[125] See Appendix I for a discussion of the methodology of this study.

[126] For a discussion of the involvement of these social groups in the separatist movement, see Ch. 6.

[127] Précis of information and reports on secret societies, Mar. 1909–Nov. 1913, PRO CO 904/12–14.

TABLE 12. Agrarian agitation in Ireland, 1907–14.

Year	Agrarian outrages	Cattle drives	Rent combinations (average per month)
1907	372	390	27
1908	576	681	45
1909	397	200	36
1910	420	188	25
1911	324	114	17
1912	307	69	17
1913	190	55	8
1914	235	127	4

Sources: Breandán Mac Giolla Choille (ed.), *Intelligence notes, 1913–16* (Dublin, 1966), 62, 124, 246; the confidential print, 1907–8, PRO CO 903/14/37–8; the confidential print, 1910–11, PRO CO 903/16/161–2; the confidential print, 1912–13, PRO CO 903/17/45–6; IG monthly reports, Jan. 1907–Dec. 1914, NA IGCI/11–15 and PRO CO 904/77–95.

TABLE 13. The occupations of the Galway secret society and the 1916 insurgents.

Occupation	Secret society members/ 1916 insurgents (%)	Galway in 1911 (%)
Farmer	34	39
Farmer's son	26	24
Shopkeeper-grazier	0	
Business	3	
Clerk/shop assistant	2	
Professional	4	
Student	0	
Artisan	18	
Labourer	13	
Number	211	

Notes and sources: see Appendix I

throughout this period, he was in regular contact with John MacBride, Sean MacDermott, Bulmer Hobson, and Tom Clarke, all of whom were members of the Supreme Council of the IRB. Martin Newell confirms that 'Kenny used to go to Dublin fairly often and became acquainted with Tom Clarke, Sean MacDermott, Austin Stack, Sean Milroy, Eoin O'Duffy, Lorcan O'Toole, Dinny McCullough, Dick Fitzgerald and many of the leaders ... [He] had come under police notice and was regarded by them

TABLE 14. The valuation of the family farm of farmers and farmers' sons involved in the secret society and the Galway Rising

Valuation (£n)	Secret society members/ Galway insurgents (%)
$n<4$	0
$4\leq n<10$	25
$10\leq n<20$	44
$20\leq n<30$	25
$30\leq n<50$	6
$50\leq n<100$	0
$n\geq100$	0
Number	16

Notes and sources: See Appendix I.

TABLE 15. The ages of the members of the Galway secret society and the 1916 rebels (in 1916)

Age	Secret society members/ Galway insurgents (%)
0–19	3
20–9	57
30–9	25
40–9	6
50–9	3
60+	6
Number	67

Notes and sources: See Appendix I.

as being a dangerous man. On his trips to Dublin and elsewhere he was always followed by two detectives.'[128] Indeed, Kenny attended an IRB meeting at the Thomond Hotel in Dublin in August 1909, leading the Under-Secretary to notify the Chief Secretary of 'the position Kenny of Craughwell seems to have attained in the I.R.B.'[129] But most of Kenny's meetings with Fenian leaders were informal. He regularly met with John MacBride, for instance, at the Royal Exchange Hotel on Parliament

[128] Martin Newell witness statement, MA BMH WS 1,562. Newell adds that 'I was familiar with the names of these men from listening to him [Kenny] telling of discussion he had with them long before they became known to the general public.'

[129] Précis of information and reports on secret societies, Sept. 1909, PRO CO 904/12.

Street, or at the GAA grounds at Jones' Road, where they associated during hurling matches.[130] The primary purpose of Kenny's visits to Dublin, however, was to attend the twice-monthly meetings of the GAA central council, of which he was a member. In this context, Kenny was closely associated with Jim Nowlan and Lawrence O'Toole, the president and secretary of the Association, and with a number of other well-known Gaelic revivalists.[131] As a prominent member of Sinn Féin, the GAA, and the IRB in Dublin, Kenny was in a position to absorb the new political and cultural ideas that were circulating in the capital, and to carry them back to the provinces. At a meeting of the Craughwell hurling club in December 1910, for example, a number of members of the team who had been influenced by Kenny stated that they had read *The Resurrection of Hungary* and were now supporters of the Sinn Féin policy.[132]

The police reported that there were 400 members of the IRB who supported Sinn Féin in the east riding of Galway in August 1907, but they provide no corresponding figure for the west riding.[133] However, the secret society was expanding in this period, with new circles being formed throughout east and west Galway between 1907 and 1909.[134] By May 1909, the secret society had been established at Athenry, Bullaun, Craughwell, Gurteen, Gurtymadden, Kilchreest, Kiltulla, Loughrea, Monivea, Moyvilla, New Inn, and Peterswell in the east riding, and at Ardrahan, Gort, Kilcolgan, and Oranmore in the west riding.[135] Throughout 1910, the society expanded further into the north of the county with circles formed at Cummer and Turloughmore,[136] and there were also circles of the secret society in neighbouring county Clare.[137] There were members of the secret society in the United Irish League, the United Estates Committee, and the Town Tenants' League, leading the police to believe that the society embraced 'a considerable number of persons',[138] and it is likely that there were between 500 and 1,000 members of the secret society in the county. Despite the relatively small membership, particularly

---

[130] Ibid., Mar. and Dec. 1909, PRO CO 904/12.

[131] Ibid., Sept. 1909 and Jan. 1910, PRO CO 904/12.

[132] *Connacht Tribune*, 24 Dec. 1910.

[133] CI monthly report, east Galway, Aug. 1907, NA IGCI/12. There were forty-nine members in the Kilreekle branch of Sinn Féin, and if there were a similar number of members in each of the other six branches, there would have been approximately 343 members of Sinn Féin in Galway in 1907, *Sinn Féin*, 3 Nov. 1906.

[134] IG monthly report, Feb. 1913, PRO CO 904/89; IG monthly report, Mar. 1911, PRO CO 904/83.

[135] CI monthly reports, east Galway, Feb. 1909 and May 1909, PRO CO 904/77–8.

[136] Précis of information and reports on secret societies, Nov. 1910, PRO CO 904/119.

[137] IG monthly report, Feb. 1913, PRO CO 904/89.

[138] CI monthly report, east Galway, Feb. 1909, PRO CO 904/77.

when compared to that of the United Irish League, the secret society was reported to 'dominate everything' in the Loughrea and Athenry police districts.[139]

The early Sinn Féin movement in Galway was established on the basis of a republican, radical agrarian tradition that had existed in the region since the Land War. It is likely that Sinn Féin branches in the rest of Connacht emerged from a similar political tradition. Certainly, the police confirmed that the members of Sinn Féin in the provinces were generally also members of the Irish Republican Brotherhood. And, following the IRB's adoption of a radical agrarian policy in the 1870s, many Fenians in the west of Ireland were undoubtedly small farmers and landless men who were committed to a radical policy of land redistribution.[140] It was no accident that the Sinn Féin branch at Kilreekle invoked the memory of Matthew Harris by styling itself the 'Matt Harris' branch.[141] Neither should it surprise us that the same branch commemorated the execution of a Ribbonman, Anthony Daly, who had been hanged at Craughwell in 1819.[142] The roots of Sinn Féin in the west of Ireland were deep, and closely interwoven with long-standing traditions of agrarian protest, going back perhaps as far as the early nineteenth century.

II

After 1909, the Sinn Féin movement in Ireland fell into decline. The 1909 Land Act restored the faith of provincial nationalists in the effectiveness of parliamentary agitation, and the two general elections of 1910 changed the balance of power in the House of Commons, so that the Liberal Party was once again dependent on nationalist support. Home Rule was, therefore, back on the political agenda, and with the removal of the House of Lords' power of veto in 1911, its implementation seemed inevitable. The membership of the United Irish League, which had decreased considerably in 1907, gradually returned to its former level, and the number of subscribing Sinn

---

[139] CI monthly report, east Galway, Mar. 1910, PRO CO 904/80.

[140] A number of provincial Sinn Féin branches were engaged in agrarian agitation, notably in north Clare, King's county, and north Tipperary. Precis of information received in Crime Special Branch, Dec. 1907, Oct. and Nov. 1908, PRO CO 904/117–18.

[141] *Sinn Féin*, 3 Nov. 1906. On Matthew Harris, see Ch. 1.

[142] *Sinn Féin*, 16 Feb. 1907. See also David Ryan, 'The trial and execution of Anthony Daly', in Joseph Forde, Christina Cassidy, Paul Manzor, and David Ryan (eds.), *The district of Loughrea, i: History, 1791–1918* (Galway, 2003).

Féin clubs began to decline.[143] Sinn Féin's abstentionist policy, which had gained so many adherents in 1907, was now discredited by the Irish Parliamentary Party's successes at Westminster. Griffith, and his party, fell back to their pre-1906 position of awaiting the results of the Party's attendance at Westminster.[144] Sinn Féin did not, however, cease to exist. In the 1910–13 period, the annual congress continued to be held, the *Sinn Féin* weekly was published, industrial exhibitions were organized, and a number of provincial branches were maintained. Indeed, P. S. O'Hegarty's claim that there were only two or three Sinn Féin clubs left in Ireland in 1912 is probably incorrect.[145] In addition to the Dublin branch, the Galway clubs continued to meet and provincial delegates also attended the Sinn Féin executive meetings, suggesting the existence of active branches elsewhere in the country, particularly in Wexford and south Tipperary.[146] After 1910, however, Sinn Féin was not the vital organization that it had been in the aftermath of the Irish Council Bill crisis.

In Galway, local developments also caused the influence of the secret society and Sinn Féin to fall into decline. The first six months of 1910 probably constituted the high point of pre-1916 Sinn Féin power in county Galway. In January 1910, Padraic Ó Maille, a local Sinn Féin candidate, intended to contest William O'Malley's Connemara seat. However, at a meeting of the Galway county committee of Sinn Féin it was decided that he should not stand because 'it was the expressed desire of the National Council not to force the contests in Ireland at the present, lest the general national progress of Sinn Fein might be hampered by the violent political passions which would be aroused' and because 'parliamentarianism if left unopposed will condemn itself in a few years'. Even so, the police believed that 'he would probably have carried the seat if he [had] persisted'.[147] In the east of the county, Kenny's power reached its high point in June 1910. Following the release of Thomas Hynes and Michael Dermody, who had been accused of the killing of Constable Goldrick at Craughwell, 'the demeanour of Tom Kenny and his gang at Craughwell ... [became] more truculent and defiant towards the police. He goes about at night singing Fenian songs at the top of his voice. He conducts strangers openly and boastfully over the scene of the murder, and the accused, Dermody and

---

[143] United Irish League membership figures, PRO CO 904/20/2; Davis, *Arthur Griffith*, 81–2.

[144] IG monthly report, Sept. 1911, PRO CO 904/85.

[145] Quoted in Davis, *Arthur Griffith*, 86. O'Hegarty was a civil servant in London, born in Cork, and a member of Sinn Féin. Maume, *The long gestation*, 85.

[146] Davis, *Arthur Griffith*, 173–6.

[147] Précis of information received in Crime Special Branch, Jan. 1910, PRO CO 904/119.

Hynes, are taken about to various gaelic sports and other meetings where they are publicly greeted as heroes.'[148] At the same time, the secret society was described as exercising 'supreme power' in the Athenry and Loughrea districts of the east riding.[149] But Kenny had also made many enemies during his extraordinary rise to power. As well as disliking him personally, the local United Irish League officers resented his ability to influence young Leaguers into defecting to Sinn Féin.[150] Similarly, the Roman Catholic hierarchy were concerned that the secret society was becoming more influential than the Church in the riding. Finally, the Royal Irish Constabulary were determined to destroy Kenny's power, particularly after the shooting of Constable Goldrick which they attributed to members of his secret society.[151]

In the winter of 1910, a systematic campaign was initiated by the United Irish League against the members of the secret society. Over the following year, there were a large number of violent incidents in the village, including physical beatings, the firing of shots at Sinn Féiners, and a number of attempts on Kenny's life.[152] At a meeting of the south Galway UIL executive at Loughrea on 11 June 1911, for example, 'when Kenny attempted to speak he was set upon by the Leaguers and severely beaten about the face and body. All those attending the meeting seemed hostile to him, and he had to be escorted from the Hall by Mr Duffy, MP.' Later, 'Kenny himself stated he would have been killed but for the intervention of Mr Duffy.'[153] Consequently, a significant number of Kenny's supporters rejoined the Craughwell United Irish League branch.[154] The intimidatory tactics of the local United Irish Leaguers also ensured that Kenny's forge was 'deserted' by January 1911, and that his most important customer, Mr Concannon, the owner of the local kennels, was instructed to send his horses elsewhere, resulting in a loss of £60 per annum to Kenny.[155] In July 1911, the County Inspector observed that, 'If the present state of things continues, Kenny

[148] CI monthly report, east Galway, June 1910, PRO CO 904/81.

[149] CI monthly report, east Galway, Dec. 1909, PRO CO 904/79.

[150] CI monthly report, east Galway, Jan. 1911, PRO CO 904/83. According to Martin Newell, the Leaguers' dislike of Kenny was 'due to the fact that he and his associates were attracting many recruits to Sinn Féin from the United Irish League', Martin Newell witness statement, MA BMH WS 1,562.

[151] Martin Newell suggests that the United Irish League's campaign against Kenny was supported by the RIC. Martin Newell witness statement, MA BMH WS 1,562.

[152] See Ch. 4.

[153] Precis of information received in Crime Special Branch, June 1911, PRO CO 904/119.

[154] CI monthly report, east Galway, May 1911, PRO CO 904/84.

[155] CI monthly report, east Galway, Jan. 1911, PRO CO 904/83; *Connacht Tribune*, 15 June 1912. According to Martin Newell, Kenny was dismissed from his work at the kennels as a result of UIL pressure. Martin Newell witness statement, MA BMH WS 1,562.

must sooner or later leave the country as he is now absolutely without any viable means.'[156] Indeed, by the end of 1911, Kenny had lost his livelihood and most of his local support.[157] Such was the level of opposition against him that at a meeting of the south Galway UIL executive in Loughrea, he said that he 'had to fight the Church, State and U.I. League'.[158] Kenny's power was crushed by this onslaught, and the United Irish League regained its dominance in east Galway. However, the conflict at Craughwell was— at least partially—resolved in the autumn of 1912 when a member of the Clan na Gael from Boston effected a reconciliation between Kenny and the United Irish Leaguers. As a result, Kenny was restored to 'lucrative employment', and the police believed that it was just a matter of time before he regained 'his old ascendancy'.[159]

The fortunes of both Dublin and provincial separatists were transformed by the formation of the Irish Volunteers at the Rotunda Rink, Dublin in November 1913. After the introduction of the Home Rule Bill in the House of Commons in April 1912, the Ulster Volunteer Force (UVF) was formed to resist its implementation. In response to developments in Ulster, the Irish Volunteers were established to ensure that the UVF did not obstruct the introduction of Home Rule. The Irish Volunteers were not founded by members of the Irish Parliamentary Party, but by a number of prominent cultural nationalists and separatists. Eoin MacNeill, the professor of early and medieval Irish history at University College, Dublin, and vice-president of the Gaelic League, who became the chief of staff of the new organization, stated that the aim of the Irish Volunteers was to 'secure . . . the rights and liberties common to all the people of Ireland'.[160] He believed that the threat of nationalist force would guarantee the implementation of Home Rule. However, the driving force behind the formation of the Irish Volunteers was the Irish Republican Brotherhood, and when a Provisional Committee was established, as the organizational basis of the new movement, twelve of its thirty members were members of the IRB.[161] The IRB, unlike MacNeill, viewed the Irish Volunteers as a potential military force capable of staging an insurrection. In Dublin, many prominent Sinn Féiners joined the Irish Volunteers. Bulmer Hobson and Sean MacDermott, both of whom had been members of Sinn Féin, were

---

[156] CI monthly report, east Galway, July 1911, PRO CO 904/84.

[157] Interview with Gerry Cloonan, 23 Nov. 1997.

[158] Précis of information received in the Crime Special Branch, May 1911, PRO CO 904/13/145.

[159] IG monthly report, Aug., Sept., and Dec. 1912, PRO CO 904/87–8.

[160] Lyons, *Ireland since the Famine*, 322.

[161] Ibid.

founding members of the Provisional Committee.[162] There were also four designated Sinn Féin representatives on the Provisional committee, established in May 1914, including Eamon Ceannt, a Galway-born clerk, and The O'Rahilly, a Kerry 'country gentleman'.[163]

The first branch of the Irish Volunteers in county Galway was formed at a public meeting held at Galway Town Hall on 12 December 1913. Among the speakers were Eoin MacNeill, Patrick Pearse, and Roger Casement, all of whom were members of the Provisional Committee, and George Nicholls, a solicitor and a prominent Galway Fenian and Sinn Féiner. 'Mr. Pierce [*sic*]' explained the rationale for the new movement, telling the 'packed' hall that 'Ireland armed would be able to make a better bargain with the Empire [for Home Rule] than Ireland unarmed.'[164] At the end of the meeting 248 persons were enrolled, and the activists who had attended the meeting began to establish Volunteer companies throughout the county.[165] Patrick Callanan, for example, lost no time in founding a company of the Volunteers: 'Coming home from [the] Galway [meeting] he dismounted from his bicycle at Clarinbridge and got into conversation with some twenty young men standing, as men did in those days of limited amusement, at the gable of Jordan's public house. After an hour's conversation he had a dozen "prospects" and was well satisfied.' A week later, 'a large number of young men' at Clarinbridge were formally enrolled into the Volunteers.[166] As a result of the efforts of Nicholls and other Volunteer organizers, there were thirty branches of the Galway Volunteers with 3,037 members by the following May.[167]

In Galway, the Irish Volunteer movement was established and (in many cases) led by local members of the IRB, Sinn Féin, and the secret society. Indeed, the members of the Galway IRB deliberately set out to take over the Volunteer movement in the county. Peter Howley, the captain of the Ardrahan company, recalled:

My father told me that he was a member of the Irish Republican Brotherhood and that some of the most active of the Land Leaguers were also members. He took the oath as a young man. At the time of the formation of the Volunteers in Galway in 1914 he expressed the opinion that the Volunteer movement would not be a success without an inner circle, meaning the I.R.B.[168]

[162] Breandán Mac Giolla Choille, *Intelligence notes, 1913–16* (Dublin 1966), 106; Davis, *Arthur Griffith*, 67.

[163] The others were Sean FitzGibbon and Peter Macken, Davis, *Arthur Griffith*, 71; Foster, *Modern Ireland*, 473, 444.   [164] *Connacht Tribune*, 13 Dec. 1913.

[165] CI monthly report, east Galway, Nov. 1913, PRO CO 904/91.

[166] *Connacht Tribune*, 2 Apr. 1966.

[167] CI monthly reports, east and west Galway, May 1914, PRO CO 904/93.

[168] Peter Howley witness statement, MA BMH WS 1,379.

Evidently, many members of the Galway Volunteers took William Howley's advice. Michael Kelly, a member of the IRB and the Rockfield Volunteers, told the Bureau of Military History: 'It was . . . the general policy of the I.R.B. to fill officerships in the Irish Volunteers by members of the I.R.B.'[169] Alfred Monaghan, a Belfast-born Sinn Féin organizer sent to Clarinbridge in January 1916, also confirms that 'In setting up company, battalion and brigade councils, and in appointing officers, care was taken that members of the I.R.B . . . .were put into all the key positions.'[170] Consequently, many of the officers of the Irish Volunteers in county Galway were members of the Irish Republican Brotherhood. George Nicholls was 'head centre' of the Galway city IRB, a member of the national Sinn Féin executive, and now became the commandant of the Galway city Volunteers.[171] At Athenry, Lawrence Lardner and Stephen Jordan, both veterans of the TTL, the secret society, Sinn Féin, and the IRB, became Volunteer officers when a company was established in the town in January 1914.[172] At Mount Bellew, James Haverty, the Sinn Féiner and Fenian, was captain of the local Volunteer company.[173] And at Clarinbridge, Patrick Jordan, 'a veteran of the I.R.B. and Land League', presided at the inaugural meeting of the Volunteers.[174]

In south Galway, Tom Kenny, who had lost a great deal of his influence as a result of the Craughwell dispute, became a prominent Volunteer organizer with the power to 'make and unmake its officers'.[175] Although Kenny was not formally appointed as an officer of the Volunteers, his influence behind the scenes was often decisive. Martin Newell recalls that when the Rockfield company was first established in June 1914, Kenny did not approve of the captain, Morgan Healy. 'After about four or five weeks, a meeting of the Craughwell I.R.B. Circle was held. Kenny pointed out that Healy was not suitable for the job, and the Circle decided to have him removed. Subsequently this was done, and Gilbert Morrissey was elected captain. Gilbert was an I.R.B. man.' A significant proportion of the membership of the Rockfield Volunteers (twenty of the forty) were

[169] Michael Kelly witness statement, MA BMH WS 1,564.

[170] 'Document from Ailbhe O'Monachain [Alfred Monaghan], January 1939', Desmond Greaves Archive, Dublin (DGAD).

[171] John Hosty witness statement, MA BMH WS 373; Davis, *Arthur Griffith*, 175; *Connacht Tribune*, 4 July 1914.

[172] 'Document from Ailbhe O'Monachain, January 1939', DGAD; Stephen Jordan witness statement, MA BMH WS 346; *Connacht Tribune*, 4 July 1914.

[173] Haverty, 'Memoirs of an ordinary republican', MA BMH CD 72; *Connacht Tribune*, 4 July 1914.

[174] Patrick Callanan witness statement, MA BMH WS 347.

[175] *Connacht Tribune*, 2 Apr. 1966.

also members of the Brotherhood.[176] Indeed, the Volunteers in south Galway were largely controlled by members of Kenny's secret society. In August 1914, the Inspector General observed: 'In [the] districts of Galway and Clare which are dominated by Secret Societies, the leaders of these Societies appear to command the Volunteers.'[177] At Clarinbridge, the County Inspector stated that 'Nearly every member of the Branch [of the Volunteers] is a member of a Secret Society & a moonlighter . . . These people seem to be under the impression that all law has been abrogated in their favour because they are Volunteers & that they can indulge in . . . carrying out their bandit work after dark.'[178] Similarly, at Athenry, Loughrea, and Mount Bellew, the Volunteers were 'dominated' by Kenny and were described by the police as 'entirely disloyal, Anti-English & Pro-German. They are bitterly opposed to recruiting in the Army, Anti-enlisting . . . [and] hostile to the British Empire.'[179] Although there were pro-Redmond Volunteer companies, the leadership of the Irish Volunteer movement in much of east Galway was a continuation of the earlier IRB, secret society, and Sinn Féin organization. The formation of the Irish Volunteers provided a new forum for Kenny, and he appears to have regained a great deal of influence in the county as a consequence. However, at Craughwell his enemies remained in power, as the local Volunteer company was 'started and controlled by the U.I.L.'[180]

Initially, the Irish Parliamentary Party opposed the Volunteers, regarding it with suspicion as a front organization for the Irish Republican Brotherhood. The rapid expansion of the Volunteers, which suggested that it might even supersede the United Irish League, caused Redmond to identify himself with the new movement. By May 1914, just six months after its formation, there were 191 corps of the Irish Volunteers with 25,000 members in 25 counties.[181] At a meeting on 15 June, Redmond forced the Provisional Committee to accept twenty-five Irish Parliamentary Party nominees, thereby securing a safe majority for the Home Rule movement. As a result, 'the extreme section . . . are now only a small minority of the membership [of the Irish Volunteers], and are also outnumbered on the governing committee'.[182] With the official support of both the Irish Parliamentary Party and the Roman Catholic Church, membership

---

[176] Martin Newell witness statement, MA BMH WS 1,562.
[177] IG monthly report, Aug. 1914, PRO CO 904/94.
[178] CI monthly report, west Galway, Aug. 1914, PRO CO 904/94.
[179] CI monthly report, east Galway, Oct. 1914, PRO CO 904/95.
[180] Martin Newell witness statement, MA BMH WS 1,562.
[181] IG monthly report, Apr. 1914, PRO CO 904/93.
[182] IG monthly report, June 1914, PRO CO 904/93.

of the Irish Volunteers soared, reaching a peak of 184,000 in August,[183] making it 'the largest Nationalist organisation [in Ireland]'.[184] In Galway, the membership of the Irish Volunteers increased to 9,969 men in 110 companies.[185] However, the beginning of the Great War had a profound impact on the members of the Irish Volunteers.

The outbreak of hostilities elicited a response from Redmond which led to a split in the Irish Volunteers. On 20 September, in a speech at Woodenbridge, county Wicklow, Redmond called on the Irish Volunteers to support the war effort by enlisting in the British army.[186] The split did not occur immediately, but it was inevitable. Redmond and his supporters on the Provisional Committee were now 'urging Irishmen to fight in the British Army'.[187] Eoin MacNeill and the separatists on the committee, on the other hand, were vehemently opposed to recruiting, and began to campaign against it through 'the circulation of seditious and anti-recruiting leaflets and placards, to stir up ill-feeling against England and sympathy with Germany, and to prevent Nationalists [from] enlisting in the Army'.[188] The two groups on the Provisional Committee could not have been more polarized. In November, the separatist section of the Irish Volunteers, under the leadership of Eoin MacNeill, detached itself from the main body, retaining the name 'Irish Volunteers', while the remaining Redmondite Volunteers now became the 'National Volunteers'. The Redmondite National Volunteers were by far the larger of the two groups, with 147,050 members, while the MacNeillite Irish Volunteers, on the other hand, numbered only 9,700.[189] Despite Redmond's plea, however, most of the members of the National Volunteers did not enlist. At the end of 1915, the Inspector General noted that the results of recruiting meetings held throughout the country had 'not been commensurate with the trouble and expense incurred'.[190] And although Ireland's contribution to the war effort was in the region of 206,000, this was a comparatively small figure when compared to the five million or so recruits raised in the rest of the United Kingdom.[191] Most of the members of the National Volunteers were farmers' sons, and members of this social group were reluctant to

183 IG monthly report, Aug. 1914, PRO CO 904/94.
184 IG monthly report, July 1914, PRO CO 904/94.
185 CI monthly reports, east and west Galway, Aug. 1914, PRO CO 904/94.
186 Foster, *Modern Ireland*, 472.
187 IG monthly report, Oct. 1914, PRO CO 904/95.
188 IG monthly report, Sept. 1914, PRO CO 904/94.
189 IG monthly report, Dec. 1914, PRO CO 904/95.
190 IG monthly report, Nov. 1915, PRO CO 904/98.
191 David Fitzpatrick, 'The logic of collective sacrifice: Ireland and the British army, 1914–1918', *Historical Journal*, 38/4 (1995), 1017–18.

join the colours.[192] In Galway, for instance, recruiting was reported to be slow and 'entirely confined to the towns' in 1914; during 1915 only 647 men joined the colours; and in 1916, according to police intelligence, 'recruiting is dead'.[193]

After the beginning of the Great War, there was great concern among many sections of Irish society that conscription would be applied to Ireland. Initially, this was confined to the Volunteers, who believed that their involvement in drilling could lead to their being 'compulsorily enlisted'.[194] As a result, the membership of the National Volunteers fell into a steep and irreversible decline. Between December 1914 and February 1916, the membership of the National Volunteers declined from 147,050 to 102,128 (a decrease of 31 per cent).[195] As early as October 1914, the Inspector General recognized that the membership of the Volunteers was 'now steadily on the decline' because of the members' 'dread of being called on for military service in the War'.[196] By the spring of 1915 'Apathy . . . [was] everywhere noticeable in the [National] Volunteer movement which is steadily on the decline'.[197] On the eve of the Rising, although the movement still claimed over 102,000[198] members, it was described as 'practically dead'[199] and 'non-existent'.[200] In contrast, the membership of the MacNeillite Irish Volunteers increased rapidly over the same period, increasing from 9,700 to 12,215 between December 1914 and February 1916, an increase of 26 per cent.[201] It is also significant that the Irish Volunteers were described by the police on the eve of the Rising as 'foremost among [nationalist] political societies, not by reason of their numerical strength, but on account of their greater activity'.[202]

In Galway, after the split, most Volunteers remained committed to

[192] This observation became a commonplace in police reports during the Great War. See, for example, IG monthly report, June 1915, PRO CO 904/97; CI monthly report, Roscommon, Jan. 1915, PRO CO 904/96; CI monthly report, west Galway, May 1915, PRO CO 904/97.

[193] CI monthly report, east Galway, Feb. 1915, PRO CO 904/96; Mac Giolla Choille, *Intelligence notes, 1913–16*, 152 and 218.

[194] IG monthly reports, Sept. and Oct. 1914, PRO CO 904/94–5; CI monthly report, east Galway, Sept. 1914, PRO CO 904/94.

[195] IG monthly report, Dec. 1914, PRO CO 904/95; IG monthly report, Feb. 1916, PRO CO 904/99.

[196] IG monthly report, Oct. 1914, PRO CO 904/95.

[197] IG monthly report, Apr. 1915, PRO CO 904/96.

[198] The figure is 102,128 in February 1916, IG monthly report, Feb. 1916, PRO CO 904/99.

[199] IG monthly report, Jan. 1916, PRO CO 904/99.

[200] IG monthly report, Feb. 1916, PRO CO 904/99.

[201] IG monthly report, Dec. 1914, PRO CO 904/95; IG monthly report, Feb. 1916, PRO CO 904/99.

[202] IG monthly report, Mar. 1916, PRO CO 904/99.

Redmond. In the spring of 1915, for example, there were 5,809 National Volunteers, and only 742 Irish Volunteers.[203] The majority of Volunteer companies followed the pattern of that at Ardrahan, described by Peter Howley:

> I remember very well the night the split occurred. Naughton, the instructor, came as usual from Athenry. The company fell in and Naughton addressed them. As far as I can remember, he put two view points before us—that we could guard the shores of Ireland for England against any foreign invasion or simply guard the shores of Ireland for Ireland. He then said that any Volunteer who was not satisfied to guard the shores of Ireland for England against the invasion was at liberty to leave the company. The Home Rule Bill was on the Statute Book at the time. Out of the eighty or so men on parade only five left the ranks.[204]

At Mullagh, the company adjutant, Michael Manning, recalled: 'After John Redmonds [*sic*] appeal for recruits for the British Armed Forces had split the Volunteer ranks, the majority of Mullagh company elected to follow Redmond's lead and joined the National Volunteers. The minority (about ten) resolved to carry on under the original leadership of the Irish Volunteers.'[205] Similarly, in Galway city after a meeting of Volunteers at the Town Hall, the majority went 'over to Redmond to assist him in his recruiting campaign for the British army'.[206] However, those companies that did support Redmond tended to become inactive, and often ceased to exist soon after the split. Patrick Connaughton, a member of the Closetoken National Volunteers, recalled that following the split, 'our company dwindled until it finally fizzled out'.[207] And at Ardrahan, the company of National Volunteers 'disintegrated' in late 1914.[208] The tendency for National Volunteer companies to become inactive and merely nominal during the Great War is reflected in the statistics compiled by the police. Between August 1914 and January 1916, the Galway National Volunteers' membership had dropped by 4,961 (50 per cent), leaving 56 companies with 5,008 members most of which were described by the police as 'inactive'.[209]

The membership of the Irish Volunteers in Galway, on the other hand,

---

203 CI monthly report, east Galway, Feb. 1915, PRO CO 904/96; CI monthly report, west Galway, Mar. 1915, PRO CO 904/96.

204 Peter Howley witness statement, MA BMH WS 1,379.

205 Michael Manning witness statement, MA BMH WS 1,164.

206 Frank Hardiman witness statement, MA BMH WS 406.

207 Patrick Connaughton witness statement, MA BMH WS 1,137.

208 Peter Howley witness statement, MA BMH WS 1,379.

209 CI monthly reports, east and west Galway, Aug. 1914, PRO CO 904/94 and CI monthly reports, east and west Galway, Jan. 1916, PRO CO 904/99.

increased after the split. By April 1916, there were 1,791 Irish Volunteers in the county, signifying an increase of 141 per cent since the spring of 1915.[210] Moreover, the MacNeillite Volunteers were the most active political organization in Galway.[211] Those Volunteer companies that supported MacNeill after the split tended to be located in the south-east of the county (except in the town of Loughrea), where the secret society was most densely organized. James Barrett, a member of the Athenry company, recalled:

At the split in the Volunteers caused by John Redmond's speech at Woodenbridge, a special meeting of the Company was held to decide which side the Volunteers would take. The position was explained by Captain L.[awrence] Lardner who said that anyone who did not stand behind McNeill [sic] was free to leave; no one left.[212]

Similarly, the testimonies of members of the Volunteer companies at Rockfield, Clarinbridge, and Castlegar indicate that they 'stood solid behind McNeill'.[213] Michael Kelly, of the Rockfield company, explained that 'There was no split in either the Clarenbridge [sic] or Rockfield Companies, as these were Sinn Féin areas and both Companies were controlled by the I.R.B.'[214] This was also the view of the police, who pointed out that companies of the Irish Volunteers tended to be established in 'localities [that] had always been disturbed, [and] were honeycombed with secret society influence'.[215] Elsewhere, and particularly in the towns (with the exception of Athenry), separatist Volunteers often met with violent opposition.[216] According to Thomas Hynes of the Galway city Volunteers: 'we tried to break up recruiting meetings but we generally got beaten up ourselves as at least eighty per cent. of the population were hostile to Sinn Féin, for a number of their husbands and sons were in the English army and navy.'[217] And at Loughrea, the Volunteers 'deposed'[218]

[210] CI monthly report, east Galway, Feb. 1915, PRO CO 904/96; CI monthly report, west Galway, Mar. 1915, PRO CO 904/96; *The Royal Commission on the Rebellion in Ireland: minutes of evidence and appendix of documents*, HC (1916), [Cd. 8311], xi. 260, 262.

[211] IG monthly report, Mar. 1916, PRO CO 904/99.

[212] James Barrett witness statement, MA BMH WS 343.

[213] Brian Molloy witness statement, MA BMH WS 345; Patrick Callanan witness statement, MA BMH WS 347; Gilbert Morrissey witness statement, MA BMH WS 874.

[214] Michael Kelly witness statement, MA BMH WS 1,564.

[215] *The Royal Commission on the Rebellion in Ireland: minutes of evidence and appendix of documents*, HC (1916), [Cd. 8311], xi. 260.

[216] Martin Dolan confirms that, 'the towns, in general, did not take kindly to the I.R.B. nor to the Irish Volunteers', *Connacht Tribune*, 2 Apr. 1966.

[217] Thomas Hynes witness statement, MA BMH WS 714.

[218] IG monthly report, Sept. 1914, PRO CO 904/94.

their pro-German leaders, and smashed the windows of Sinn Féiners in the town in November 1915.[219]

The outbreak of the Great War also transformed Irish separatist politics. For the Irish Republican Brotherhood, 'England's difficulty was Ireland's opportunity', and in August 1914 physical force republicans began to plan an insurrection.[220] A number of officers on the governing council of the Irish Volunteers were prominent members of the Irish Republican Brotherhood. In May 1915, these officers, together with the executive of the IRB Supreme Council, formed a military council to organize a rebellion.[221] The arrangements for the rebellion extended into the provinces. In the spring of 1915, the Irish Volunteer executive began to organize the Volunteers in a number of counties, with a view to preparing for the projected rebellion. The Inspector General observed in April that 'Organizers, holding advanced views, were busy among the Sinn Fein Volunteers in the counties of Limerick, Kerry, Kilkenny, Waterford, Wexford, Galway, Londonderry, and King's County.'[222] 'These mischievous agents are ostensibly organizing and recruiting for the Irish Volunteers (Sinn Fein), but there are good grounds for believing that some of them at least are also engaged in secret society work; and as they advocate resistance to conscription it is not unlikely that they will be successful in attracting new followers.'[223] Liam Mellows was appointed a permanent organizer in Galway, and he took up residence at Athenry in March 1915.[224] Mellows was born at Ashton-under-Lyne in 1892, and reared at Macoyle in north-east Wexford. After being educated at the Royal Hibernian Military School in Cork, he became a clerk in Dublin in 1905, where he joined the IRB in 1912.[225] Alfred Monaghan later observed that the military council 'had reasons for having Galway very specially organised and equipped for the coming Rising'.[226] Indeed, it is likely that the military council, of which John MacBride was a member, recognized that Kenny's secret society could be mobilized to support the proposed Rising. This is borne out by the fact that when Mellows arrived in Galway, he immediately

[219] CI monthly report, east Galway, Nov. 1915, PRO CO 904/98.

[220] Laffan, *The resurrection of Ireland*, 34.

[221] Lyons, *Ireland since the Famine*, 341–2.

[222] IG monthly report, Apr. 1915, PRO CO 904/96.

[223] IG monthly report, May 1915, PRO CO 904/97.

[224] 'Document from Ailbhe O'Monachain, January 1939', DGAD.

[225] Desmond Greaves, *Liam Mellows and the Irish revolution* (2nd edn., London, 1987), 35–40.

[226] 'Document from Ailbhe O'Monachain, January 1939', DGAD; Michael Kelly witness statement, MA BMH WS 1,564.

'rallied to his standard all the young men who were members of secret societies, with pronounced disloyal feelings'.[227]

Although Mellows would later be regarded as a heroic figure in county Galway, the first impression which he conveyed to the Athenry Volunteers in early 1915 was somewhat less auspicious. Frank Hynes, the captain of the Athenry company, recalled his first encounter with Mellows:

I think it was in January, 1915, we got word from Dublin that an officer was being sent down to organise and train the Volunteers in County Galway. He was to be with us for one week only. We all were very excited over the matter. When the night arrived, Larry [Lardner] told me to call the company on parade while he went to the train to meet the officer. When he arrived I was introduced to a little fellow with glasses. My impression of him was that he may be a clever lad—he was about 22 years—but couldn't be much good at fighting. His name by the way was Liam Mellows. He came in when the men were lined up, six footers most of them. Liam addressed them 'Now men I was sent down to get you to do a bit of hard work, so I want you to be prepared for a week of very hard work'. I could see the faintest trace of a supercilious smile on some of the men. When he was finished talking Larry and himself went off to arrange about digs. Then the smiles broke out to laughing. 'Who is the ladeen?', asked one fellow, 'who talks to us about hard work'.

In time, however, Mellows won the support and respect of the majority of Irish Volunteers in Galway, as Hynes observes: 'before the first night under his command was over . . . they loved and respected him.'[228] The local separatist leaders, notably Tom Kenny and Lawrence Lardner, were less inclined to welcome the new leader. Kenny, in particular, resented Mellows, who gradually replaced him as the most influential separatist in east Galway. In part, this was because Kenny lacked military training and was, therefore, 'unfit to hold any rank in any one of the companies he had helped to create'. Mellows, on the other hand, 'arrived in Galway with a knowledge of drill and arms far beyond that of anyone there and this knowledge gained him his commanding position among the Volunteers while Kenny's stock declined accordingly'.[229] Later, Kenny would allege that Mellows was an inadequate military leader, and write, 'Fairheaded Bill you are good for nothing only drinking tea over at Walshe's of Killeeneen, and going up to Pádraig Fahy's, Ballycahalan.'[230] There was also a certain

---

[227] County Inspector G. B. Ruttledge to the Royal Commission on the Rebellion, 27 May 1916, *The Royal Commission on the Rebellion in Ireland: minutes of evidence and appendix of documents*, HC (1916), [Cd. 8311], xi. 260.

[228] Frank Hynes witness statement, MA BMH WS 446.

[229] *Connacht Tribune*, 2 Apr. 1966.

[230] Patrick Callanan witness statement, MA BMH WS 405. Hubert Walshe and his wife were national school teachers in Killeeneen, and they were also Irish language enthusiasts

amount of tension between Mellows and Lardner. This arose largely from the ambivalence of Mellows's position in Galway. Although Lardner was the commanding officer of the Galway brigade, Mellows

was generally known as the 'Captain' . . . [and] had the backing of the Volunteer Executive . . . and had authority over Lardner. He had, too, the respect and admiration of the ordinary Volunteer who looked upon him as being the superior officer of the county. He had, too, the support of the officers, most of whom were in the IRB . . . [T]here was constant friction between Lardner and Mellowes [*sic*] and the former was kept very much in the dark at times.[231]

Notwithstanding these tensions, the activism of Mellows and other organizers led to the expansion of the Irish Volunteers in east Galway during 1915 and 1916. By December 1915, there were six companies of the Irish Volunteers in west Galway, three of which were established after a public Volunteer meeting at Athenry in November when 'the members of three branches of Mr. Redmond's Volunteers . . . turned over and joined the Sinn Fein section'.[232] In east Galway, the Athenry meeting also resulted in the formation of five new Irish Volunteer companies 'in and around Loughrea and Athenry'.[233] This meeting, which was attended by 670 Irish Volunteers, 161 of whom were armed, was viewed by the police as constituting a turning point in the fortunes of the separatist movement in Galway.[234] After a series of 'inflammatory' speeches by Laurence Ginnell, The O'Rahilly, George Nicholls, and Liam Mellows,

shots were discharged in the field [where the meeting was held], a number of shots at Athenry Railway Station, and some along the roads. This meeting has had a bad effect in the neighbourhood of Athenry, where a feeling of resentment had been growing amongst the more respectable people against the Sinn Feiners, and public opinion was beginning to assert itself on the side of law and order. This feeling has now been checked, as the people concerned are afraid and have been completely

(as were their children Paddy, Gretta, Bridie, and Tess). Pádraig Ó Fathaigh, a Gaelic League travelling teacher (*múinteoir taistil*) from Lurgan (near Gort), stayed with the Walshes when he taught in the area, and the Walshe house was Mellows's base before the Easter Rising. *Connacht Tribune*, 2 Apr. 1966; Mrs S. Malone (Brighid Breathnach) witness statement, MA WS 617; T. G. McMahon, *Pádraig Ó Fathaigh's War of Independence* (Cork, 2000), 1–5.

[231] *Connacht Tribune*, 2 Apr. 1966.
[232] CI monthly report, west Galway, Dec. 1915, PRO CO 904/98. *The Royal Commission on the Rebellion in Ireland: minutes of evidence and appendix of documents*, HC (1916), [Cd. 8311], xi. 260.
[233] County Inspector E. M. Clayton to the Royal Commission on the Rebellion on 27 May 1916. *The Royal Commission on the Rebellion in Ireland: minutes of evidence and appendix of documents*, HC (1916), [Cd. 8311], xi. 262.
[234] Ibid.

over-awed by the display of armed and unlawful force, which they believe the Government are too weak to resist.[235]

According to Patrick Callanan, 'Everything went very well after that [meeting].'[236] Throughout the winter of 1915 and the spring of 1916, Irish Volunteer organizers including George Nicholls, Patrick Callanan, Stephen Jordan, Lawrence Lardner, Pádraig Ó Fathaigh, and Liam Mellows travelled around the county forming new companies, and teaching basic military procedures (including drilling, target practice, and conducting 'sham' battles).[237]

On the eve of the Easter Rising, there were 1,070 Irish Volunteers in west Galway, in an unspecified number of companies, and 721 in east Galway, half (371) of whom were members of eleven companies while the other half (350) were not affiliated to any company.[238] It is clear that both the decline of the National Volunteers and the growth of the Irish Volunteers in Galway were primarily caused by the fear that Irishmen would be conscripted.[239] The County Inspector observed in September 1914 that the members of the Volunteers 'believe that if they go on drilling they will be in some way or another forced to enlist for service at the front'.[240] On the other hand, after the beginning of the war, the MacNeillite Volunteers initiated an extensive anti-recruiting campaign, and pledged themselves 'to resist conscription with arms'.[241] This policy was emphatically conveyed at the Athenry meeting held on 14 November 1915, and attended by over 2,000 people,[242] when Mellows stated that the question of conscription 'resolved itself into a mathematical problem. It would not be worth the trouble if when England enforced conscription she lost two men to gain

[235] CI monthly report, east Galway, Nov. 1915, PRO CO 904/98. Ginnell, who revealed Sinn Féin sympathies as early as 1906, described himself as an independent nationalist between 1910 and 1917, and a Sinn Féiner thereafter. Maume, *The long gestation*, 229.

[236] Patrick Callanan witness statement, MA BMH WS 347.

[237] CI monthly report, west Galway, July 1915, PRO CO 904/97; CI monthly report, west Galway, Nov. 1915, PRO CO 904/98; CI monthly report, east Galway, Dec. 1915, PRO CO 904/98; Patrick Callanan witness statement, MA BMH WS 347; Frank Hynes witness statement, MA BMH WS 446; Peter Howley witness statement, MA BMH WS 1,379; Michael Manning witness statement, MA BMH WS 1,164.

[238] *The Royal Commission on the Rebellion in Ireland: minutes of evidence and appendix of documents*, HC (1916), [Cd. 8311], xi. 260, 262.

[239] Fear of conscription was endemic in Galway during the Great War. In November 1915, for instance, '6 young men emigrated through fear of conscription and 94 others who were on their way were turned back from Liverpool'. CI monthly report, west Galway, Nov. 1915, PRO CO 904/98.

[240] CI monthly report, east Galway, Sept. 1914, PRO CO 904/94.

[241] IG monthly report, Oct. 1915, PRO CO 904/98.

[242] *Connacht Tribune*, 20 Nov. 1915; CI monthly report, east Galway, Nov. 1915, PRO CO 904/98.

one.'[243] A month later, the police observed that 'The Sinn Fein people are active and the movement is spreading. It is a comfortable doctrine in these days of contemplated conscription.'[244]

Interestingly, the Irish Volunteers won the support of a significant number of young curates in east Galway. No less than ten priests were present on the platform at the Athenry meeting of November 1915, and this was 'looked upon as a victory for the Sinn Feiners, and ... a matter of great surprise to the well-disposed'.[245] Two of the most influential separatist priests in pre-Rising Galway were Father John William O'Meehan, a native of Clarinbridge and the curate at Kinvara, and Father Henry Feeney of Castlegar who was the curate at Clarinbridge.[246] At Kinvara, O'Meehan was responsible for recruiting Irish Volunteers, distributing separatist newspapers, and teaching Irish classes. Consequently, he was regarded by the local Volunteers as 'an inspiration to us by his addresses ... [and] lectures'.[247] Father Feeney was equally influential at Clarinbridge where 'he threw himself wholeheartedly into the advancement of the Volunteers and did everything in his power to encourage us. Meetings of the officers were held in his house, and even bombs were manufactured there. He always attended our parades.'[248]

Given the origins of the Irish Volunteers in the anti-clerical tradition of the secret society, the involvement of these priests in the separatist movement appears paradoxical. However, two factors may explain their participation in the Irish Volunteers. First, both had been reared in localities where there were strong separatist and radical agrarian traditions. O'Meehan's sister Mary Leech recalled:

During his vacations from Maynooth ... [Father O'Meehan] always sought the company of old people, to hear them speak of their younger days, to learn Irish from them and to listen to their stories about the Land League and the hardships they underwent in that period. The people were very fond of him and liked to tell him all they knew or had heard of the Penal Days and Land League period. I understood from him that he had no love for the landlord class. He was always denouncing the custom of those people who were cringing and debasing themselves before the landlords.[249]

---

[243] *Connacht Tribune*, 20 Nov. 1915. In his speech, the Sinn Féiner Bryan Cusack encouraged the audience not to emigrate, but 'when their friends there [in the United States] sent them their passage, to buy a rifle with it'.

[244] CI monthly report, west Galway, Dec. 1915, PRO CO 904/98.

[245] CI monthly report, east Galway, Nov. 1915, PRO CO 904/98.

[246] Patrick Callanan witness statement, MA BMH WS 347.

[247] Thomas Reidy witness statement, MA BMH WS 1,555; Michael Hynes witness statement, MA BMH WS 1,173.

[248] Martin Newell witness statement, MA BMH WS 1,562.

[249] Mary Leech witness statement, MA BMH WS 1,034.

It is likely that these traditions influenced some of the young priests in east Galway to embrace separatist politics during the Great War. And second, some of these priests probably believed that they were playing a moderating role within the Irish Volunteers. At Kinvara, O'Meehan instructed Thomas Reidy 'not to insult the R.I.C. as he was of opinion that they would change over and join with us when the time came to fight', and he later discouraged violent land agitation during 1920.[250] Kenny would have had different views of both matters, and clerical involvement in the Irish Volunteers may have been intended as a safeguard against the more radical urges of the secret society.

The prelude to the Easter Rising was as confused in Galway as it was elsewhere. Although the officers of the Irish Volunteers who were also members of the IRB had known about the planned insurrection for some time, the events of Holy Week created an air of confusion as to when the rebellion was to take place.[251] On the Monday before Easter, Eamon Corbett, a small farmer from Killeeneen and prominent member of the Galway IRB, attended a meeting of the Military Council in Dublin at which he was told the Rising would begin on Easter Sunday night at 7.30.[252] However, a series of contradictory messages were subsequently received, and on Easter Saturday a meeting of all the Galway officers was held at George Nicholls's house on University Road at which it was decided to send John Hosty to Dublin to clarify the position.[253] The following day, Hosty met MacNeill in Dublin who said that 'he had already sent out countermanding orders calling the mobilisation off'. Hosty then conveyed this information to Lardner at Athenry and Nicholls in Galway, both of whom had already heard 'that things were off'.[254] The plan for the Galway Rising had been that the Irish Volunteers would assemble after second mass on Easter Sunday (at which they were to receive communion and go to confession) for three days of route marching, drilling, and manoeuvres.[255] The insurrection would then begin on the Sunday evening. On the following day, rifles from the German gunboat the *Aud* would be distributed by rail from Tralee to Volunteer companies throughout the west. The

---

[250] Thomas Reidy witness statement, MA BMH WS 1,555; see Ch. 6.

[251] Mícheál Ó Droighneáin, for instance, had a two-hour conversation with Pearse in August 1915 about the proposed rebellion. Michael Ó Droigheneain witness statement, MA BMH WS 374.

[252] 'Document from Ailbhe O'Monachain, January 1939', DGAD.

[253] Ibid.

[254] John Hosty witness statement, MA BMH WS 373.

[255] The majority of the rank and file did not know that a Rising was planned and believed that they were to meet on Easter Sunday for three days of route marching and training.

Galway Volunteers had been instructed to attend a parade at Gort on Easter Monday, at which the German rifles were to be distributed.[256] But MacNeill's countermand undermined these plans and left the Irish Volunteers in a state of disarray, and many Volunteer companies that had been mobilized on Easter Sunday morning were dismissed that evening. This confusion was further intensified when the *Aud* was captured, and the proposed Gort meeting called off.

As events unfolded, the leaders of the Galway Volunteers were forced to reassess their objectives. At the outset, the aim of the western Volunteer officers was to take control of their counties, and to hold a line along the Shannon. In early 1916, Pearse had visited Lardner at Athenry and told him that when the Rising took place he should 'hold a line on the river Suck near Ballinasloe'.[257] John Broderick, a building contractor and officer of the Athenry Irish Volunteers, recalled that the 'original plan was that each Company was to attack and capture all police Barracks in its area'.[258] In Galway city, Nicholls also planned to 'take a few prominent men— Martin McDonagh (Máirtín Mór), Joe Young, etc., and [to] occupy the Post Office'.[259] However, the capture of the *Aud* meant that the Galway Volunteers were insufficiently well armed to engage the British forces and the RIC, and an alternative strategy needed to be devised. On Easter Sunday, Mellows discussed the situation with Father Connolly, a professor at Garbally College, Ballinasloe, and a supporter of the Irish Volunteers:

> Fr. Connolly very sensibly pointed out that without the promised rifles the line of the Shannon could not be held as the river ran through flat land where the rebels would be particularly vulnerable to artillery and machine-gun fire . . . He further pointed out that, owing to the cancellation by MacNeill, a chaotic situation would result, that the other counties might not rise and that the Galway men might find themselves isolated and cut-off in a countryside almost devoid of cover.
>
> The possibility of a limited rising was then discussed and Mellowes evolved a plan of beginning the insurrection in the Athenry-Loughrea-Gort-Kinvara-Oranmore area with the rest of the county giving it initial support by the cutting of railway lines, the blocking of roads, the destruction of bridges, and other acts of sabotage. He believed that starting with the proposed area, the rebellion would increase by concentric waves which could conceivably spread throughout the province.[260]

Alfred Monaghan recalled in 1939 that 'when they went out', the Galway

---

256 A Galway man, 'Galway and the 1916 Rising', *An t-Óglach*, Feb. 1936.
257 Pat Callanan witness statement, MA BMH WS 347.
258 John Broderick witness statement, MA BMH WS 344.
259 Thomas Hynes witness statement, MA BMH WS 714. Joe Young was a prominent Galway city businessman.   260 *Connacht Tribune*, 2 Apr. 1966.

Volunteers 'did not hope to do anything big. Badly armed as they were, their only hope was to bottle up the British garrison and divert the British from concentrating on Dublin.'[261] In these circumstances, the Galway Rising could easily have been called off. Kenny, who had met with Clarke and MacDermott on Easter Sunday, 'was against it ... he believed the time was not ripe',[262] and Lardner at Athenry was 'funking it' and probably suffering from nervous exhaustion.[263] Mellows, however, was 'determined on revolt even if he had only Clarinbridge to follow him'.[264]

III

At about one o'clock on Easter Monday, a Miss Farrelly brought a message from Pearse to Lardner at Athenry, 'We are out from twelve o'clock today. Issue your orders without delay. P.H.P.'[265] Frank Hynes, who was at home on his lunch break, 'got a message to call down to the hall. When I went down Larry was there and his face was a placard in which trouble could be read easily. He handed me a despatch from Pearse—"Going out today at noon; issue your orders". There was a kettle of fish! What were we going to do? We notified all the companies we could get in touch with.'[266] James Barrett was sent to Killeeneen to pass on the news to Mellows, as he recalls: 'I went to Fleming's house in Clarinbridge and gave the dispatch to one of the Flemings who was also a Volunteer, to deliver to Mellows.'[267] Fleming then called on Father Feeney, and 'at about 2 p.m. on Easter Monday, Fr. Feeney rushed into Walsh's with the news that Dublin was out since 12 noon':[268]

Mellowes [*sic*], who was reading. jumped to his feet and dashing his book to the floor, directed: 'Call out the lads and put a guard around the house' . . . The first mood of elation changed when Lardner's despatch was fully digested. Dublin was 'out' certainly but the likelihood of the whole country rising was very poor . . . The pros and cons were discussed and no decision could be arrived at.

The arrival of Mattie Neilan settled the matter. Having listened for a few minutes to the outline of the dilemma, he interrupted Mellowes saying: 'Listen, Liam! Whatever you're going to do, do it now'.

[261] 'Document from Ailbhe O'Monachain, January 1939', DGAD.
[262] Gilbert Morrissey witness statement, MA BMH WS 874.
[263] Frank Hynes witness statement, MA BMH WS 446.
[264] *Connacht Tribune*, 2 Apr. 1966.
[265] 'Document from Ailbhe O'Monachain, January 1939', DGAD.
[266] Frank Hynes witness statement, MA BMH WS 446.
[267] James Barrett witness statement, MA BMH WS 343.
[268] Patrick Callanan witness statement, MA BMH WS 347.

'What do you think yourself, Mattie?' asked Mellowes. 'I think we should go out', was the reply.[269]

Mellows immediately issued instructions to all Volunteer captains to mobilize their men.[270] The Clarinbridge Volunteers were told to gather at Killeeneen school house that evening.[271] Patrick Callanan was sent to mobilize the Volunteers at Maree, Oranmore, Claregalway, and Castlegar.[272] Michael Kelly delivered a dispatch to Peter Howley at Ardrahan, instructing him to mobilize his company and 'take it to Tullyra, where we were to remain and guard the Galway/Ennis road', and also asking him to mobilize the Ballycahalan company.[273] Gilbert Morrissey received a dispatch on Tuesday morning telling him that there was fighting in Dublin and to mobilize the Rockfield company.[274] Pádraig Ó Fathaigh was sent to Kinvara to mobilize the company, and to bring Father O'Meehan to Killeeneen, but he was arrested before he could do so.[275] The Kinvara company was later mobilized by Father O'Meehan.[276] On Wednesday morning, Thomas McInerney, the brigade scout, visited the companies at Gort, Kiltartan, Ballycahalan, Kinvara, and Ballinderreen, and 'found them all mobilised and standing to arms in their respective areas'.[277] However, due to both the countermand and the poor communications of the time, a number of companies received no word from Mellows. At Mount Bellew, Loughrea, and Mullagh, the Volunteers

269 *Connacht Tribune*, 2 Apr. 1966. Neilan was a native of Kilcolgan, a student at University College, Galway, and a member of the Irish Volunteers. Seán Spellissy, *The history of Galway: city and county* (Limerick, 1999), 299.

270 This narrative account of the Easter Rising in Galway has been compiled from a variety of sources generated by both the British Government and the republican movement: A Galway man, 'Galway and the 1916 Rising', *An t-Óglach*, Feb. 1936; Bureau of Military History witness statements and contemporary documents; CI monthly reports, east and west Galway, Apr. 1916, PRO CO 904/100; Mhiceáil Uí Coincheannain, Móinteach, baile Chlár na Gaillimhe, 'Eirghe amach na Cásca 1916 i mbaile Chlár na Gaillimhe. [The 1916 Easter Rising in Claregalway]', DIFUCD IML 781, 381–92; *Connacht Tribune*, 29 Apr. and 6 May 1916; 'Document from Ailbhe O'Monachain, January 1939' and Ailbhe Ó Monachain, 'After Easter week', DGAD; Martin Dolan, 'The Rising in Galway', *Connacht Tribune*, 2, 9, 16 and 23 Apr. 1966; *Gaelic American*, 20 Jan. 1917; IG monthly report, 1 Apr.–31 May 1916, PRO CO 904/100; Weekly Irish Times, *Sinn Féin rebellion handbook* (Dublin, 1917); *The Royal Commission on the Rebellion in Ireland: minutes of evidence and appendix of documents*, HC (1916), [Cd. 8311], xi. 185; reports on east and west Galway in 1916, PRO CO 904/120 and War Office files, PRO WO 35/69/1/1–3.

271 *Connacht Tribune*, 9 Apr. 1966.

272 Patrick Callanan witness statement, MA BMH WS 347.

273 Peter Howley witness statement, MA BMH WS 1,379.

274 Gilbert Morrissey witness statement, MA BMH WS 874.

275 McMahon, *Pádraig Ó Fathaigh's War of Independence*, 7.

276 Thomas Reidy witness statement, MA BMH WS 1,555.

277 Thomas McInerney witness statement, MA BMH WS 1,150.

awaited instructions, but to no avail.[278] Similarly, no message was conveyed to the Volunteers west of Spiddal, as Peter McDonnell recalls: 'During Easter Week 1916 West Galway was completely cut off from the rest of the country, and no information—except rumour—could be had as to what was happening, and no instructions were received.'[279] Other companies did receive instructions, but did not act. At Moycullen, Pádraig Thornton could not be persuaded by Patrick Callanan and Brian Molloy to mobilize his men, complaining, 'what's the use against the army without guns'.[280] And although both George Nicholls and Mícheál Ó Droighneáin received a message from Pearse on Easter Monday afternoon instructing them to 'carry out your orders', they 'decided that we would do nothing until we got more information'.[281] A few hours later, they were both arrested and escorted to a naval mine sweeper, the *Laburnum*, in Galway bay, so that they could not easily be rescued.[282]

On Easter Tuesday morning, Liam Mellows led the Clarinbridge Volunteers from Killeeneen to Clarinbridge, where they mounted an attack on the RIC barracks.[283] Mellows selected twelve young men to lead the attack: 'His plan was to form up the attacking party in two groups of six each on the green opposite [the barracks]. At a given signal they would leap the walls, rush through the door, which then lay open, and seize the barracks.' The Volunteers gained access to the barracks, but once they had done so, they found themselves caught in the cross-fire as the police on the second floor opened fire on the Volunteers outside, so that 'around the interior walls of the stone-built barracks the bullets screamed and ricochetted, wounding Mick Callanan'. The young and inexperienced Volunteers then 'backed out on the street for instructions as to how they should deal with the situation', and as they did so the police rushed down the stairs and bolted the door.[284] When Michael Kelly arrived in the village a short time later, he observed that 'The whole company was there, all firing at the barracks at a range of about fifty yards. There was a barricade on the Oranmore Road made of Mineral water boxes, with Volunteers behind the barricades to prevent reinforcements from reaching the barracks. All the approaches to the village were barricaded and all traffic held up.'[285] However, the police

[278] Patrick Coy witness statement, MA BMH WS 1,203; Haverty, 'Memoirs of an ordinary republican', MA BMH CD 72; Michael Manning witness statement, MA BMH WS 1,164.
[279] Peter McDonnell witness statement, MA BMH WS 1,612.
[280] Thomas Courtney witness statement, MA BMH WS 447.
[281] Mícheál Ó Droighneáin witness statement, MA BMH WS 374.
[282] PRO War Office 35/69/1/2.
[283] There were seventy-four men in the Clarinbridge company armed with six rifles and twenty-four revolvers. *Connacht Tribune*, 9 Apr. 1966.
[284] Ibid.   [285] Michael Kelly witness statement, MA BMH WS 1,564.

were barricaded inside the building, and the rebels were unable to take the barracks by force. During the attack, the local parish priest, Father Tully, 'spoke to them and told them the curse of God would be on them if they used any violence', and demanded that they call off the attack.[286] 'Mellows refused to do so unless the R.I.C. surrendered. He asked Fr. Tully to call on the police to surrender. Fr. Tully did so, but they refused, and we resumed the attack.' After a few hours, Mellows called off the rebels, and ordered his men to march towards Oranmore, with the intention of attacking the barracks there. There was only one casualty at Clarinbridge, as Martin Newell recalls: 'Shortly after the attack had started, a policeman cycling from Clarenbridge to Kilcolgan was called on by the outpost to halt and put up his hands. He made an attempt to draw his revolver and one of the outpost—my brother Ned—opened fire on him and wounded him.'[287]

An attack on the barracks at Oranmore had already been initiated by the captain of the local Volunteers, Joe Howley. Having mobilized the two neighbouring Volunteer companies at Oranmore and Maree, Howley assembled the combined force of 106 men in Oranmore on Easter Tuesday morning. 'The officers had revolvers; many of the men had shotguns; some had hayforks; no one had a rifle.'[288] In the village, a policeman stood in the doorway of the barracks, and every now and again walked out a few paces and then walked back again. The Volunteers planned to capture him as he walked out, 'leaving the way clear to rush into the barracks'. But the policeman was on the alert, and 'at the first sound of heavy boots leaped for the doorway, slammed the door and bolted it'. Once again, the police held the barracks, and Howley withdrew his men to join Mellows at Clarinbridge.[289] The two groups of Volunteers, under the command of Mellows and Howley, met on the road between Oranmore and Clarinbridge, and decided to renew the attack on Oranmore barracks. As the 180 men marched back towards Oranmore, however, they came under fire from a party of police on the road outside the village, hidden behind heavy furniture.[290] At the same time, Mellows was informed that a party of police were travelling by train from Galway to Oranmore, and

---

[286] Brighid Breathnach witness statement, MA BMH WS 617; report on west Galway in 1916, PRO CO 904/120. Dolan implausibly suggests that Tully did not object to the attack and instead 'smiled grimly' when he heard that the men were 'in revolt against England'. *Connacht Tribune*, 9 Apr. 1966.

[287] Martin Newell witness statement, MA BMH WS 1,562. The man was Constable David Manning who was wounded in the nose and detained by the rebels until 29 April. According to the War Office, he was unarmed and agreed to surrender when requested to do so. PRO WO 35/69/1/1 and 3.

[288] *Connacht Tribune*, 9 Apr. 1966.   [289] Ibid.   [290] Ibid.

he sent Michael Commins to see if this force had arrived at the station.[291] The extra Constabulary had already arrived at the station when Commins got there, and they 'spotted the Volunteer and opened fire on him. The Volunteer jumped on his bike and in a stooped position and under cover of a wall got safely away and reported to Mellows that the police had got off the train.'[292] A further group of police, under County Inspector Clayton, and ten Connaught Rangers, under Captain Sir Andrew Armstrong, arrived by road from Galway, and Mellows instructed the Volunteers to retreat back along the Oranmore–Athenry road.[293] As his men retreated, 'Mellows remained behind; he was the last to leave and took cover at the gable of Reilly's public-house until the R.I.C. arrived in the village from the station and, when they were about to enter the R.I.C. barrack, he opened fire on them, with, I think, an automatic pistol from a distance of 25 yards.'[294]

The rebels were about a mile from Athenry when they encountered the Athenry company, who were marching to Oranmore to join up with Mellows. At Athenry, Lardner had decided that an attack on the RIC barracks in the town would be disastrous. The barracks was surrounded by houses, all occupied by the RIC, who would have been able to open fire on the attacking rebels.[295] Consequently, the company decided to 'retreat towards Oranmore and meet Mellows and his contingent and leave it to him to decide what was best to do'. At the point in the road where the two groups of Volunteers met, there was an Agricultural College, and 'Liam decided to take possession of that for the time being.'[296] That evening the Volunteers from Clarinbridge, Oranmore, Maree, and Athenry were united at the College, and later joined by the Rockfield, Newcastle, Derrydonnell, Cussaun, and Kilconieron companies.[297] The Volunteers were accompanied by Father Feeney, who acted as chaplain to the rebels during Easter week, and also 'the girls of Cuman na mBan' who 'generally looked after the cooking'.[298] At the College, 'the women lay in the beds normally used by students and many of the leaders and men also found orthodox beds',[299] but most of the rank and file slept in the outhouses

---

[291] Ibid.
[292] Martin Newell witness statement, MA BMH WS 1,562.
[293] *Connacht Tribune*, 9 Apr. 1966.
[294] Martin Newell witness statement, MA BMH WS 1,562.
[295] *Connacht Tribune*, 9 Apr. 1966; Frank Hynes witness statement, MA BMH WS 446.
[296] Frank Hynes witness statement, MA BMH WS 446.
[297] Martin Newell witness statement, BMH WS 1,562; *Connacht Tribune*, 9 Apr. 1966; Gilbert Morrissey witness statement, MA BMH WS 874.
[298] 'Document from Ailbhe O'Monachain, January 1939', DGAD.
[299] *Connacht Tribune*, 9 Apr. 1966.

of the college, on beds of hay and straw.[300] Early the next morning, the Volunteers were drilled and

We were ordered by an officer—I cannot remember who he was—to yoke the horses to the carts and load them up with potatoes etc. While we were doing so, a scout named Casserly came with the news that Castlegar and Claregalway companies had ambushed a convoy of R.I.C. at Carnmore Crossroad and were on their way after him across the mountain to join the main body at the farmyard.[301]

On Easter Tuesday, the Castlegar and Claregalway Volunteers had also been mobilized, and marched towards Oranmore to join forces with Mellows.[302] However, *en route* to Oranmore, they 'were informed that the companies we were to link up with there had gone to Athenry'.[303] Tom Newell was sent to Mellows in Athenry for further instructions, and the two companies spent that night in farmhouses and barns at Carnmore and Kiltullagh.[304] Early on Wednesday morning, Michael Newell was leading the Castlegar company to Carnmore crossroads where they were to meet the Claregalway company:

It was then about 5 a.m. on Wednesday. I noticed a girl on a hill at Kiltullagh waving a white apron, apparently in order to attract our attention. She was Miss Sheila (Bina) King. I looked to see what was wrong and saw a number of motor cars about half a mile away coming in our direction from Galway City. We at first thought it was the Galway City Volunteers coming to join with us. Captain Molloy ordered us to take cover behind the walls. Just as we had taken cover, fire was opened on us. The cars proceeded to about one hundred yards from our position and then halted. The enemy advanced on foot on our position, firing all the time. Captain Molloy ordered us to open fire which we did, but the enemy fire was so intense and the bullets striking the top of the walls, we were compelled to keep down, and we were only able to take an occasional shot. The enemy advanced up to the cross roads and Constable Whelan was pushed by District Inspector Herd [*sic*] up to the wall which was about four feet high, the District Inspector standing behind Whelan and holding him by the collar of his tunic.

Constable Whelan shouted, 'surrender, boys, I know ye all'. Whelan was shot dead and the District Inspector fell also and lay motionless on the ground. The enemy then made an attempt to outflank our position but were beaten back. The enemy then retreated and continued to fire until well out of range of our shotguns They got back into the cars and went in the direction of Oranmore.[305]

After the engagement at Carnmore, the sixty men of the Claregalway and

---

300 Martin Newell witness statement, MA BMH WS 1,562.
301 Ibid.   302 *Connacht Tribune*, 9 Apr. 1966.
303 Michael Newell witness statement, MA BMH WS 342.
304 Ibid.   305 Ibid.

Castlegar companies, armed only with thirty shotguns, marched to the Department of Agriculture farm, where they met up with Mellows and the other rebel companies on Wednesday morning.[306] Altogether, there were now about 500 men at Athenry,[307] armed with little more than 25 rifles, 60 revolvers, 300 shotguns, 60 pikes, and 'some assorted hayforks, bayonets and other extemporised weapons'.[308]

On Wednesday morning, a small contingent of police attempted to attack the rebel position at the Agricultural College. Martin Newell recalls:

A scout came in from the Athenry direction with the news that a number of R.I.C. men had moved out of Athenry and had gone into the Agricultural College land on the opposite side of the road and were moving in a south westerly direction towards the farmyard. Captain Eamon Corbett got five or six men armed with rifles across the main road into the Mulpit road and opened fire on the R.I.C. men who were advancing towards them. The police returned the fire and retreated back into the town.[309]

Although there were no casualties on either side, this incident appears to have demonstrated to the rebel leaders that the Agricultural College was a vulnerable location, which could easily be attacked by both the police and the military. A 'Council of War' was held that morning, at which 'Tom Ruane suggested that we should break up into small columns and fight the police as we would meet them. The meeting was unanimously against doing so. It was decided to move to Moyode Castle.'[310] The captain of the Athenry company, Frank Hynes, explains the decision to decamp to Moyode in the following terms:

Anyone reading this account would be inclined to think that we were acting in a rather cowardly manner—why did we not attack the barrack in Athenry? Why did we keep retreating, etc, etc. The Volunteers who were out in Galway numbered between five and six hundred; we had about fifty full service rifles and about thirty rounds for each rifle. The rest were old shot guns, .22 rifles, about one dozen pikes and a good many more were not armed at all, so that if we wasted our ammunition on attacking the barrack we had nothing to fight with after that; and as for bombs, we made some hopeless attempts at making bombs. If one of them exploded in a man's hand it would not injure him. After the scrap with the peelers we called a meeting and decided to retreat to a place called Moyode. This was a castle which was owned by one of the big landlords called Perse [*sic*]. It was about five miles

306 Ibid.   307 'Document from Ailbhe O'Monachain, January 1939', DGAD.
308 *Connacht Tribune*, 16 Apr. 1966.
309 Martin Newell witness statement, MA BMH WS 1,562.
310 Patrick Callanan witness statememt, MA BMH WS 347.

from us. The argument in favour of Moyode was that we could defend it at least until our ammunition would be spent. The castle was in charge of a caretaker so there was no trouble in capturing it.[311]

On Wednesday evening, the rebel force made the 5-mile journey south to the deserted castle at Moyode, where they arrived at between seven and eight on Thursday morning.[312]

The following afternoon, Tom Kenny rode into Moyode Castle on his white horse and held a meeting with Mellows. He said that he had met a man from Ballinasloe who told him that 'a battalion of soldiers 900 strong, had arrived in that town and was ready to march to Galway'.[313] Writing in the 1940s, Frank Hynes suggested that Kenny had deliberately conveyed a false rumour to Mellows 'to get us to give up and go home and have sense'.[314] Whether this is true or not,[315] Kenny's intervention generated a sense of panic among the Volunteers: 'We called a meeting and I'm afraid that one or two of our officers were anxious to take him seriously and take his advice to go home. Liam got disgusted and said he would not disband the men. He handed over to Larry, but Larry would not disband them. Liam after about an hour took over again and called for the Volunteers to go out the roads to see if there were any soldiers.'[316] At 3 o'clock, Mellows and some of the other officers set out in a motor car and drove 12 miles east in the direction of Ballinasloe, finding only a vacant RIC barracks at New Inn, and no evidence of British forces. On his return, Mellows 'told his staff that Kenny had been misinformed . . . and that it seemed as if the country-side was still clear of British troops'.[317] However, a subsequent rumour 'of the same nature' provoked the officers to hold a further meeting at which Frank Hynes 'proposed that the officers all stick together whatever comes' but that 'the men . . . be informed of the situation and given the option of going or staying'. The majority of the rank and file had been mobilized on Easter Tuesday believing simply that they were to take part in a route march, but they now found themselves engaged in open rebellion. Both Frank Hynes and Father Feeney felt that these men should be given the option of going home, should they want to.[318] Consequently:

On Thursday night, all the Volunteers were instructed to assemble in the yard.

311 Frank Hynes witness statement, MA BMH WS 446.
312 James Barrett witness statement, MA BMH WS 343.
313 *Connacht Tribune*, 16 Apr. 1966.
314 Frank Hynes witness statement, MA BMH WS 446.
315 According to Dolan, 'the story was false, but Kenny did not know that'. *Connacht Tribune*, 16 Apr. 1966.
316 Frank Hynes witness statement, MA BMH WS 446.
317 *Connacht Tribune*, 16 Apr. 1966.   318 Ibid.

Mellows and Alf Monaghan addressed us and pointed out that any man who was not prepared to continue with them was free to leave and that they could do so honourably and that nothing worse would be thought of him. When some of the men were leaving, Martin [Mattie] Niland was standing on the archway leading to the yard. He was waving a tricolour and saying in solemn tones: 'This is the flag, boys, this is the flag'.[319]

About two hundred men left, although some of them returned to Moyode the following morning.[320]

During his meeting with Mellows, Kenny also appears to have suggested that the Volunteers should attack the RIC barracks at Craughwell.[321] The Craughwell National Volunteers, including the officers of the United Irish League, had offered their services to the local Constabulary, and were hiding out in the barracks partly for their own safety.[322] While an attack on the barracks would fit with the broader plan of the Galway Rising, it would also contribute to the wider struggle of the secret society against the bourgeois leadership of the United Irish League. Mellows, sensing that Kenny was attempting to guide the Galway Rising in a more radical direction, refused his request, much to Kenny's annoyance.[323] However, an attempt was made by Mellows to encourage those members of the National Volunteers at Craughwell, some of whom were former members of Kenny's secret society, to join the rebels.[324] Martin Newell and Darby Deely were sent to Craughwell 'to contact the prominent members of the Redmond Volunteers. Our instructions from Mellows was to tell them that they would be gladly accepted if they came. We carried out these instructions by interviewing several prominent members, but they refused.'[325] Later, Mellows would adopt a socialist republican position, but his politics during the Galway Rising were relatively conservative. Throughout the Galway Rising, the Volunteers were forced to seize cattle and other provisions to feed themselves, although they did so only from 'wealthy shopkeepers and big farmers'.[326] Perhaps fearing that the seizure of cattle might introduce an agrarian dimension to the Galway Rising,

[319] Martin Newell witness statement, MA BMH WS 1,562.
[320] *Connacht Tribune*, 16 Apr. 1966.
[321] Patrick Callanan witness statement, MA BMH WS 405.
[322] CI monthly report, east Galway, Apr. 1916, PRO CO 904/99.
[323] Kenny was later openly critical of Mellows's leadership of the Galway Rising. See Patrick Callanan witness statement, MA BMH WS 405.
[324] Patrick Callanan points out that 'most of those I knew in the I.R.B. in Craughwell from 1905–1916, aided the R.I.C. in Craughwell during Easter week, 1916'. Patrick Callanan witness statement, MA BMH WS 347.
[325] Martin Newell witness statement, MA BMH WS 1,562.
[326] James Barrett witness statement, MA BMH WS 343.

Mellows 'was reluctant to slaughter bullocks for his men'.[327] When James Barrett arrived at Moyode with 'twenty-one of the finest bullocks to be got anywhere . . . the property of the Dalys of Dunsandle', Mellows ordered him to return them.[328]

On the Thursday evening, there was a sense of impending doom at Moyode. Michael Kelly recalled that 'The rumours about the British advance and the uncertainty, along with the withdrawal of the two hundred men, had a disturbing effect on all the Volunteers . . . We got no sleep that night.'[329] The next day, there were further rumours that British forces were approaching, until 'On Friday evening we got word from one of our scouts who were watching the railway, that 900 soldiers were in Attymon and were marching on Moyode. There was no question of trying to defend the castle under the circumstances, so the question was, would we disband or retreat in order; so we decided on the latter.'[330] Mellows appears to have still believed that Clare and Limerick might rise,[331] and he proposed 'trying to get down through Clare county and if we got enough help to fight our way to Limerick'.[332] As the rebels marched south past Craughwell, they were overtaken by two priests, Father Tom Fahy and Father O'Farrell, 'who told us we were marching to certain death. They had definite information that Dublin had given in and that the soldiers in Galway were aware of our movements and were marching to meet us.'[333] Indeed, two groups of 100 marines had been posted to Galway city from Queenstown and HMS *Gloucester* by the War Office on 27 April.[334]

There was a deserted Big House near Peterswell, at Limepark, and the Volunteers 'decided to hold council there'.[335] Father Fahy 'tried to reason with Mellows that the only sensible thing to do was to disband his men, otherwise they were likely to be surrounded and caught. He said no; he would fight it out to the end. These men had joined him voluntarily and he would never ask them to go away . . . I suggested to Mellows that at least a meeting of the officers should be held to discuss the question. He agreed to this.'[336] At Limepark, Michael Kelly of the Clarinbridge Volunteers

happened to be sitting on the window sill of the room in which the meeting was

327 *Connacht Tribune*, 16 Apr. 1966.
328 James Barrett witness statement, MA BMH WS 343.
329 Michael Kelly witness statement, MA BMH WS 1,564.
330 Frank Hynes witness statement, MA BMH WS 446.
331 Patrick Callanan witness statement, MA BMH WS 347.
332 Frank Hynes witness statement, MA BMH WS 446.
333 Ibid.   334 PRO WO 35/69/1/2.
335 Frank Hynes witness statement, MA BMH WS 446.
336 Father Tom Fahy witness statement, MA BMH WS 383.

held. I heard one of the priests telling all the officers assembled about the surrender in Dublin. A discussion then arose mainly between the priest and Mellows. The priest was trying to convince the meeting that, as the Volunteers in Dublin had surrendered, the Galway Volunteers should disperse as the position was hopeless in the circumstances. The priests asked Mellows whether he would be agreeable to put it to the men whether they would disperse or carry on. Mellows said that he had already put it to the men in Moyode and that every man in Limepark had agreed to carry on. The priest said that as Dublin had been dispersed, the British Forces could concentrate fully on Galway. Mellows still refused to go to the men for a decision as he maintained it had already been taken. The priests asked him then if he would allow them to put it to the men and after some hesitation he agreed.[337]

Father Fahy then addressed the 350 remaining men, gathered on the lawn in front of the Big House, telling them that if they did not disband they would be killed by the advancing British forces: 'They had made their gesture, he told them, and now they must preserve their lives for the next fight.'[338] Mhiceáil Uí Coincheannain, of the Claregalway company, recalled:

Tháinig scéal ansin go páirc an aoil an áit a raibh said compáilti ag Liam Mellows, agus ag Father Feeney, agus ag na ceannphoirt a bhí go raibh loingeachaí móra istigh i gcuan na Gaillimhe, agus go raibh an t-arm a' tígeacht amach as Gaillimh ar a' mbóthar acab le gunnaí beaga is le gunnaí móra, agus nach mbeadh aon ghnaithe acab le na gcuid gunnaí gróin[?] a' cainnt ar seasamh in aghaidh rifles, agus in aghaidh gunnaí móra . . .

Fuair said cómhairle ansin ó na ceannphoirt dul abhaile thríd na haicearraí, agus iad féin a comhaint comh maith is a bheadh said in ann ar a námhaid.

[The news then arrived at Limepark, the place they were camped with Liam Mellows and Father Feeney, and the other leaders, that large ships had landed in Galway Bay and that the army was coming out to them from Galway with big guns and small guns, and that they would have no business with their defective weapons making a stand against rifles and against big guns . . .

They got advice then from the leaders to go home through the short cuts and to protect themselves immediately as best they could from the enemy.[339]]

Indeed, the poorly armed force would surely have been massacred by the British marines if they had remained at Limepark. After a great deal of discussion, the Volunteers decided to disband, and on Saturday, 29 April, five days after the Galway Rising had begun, the 350 rebels returned to their homes, while Mellows and the other leaders went on the run.[340] Liam Mel-

---

[337] Michael Kelly witness statement, MA BMH WS 1,564.
[338] *Connacht Tribune*, 16 Apr. 1916.
[339] Mhiceáil Uí Coincheannain, 'Eirghe amach na Cásca 1916 i mbaile Chlár na Gaillimhe. [The 1916 Easter Rising in Claregalway]', DIFUCD IML 781, 391–2. I am grateful to Tony Varley for translating this document.   [340] *Connacht Tribune*, 16 Apr. 1966.

lows and Patrick Callanan escaped to New York, Eamon Corbett made his way to California, Lawrence Lardner went into hiding in Belfast, and Tom Kenny travelled to Boston, where he remained until 1923.[341] Father Feeney was 'banished' to the United States for five years.[342] Most of the rebels were arrested the following week, and imprisoned in English and Scottish jails (Glasgow, Knutsford, Lewes, Perth, Stafford, Wakefield, Wandsworth, and Woking), before being transported to Frongoch in south Wales, where the rank and file were detained until July.[343] The more prominent rebels were finally released at Christmas 1916.

Who were the Galway rebels? The Inspector General described the Irish Volunteers as 'persons of no importance' or 'men of no position in the country', adding that 'nearly everybody of stake is opposed to them'.[344] In west Galway, the County Inspector claimed in February 1915 that the Irish Volunteers were 'persons of no influence'.[345] Three months later, he explained more precisely: 'There is a great deal of Sinn Fein amongst the agricultural class of young men & the shop boys', and after the rebellion he noted that 'at the time the rebellion broke out a large percentage of the labourers, farmer's sons, and shop assistants, were either active Sinn Feiners or in favour of its policy'.[346] The County Inspector for east Galway also described the social composition of the rebel forces in his responses to the questions of the Royal Commission on the Rebellion:

1773. Now many of the Sinn Feiners were pretty well known weren't they?—Yes.
1774. Were there any people in it among them of the superior class and education?—No.
1775. What class did they come from?—Well, one of the leaders, this man Kenny, is a blacksmith, another was a publican [Lardner]. There were shopkeepers and farmers' sons.
1776. There was nobody of a literary type a Sinn Feiner?—No.
1777. There was no person of any considerable position?—No.[347]

A study of the social background of 211 (43 per cent) of the Galway insurgents has been undertaken to ascertain the accuracy of these observations (see Tables 13, 14 and 15). This analysis indicates that most of the

---

[341] Greaves, *Liam Mellows*, 101; interview with Kitty Lardner (Lawrence Lardner's daughter) at Athenry, 15 Dec. 1994; Patrick Callanan witness statement, MA BMH WS 405.
[342] Brighid Breathnach witness statement, MA BMH WS 617.
[343] Sean O Mahony, *Frongoch: university of revolution* (Dublin, 1987), 16.
[344] IG monthly reports, Sept.–Oct. 1914, PRO CO 904/94–5.
[345] CI monthly report, west Galway, Feb. 1915, PRO CO 904/96.
[346] CI monthly report, west Galway, May 1915, PRO CO 904/97; reports on west Galway in 1916, PRO CO 904/120.
[347] *The Royal Commission on the Rebellion in Ireland: minutes of evidence and appendix of documents*, HC (1916), [Cd. 8311], xi. 263.

rebels were farmers (34 per cent) or farmers' sons (26 per cent), occupying small farms. As Table 14 indicates, 69 per cent of the farmer-insurgents occupied small farms, valued at less than £20. The next largest group were skilled and unskilled labourers. Almost one-fifth (18 per cent) of the rebels were tradesmen, primarily from urban backgrounds, and a further 13 per cent were agricultural labourers. Of the remainder, 4 per cent were professionals, generally teachers and solicitors; 3 per cent were small shop-keepers; and 2 per cent were shop assistants. The rebels were all Roman Catholic, and almost all of them were literate (98 per cent), unmarried (83 per cent), and young (85 per cent of them were aged under 40 in 1916). In 1911, only 16 per cent of them were deemed by the censal enumerators to be the heads of their families. While many of them were members of the Gaelic League, less than half were Irish speakers (44 per cent). Overall, then, the observations of the police were correct: the Galway rebels were young, literate (if not literary) Catholics from small farm, artisan, and labouring backgrounds.

The Galway Rising emerged from the republican and radical agrarian tradition of the secret society. In the first instance, it was conceived by the local leadership as a contribution to a nationwide insurrection intended to force the British out of Ireland. But it also contained radical agrarian elements. The buildings occupied and attacked by the rebels were symbols of the power of the landlord, the grazier, and the state, against which the Galway secret society had been agitating since the 1870s.[348] The insurgents, many of whom were also members of the secret society, were small farmers, artisans, and landless labourers. Indeed, the police reported that the Galway Rising had been carried out by the secret society,[349] a belief that was confirmed by the low level of agrarian agitation during 1916 due to 'the fact that most of the persons who organised and committed agrarian crimes in the past were interned'.[350] Symbolically, one of the guns used in the Rising had been taken from the soldier who was shot with Walter Bourke by the Galway IRB in 1882.[351] Martin Newell later recalled that it was Kenny who had inspired him to take part in the Galway Rising:

In my opinion . . . were it not for Tom Kenny and his activities for over ten years prior to Easter 1916, there would certainly have been no Rising in County Galway.

[348] In particular, the Department of Agriculture farm at Newford and the Big House at Limepark were both the objects of ongoing agrarian agitation orchestrated by the secret society. See CI monthly report, east Galway, Oct. 1907 NA IGCI/12; CI monthly report, west Galway, July 1916, PRO CO 904/100.

[349] CI monthly report, west Galway, July 1916, PRO CO 904/100.

[350] Report on west Galway in 1916, PRO CO 904/120.

[351] Tom Kenny's obituary, *Connacht Tribune*, 5 Apr. 1947.

For my part anyway, and the same holds for many of my comrades, I would not have been involved in the Galway Rising. The teaching and example of Kenny ... exercised a profound influence on many of us.[352]

Most of the Galway rebels had not benefited from the various Land Acts passed by the British Government, and probably held firm to the belief that the land question could only be solved by an independent Irish Republic. It was for this reason that they staged an insurrection against both the British state in Ireland, and the landlords who owned the thousands of acres of grazing land which surrounded their small holdings. In their responses to the questions put to them by the Royal Commission on the rebellion, the insurgents generally explained their motivation in nationalistic terms. When asked if he knew what he was doing when he joined the Galway rebellion, Michael Kelly 'answered that I did, and [said] that I was looking for the freedom of my country as any decent man would do in an unfree country'.[353] However, the rebels' conception of 'freedom' encompassed economic as well as political liberty, and the two struggles against the British state and the landlord class were viewed as one and the same.[354] The Galway Rising was, in the words of Martin Dolan: 'A Rising of common men who had learned their patriotism from their parents, from patriotic teachers, [and] from those who were steeped in the traditions of the secret societies which had always resisted ... the British and ... [the] landlords.'[355]

IV

The expansion of the Sinn Féin movement between the Easter Rising and the December 1918 general election has been discussed at length elsewhere, and I will not describe those developments in detail here.[356] However, it is clear that four critical factors converted the marginal pre-1916 Sinn Féin party into the mass movement of December 1918. First, the government's repressive response to the Easter Rising of 1916 radicalized Irish nationalists and caused many of them to adopt the more separatist politics of

---

[352] Letter from Martin Newell, *Connacht Tribune* 19 Feb. 1966.
[353] Michael Kelly witness statement, MA BMH WS 1,564. See also Martin Newell witness statement, MA BMH WS 1,562.
[354] Gilbert Morrissey witness statement, MA BMH WS 1,138.
[355] *Connacht Tribune*, 2 Apr. 1966. Undoubtedly, the Galway Rising was more than a 'skirmish', as it is portrayed in Laffan, *The resurrection of Ireland*, 43.
[356] See, for instance, Laffan, *The resurrection of Ireland*, Chs. 3 and 4.

Sinn Féin.[357] Second, the failure of the Irish Parliamentary Party to secure a Home Rule settlement after the Rising suggested the inefficacy of parliamentary agitation as a means of achieving political independence.[358] Third, the identification in the popular mind of Sinn Féin as the anti-conscription party during the conscription crisis of April 1918 caused young men to flock into its ranks.[359] And fourth, Sinn Féin's adoption of a radical agrarian policy (at a time when the Irish Party were urging their supporters to put their hunger for land on hold) enabled the new party to win the support of the small farmer.[360] The membership of Sinn Féin increased rapidly from 11,000 in June 1917 to 112,000 in December 1918,[361] and the membership of the United Irish League gradually declined over the same period from 120,403 to 105,720.[362]

During the Rising, most of the population of county Galway did not support the rebels. In the east riding, 'The feeling of the people generally was one of intense indignation at the action of the rebels . . . [I]n the district of Athenry, the rebels had large numbers of sympathisers and also in some places in Loughrea district, but in the rest of the Riding the feeling was wholly against them.'[363] In west Galway, on the other hand, 'When the rebellion broke out, a large area became involved, and most of the Districts of Galway, Gort, and Tuam became very disaffected and disturbed. A large percentage of the young men in these Districts were guilty of overt acts of rebellion.'[364] The Rising was condemned by Galway county council who 'rejoice[d] that this dastardly attempt has failed', and by the various rural district councils throughout the county.[365] In Galway city, the arrested rebels also encountered great hostility from the townspeople. Mícheál Ó Droighneáin recalls that when the leaders of the Irish Volunteers in Galway city were arrested on Easter Monday and carried by sidecar to the docks, they were 'pelted with mud off the streets by the mothers of men serving with the British Forces—Hardiman and Carter

---

[357] IG monthly report, June 1916, PRO CO 904/100.
[358] See, for example, IG monthly report, Oct. 1916, PRO CO 904/101; *Connacht Tribune*, 5 Aug. 1916 and 14 July 1917.
[359] IG monthly report, Mar. 1918, PRO CO 904/105.
[360] For a full discussion of Sinn Féin's agrarian policy, see Ch. 6.
[361] IG monthly report, June 1917, PRO CO 904/103; IG monthly report, Dec. 1918, PRO CO 904/107.
[362] United Irish League membership figures, PRO CO 904/20/2.
[363] Report on east Galway in 1916, PRO CO 904/120.
[364] Report on west Galway in 1916, PRO CO 904/120.
[365] Galway county council minutes, 3 May 1916, Galway county council offices (GCCO). For a discussion of Loughrea Town Commissioners' response to the Rising, see *Connacht Tribune*, 6 Mar. 1920.

receiving lumps of mud in their faces'.[366] However, as the police observed, 'the alleged excesses committed by the military in Dublin, and the execution of the leaders of the insurrection, subsequently stirred up a considerable amount of sympathy with the rebels, even amongst persons who were hitherto regarded as loyal'.[367] Sinn Féin, although it had not officially been involved in the Easter Rising, benefited from the increased sympathy for the rebels displayed by the wider nationalist community. Even so, at the end of 1916 the police could still report that life in Galway had gone on much as usual: 'Apart from the rebellion, nothing important occurred during the year.'[368]

In the seventeen months between May 1916 and December 1918, the membership of Sinn Féin in Galway expanded from 200 (in one branch) to 7,530 (in eighty-four branches).[369] In the initial phase of expansion, between May 1916 and September 1917 (when there were 1,822 Sinn Feiners in twenty-six branches),[370] the new members of Sinn Féin were generally the released internees and former Irish Volunteers, who had numbered just under 2,000 on the eve of the Rising. These men, many of whom were also veterans of the secret society, became the leaders of Sinn Féin in Galway after the Rising. A study of the previous political involvements of forty-one Sinn Féin officers in Galway in 1917–18 quantifies these continuities (see Table 16).[371] Over one-quarter (27 per cent) had been involved in the first Sinn Féin party, while just under a quarter (24 per cent) were graduates of both the IRB and Kenny's secret society. There was also a high level of continuity between the rebels of 1916 and the officers of Sinn Féin: at least 41 per cent of Sinn Féin leaders in Galway had been 'out' in 1916. Far fewer were veterans of the United Irish League: only 10 per cent of the forty-one Sinn Féin officers examined here were former members of the UIL, and these tended to be Fenians and members of the 'secret League'. Most prominent among these defectors was Martin Finnerty, the former secretary of the east Galway UIL executive.[372] As a Fenian and agrarian agitator, he was typical of the United Irish Leaguers who defected to Sinn Féin in Galway.[373]

---

[366] Mícheál Ó Droighneáin witness statement, MA BMH WS 374.

[367] Report on west Galway in 1916, PRO CO 904/120.

[368] Report on east Galway in 1916, PRO CO 904/120.

[369] CI monthly report, east Galway, May 1916, PRO CO 904/100; CI monthly reports, east and west Galway, Dec. 1918, PRO CO 904/107.

[370] CI monthly reports, east and west Galway, Sept. 1917, PRO CO 904/104.

[371] For the methodology used to carry out this study, see Appendix I.

[372] On Finnerty, see Ch. 3.

[373] Of the ninety-nine Galway Leaguers under review, 7 % defected to Sinn Féin. The defectors included four farmers, two farmers' sons, and one town labourer. An examination

TABLE 16. Previous political and social involvements of Sinn Féin officers in Galway in 1917–1918

Affiliation	Sinn Féin officers (%)
UIL (1909–16)	10
Local council	5
AOH	0
GAA	27
Gaelic League	15
Sinn Féin (1906–10)	27
IRB	24
Secret society	24
1916 Rising	41
Number	41

Notes: UIL (1909–16): involved in the United Irish League between 1909 and 1916; Local council: member of the county council or of urban or rural district councils; AOH: member of the Ancient Order of Hibernians; GAA: member of the Gaelic Athletic Association; IRB: member of the Irish Republican Brotherhood.

Sources: See Appendix I.

At least half of the leaders of Sinn Féin in Galway joined the new party after the Rising. Indeed, the extraordinary expansion of Sinn Féin in Galway can be attributed largely to the party's involvement in agrarian agitation during the spring of 1918, and to the conscription crisis of April 1918. In the spring of 1918, Sinn Féin promoted an agrarian policy which effectively outflanked the Irish Parliamentary Party on the land question, and many of the rural poor in the county quickly identified themselves with the new party. As a result, Sinn Féin membership increased dramatically from 4,742 to 6,343 between March and April 1918.[374] During the conscription crisis of April 1918, the new party also won the support of the Catholic clergy, and Sinn Féin membership in Galway soared from 6,343 in April to 7,524 in May.[375] These factors were summarized by the compiler of the *Intelligence notes* in 1918:

The Sinn Fein movement [in the east riding of county Galway] progressed enormously during the year. At the beginning of the year the general public

of the landholdings occupied by the farmers and farmer's sons indicates that two were middle sized (valued at between £20 and £50), two were small (valued at less than £20), one was congested (valued at less than £10), and one was not possible to identify. In addition, three of the defectors were well-known members of the IRB.

[374] CI monthly reports, east and west Galway, Mar. and Apr. 1918, PRO CO 904/105.
[375] CI monthly reports, east and west Galway, May 1918, PRO CO 904/106.

appeared to take little interest in Sinn Fein, and where Sinn Fein clubs existed their objects were in most cases purely agrarian. The young priests, while Sinn Fein in their tendencies, were fairly discreet and were kept in check by the Bishops. However, the moment the anti-conscription movement amalgamated the clergy and Sinn Fein, the former appears to have thrown off all restraint and indulged in the most extreme Sinn Fein propaganda, utilising their position as priests to push their political opinions. The Sinn Feiners here, as in other parts of Ireland, took a prominent part in opposing the application of conscription to Ireland, and the failure of the Government to enforce it has greatly improved the position of Sinn Fein, as that body gets the chief credit for defeating conscription. At the beginning of the year about 20 or 25 per cent. [*sic*] of the population were Sinn Feiners, now they are about 80 per cent.[376]

The small Sinn Féin party, first established in Galway in 1906, thus became the largest and most influential political organization in the county by 1918.[377]

The evidence presented in this chapter suggests that it may not be possible to apply all aspects of Fitzpatrick's Clare model to neighbouring Galway.[378] Far from being established on the basis of the 'Home Rule tradition', Sinn Féin emerged from the radical agrarian and republican political culture of Kenny's secret society. In Galway, the early Sinn Féin movement mobilized the support of the members of a pre-existing secret society, and the new Sinn Féin ideas were incorporated into the republican and anti-grazier ideology of the secret society. There was, in the view of the police, a natural kinship between the ideas of Sinn Féin and the secret society: '[In] the secret society area, which comprises the greater portion of the Districts of Galway, Gort, and Tuam . . . the people have ever been hostile to everyone and everything connected with the Government, and it was as a second nature to them to obey the dictates of . . . Sinn Fein.'[379] Indeed, it is possible that Sinn Féin may have established itself on the basis of pre-existing secret societies elsewhere in Ireland. 'In Clare the County Inspector regards Sinn Fein as the nearest approach to an oathbound Secret Society, and he believes it is responsible for many [agrarian] outrages.'[380] As in Galway, Sinn Féin in Clare was engaged in an agitation to redistribute grazing land, and was prepared to use violent means

---

[376] The confidential print, 1918, PRO CO 903/19/4/48.

[377] On 21 September 1917, Galway Sinn Féiners purchased the unionist newspaper the *Galway Express*, and this played a critical role in disseminating republican ideas. CI monthly report, west Galway, Sept. 1917, PRO CO 904/104.

[378] Sinn Féin did, undoubtedly, inherit the United Irish League's organizational structure of parish branches, and constituency, provincial, and national executives.

[379] Report on west Galway in 1916, PRO CO 904/120.

[380] IG monthly report, Jan. 1912, PRO CO 904/86.

to achieve its objectives.[381] In addition, there were strong links between members of the secret society in north Clare and south Galway, leading the Inspector General to suppose that 'In Galway, and portions of Clare ... there are a number of secret society circles, under the leadership of a blacksmith at Craughwell named Kenny, which are the chief cause of the disturbed condition of those counties.'[382] Further research is required to examine the continuities between the members of the Clare secret society and post-Rising Sinn Féin in the county, but these examples suggest that Galway Sinn Féiners may not have been dissimilar to their colleagues in other parts of the west of Ireland.

This study also suggests that the personnel of Sinn Féin in Galway were not, by and large, the old Home Rule wine decanted into new bottles. However, even in Clare the evidence for continuity is not as high as we may have expected. Of 913 separatists, only 116 (13 per cent) had been members of Home Rule organizations in Clare.[383] While this demonstrates that there was a significant overlap, it does not substantiate the assertion that there was a 'thick strand of continuity' between the two movements, or the statement that separatists were 'almost exclusively' Home Rulers.[384] What can be said, based on this evidence, is that about one in eight separatists (in Clare) had formerly been involved in Home Rule organizations. The combined evidence from Clare and Galway suggests that the level of continuity between the two movements in Ireland is likely to have been between 3 and 13 per cent: at least 87 per cent of provincial Sinn Féiners, then, were not former members of the Home Rule movement.[385] Many of the officers of Sinn Féin in Galway after the Rising were also members of Kenny's secret society, and in the next chapter I will consider the influence which these men had on Sinn Féin's agrarian policy both in Galway and at the wider national level.

---

[381] IG monthly report, Jan. 1912, PRO CO 904/86; IG monthly report, Feb. 1912, PRO CO 904/86; IG monthly report, Aug. 1912, PRO CO 904/87; IG monthly report, Feb. 1913, PRO CO 904/89.   [382] IG monthly report, Feb. 1913, PRO CO 904/89.
[383] Fitzpatrick, *Politics and Irish life*, 289.   [384] Ibid. 138.
[385] Although Marie Coleman discusses a small number of senior Home Rulers who defected to Sinn Féin, she provides no systematic statistics on the continuities between the two movements in Longford. See Marie Coleman, *County Longford and the Irish revolution, 1910–1923* (Dublin, 2003), 74–6.

6

Land and Revolution in the West of Ireland, 1918–1921

> [T]he land agitation . . . is sweeping through the West like a prairie
> fire . . . [W]hatever we may think of the means, the object aimed
> at [land redistribution] is being secured with a rapidity that all the
> British land laws of the past hundred years never attained . . . [T]he
> landless men of Ireland are proceeding by rough and ready methods
> to settle the [land] question for themselves.
>
> (*Connacht Tribune*, 3 Apr. 1920)

Did Ireland experience a revolution between 1916 and 1923 and, if so, what
kind of revolution was it? Recently, a debate has begun among Irish historians as to the nature of the Irish revolution, and Peter Hart has provided a
useful definition of what is meant by the term the 'Irish revolution'. Following Charles Tilly, Hart suggests that the Irish revolution was a period during which two distinct blocs made competing claims to the state (beginning
with the Easter Rising), resulting in a period of multiple sovereignty which
was only concluded in May 1923, when the anti-Treaty republicans gave up
their attempt to dispute the existence of the southern state.[1] This political
revolution was not accompanied by a social revolution as there was no
transformation of class structures.[2] Broadly speaking, the Irish revolution
is depicted as essentially political in nature—involving the transfer of state
power from one elite to another—without any accompanying change in
social structures. Other historians have gone further than Hart in suggesting not simply that there was no social revolution in Ireland between 1916
and 1923, but that there was not even an attempt to challenge the social

---

[1] Peter Hart, 'Definition: defining the Irish revolution', in Joost Augusteijn (ed.), *The
Irish revolution, 1913–1923* (Basingstoke, 2002), 17–18.

[2] This definition of social revolution is derived from Theda Skocpol, *States and social
revolutions: a comparative analysis of France, Russia and China* (Cambridge, 1979), 4–5.

order. In *The resurrection of Ireland*, Michael Laffan claims that 'the Irish
revolution took nationalist, political and military forms, but it did not
seriously attempt—let alone achieve—a change in the social balance of
power.'[3] Underpinning this interpretation is Kevin O'Higgins's famous
retrospective observation that 'We were the most conservative minded
revolutionaries that ever put through a successful revolution.'[4] However,
O'Higgins represented only one wing of the revolutionary movement.
There were radical impulses, and although many of them were defeated,
they demonstrate that the revolution was neither innately nor inevitably
conservative. This chapter will examine the broader social dynamics of
the Irish revolution in the west of Ireland between the general election of
December 1918 and the Truce of July 1921, and consider the extent to which
Irish society was transformed between these years.

I

The members of Sinn Féin were not the old Home Rule wine decanted into
new bottles; but were the new representatives of nationalist Ireland drawn
from different social backgrounds to their opponents in the United Irish
League? In order to assess the extent to which the 1918 general election
inaugurated a transformation in the social composition of nationalist
politics, I have carried out a prosopographical study of the officials of Sinn
Féin and the United Irish League in east Galway. Altogether, biographical
information on 122 Sinn Féin officials (14 per cent of the total in east
Galway in January 1919), and 99 United Irish Leaguers (10 per cent of the
total in east Galway in March 1916) was compiled, and the results of this
analysis are presented in Tables 17,18,19 and 20.[5]

The majority of Sinn Féin officials were drawn from the ranks of the
rural poor. More than half (55 per cent) were small farmers (16 per cent),
their sons (29 per cent), and agricultural labourers (10 per cent). Whereas
farmers were under-represented, in terms of their numbers in the Galway
adult workforce, farmers' sons were slightly over-represented, suggesting
that the party was particularly popular with this group. Most farmers' sons
would not inherit their family farm, and together with the agricultural
labourers, these were the landless men who required land if they were to

---

[3] Laffan, *The resurrection of Ireland*, 315.
[4] Quoted in J. J. Lee, *Ireland, 1912–1985: politics and society* (Cambridge, 1989), 105.
[5] See Appendix I for the methodology of this study.

TABLE 17. The occupations of United Irish League and Sinn Féin
officials in east Galway, 1899–1918

Occupation	United Irish League, 1899–1918 (%)	Sinn Féin, 1916–18 (%)	Galway, 1911 (%)
Farmer	41	16	39
Farmer's son	12	29	24
Shopkeeper-grazier	7	0	
Business	27	13	
Clerk	1	6	
Professional	3	6	
Student	0	1	
Agricultural labourer	1	10	
Town labourer	1	6	
Artisan	7	13	
Number	99	120	

Notes and sources: See Appendix I

TABLE 18. The valuation of the farms occupied by the farmers, farmers'
sons, and shopkeeper-graziers who were members of the United Irish
League and Sinn Féin, 1899–1918

Valuation (£n)	United Irish League, 1899–1918 (%)	Sinn Féin, 1916–18 (%)
$n<4$	5	10
$4\leq n<10$	24	28
$10\leq n<20$	28	31
$20\leq n<30$	19	24
$30\leq n<50$	13	7
$50\leq n<100$	7	0
$n\geq100$	4	0
Number	54	29

Notes and sources: See Appendix I

avoid the emigrant ship.[6] Even those farmers' sons who did inherit,
as well as the farmers who were members of Sinn Féin, occupied small
farms which enabled them to live just above the poverty line. More than

[6] On inheritance patterns in Ireland, see Liam Kennedy, 'Farm succession in modern
Ireland: elements of a theory of inheritance', *Economic History Review*, 44/3 (1991).

TABLE 19. The ages of officials of the United Irish League and
Sinn Féin in 1918, and the United Irish League in 1899

Age	United Irish League, 1918 (%)	Sinn Féin, 1918 (%)	United Irish League, 1899 (%)
0–19	0.0	3.3	0
20–9	2.5	40.0	10
30–9	12.5	33.3	38
40–9	20.0	12.2	19
50–9	37.5	2.2	19
60+	27.5	9.0	14
Number	80	90	21

Notes and sources: See Appendix I.

TABLE 20. Other affiliations of United Irish League and Sinn Féin
officers

Affiliation	United Irish League, 1914–18 (%)	Sinn Féin, 1916–18 (%)
NL/UIL (1899)	35	2
Local council	45	5
AOH	15	0
GAA	5	27
Gaelic League	5	15
IRB	5	24
Secret society	5	24
1916	0	41
United Irish League (1909–16)	100	10
Sinn Féin	0	100
Number	20	41

Notes: NL/UIL (1899): involved in the National League (1882–91) or the United Irish League in 1899; Local council: member of the county council or of urban or rural district councils; AOH: member of the Ancient Order of Hibernians; GAA: member of the Gaelic Athletic Association; IRB: member of the Irish Republican Brotherhood; 1916: involved in the 1916 Rising in Galway.

Sources: See Appendix I.

two-thirds (69 per cent) of farmers and farmers' sons who were members of Sinn Féin lived on small holdings (valued at less than £20), while a substantial proportion (38 per cent) lived on farms which the CDB defined as too small to provide a reasonable standard of living for the occupier and his family.[7] These small farmers required additional land if they were to make their landholdings viable.

The social composition of Sinn Féin was similar to that of the 1916 insurgents, many of whom had joined the new party after their release. Skilled and unskilled labourers had played an important part in the Galway Rising, and artisans (13 per cent) and town labourers (6 per cent) constituted almost one-fifth of Sinn Féin officials (19 per cent). In part, this was because artisans in Ireland were traditionally associated with separatist politics.[8] Throughout the nineteenth century, tradesmen had argued that the Act of Union undermined Irish industrial development, and claimed that Irish manufacturing industries could only be revived by the achievement of political independence.[9] For this reason, the Fenian movement of the 1860s had been dominated by tradesmen, and they remained extremely influential in Sinn Féin. Of 1,086 Fenians arrested under the Habeas Corpus Suspension Act, 520 (48 per cent) were tradesmen.[10] The Sinn Féin policy appealed directly to them because it was committed to Irish industrial development, and to a protectionist policy that would benefit small producers.

There were a significant number of businessmen in the ranks of Sinn Féin in Galway. Almost one-seventh (13 per cent) of Sinn Féin officials were members of the provincial bourgeoisie. While there were also businessmen in the United Irish League, Sinn Féin tended to attract the support of the smaller business interests in the county. In this respect, the composition of Sinn Féin was similar to that of the IRB. According to Garvin, one-fifth of Fenian activists between 1880 and 1902 were 'shopkeepers, usually in a rather small line of business'.[11] However, there were a variety of businesses represented in Sinn Féin including publicans, building contractors, newsagents, general merchants, and jewellers. Sinn Féin's economic policy was attractive to these small business interests as it promised to impose high tariffs on imported goods and to protect and encourage Irish industrial development. Small provincial retailers, who stocked Irish-made goods, would also have benefited from the Sinn Féin campaign to ensure that its members should buy Irish.[12]

---

[7] *Royal Commission on Congestion: final report*, HC (1908), [Cd. 4097], xlii. 744.

[8] R. V. Comerford, 'Patriotism as pastime: the appeal of Fenianism in the mid-1860s', *Irish Historical Studies*, 22/87 (Mar. 1981), 241.

[9] Maume, *The long gestation*, 49; see also Maura Cronin, *Country, class or craft? The politicisation of the skilled artisan in nineteenth century Cork* (Cork, 1994).

[10] Comerford, 'Patriotism as pastime', 241.

[11] Tom Garvin, *Nationalist revolutionaries in Ireland, 1858–1928* (Oxford, 1987), 38.

[12] John Cunningham, *Labour in the west of Ireland: working life and struggle, 1890–1914* (Belfast, 1995), 141.

Finally, Sinn Féin attracted the support of young educated Catholics. Young professionals (6 per cent), clerks (6 per cent) and students (1 per cent) constituted more than one-seventh of the leadership of Sinn Féin in Galway. In urban areas, Sinn Féin was dominated by solicitors and academics,[13] and some of the latter were probably responsible for converting University College, Galway, into 'a hotbed of Sinn Feinism'.[14] Clerks and shop assistants were also prominent members of Sinn Féin in both urban and rural areas: Richard Ford, a shop assistant, was the vice-president of Sinn Féin at Gurteen, and at Tuam, James Daly, a clerk, was a leading Sinn Féiner.[15] The involvement of each of these groups may have been motivated by the lack of employment opportunities open to educated Catholics in Edwardian Ireland. Although there were a large number of Catholics who had received second-and-third level education by the turn of the century, there is evidence that the top jobs in Irish society were still going to Protestants.[16] In this context, young middle-class Catholics may have viewed the achievement of political independence as a means of securing upward social mobility, and this would explain their involvement in Sinn Féin.[17] The preoccupation of leading Galway Sinn Féiners with gaining lucrative county council appointments lends some substance to this interpretation of middle-class involvement in separatist politics.[18]

This study of a local Sinn Féin elite suggests some interesting contrasts with the 'national' leadership of the movement. Garvin has examined the social composition of the Republican elite between 1918 and 1921, and found that it was dominated by members of the professions.[19] While

---

[13] In Galway city, for instance, the leaders of Sinn Féin were George Nicholls (solicitor), Louis O'Dea (solicitor), Dr Thomas Walsh (professor of pathology at University College, Galway (UCG)) and Dr Steinberger (professor of modern languages at UCG). See Appendix I.

[14] The confidential print, 1917, PRO CO 903/19/3/17. It is likely that the proportion of students in Sinn Féin was higher than 1 %, but in the absence of a membership list for the UCG club, it is impossible to quantify the extent of student involvement in the movement.

[15] Cunningham, *Labour in the west of Ireland*; see Appendix I.

[16] Fergus Campbell, 'Elites, power and society in Ireland, 1879–1914', paper delivered to the American Conference of Irish Studies, New York City, June 2001.

[17] John Hutchinson, *The dynamics of cultural nationalism* (London, 1987), 266–76.

[18] In 1918, George Nicholls was disappointed not to be appointed to the recently vacated county solicitorship and his rivalry with Louis O'Dea (who was appointed to the vacancy) created a brief split in the Galway city Sinn Féin club. 'Report on the correspondence of 97 Irish internees, July–October [1918]', PRO HO 144/1496/362269.

[19] The republican elite, as defined by Garvin, includes all Sinn Féin and Republican Labour TDs elected to the first and second Dáils; all IRA leaders and officers of Cumann na mBan included in Padraic O'Farrell's *Who's who in the Irish War of Independence 1916–1921* (Dublin, 1980); all members of the IRB Supreme Council in 1920; and all sixteen leaders executed after the 1916 Easter Rising. Garvin, *Nationalist revolutionaries*, 49.

professionals constituted only 6 per cent of Galway Sinn Féin officials, they accounted for 35 per cent of the national leadership.[20] This suggests that the professionals in the provincial movement tended to become influential in the higher reaches of the Sinn Féin party. In Galway this process is illustrated by the rise to prominence of Patrick Hogan (first Minister of Agriculture in the Irish Free State),[21] George Nicholls (chairman of Galway county council, 1920–25),[22] Frank Fahy (TD for south Galway)[23] and Bryan Cusack (TD for north Galway).[24] The small farmers and their sons, however, who dominated the local movement, were much less numerous in the 'national' elite. Whereas farmers and farmers' sons constituted almost half of the provincial elite (45 per cent), only one-fifth of the national leadership were farmers.[25] Peter Hart's more impressionistic study of 131 Sinn Féin officers throughout provincial Ireland suggests that outside Connacht leading Sinn Féiners were less likely to be farmers or farmers' sons (27 per cent), and more likely to be tradesmen (19 per cent) and shop assistants or clerks (18 per cent).[26]

In east Galway, Sinn Féiners tended to be small farmers, labourers, shop assistants, artisans, and small shopkeepers. The officials of Sinn Féin in Galway were also Catholic (100 per cent), male (100 per cent),[27] and young (77 per cent of them were not yet 40). As they were still comparatively

[20] Garvin, *Nationalist revolutionaries*, 52.

[21] Patrick Hogan (1891–1936), born at Kilreekle; educated at St Joseph's college, Ballinasloe, and University College, Dublin; a solicitor; joined Sinn Féin in 1917; Cumann na nGaedheal TD for Galway, 1921–36, and Minister for Agriculture, 1922–32.

[22] George Nicholls (1886–?) graduate of the Royal University; a solicitor; joined Sinn Féin in 1910; IRB centre for Galway city, 1916; chairman Galway county council, 1920–5, and elected TD for Galway, 1922.

[23] Frank Fahy (1880–1953), born at Kilchreest; educated at Mungret College, Limerick, and graduate of the Royal University; a secondary school teacher; fought in Dublin in 1916; Sinn Féin TD for south Galway, 1918–21; TD for Galway, 1921–39, and for east Galway, 1948–53; opposed the Treaty and joined Fianna Fáil in 1926; speaker of the Dáil, 1932–52.

[24] Bryan Cusack was educated at University College, Galway; a medical doctor; Sinn Féin TD for north Galway, 1918–21 and represented county Galway as an anti-Treaty member, 1921–3.

[25] In Garvin's study of the social composition of the republican leadership, the professions account for 35 %, the 'retail trade' (shopkeepers and merchants) account for 16 %, clerks and civil servants account for 15 %, and farmers for a further 20 % (a total of 86 per cent). The occupational background of 14 % of the republican leadership is not provided. Garvin, *Nationalist revolutionaries*, 52.

[26] Peter Hart, 'The social structure of the Irish Republican Army, 1916–1923', the *Historical Journal*, 42/1 (1999), 221–2.

[27] Although the officials of the Sinn Féin branches under review were all male, Sinn Féin did (unlike the UIL) have female members. In county Limerick, for example, 9 % of Sinn Féiners (401 of a total membership of 4,698) were women, see David Fitzpatrick, *The two Irelands, 1912–1939* (Oxford, 1998), 37, 246.

young, most of them (86 per cent) were unmarried, and they were generally not identified as the heads of their households by the census enumerators in 1911 (72 per cent of them were not the heads of their families). The vast majority of them had received at least a primary education (96 per cent were literate), and although many of them were members of the Gaelic League, only one-third (36 per cent) were Irish speakers. Overall, the majority of Galway Sinn Féin officials were young Catholic men from small farm and labouring backgrounds, although the leaders were often drawn from the artisanate and the professional classes in the small towns.

As we might expect from an organization that was committed to improving the circumstances of farmers, the United Irish League was dominated by the farming class. Almost two-thirds of the Galway Leaguers (60 per cent) were farmers (41 per cent), their sons (12 per cent), and shop-keeper-graziers (7 per cent).[28] Unlike Sinn Féin, however, there were far more farmers than farmers' sons, reflecting both the seniority and higher status of members of the UIL. Even where farmers' sons were members, they were older than their colleagues in Sinn Féin. In contrast to Sinn Féin, there were very few agricultural labourers (1 per cent). Instead the UIL contained a significant number of shopkeeper-graziers (7 per cent), who were among the wealthiest members of the local agrarian economy. William Duffy, for instance, owned a 71-acre grazing farm in addition to his shop and public house in Loughrea.[29] The UIL farmers, farmers' sons, and graziers lived on holdings of various sizes. While more than one in ten (11 per cent) were graziers (their farms were valued in excess of £50), there were also a considerable number of small farmers (57 per cent), about half of whom were congested tenants.[30] As the United Irish League programme appealed to the occupiers of both large and small holdings, the UIL attracted the support of both the poorest and the wealthiest tenant farmers.

The United Irish League also attracted the support of the business community in the county. More than one-third (34 per cent) of the UIL officials in Galway were businessmen (27 per cent) and shopkeeper-

[28] Shopkeeper-graziers, who were both businessmen and farmers, have been included in the discussion of both farm and business involvement in the UIL.

[29] Duffy had purchased a 122-acre grazing farm from the Estates Commissioners for redistribution among local congests, but rather than dividing it all among the rural poor, he kept 71 acres of the best grazing land for himself. CI monthly report, east Galway, Feb. 1916, PRO CO 904/99.

[30] More than one-quarter (29 %) of UIL farmers and farmers' sons occupied congested landholdings (valued at less than £10), and more than half (57 %) lived on small farms (valued at under £20). The comparable figures for Sinn Féin are slightly higher: 38 % of Sinn Fein farmers occupied congested holdings, and 69 % were small farmers.

graziers (7 per cent). A variety of business interests were represented in the UIL, ranging from the village shopkeeper-publican to the larger manufacturing companies in Galway City. More than one-fifth (21 per cent) of UIL businessmen were rural shopkeeper-publicans, and a further 29 per cent were shopkeeper-publicans, spirit dealers, and wine merchants in urban areas. In the smaller towns, drapers, building contractors, ironmongers, hotel owners, and tea merchants were also members of the League. In Galway city, however, many of the substantial businessmen were members of the UIL. The most prominent was Máirtín Mór McDonagh. He owned 'Thomas McDonagh and Sons', the largest employer in Connacht, which sold timber and furniture as well as being a manure manufacturer. In addition, he owned a substantial grazing farm at Monatigue, near Craughwell, and bred racehorses. According to Stephen Gwynn who recalled this 'Galway Merchant' in his *Memories of enjoyment*, McDonagh was 'rich by Irish standards, and bountiful by any'.[31] In the city, the UIL branch repeatedly campaigned on behalf of local entrepreneurs.[32]

The United Irish League was dominated by farming and business interests, and Catholic professionals and artisans were scarcely represented. Only 4 per cent of Leaguers were professionals (3 per cent) or clerks (1 per cent), whereas these groups constituted more than one-tenth (12 per cent) of Sinn Féiners. Similarly, less than a tenth of Leaguers were town labourers (1 per cent) or artisans (7 per cent), while artisans and town labourers accounted for almost one-fifth (19 per cent) of the membership of Sinn Féin. Both Catholic professionals and the labour force were far more likely to join Sinn Féin than the United Irish League. Where members of these occupational groups did join the United Irish League, they were generally substantially older than their colleagues in Sinn Féin. There is also some evidence that the more prosperous members of these groups joined the UIL. P. S. MacDonnell, for example, was a solicitor in the city who was also a director of the Galway Woollen Manufacturing Company.[33] Similarly, a number of the UIL artisans were senior members of their trade: John Griffin, for example, a prominent city Leaguer, was a master baker.

It should be emphasized, however, that not all members of the United

---

[31] Stephen Gwynn, *Memories of enjoyment* (Tralee, 1946), 96.

[32] During the Great War, for example, the UIL demanded that a munitions factory be established in the city, as this would benefit the businessmen who were members of the branch, *Connacht Tribune*, 5 Feb. 1916. The branch also campaigned for a transatlantic port to be established in the city, *Connacht Tribune*, 16 Nov. 1918.   [33] See Appendix I.

Irish League were drawn from the better-off sections of Galway society. While Catholic graziers, shopkeepers, and businessmen were prominent members of the UIL, there were also a large number of small farmers in the League who were among the poorer members of the community. Both of these groups played a leading role in UIL branches, and they appear to have represented the two wings of the League in Galway—the radical agrarian small farmers, and the more conservative shopkeepers and large farmers. While some of the members of the radical agrarian wing defected to Sinn Féin in 1917–18, most of the small farmers in the UIL remained within the Home Rule camp. In December 1918, over one-quarter (26 per cent) of UIL officials in Galway were small farmers, and their continued involvement in the League may be attributable to their age.[34]

Even if all of the members of the United Irish League were not men of stake in the country, they were significantly older than their rivals. Almost all (85 per cent) of the UIL officials were over 40, and most of them were in their fifties (37.5 per cent) and their sixties (27.5 per cent). The Sinn Féiners, on the other hand, had generally not yet reached their fortieth birthday (76.6 per cent of them were under 40), while most of them were in their twenties (40 per cent) and their thirties (33.3 per cent). At a time when there was considerable fear of conscription (which would have applied to all adult males in Ireland aged between 18 and 40) this was a crucial distinction. The seniority of the Leaguers meant that most of them were either married (56 per cent) or widowers (12 per cent), and identified by the censal enumerators in 1911 as the heads of their families (76 per cent). They were slightly less literate than their adversaries (94 per cent were literate as opposed to 96 per cent of Sinn Féiners), but they were far more likely to be bilingual (67 per cent could speak both Irish and English).[35]

The small farmers who did not defect to Sinn Féin, and who retained their membership of the UIL, probably did so because of their long-standing commitment to Home Rule. Having supported the Irish Parliamentary Party for most of their adult lives, these small farmers were unwilling to desert the Home Rule cause in middle age. More than one-third of those who held office in the UIL between 1914 and 1918 had been involved in the National League (1882–91) or the UIL in 1899, suggesting a level of attachment to Home Rule that could not easily be severed (see Table 20). In later life, William Duffy, who bitterly regretted his electoral defeat in December 1918, even suggested that he should have defected to

---

[34] Most of the small farmers in the League (79 %) were over 50 years old, whereas the majority (55 %) of small farmers in Sinn Fein were less than 30 (75 % of them were under 50).   [35] Only 36 % of Sinn Féiners were bilingual.

Sinn Féin in order to be re-elected. According to J. B. Donohoe, who was a close friend of Duffy, 'I often had long chats with him [William Duffy] in his final years and the lasting impression was that he never "got over" the electoral rejection of 1918 . . . He told my father on one occasion that he would have been better to have stood for Sinn Féin himself rather than sticking with the other side.'[36] That he did not do so, however, demonstrates the powerful pull that a lifetime of involvement in Home Rule politics exercised on middle-aged Leaguers.

This study demonstrates that the United Irish League and Sinn Féin were composed of two different constellations of social and generational groups. In Galway, Sinn Féin attracted the support of a number of social groups including a section of the Catholic middle class, the artisanate, town labourers, small businessmen, and the rural poor. These apparently diverse groups were united by their youth, and by their fear of being conscripted, but also by their dissatisfaction with the status quo. Young professionals felt that opportunities for promotion were restricted, some artisans and small businessmen believed that Irish industrial production had been undermined by the Act of Union, and the rural poor required more land to attain a reasonable standard of living. In different ways, each of these groups may have felt marginalized within the old Home Rule order, and Sinn Féin promised to address their grievances by providing them with jobs, industrial development, and land.

The social composition of the United Irish League was more complex than that of Sinn Féin. In effect, the UIL contained two distinct sections. On the one hand, the UIL was the party of the Catholic economic elite, including big business interests, shopkeeper-publicans, and graziers. These social groups joined the UIL for three reasons. First, their involvement in the League enabled them to control and moderate radical initiatives that might threaten their own property.[37] Second, the League campaigned on behalf of their interests. The Galway city UIL branch, which was dominated by businessmen, petitioned both the Irish Parliamentary Party and the Government for measures that would be beneficial to the entrepreneurial community in the town. In rural areas, League branches agitated to force landlords to sell their estates at prices determined by the tenants, a policy beneficial to the grazier as well as the small tenant farmer. And third, the UIL provided these groups with a route to influential positions in local government, most of which could only be obtained with League support. Almost half (43 per cent) of the officers of the UIL were

---

[36] Letter to the author, 5 Apr. 1996.   [37] See Ch. 4.

county and rural district councillors. The conservative section of the UIL were the nationalist establishment, who hoped to become the economic and political elite in Galway when Home Rule was implemented. On the other hand, the UIL also contained a significant number of small farmers and congested tenants, who required more land if they were to make their holdings viable.

The electoral victory of Sinn Féin, therefore, constituted a significant transformation in the composition of nationalist politics in east Galway. In December 1918, the middle-aged businessmen, large farmers, and shopkeeper-graziers who had dominated the UIL between 1910 and 1918 were dramatically pushed aside by the young professionals, small farmers, artisans, and landless labourers of Sinn Féin. This new Sinn Féin elite was composed of a new set of social and generational groups. For the first time, the lower social orders and the young took their place among the local political elite. As Kathleen Fallon told Stephen Jordan in March 1919, 'the spirit of Sinn Fein has taken possession of the young hearts of Loughrea'.[38] These younger and more plebeian nationalists, many of whom were members of the Galway secret society, also ensured that Sinn Féin adopted a more radical agrarian policy than their old Home Rule adversaries.

II

During the Great War, the Irish Parliamentary Party was opposed to the renewal of agrarian agitation. In the first instance, the leaders of the Party believed that agrarian conflict would damage the cause of Home Rule in the House of Commons. William O'Malley told his constituents at Letterfrack that 'We are afraid to do anything that would give the enemy a handle, and jeopardise the movement. My conviction is, that cattle-driving is the only solution of the grass-farm problem in Connemara . . . It is only a pity that at this last moment it is being done to the disadvantage of our cause.' He explained the English view of agrarian agitators—'They look upon the Irish people [involved in agrarian conflict] as cut-throats, prepared to cut landlords' throats'—and that this hindered the progress of Home Rule in the House of Commons: 'Anxious as I am to see the tenants here in possession of the grass lands; anxious as I am to see them living in better houses, I am more anxious to see Ireland in the possession

---

[38] Kathleen Fallon to Stephen Jordan, 3 Mar. 1919, '9th & Final Report on the Correspondence of the Irish Internees', PRO HO 144/1496/362269.

of her own Parliament.'[39] Consequently, they should be patient and only 'pressure within the law' should be applied to the graziers and the landlords.[40] Western Leaguers, therefore, were encouraged to defer their hunger for land until the advent of an Irish parliament. William Duffy, for instance, told the farmers of Annaghdown that once an Irish parliament was in place 'you will have the landlords and graziers tumbling over one another in their anxiety to sell'.[41] The Irish Party's policy on the land question between the introduction of the third Home Rule Bill and the December 1918 general election was clearly articulated: agrarian agitation should be kept within legal limits, and once Home Rule was implemented the land question would be quickly solved. Although there were a number of isolated outbreaks of agrarian conflict,[42] the rank and file members of the UIL appear to have accepted the moderate agrarian policy espoused by the Irish Parliamentary Party leadership. As Table 21 demonstrates, there was a steep decline in agrarian agitation in Ireland after the beginning of the war, which resumed only when Sinn Féin initiated agrarian conflict in late 1917.

But while Ireland waited for Home Rule, agrarian grievances multiplied. First, land purchase was widely perceived as proceeding too slowly. In October 1912, the Inspector General commented that 'the necessity for accelerating the matter [land purchase] is universally felt'.[43] Indeed, Table 3 indicates that only just over half (54 per cent) of the land of Ireland had been transferred from the landlord to the tenant by 1913. In order to address this problem, Birrell drafted a second Land Bill in 1913 which would have amended the 1909 Act, but unfortunately he did not persevere with it, and the proposed bill was dropped.[44] Land purchase continued to proceed at a slow rate, and at the end of the Great War as much as one-third of tenanted land remained unpurchased.[45] And second, untenanted land was not distributed rapidly, leading many commentators to believe that the 1909 Act had failed. Although over one million acres of untenanted land were purchased by the CDB between 1909 and 1919, there was a long delay before redistribution could take place, and the problem

[39] *Connacht Tribune*, 17 Jan. 1914.
[40] Letter from O'Malley that was read out at a meeting at Oughterard, *Connacht Tribune*, 26 July 1913.   [41] *Connacht Tribune*, 3 Feb. 1912.
[42] See Varley, 'The politics of agrarian reform', 200 n. 120, 208–9; *Connacht Tribune*, 11 Sept. 1915; CI monthly report, west Galway, Jan. 1914, PRO CO 904/92.
[43] IG monthly report, Oct. 1912, PRO CO 904/88.
[44] Mullen, 'The origins and passing of the Irish Land Act of 1909', 145.
[45] See Table 3 on land purchase figures. There were between 50,000 and 70,000 unpurchased tenants in Ireland in 1916. J. T. Sheehan, 'Land purchase policy in Ireland, 1917–23' (National University of Ireland, Maynooth, MA, 1993), 144.

TABLE 21. Agrarian agitation in Ireland, 1914–1918

Year	Cattle drives	Agrarian 'outrages'	No. of unlet grazing farms
1914	127	235	46
1915	36	183	33
1916	51	158	26
1917	64	169	12
1918	245	350	16

Sources: Breandán Mac Giolla Choille (ed.), *Intelligence notes, 1913–16* (Dublin, 1966), 124, 187, 254; the confidential print, 1917, PRO CO 903/19/3/30; the confidential print, 1918, PRO CO 903/19/4/56, 61, 63.

of congestion remained largely unsolved.[46] On the eve of the Great War (in 1913), for example, over a third of Irish farmers still lived on congested landholdings.[47] The situation worsened considerably in August 1914, when land purchase operations were suspended for the duration of the war. While the Congested Districts Board was allowed to continue with negotiations on estates where offers had already been made, the Board could not make new offers. This policy was roundly criticized by United Irish League activists in the west, and there was concern that in the absence of land reform an illegal agrarian agitation would be resumed.[48]

The Congested Districts Board lost further credibility during the Great War when it began letting untenanted land to graziers on the eleven-months system. Between 1910 and 1914, the Board had acquired untenanted land faster than it could redistribute it, and a good deal of land had not yet been redistributed when purchase operations were suspended in 1914. In 1917, for example, the Board owned at least 70,000 acres.[49] Rather than letting this land to small farmers and congested tenants, it was leased to graziers in order to maximize the Board's profits during the war.[50] Although CDB officials claimed that these profits would be used to reduce the purchase prices paid by tenants after the war,[51] this policy undermined

[46] Under the terms of the 1909 Land Act, the Congested Districts Board purchased 1,400,000 acres of untenanted land between 1909 and 1919, whereas only 380,000 acres of untenanted land had been purchased by the Board before 1910. See Mullen, 'The origins and passing of the Irish Land Act of 1909', 147.

[47] In 1913, 186,378 (34%) of 552,245 Irish farmers occupied farms of between 1 and 15 acres. *Agricultural statistics of Ireland ... for the year 1913*, HC (1914), [Cd. 7429], xcviii. 635.

[48] Varley, 'The politics of agrarian reform', 201–2.

[49] Ibid. 202, n. 130.   [50] Ibid. 205.

[51] Ibid. 268.

popular nationalist confidence in the Board.[52] By letting untenanted land to graziers, the Board was perceived to be upholding the very system that it had been established to destroy.

During the final years of the Great War, Sinn Féin promoted a more radical agrarian policy than that espoused by the United Irish League. In two critical policy documents, the new party outlined its position on the land question. In an official Sinn Féin pamphlet published in 1917, Laurence Ginnell called for the immediate amelioration of a series of agrarian grievances, including the 'immediate restoration of all evicted tenants and descendants of such still unprovided for; compulsory sale of all land remaining unsold; distribution of all ranches; amelioration of the condition of agricultural labourers; [and the] drainage of flooded areas'. In order to achieve these objectives, Ginnell proposed the adoption of a widespread and multi-faceted agrarian campaign, similar to the Ranch War. Through a nationwide series of rent combinations and cattle drives, Ginnell believed that evicted tenants would be reinstated, estates would be sold, and grazing ranches divided:

[I]t is for the people familiar with facts and local conditions to consider the best methods for all the abandoned evicted tenants to pursue, and to put those methods in operation, not at different times, but simultaneously, thus preventing any great concentration of force against any individual or group, and securing victory for all. At the same time as this action, whatever it may be, those tenants who have not yet got a chance of purchasing on fair terms will also have their plans matured for acting simultaneously [and not paying their rents] ... Young landless people can easily be ready, concurrently with the foregoing operations, to clear cattle off every ranch, and keep them cleared until distributed. The simultaneity of the operations will paralyse opposition of every kind and command success . . . Such a crisis can thus be created that landlords who have not sold and ranch owners will call upon their friends, the Government, more imperatively than the people ever did to release them from a position no longer tenable.

In this way, Ginnell explained, 'the land question will at last be settled'.[53]

A more cautious view of the land question was put forward by the Sinn Féin standing commitee in a 'Special circular re cattle driving', published in February 1918. The document was produced in response to a letter from Tim Considine of Feakle, county Clare, who claimed that Sinn Féin agitations were being organized against 'relatively small farmers'. After due consideration, the standing committee, including Griffith, Plunkett,

---

[52] A member of the north Galway UIL executive called on the League to fight the CDB 'as the landlords of the past were fought'. *Connacht Tribune*, 8 Apr. 1916.

[53] Laurence Ginnell, 'The land question' (Dublin, n.d. [1917?]), 19–20.

Cosgrave, and Stack, resolved that it was legitimate for Sinn Féin clubs to drive the cattle of farmers who occupied 'ranches strictly known as such', but that they must distinguish between untenanted land and 'land occupied by relatively small farmers'.[54] Although it has been argued that this document demonstrates that Sinn Féin was opposed to agrarian agitation, the circular had a more complex purpose. During the Ranch War, the United Irish League had been careful to define which land was a legitimate target for the agrarian agitation;[55] and, in this circular, Sinn Féin was following the precedent set by its predecessor. While the agitation against 'relatively small farmers' was condemned, Sinn Féin branches were allowed to pursue an agitation against graziers who occupied 'ranches strictly known as such, that is . . . land untenanted or non-residential'. In this document, therefore, the Sinn Féin leadership supported the agitation against graziers, and the driving of graziers' cattle was deemed to be justifiable.[56]

This policy was also articulated by leading Sinn Féiners at a series of public meetings in 1917. In the course of the north Roscommon by-election campaign, for example, both Laurence Ginnell and Eamon de Valera, the future president of Sinn Féin, called on Sinn Féiners to initiate an agitation for the redistribution of grazing land. At a meeting at Elphin on 28 January 1917, Ginnell told his audience 'to seize the present opportunity to have every sod of ranch land broken up and force the Government to send down steam ploughs, turn them up, and divide them into holdings'.[57] This policy was restated by de Valera in February, when he called on 'every [Sinn Féin] Club . . . to divide the land evenly'.[58] Later in the year, Father Michael O'Flanagan, the radical agrarian priest, chaired a meeting of the Crossna Sinn Féin club in Roscommon which resolved that grazing farms should be 'bought up and divided into reasonable sized tillage farms and not added to large farms or grazing ranches'.[59] The immedi-

---

[54] 'Special circular re cattle driving', 23 Feb. 1918, Sinn Féin funds case, papers. Minutes of the standing committee of Sinn Féin, book 19. NA 2B. 82. 116. According to Darrell Figgis, two members of the standing committee supported the agitation but were overruled by the Ard Chomhairle or High Council of Sinn Féin, see Darrell Figgis, *Recollections of the Irish war* (London, 1927), 186.

[55] There is a copy of the UIL circular letter on 'untenanted land', dated 27 Oct. 1905, in the confidential print. See 'The United Irish League and untenanted land', the confidential print, 1905, PRO CO 903/12/163–4.

[56] 'Special circular re cattle driving', NA 2B. 82. 116.

[57] The Sinn Féin movement, PRO CO 904/23.

[58] IG monthly report, Feb. 1918, PRO CO 904/105.

[59] Varley, 'The politics of agrarian reform', 226. See Denis Carroll, *'They have fooled you again': Michael O'Flanagan, 1876–1942: priest, republican, social critic* (Dublin, 1993).

ate context for Sinn Féin's involvement in agrarian agitation was the food crisis of the terrible war winter of 1917–18. As a result of food short-ages and the Government's compulsory tillage order, the poor and the hungry petitioned landowners to rent them small tillage plots (conacre).[60] In cases where terms for conacre could not be agreed with landowners, fields were simply commandeered by crowds of up to 500 men, usually carrying spades, and marching in military formation under the tricolour. Significantly, even when plots were seized, rents were fixed in the name of the Irish Republic.[61] This tillage agitation was carried out throughout Connacht in the spring of 1918, and was often led by local Sinn Féiners.[62]

In the west of Ireland, the local Sinn Féin leadership also advocated the redistribution of grazing land. The east Galway Sinn Féin executive, for example, resolved in March 1918 that

the land is a question of national and vital importance, and . . . the people have a grievance in not getting the land they are able and willing to till, and . . . there can be no peace until this economic hardship is removed by [the] just and equitable distribution of the ranches. Each district should look after its own interests in this respect, and the people concerned should have the help of the public and of the Sinn Féin clubs in their efforts to get the land.[63]

The agrarian agitation in Galway was carried out by individual Sinn Féin branches. In February 1918, the Caltra Sinn Féin club expressed their sup-port for the tenants on the Clonbrock estate who had initiated an agitation to divide a local grazing farm, and they called on other Sinn Féin clubs in the locality to assist the Clonbrock tenants in their endeavours.[64] Two years later, the Loughrea Sinn Féin club sent a deputation to J. J. Smyth of Masonbrook, 'for the purpose of putting forward a claim on behalf of landless young men in the locality to portion of certain lands'.[65] At Ballinderreen, the police seized the minute books of the Sinn Féin branch which included a letter from the captain of the local Irish Volunteer com-pany 'requesting the Club to take up the question of the grazing farms in the parish for the benefit of small tenants'.[66] Sinn Féin in Galway, then, was an agrarian movement, which aimed to redistribute grazing land among small farmers and landless men. As the County Inspector for west

[60] Fitzpatrick, *Politics and Irish life*, 156, 168; Varley, 'The politics of agrarian reform', 212–15.   [61] Varley, 'The politics of agrarian reform', 215.   [62] Ibid. 212–15.
[63] *Galway Express*, 23 Mar. 1918. Although the executive also pointed out that Sinn Féin should 'concentrate all its forces on its primary object – the complete independence of Ireland'.   [64] *Galway Express*, 9 Feb. 1918.
[65] *Connacht Tribune*, 3 Apr. 1920. The Smyth estate at Masonbrook consisted of 9,670 acres valued at £5,049 in the late 1870s. Melvin, 'The landed gentry of Galway, 1820–80', 512.
[66] CI monthly report, west Galway, Mar. 1918, PRO CO 904/105.

Galway rather pejoratively put it in March 1918: 'The success of Sinn Féin in this Riding is because it assists the people in their greed for land.'[67] This is confirmed by Thomas Hussey, a shop assistant and member of the Belclare Sinn Féin club: 'I would say that some of the members joined the club in the hope of obtaining land.'[68]

The Sinn Féin movement in other parts of Connacht also implemented a radical agrarian policy. In north Roscommon, the Sinn Féin executive called on all the clubs in the constituency to initiate an agitation that would 'secure the ranches for the landless men of Ireland'.[69] The aim of the agitation, the executive explained, was to commence a campaign of boycotting that would leave the ranches 'derelict and unattended, and thus compel their division'.[70] Grazing land was forcibly seized by the agitators, who branded their cattle 'SF' and flew tricolours above the occupied farms.[71] According to the *Roscommon Herald*, by May 1920 the 'agitation for the division of the grass ranches in the Castlerea district has assumed a victorious aspect for the Sinn Féin party'.[72] A similar policy was adopted by the south Sligo Sinn Féin executive in 1919. Alex McCabe stated in March 1919 that it was his intention to persuade Dáil Éireann to revise all land transactions made 'without the consent of the local Sinn Féin club' since 1917.[73] In south Mayo, too, Sinn Féin organized cattle drives in order to force the redistribution of grazing land.[74]

Sinn Féin's agrarian policy marked a radical departure from that of the Irish Party by establishing new land purchase agencies. In part, this was necessitated by the virtual cessation of land purchase during the war, but it also enabled Sinn Féin to capitalize on the widespread disenchantment with the CDB's grazing practices. From 1917 onwards, Sinn Féin executives and branches undertook the direct redistribution of grazing land. In south Sligo, for example, the Sinn Féin executive divided between 4,000 and 5,000 acres of land 'among tenants and landless men' in 1919.[75] The Sinn Féin clubs in Galway also purchased grazing farms which they then distributed among their members. In January 1918, the New Inn Sinn Féin club aimed to begin dividing up a local grazing farm, owned by the Congested Districts Board, among farmers' sons in the parish.[76] Later in

---

[67] Ibid.   [68] Thomas Hussey witness statement, MA BMH WS 1,260.
[69] *Galway Express*, 29 Dec. 1917.   [70] Varley, 'The politics of agrarian reform', 235.
[71] Tony Varley, 'Agrarian crime and social control: Sinn Féin and the land question in the west of Ireland in 1920' in Ciaran McCullagh et al. (eds.), *Whose law and order? Aspects of crime and social control in Irish society* (Belfast, 1988), 58.
[72] Varley, 'The politics of agrarian reform', 250.
[73] Ibid. 235 n. 14.   [74] Ibid. 236.   [75] Ibid.
[76] CI monthly report, east Galway, Jan. 1918, PRO CO 904/105.

the year, the Abbey Sinn Féin club posted the following notice outside the chapels of Abbey, Tynagh, and Ballinakill:

The public are requested to note that it is the intention of the Abbey Sinn Fein Club to take up the lands known as Castle Pinch [at Lisdurra] on the Lewis Estate for the express purpose of first supplying the needs of congests in the neighbourhood with grass for their cows, and, secondly, for reserving any surplus grass for deserving applicants within the said Sinn Fein Club . . . [I]t is our determined intention to take up this land for the purposes of the Abbey club.

The members of the club then drove the cattle off the farm, and placed their stock on it.[77] According to the police, 'the Abbey Sinn Fein club . . . wants the land for its members'.[78] Similarly, at Kilchreest a land committee led by Martin Forde, the president of the local Sinn Féin club, purchased untenanted land from Major Persse for division among smallholders and the landless. As Forde explained: 'You must understand the buying or getting of land through the Estates Commissioners or Congested Districts Board is a thing of the past. By buying the land ourselves, as we mean to do, it will enable the small landholders to get an increase, and the young men who should otherwise emigrate to get holdings (hear, hear).'[79]

The members of the Galway secret society did influence the agrarian policy adopted by Sinn Féin in the county. At Craughwell, at least five members of the Sinn Féin club in 1918 were members of Kenny's secret society, one of whom had been involved in the shooting of Martin Goldrick in 1909.[80] During the spring of 1919, the members of the club initiated an agitation to redistribute three large grazing farms on the Moyode estate—at Carrownamorrissey, Garrankyle, and Lickerrig—among local smallholders. The strategies used by the agitators were those of the secret society. On 24 February, Michael Costelloe, a butcher in the city, who grazed the Lickerrig farm on the eleven-months system, received a threatening letter demanding that he give up the farm.[81] Two months later, on 28 April, sections of the walls surrounding the three grazing farms were knocked down, and gates were pulled down and thrown into a nearby river, causing damages of £500. According to the police, 'A large number of men

[77] IG monthly report, May 1918, PRO CO 904/106; *Connacht Tribune*, 1 June 1918.

[78] IG monthly report, May 1918, PRO CO 904/106.

[79] *Galway Express*, 28 Feb. 1920.

[80] *Galway Express*, 19 Jan. 1918; interview with Gerry Cloonan at Craughwell, 16 May 1996; Patrick Callanan witness statement, MA BMH WS 448, and Gilbert Morrissey witness statements, MA BMH WS 874 and 1,138. The police continued to identify Sinn Féin after 1918 as a continuation of the Galway secret society. See CI monthly reports, west Galway, Jan., Feb. Apr., and Oct. 1919, and July 1920, PRO CO 904/108–12.

[81] CI monthly report, east Galway, Mar. 1919, PRO CO 904/108.

probably 100 must have been engaged in this work of destruction.'[82] In May, the Sinn Féin club purchased the Carrownamorrissey farm from Mr Kenny of Eyrecourt, but the police believed that this would lead to the intensification of the agitation to divide the other farms: 'from my knowledge of the locality I have little doubt that as soon as the Sinn Féin club sets about dividing Carrownamorrissey farm further trouble is certain to arise as the members of the club who will not get divisions will commit outrages on the others.'[83] A month later, the police reported that the agrarian agitation on the Moyode estate had 'practically ceased', as Michael Costelloe had agreed to sell the Lickerrig farm to the Sinn Féin club.[84] In the absence of Tom Kenny, the members of the secret society continued to agitate for a more equal distribution of land through the agency of Sinn Féin.

Elsewhere in the county, Sinn Féin also seems to have been established on the basis of the old secret society. In October 1919, the police observed that 'Sinn Féin is supported by the Galway secret society which spreads from Gort to Tuam'.[85] And it was this 'extreme element in Sinn Féin' that was responsible for promoting renewed agrarian agitation 'to obtain grazing lands'.[86] At Kilbeacanty, for instance, Michael Reilly, a Sinn Féiner and member of the IRB, recalled:

Some of its [the IRB's] meetings were in connection with the division of land. Pressure was brought on the landlords to compel them to give some of their acres to the Land Commission for division amongst the tenants.

In this connection I remember that a local landlord—Baggot of Ballyturn [*sic*]— was compelled as a result of agitation by the I.R.B. to go into the Sinn Féin Land Court sitting in Loughrea in the year 1919. The agitation included boycotting.[87]

However, the national leadership of Sinn Féin were keen to restrict the influence of the western radicals on the party. As early as October 1917, Cathal Brugha, the IRA chief of staff, wrote the following letter to Father Bourke in Galway regarding the forthcoming Sinn Féin convention:

I understand you have been named as one of the delegates to represent Galway at the Sinn Féin Convention. I hope there will be no doubt of your coming up. It is most essential that you should be present as the closer the connection between the clergy of the right kind and this movement the better for both, and for the country as a whole. It is especially important that this connection should be

[82] CI monthly report, east Galway, Apr. 1919, PRO CO 904/108.
[83] CI monthly report, east Galway, May 1919, PRO CO 904/109.
[84] CI monthly report, east Galway, June 1919, PRO CO 904/109.
[85] CI monthly report, west Galway, Oct. 1919, PRO CO 904/110.
[86] CI monthly report, west Galway, May 1919, PRO CO 904/109.
[87] Michael Reilly witness statement, MA BMH WS 1,358.

established and maintained in the West; as doubtless you are aware that in other movements attempts have been made there to introduce some of the most objectionable methods of the land campaign. The people responsible for this are the type who are always glad to make use of any movement to accomplish their own ends. Now it is to be hoped that none of this class has come into Sinn Féin as yet, but we must not take it for granted. What we have to do is to see that those elected to positions at the head of the movement are persons whose character is above reproach. You must come up therefore as you would be more likely to know the people whose names will be suggested to represent the West than some of us in Dublin.[88]

While there can be no doubt that the Sinn Féin party was in favour of a radical agrarian policy, there were two main views of the land question among the leadership of the party. The first, outlined in Ginnell's pamphlet, favoured both land redistribution and the use of direct action to achieve it. This view was popular among the rank and file members of Sinn Féin in the west of Ireland. A second view, held by Arthur Griffith, was in favour of land redistribution in principle, but opposed to direct action. Griffith's commitment to the redistribution of grazing land was overshadowed by his belief in the importance of 'conciliating all parties' in Irish society. He had observed the conflict in Dublin during the 1913 lock-out, and was determined to avoid social struggles that might fragment the cross-class appeal of Sinn Féin.[89] As land redistribution would alienate the support of large farmers and graziers, Griffith wanted the party to adopt a more cautious agrarian policy than that espoused by Ginnell. These two perspectives provided the context in which the leadership of Sinn Féin formulated a response to the outbreak of serious agrarian conflict in the west of Ireland in the spring of 1920.

III

According to Kevin O'Shiel, a Tyrone-born barrister and Sinn Féiner, who was sent by Dáil Éireann to investigate the situation in the west in early 1920, 'all bonds were broken and the fever [of agrarian agitation] swept with the fury of a prairie fire over Connacht and portions of the other provinces[,] sparing neither great ranch nor medium farm and inflicting in its head-

---

[88] Cathal Brugha to Father Bourke, 21 Oct. 1917, MA BMH CD 161/2. The republican small farmers and landless labourers were able to influence Sinn Féin policy in Galway, but they were much less influential than the members of the professions in determining the 'high' politics of the republican movement.

[89] Varley, 'The politics of agrarian reform', 219–20.

long course, sad havoc on man, beast, and property'.[90] This agitation—
which O'Shiel characterized as 'the last land war'—spread into sixteen
counties between March and June 1920 and resulted in the commission
of more 'agrarian outrages' in Ireland than in any year since 1882.[91] This
'outbreak' of agrarian agitation was caused by four main factors. First, the
problem of congestion in the west of Ireland remained largely unsolved,
and one-fifth of farmers continued to occupy holdings that were too small
to provide a reasonable standard of living.[92] These farmers required additional land to make their holdings viable, and they initiated the agitation
of 1920 in order to gain this land. Second, as a result of the restrictions on
wartime emigration, by 1920 there were a large number of surplus non-
inheriting farmers' sons and landless labourers who demanded land so
that they might be able to continue living in Ireland.[93] This body of men,
who would have emigrated if they had been able to do so, now joined
the agitation to acquire grazing land, leading to a dramatic increase in
the ranks of the rural poor. Thirdly, wartime and post-war prosperity
made the acquisition of grazing land an even more attractive prospect.
The prices for most agricultural produce trebled between 1913 and 1920,
and landless labourers and small farmers were keen to ensure that graziers
were not the only members of the agricultural community to benefit from

[90] Kevin O'Shiel, 'The last land war', *Irish Times*, 22 Nov. 1966. O'Shiel was a barrister who
was appointed as a special judicial commissioner of Dáil Éireann for agrarian disputes in
May 1920, and appointed judicial commissioner of the Dáil Land Commission in September
1920. Fergus Campbell, 'The last land war? Kevin O'Shiel's memoir of the Irish revolution
(1916–21)', *Archivium Hibernicum*, 57 (2003), 157–8.

[91] According to the surviving police reports, for March and July 1920, the agrarian
agitation affected east and west Galway, Leitrim, Mayo, and Roscommon in Connacht;
Carlow, Queen's County, Westmeath, and Meath in Leinster; Clare, Kerry, north and
south Tipperary, and Waterford in Munster; and Cavan, Tyrone, and Donegal in Ulster. IG
monthly reports, Mar. and July 1920, NA IGCI/15. The agitation was also promoted in Sligo.
Varley, 'The politics of agrarian reform', 238. There were 1,114 agrarian outrages recorded in
1920. Varley, 'Agrarian crime and social control', 69 n. 2.

[92] In 1917 (the last year for which figures are available), 111,091 of 561,617 occupiers held
farms of between 1 and 15 acres. *Agricultural statistics of Ireland . . . for the year 1917*, HC
(1921), [Cmd. 1316], xli. 166. The Irish land question remained sufficiently unsolved in 1920
for the British Government to draft a new Land Bill that would implement compulsory
purchase of untenanted land in the congested districts for redistribution among congests,
and compulsory purchase of all tenanted land. The bill was given a second reading in the
House of Lords, but did not receive the final sanction of the cabinet and was allowed to lapse.
Sheehan, 'Land purchase policy in Ireland, 1917–23', 78–9.

[93] An editorial in the *Connacht Tribune* ('The land hunger again') explained that 'An
anti-emigration society exists in policy, if not in name, and efforts are being pushed forward
to provide opportunities to enable the most enterprising of our youth to join together to
purchase large areas of land for redistribution amongst themselves', *Connacht Tribune*, 13
Mar. 1920.

the boom in prices.[94] And fourthly, the coercive apparatus of the state was undermined and weakened by the activities of the IRA, so that there was very little opposition from the RIC to agrarian agitation in the spring months of 1920.[95]

In Connacht, the agitation was directed primarily against the grazing or eleven-months system. As Kevin O'Shiel recalled in 1966, one of the principal aims of the campaign was to prevent graziers from letting land on the eleven-months system:

In the spring of 1920, reports appeared in the press of opposition to holders of lettings or 'takes' of land, auctioned out on the eleven months system … They were a cause of great irritation in badly congested areas, where the tenants of unviable holdings, who for years were expecting allotments on such constantly let lands, had their hopes annually frustrated by those eleven months 'lettees'.[96]

However, the agitation also aimed to force landlords and large farmers who owned grazing land to redistribute it among the rural poor. At Headford, for example, a crowd of 'between two and three hundred people' demanded that James G. Alcorn give up the grazing farms on his estate to his tenants; and at Ballymacward, the *Connacht Tribune* reported that 'owners of land are being requested to deliver them [their grass farms] up for distribution amongst small farmers and landless men'.[97] In addition, the agitation was directed against the Congested Districts Board, which had allowed graziers to stock grass farms in its possession during the Great War. The agitators attempted to force the Board to redistribute these farms by preventing graziers from stocking them. In Roscommon, for example, posters were placed around CDB farms, warning graziers not to stock them; and, on the day when stock were due to be taken in (1 May), crowds assembled to oppose the graziers, and to demand the farms for 'the landless young men'. As a result, all the CDB farms in Roscommon were reported to be 'derelict of stock' in May 1920.[98] The *Galway Express* explained the objective of the new agitation in the following terms:

The universality of the demand for la[n]d in the district [of north Galway] strikes the casual observer that the people are 'land mad', but those acquainted with the history of the country will not see anything weird or uncanny in the present agitation, and all will agree that the time has come for the landless to strike a blow

[94] Varley, 'The politics of agrarian reform', 233.

[95] The ratio of detections to offences declined, and many rural RIC barracks were evacuated in November 1919. Varley, 'The politics of agrarian reform', 235.

[96] O'Shiel, 'The last land war'.

[97] *Connacht Tribune*, 3 Apr. 1920. Mr James G. Alcorn of Kilroe House, Headford, was JP and High Sheriff for county Galway.   [98] Varley, 'The politics of agrarian reform', 244.

for the rights which have been denied them . . . If the land of the country was equally divided, and the demand of the landless met reasonably, all would have enough and to spare, and our people would find suitable employment at home, without having to emigrate.[99]

The majority of the agitators were small farmers, congested tenants, and landless labourers. Although David Fitzpatrick has claimed that 'many cattle-drives [between 1918 and 1921] were . . . organised not by labourers or "uneconomic holders", but by greedy strong farmers or shopkeepers eager to multiply their newly won wealth', the bulk of the evidence suggests that this was not the case.[100] In east Galway, the County Inspector observed in February 1920: 'The small farmers, their sons and labourers are taking advantage of the general unrest to force owners and occupiers of grazing lands . . . to surrender their lands for division among the agitators.'[101] The situation was the same in the west of the county, where 'the young [farmers' sons] . . . are hungering for land'.[102] In Roscommon, a priest giving evidence at the trial of eighteen cattle drivers stated that 'all the defendants were respectable small farmers living on 10 or 12 acres each of bad land'. And in south Mayo, Tom Maguire, the commandant general of the IRA (second division), confirmed that the land agitation was promoted by landless labourers and congests.[103] According to Robert Lynd, a prominent Sinn Féiner, who visited Connacht in the spring of 1920, the agitators were 'men with a few starved acres or no acres at all.'[104] O'Shiel confirms that the instigators of the agitation were 'the tenants of unviable holdings, who for years were expecting allotments on . . . [grazing] lands'.[105]

The agitators used a variety of methods to achieve their objectives. In many cases, the first step was to send a deputation to the landlord or grazier, and demand that they give up their land for redistribution among the people. These deputations often had an intimidatory effect, as the police observed, 'Bands of young men are commencing to call on owners of large farms asking them what they are going to do about selling the farms. The spokesman is not threatening, but the threat lies behind the band of men.'[106] At Oughterard in early April, 'about two hundred

[99] *Galway Express*, 20 Mar. 1920.
[100] David Fitzpatrick, 'Class, family and rural unrest in nineteenth-century Ireland', in Drudy (ed.), *Ireland: land, politics and people*, 51.
[101] CI monthly report, east Galway, Feb. 1920, PRO CO 904/111.
[102] CI monthly report, west Galway, Feb. 1920. PRO CO 904/111.
[103] Varley, 'Agrarian crime and social control', 57.   [104] Ibid. 56.
[105] O'Shiel, 'The last land war'.
[106] CI monthly report, west Galway, Feb. 1920, PRO CO 904/111.

men', most of whom were tenants on the Ross estate, walking in 'military formation', visited six graziers and demanded that they give up their grazing land. Initially, three of the graziers 'refused the demand . . . but were informed that they would get a couple of days to decide before the land would be taken compulsorily. On hearing this the graziers surrendered the lands to the deputation.' When another of the graziers Mr Jackson of Rosscahill, also refused the demand of the deputation, he was told that he would be 'taken away to an unknown destination', and then agreed to give up his farm. Indeed, in five of the six cases, the graziers 'surrendered the lands to the deputation' while the sixth, Mr Mogan of Ard, demanded the £1,800 he had paid for his land at auction: 'He was informed by the deputation that he could be thankful if he got one-third of the money.'[107] These deputations also appear to have won popular approval from the wider community. A deputation that had waited on Henry Howard at Woodfield and demanded that he give up his farm at Ballymore 'drove through Eyrecourt, where they received a great ovation, and were loudly cheered on departure'.[108]

Where landlords and graziers did not agree terms with these deputations, they were subjected to other forms of intimidation. Very few victims were as amenable as H. J. Tully of Rathfaran, who after receiving a deputation on behalf of the landless of Kilmeen, gave 'in a cheery manner the lands asked for'.[109] At Moorfield, James Howard refused to give up his 163-acre grass farm, and received a threatening letter later in the week.[110] In April, the *Connacht Tribune* reported that 'threatening letters have become as common . . . as mushrooms in August', and that most of them were accompanied by sketches of a gun, or a skull and crossbones, suggesting the likely the fate of the recipient if they did not give in to the agitators.[111] Even so, some graziers refused to be intimidated by the deputations. Howard told a deputation that 'he would not surrender the farm, and would prefer to be shot sooner than do so'.[112] A week later:

over 300 young men assembled on the farm. They proceeded to clear the stock, and drove them to Mr. Howard's residence. Mr. Howard came to meet them with a double-barrelled gun. Threats and angry words followed, and some of the drivers closed and took the gun off Mr. Howard. Mr. Howard's son attacked the crowd

---

[107] *Connacht Tribune*, 3 Apr. 1920.
[108] *Connacht Tribune*, 17 Apr. 1920.
[109] *Connacht Tribune*, 10 Apr. 1920.
[110] James Howard occupied a 200-acre home farm, as well as a 163-acre 'outside' grazing farm that he held from the CDB. Ibid.
[111] *Connacht Tribune*, 3 Apr. 1920.
[112] *Connacht Tribune*, 10 Apr. 1920.

with a bill-hook but he was overpowered . . . Mr. Howard [senior] received some cuts on the head and had to be medically treated.[113]

Another fracas took place at Castlegrove, near Tuam, when 'close on 200 men' broke into Thomas Lewin's house:

An attempt was made to seize Mr. Lewin and his brother (Lieutenant-Col. Lewin), who was visiting him. The doors were smashed open and windows broken, and the crowd demanded Mr. Lewin to hear their claim for the division of his land. Fearing bodily injury the Lewins thought it better to make good their escape, but Mr. T. Lewin had to encounter some opposition. He grappled with a few of the men whom he overcame after a rough tussle and escaped through one of the windows, jumping from a height of twenty-five feet. Colonel Lewin got out the back-way and motored to Claremorris for the help of military . . . About fifty soldiers in full war equipment came out from Claremorris and met a crowd of men at Cloghan's Hill, near where Colonel Lewin resides. They fired a volley and called a halt and the officer in charge took a note of the names and addresses of those in the crowd.[114]

At Ballyturin, near Gort, more traditional secret society methods were employed to persuade J. C. Baggott to sell his land. In early April, three of his employees were attacked 'by a party of armed men disguised in female attire and with feathers Indian fashion'.[115]

In other parts of the region, cattle driving was the preferred tactic of the agitators. The agitation in south Mayo began in March, when the cattle were driven off a number of grazing farms at Kilmaine; in east Galway, cattle driving was reported to be 'widespread' in early April; at the end of April, the stock had been cleared off all the grass farms in south Roscommon; and there were cattle drives reported in south Sligo and Leitrim in May.[116] There were two primary strategies adopted by the cattle drivers. In some counties, the cattle were driven to the grazier's house, who was warned not to return them to their fields. Elsewhere, notably in Leitrim, the cattle were scattered in every direction, and 'driven along the hard roads of Connacht for miles until they died of exhaustion and hunger, and the value of all was drastically diminished'.[117] If the cattle were returned to their fields, the grazier risked further humiliation at the hands of the agitators. According to O'Shiel: 'A large grazier of Carnaglough [county Galway] had his cattle . . . driven and when he put them back, he was stripped naked and beaten through the fair of Creggs'.[118]

The agitators were also prepared to use the threat of serious violence,

[113] *Connacht Tribune*, 17 Apr. 1920. [114] *Connacht Tribune*, 10 Apr. 1920.
[115] *Connacht Tribune*, 3 Apr. 1920.
[116] Varley, 'The politics of agrarian reform', 240–1.
[117] O'Shiel, 'The last land war'. [118] Ibid.

and murder, to achieve their objectives. At Headford, James Alcorn was escorted to the shore of Lough Corrib by a crowd of people who threatened to drown him if he did not agree to sell his lands.[119] The deputation gave him two minutes to decide, and he was told that a priest was available to perform the last rites if required. Alcorn, however, relented and agreed to sell his lands to the deputation.[120] Later, he told the *Connacht Tribune* that 'the people were mad with the land epidemic'.[121] Another landowner was approached by a party of men at Headford market who demanded that he give up some of his land. When he refused, the men went away and returned with a coffin which they placed in front of him, saying 'it was the measure of his next suit' if he did not agree terms with them.[122] In Roscommon, O'Shiel recalled that a Protestant landowner was taken from his house by 'a noisy and hostile mob', and forced to sign over his property by two men who pointed revolvers at his head, while others 'began to dig a grave on the lawn in front of him'.[123] A crowd at Headford even threatened to burn one grazier to death if he did not sign over his lands to the agitators.[124] It should also be noted that many of the victims had been subjected to agrarian agitation for some time, so that the events of 1920 often represented the culmination of a protracted conflict.[125]

The threat of violence was taken seriously by landlords and graziers after the murder of Frank Shawe-Taylor in March.[126] Shawe-Taylor had refused to give up his grazing land to a series of deputations, and, as a result, had been subjected to repeated intimidation. On 4 March, as he motored to Galway fair from his house at Moorpark, he was ambushed by eight masked men, who fired two volleys at him, killing him immediately.[127] After this murder, almost all of the threatening letters posted to graziers warned them that if they did not give up their land, they would suffer the same fate as Shawe-Taylor.[128] However, Shawe-Taylor was not the only casualty of the agitation. A north Galway grazier was shot dead, and three

---

[119] *Connacht Tribune*, 3 Apr. 1920.
[120] Ibid.
[121] *Connacht Tribune*, 10 Apr. 1920.
[122] 'Coffin as argument', *Connacht Tribune*, 3 Apr. 1920.
[123] Kevin O'Shiel, 'No contempt of court', *Irish Times*, 21 Nov. 1966.
[124] Varley, 'The politics of agrarian reform', 243.
[125] For instance, there had been an agitation to force Alcorn to sell his lands since 1918 when he was wounded and his herd, William Burke, was shot dead in an agrarian attack (Burke was shot at on 31 March 1918, and died from his wounds on 11 April). *Connacht Tribune*, 27 Mar. 1920; the confidential print, 1918, PRO CO 903/19/4/49.
[126] See Ch. 2.
[127] *Connacht Tribune*, 6 Mar. 1920.
[128] See, for example, *Connacht Tribune*, 10 Apr. 1920.

herds (employed by graziers) were murdered in June and July.[129] Indeed, O'Shiel reports that

As the weeks passed, the trouble spread over wider areas and alarming stories poured into headquarters of the violent treatment meted out to any sort of an owner, or large tenant of land. More owners than Shawe-Taylor, and even owners of medium farms and their employees, lost their lives. There was, for example, the terrible case of a herd beaten to death for having ignored an anonymous command to give up working for his employer.[130]

The police reported, 'The greed for land is in the bones of the people and induces treacherous and cruel crimes.'[131] Both the extent and the violence of the new agitation also aroused clerical opposition. The Bishop of Galway, for example, preached on Easter Sunday that 'the desire for land ... is ... being carried much too far at present', before concluding, 'I beseech you, dearly beloved in Christ, to weigh these words well, and to put your soul and God before land.'[132]

The agitation against the grazing system was often successful. By the end of April, many auctions of untenanted had been disrupted, and grazing farms throughout the region were unstocked. When O'Shiel arrived in Roscommon, for example, he found that 'most of ... [the] ranches had been cleared of their stock, and roads and lanes, all over the county, were choked with wandering and half-starved beasts'.[133] Similarly, in south Mayo the ranches were reported to be 'falling rapidly into the hands of the tenants'.[134] In east Galway, the *Galway Express* observed in April:

Never has the Land Agitation, either before or since the days of the Land League, reached such a height as at the present time (and especially during the last ten or twelve days) in the Ballinasloe rural and adjoining districts, as well as throughout East Galway as a whole.

The head centre of the agitation appears to be in the Kilconnell-Ahascragh-Woodlawn area, and from this centre all the rest of the movements against grazierism, stock-jobbing, land ownership, and all else has sprung. The movement, which first began with the sporadic tumbling down of stone walls, and gate piers, developed into big cattle and stock driving.

At the present time over 30,000 acres of land has been cleared of stock, involving, as far as is ascertainable, 20,000 head of cattle and an equal amount of sheep.[135]

---

[129] Varley, 'The politics of agrarian reform', 242–3.   [130] O'Shiel, 'The last land war'.
[131] CI monthly report, west Galway, July 1919, PRO CO 904/109.
[132] The Catholic Bishop of Galway was the Most Reverend Dr Thomas O'Dea (1858–1923), a native of Carron, county Clare. *Connacht Tribune*, 10 Apr. 1920.
[133] Kevin O'Shiel, 'On the edge of anarchy', *Irish Times*, 23 Nov. 1966.
[134] Varley, 'The politics of agrarian reform', 265.
[135] *Galway Express*, 10 Apr. 1920.

In order to resolve the conflict in east Galway, a conference of landlords and graziers was held at Hayden's hotel in Ballinasloe on 3 April at which Mr Davidson represented the owners and Mr Conroy represented 'the seekers of land'. Consequently, seven 'owners' agreed 'to certain specified concessions, subject to the forthcoming sale of the lands to those requiring it', and five others 'came to some kind of an agreement'.[136] Between 27 March and 17 April, there were at least ninety-six agitations against landlords and graziers reported in the *Connacht Tribune* and, in forty-one cases, the victims agreed to give up their land to the agitators.[137] Although precise figures are not available, this suggests that the agitators redistributed a considerable amount of grazing land in the region.[138] As the north Galway correspondent of the *Connacht Tribune* confirmed: 'The new land agitation is widespread in town and country, and no Land Act was ever capable of making the radical change in outlook in so short a space of time that this movement has already done.'[139]

The leadership of Sinn Féin was opposed to the agitation. Griffith told O'Shiel that 'he took the gravest view of the western outbreak , and said that if it was not immediately dealt with, it could well wreck the entire national movement'.[140] His opposition to the agitation appears to have been based on three main factors. First, he feared that the land seizures in the west of Ireland would divide the nationalist community, and lead to the fragmentation of the cross-class support which Sinn Féin had mobilized in December 1918. While it is unlikely that support for land seizures would have divided the Sinn Féin movement in Connacht, in other regions the agitation did threaten the cross-class alliance upon which Sinn Féin was based. In Kerry, for example, labourers agitated against medium-sized farmers, who were also their employers, for an acre of land. As members of both of these social groups were likely to be members of Sinn Féin, the 1920 agitation did threaten the unity of the separatist movement in the county.[141] Second, the republican movement was engaged

---

[136] Ibid.

[137] These figures were calculated from reports of the agitation in the *Connacht Tribune*, 27 Mar., 3, 10 and 17 Apr. 1920. However, these figures underestimate the real extent of the agitation as only those disputes where the victims were named were counted, and there are many references to other more general agitations taking place. See, for instance, *Connacht Tribune*, 3 and 17 Apr. 1920.

[138] The police reports for March, April, and May 1920 have not survived and would undoubtedly have provided systematic statistical evidence on the volume of the agitation during these months.

[139] *Connacht Tribune*, 3 Apr. 1920.   [140] O'Shiel, 'The last land war'.

[141] Fitzpatrick, *Politics and Irish life*, 264; Emmet O'Connor, *Syndicalism in Ireland, 1917–1923* (Cork, 1988), 38.

in a war with the British, and internal social conflicts distracted from the military campaign. As Cathal Brugha told O'Shiel in May 1920: 'We, of the Republic... should have ... but one ... objective ... to get the English out of Ireland ... Nothing should be allowed to ... distract us from that paramount purpose.'[142] Third, and most important, Sinn Féin feared that the agitation would undermine its attempt to establish an alternative state in Ireland. The land agitators in the west of Ireland, who took the law into their own hands, and who forcibly seized the property of others, constituted a serious threat to Dáil Éireann authority. If the legitimacy of the Dáil was to be re-established, it needed to take control of the agitation.

There were two main strategies which the republican leadership could have adopted to resolve the agrarian crisis. Conor Maguire, one of the Land Settlement Commissioners, outlined the options open to Sinn Féin in 1920. Either the agitation could be forcibly suppressed by the IRA, or land courts could be established to implement the redistribution of land in a gradual and regulated manner.[143] The leaders of Sinn Féin opted for the latter course for two main reasons. First, many members of the national and local leadership of Sinn Féin supported the agitation, and even those who were opposed to it were in favour of land redistribution in principle.[144] And second, the extent and violence of the agitation in 1920 would have made it difficult to suppress, and a protracted struggle between the agitators and the IRA would have undermined the republican movement, which drew much of its support from small farmers and landless labourers. Even so, the leaders of the Irish Republican Army issued a directive condemning unregulated land agitation, and called on the Volunteers to uphold the verdicts of Dáil courts, as Patrick Callanan recalls: 'About this time [1919–20] there was considerable trouble over land. Land was being seized by people who thought they had a claim to it. Cattle were being driven off lands and walls knocked down. Instructions were received from G.H.Q. that the land agitation would have to cease until the fight for freedom was over.'[145]

Although the leaders of Sinn Féin were opposed to the unregulated and violent seizure of land, they were in favour of a policy of land redistribution. At a series of three Land Conferences held in 1920, the guiding principles of Sinn Féin's agrarian policy were outlined. At the first, held on 9 May 1920, seventy delegates and officers of the north and south Roscommon

---

[142] Kevin O'Shiel, 'Dáil courts in action', *Irish Times*, 18 Nov. 1966.

[143] Varley, 'The politics of agrarian reform', 253.

[144] The break-up of the ranches was approved by the Dáil in 1919. Varley, 'Agrarian crime and social control', 66.

[145] Patrick Callanan witness statement, MA BMH WS 448.

Sinn Féin executives resolved that 'the land movement' should be brought under Sinn Féin control. It was decided that claims to land could only be advanced by Sinn Féin branches, acting under the control of a five-member Supreme Commission. This Commission would also take responsibility for the redistribution of grazing farms already cleared by the agitators. The Commission further committed itself to the redistribution of grazing farms of 500 acres or more during 1920, and petitioned the CDB to transfer land that it was not 'immediately prepared to divide' to local Sinn Féin branches, who would redistribute it among congested tenants.[146]

The second conference was held in Galway on 19 May to establish Sinn Féin land courts in the county.[147] Arthur O'Connor, the substitute Minister for Agriculture, attended the meeting to explain the position of the Dublin Sinn Féin authorities on the land question. While the leadership were 'not in favour of anything in the nature of confiscation or ex-appropriation [sic]', he said, 'other methods' could be utilized to persuade graziers or landlords to give up their land. Although these 'other methods' were not specified, the Sinn Féin leadership appeared to be sanctioning the use of limited force to bring about a settlement of the land question in the west. O'Connor then outlined three broad principles to guide the activities of the land courts: uneconomic holdings were to be enlarged, the landless were to be provided with farms, and land was to be bought and worked on a cooperative basis. However, Father O'Meehan, who had played a prominent part in the Galway rebellion, resolved that persons who used force in land disputes would be disqualified from obtaining land through the agency of Sinn Féin courts.[148] This position was restated at the third Land Conference of Sinn Féin leaders, TDs, and IRA commandants, which included Austin Stack, the Dáil Éireann Minister for Justice, and Cathal Brugha, held in Dublin on 29 May. At this meeting, the republican leadership accepted in principle that grazing land should be redistributed, but that eviction proceedings could only be instigated with Stack's permission. These principles were later adopted by the Land Settlement Commission, which was approved by the Ministry on 26 June 1920.[149]

At each of these Land Conferences, Sinn Féin's policy on the land question was clearly articulated. The party was in favour of the redistribution of grazing land among congested farmers and the landless, but it was opposed to the use of direct action to achieve this objective. In order to implement

---

[146] Varley, 'Agrarian crime and social control', 61.
[147] For a full account of this conference, see the *Galway Express*, 22 May 1920.
[148] Varley, 'Agrarian crime and social control', 61.
[149] Ibid. 61–2.

land redistribution in an orderly and non-violent manner, Dáil courts were established to control the land agitation. Rather than landlords and graziers being forced to give up their land, the new tribunals would ensure that they were paid in full for it. Some landowners even claimed that Sinn Féin arbitration courts paid better prices for their land than the CDB had done. Robert Lynd, for example, observed in July 1920 that this was the case, and that landowners preferred to sell to Sinn Féin because it paid in cash.[150] The party's policy on the land question was summarized by a correspondent for *The Times*, who observed in May 1920 that Sinn Féin's 'principle is apparently the seizure, on an organised basis and with reasonable compensation of grazing land in which it considers the large army of landless men has a just claim'.[151] Dáil Éireann succeeded in taking control of the agitation by implementing a radical redistribution of grazing land through the agency of the land courts and the Land Settlement Commission. After June 1920, the agitators' hunger for land, which had given rise to the violent land seizures of April and May, was channelled through the 'legal' machinery of the Dáil courts.

While it is impossible to quantify the amount of land redistributed by the Dáil courts, it is possible to assess the activities of the newly formed Land Settlement Commission, ratified by the Dáil on 19 September 1920. A National Land Bank had been established in 1919, and this body was responsible for advancing the money for purchases through the new Commission. During fourteen months of work, between 1 May 1920 and 30 June 1921, the Land Settlement Commission processed 299 cases, covering an area of 63,150 acres, and 16,046 acres were sold at a purchase price of £229,088.[152] Sinn Féin may not have promoted a revolutionary land policy, but it did support the claims of the rural poor to additional grazing land; and, as a result of its efforts, numerous small farmers and landless men in the west of Ireland gained the land that they required.

IV

In the west of Ireland, there was very little IRA activity during the War of Independence. Peter Hart's study of the 'geography of revolution' demonstrates that the storm centres of the Anglo-Irish war were the

---

[150] Varley, 'The politics of agrarian reform', 267.
[151] Ibid. 283.
[152] Varley, 'Agrarian crime and social control', 67.

south-west (Clare, Cork, Kerry, Limerick, and Tipperary) and the north midlands (Longford, Roscommon, and Westmeath), with most of Connacht relatively untouched by military conflict.[153] Indeed, if we look at the figures for total IRA violence between 1917 and 1923 per 10,000 people in each province, Munster (14.8) ranks highest, followed by Connacht (5.8), Leinster, excluding Dublin city (5.15), and Ulster, excluding Belfast (3.1).[154] The quiescence of Connacht during the conflict struck contemporaries as anomalous. James Hogan, who acted successively as the director of intelligence and adjutant of the first western division, and was Patrick's brother, recalled his efforts to 'organise some companies of Volunteers in the Loughrea district' but found that 'there was after 1916 virtually no Volunteer organisation left in south or east Galway . . . Although there were active individuals and small groups, these parts of the country—once the most disturbed parts of Ireland—as, for example, Craughwell was on the eve of 1914—were now dormant.'[155]

Historians have also been surprised to find that Connacht, the most politically active province between 1879 and 1918, did not contribute significantly to the military struggle for independence between 1919 and 1921.[156] A variety of hypotheses have been put forward to explain the quiescence of Connacht during the Anglo-Irish war. The classic analysis is that of Erhard Rumpf, first published in 1959:

What was the relationship between the land question and the war of independence? The districts where the most violent agrarian unrest occurred during this period were not the centres of the national struggle. The social aspirations of landless men were not primarily expressed in terms of hostility to the British administration. To a certain extent such aspirations were directly excluded from the national struggle, for the spirit which dominated the IRA leadership at all levels inculcated a deep suspicion of any attempt to mix social aims with the pure cause of the national struggle. The social condition of many areas of the west was not favourable to an active fight.[157]

In the west, then, the IRA's policy on the land question appears to have

[153] Peter Hart, 'The geography of revolution in Ireland, 1917–1923', *Past and Present*, 155, (May 1997), 146–54.

[154] Ibid. 147.

[155] James Hogan, 'Memoir, 1913–1937', in Donnchadh Ó Corráin, *James Hogan: revolutionary, historian and political scientist* (Dublin, 2001), 188–9.

[156] For a discussion of the War of Independence in Connacht, see Michael Hopkinson, *The Irish War of Independence* (Dublin, 2002), 132–49.

[157] Erhard Rumpf and A. C. Hepburn, *Nationalism and socialism in twentieth-century Ireland* (Liverpool, 1977), 55.

dissuaded young men from joining the Irish Volunteers and participating in the military struggle of 1919–21.[158] This view is also held by Bew, who argues: 'When it became clear in the summer of 1920 that the revolutionary nationalist leadership was not prepared to sanction land seizures, the west responded by a relatively low key participation in the war of independence.'[159] However, Fitzpatrick has queried this interpretation, and suggested that the policy of the IRA leadership on land agitation did not necessarily prevent rank and file Volunteers from engaging in agrarian conflict: 'My own study of the conduct of the revolution in County Clare ... suggests that "I.R.A. engagements" were in many cases thinly disguised land seizures which Dublin headquarters had neither the ability nor, perhaps, the intention to prevent. Shopkeepers were soothed by rhetoric from Dáil Eireann; the land-hungry were little troubled by action from the Dáil.'[160] To assess the wider applicability of these interpretations, I have undertaken a study of the social composition and activities of the IRA in Galway between 1919 and 1921.

Who were the Galway IRA? As Table 22 indicates, the members of the IRA (over the whole period, 1917–21) tended to be drawn from the poorer sections of Galway society.[161] They were predominantly farmers' sons (61 per cent), artisans (15 per cent) and labourers (9 per cent). The farmers' sons who joined the IRA were also generally from quite small farming backgrounds. As Table 23 demonstrates, almost half (41 per cent) of them were drawn from farms that were valued at under £10, and defined by the Government as 'congested'. The remainder of the farmers' sons who were members of the IRA were only slightly better off than these farmers: 38 per cent stood to (possibly) inherit farms valued just above the poverty line (between £10 and £20). However, there were also a smaller proportion of Volunteers who came from better-off farming backgrounds: 21 per cent occupied middle-sized farms valued at between £20 and £50. Overall, the movement was dominated by the rural poor, although some better-off farmers, as well as students and small business people (from urban backgrounds), were also attracted to militant republicanism in the county. According to Seán O'Neill, adjutant of the Tuam battalion, the

---

[158] Rumpf suggests that in more prosperous counties, the rural poor often constituted the rank and file of the republican movement but that there was a middle-class leadership capable of channelling the 'militant instincts of the rural proletariat' into military activism. Ibid.

[159] Paul Bew, 'Sinn Fein, agrarian radicalism and the war of independence, 1919–21', in D. G. Boyce (ed.), *The revolution in Ireland, 1879–1923* (London, 1988), 234.

[160] Fitzpatrick, 'The geography of Irish nationalism, 1910–1921', 119.

[161] On the sources and methodology used for this analysis, see Appendix I.

TABLE 22. The social composition of the south Galway IRA, 1917–1921

Occupation	1917–21 (%)	1917–19 (%)	1919–21 (%)
Farmer	2	4	2
Farmer's son	61	56	63
Artisan	15	20	13
Labourer	9	9	11
Clerk/shop assistant	5	5	4
Business	4	2	4
Student	4	4	3
Number	85	55	71

Notes and sources: See Appendix I.

TABLE 23. The valuation of farms of south Galway IRA members who were farmers and farmers' sons

Valuation (£n)	1917–21 (%)	1917–19 (%)	1919–21 (%)
$n < 4$	6	6	4
$4 \leq n < 10$	35	35	38
$10 \leq n < 20$	38	39	38
$20 \leq n < 30$	17	16	18
$30 \leq n < 50$	4	3	2
$50 \leq n < 100$	0	0	0
$n \geq 100$	0	0	0
Number	52	31	45

Notes and sources: See Appendix I.

TABLE 24. Other political affiliations of the south Galway IRA, 1917–1921

Affiliation	Galway IRA involvement (%)
1916	35
Sinn Féin	26
IRB	18
Secret society	6
Number	127

Notes and sources: See Appendix I.

TABLE 25. Rurality of south Galway IRA members, 1917–1921

	1917–21 (%)	1917–19 (%)	1919–21 (%)
Urban	13	16	11
Rural	87	84	89
Number	76	104	127

Notes and sources: See Appendix I.

TABLE 26. The age of members of the south Galway IRA (in 1918)

Age	South Galway IRA (%)
0–19	15
20–9	63
30–9	20
40–9	2
50–9	0
60+	0
Number	121

Notes and sources: See Appendix I.

TABLE 27. The occupations of the officers and the rank and file of the south Galway IRA, 1917–1921.

Occupation	Officers (%)	Rank and file (%)
Farmer	0	3.5
Farmer's son	76	55.0
Artisan	8	18.0
Labourer	8	10.0
Clerk/shop assistant	4	5.0
Business	0	5.0
Student	4	3.5
Number	25	60

Notes and sources: See Appendix I.

Table 28. The valuation of farms occupied by farmers and farmers' sons who were officers and rank and file members of the south Galway IRA, 1917–1921

Valuation (£n)	Officers (%)	Rank and file (%)
$n<4$	5	6.0
$4 \leq n < 10$	37	33.5
$10 \leq n < 20$	37	39.5
$20 \leq n < 30$	16	18.0
$30 \leq n < 50$	5	3.0
$50 \leq n < 100$	0	0.0
Number	19	33

Notes and sources: See Appendix I.

towns displayed little republican 'tenacity and grit. That grit was to be found mostly in the sons of small farmers.'[162]

The members of the Galway IRA were firmly embedded in local political and radical agrarian traditions. As Table 24 indicates, more than one-quarter (26 per cent) of Irish Volunteers were also members of Sinn Féin, and these two movements appear to have been very similar in terms of their social composition. The one distinguishing feature between the two is that IRA members tended to be younger and to view even comparatively young Sinn Féiners as 'elderly'. For instance, Michael Reilly of Kilbeacanty company regarded the president of the local Sinn Féin club, Michael Fahy (who was 38 in 1918), as 'fairly elderly'![163] Table 26 indicates that the IRA were overwhelmingly young (63 per cent were in their twenties), and they also tended to be unmarried (only 1 per cent were married) and not deemed by the censal enumerators to be heads of their households (only 2 per cent were heads of their households in 1911). More importantly, some of the leading members of the IRA were veterans of the Galway secret society: 10 per cent of 'activists' (those IRA men involved in military encounters during 1920–1) were former stalwarts of the secret society. Moreover, more than one-third (35 per cent) of the IRA had been arrested for their involvement in the Galway Rising. Given that the police believed that most Galway men involved in the 1916 Rising were members of the secret society, this suggests a strong strand of continuity between the IRA and earlier movements. Indeed, many members of the Galway IRA were born into families

162 Seán O'Neill witness statement, MA BMH WS 1,219.
163 Michael Reilly witness statement, MA BMH WS 1,358.

with strong radical agrarian traditions. For instance, Laurence Kelly, the commanding officer of the south-east Galway brigade and a convicted land agitator, was the son of P. J. Kelly of Killeenadeema, the prominent Fenian and agrarian agitator.[164]

The Galway evidence presents a rather different picture of the social composition of the IRA from that suggested by Peter Hart.[165] Hart argues that 'the IRA drew members from every walk of life and from every sector of the Irish economy. The appeal of militant republicanism crossed all occupational boundaries.'[166] While this hypothesis may be sustainable for members of the IRA throughout Ireland (Hart examined the social background of about 5,000 activists), it does not accurately reflect the nature of the IRA in Galway, where members did not cross as many occupational boundaries as Hart suggests. Certainly, the Galway IRA was a cross-class organization, which included small farmers, labourers, artisans, as well as a smattering of middle-sized farmers, small businessmen, and students. But the Galway IRA was, by and large, a coalition of the poorer classes in Galway society, who were looked down upon by the more prosperous elements of the nationalist community.[167] Moreover, Hart also suggests that most guerrillas were from urban backgrounds. In Galway, the reverse was the case. Table 25 indicates that the Galway IRA tended to become more rural as the revolution progressed, and a large number of key activists in the 1920–1 period, including Laurence Kelly, were drawn from farming backgrounds.

Indeed, all of the major studies of the social composition of the IRA, except that by Hart, suggest that the IRA drew most of its membership from rural communities. The evidence from Galway, as we have seen, indicates that farmers' sons dominated the Galway IRA between 1917 and 1921, and that their involvement increased as the revolution progressed from 56 per cent (in 1917–19) to 63 per cent (in 1919–21). Even more significantly, the proportion of farmers' sons who were officers in the Galway IRA (76 per cent) was even higher than that in the rank and file (55 per cent), suggesting that this social group were the driving force behind the IRA in

---

[164] On Laurence Kelly's conviction, see CI monthly report, east Galway, Feb. 1919, PRO CO 904/108 and GPB DORA files box 4. On P. J. Kelly, see Ch. 4. Many members of the Galway IRA came from families that had been involved in previous agrarian agitations. See, for instance, Michael Healy witness statement, MA BMH WS 1,064; Daniel Ryan witness statement, MA BMH WS 1,007; John Fahy witness statement, MA BMH WS 1,331.

[165] Hart, 'The social structure of the Irish Republican Army, 1916–1923'.

[166] Ibid. 210. Hart's assertion that the IRA drew its membership from 'every sector of the Irish economy' seems overly capacious: there were certainly no landlords or substantial businessmen involved in the Volunteers.

[167] See, for instance, Martin O'Regan witness statement, MA BMH WS 1,202.

Galway.[168] The Galway evidence is, broadly speaking, supported by that from Clare, Mayo, Londonderry, Tipperary, Wexford, and county Dublin. Fitzpatrick found that 74 per cent of the rank and file and 71 per cent of the officers in the Clare IRA were drawn from farming backgrounds, although the officers tended to be 'men of social stature' who occupied relatively substantial farms (of more than 50 acres).[169] Similarly, in the five counties which he surveyed, Augusteijn found that 'the larger part of the rank and file in the provinces was rural', many of whom were from farming backgrounds.[170] Hart's controversial contention that members of the IRA 'were disproportionately skilled, trained and urban',[171] then, may require some revision. Although Hart claims that his conclusions are applicable nationally, his evidence is drawn primarily from Munster counties. For instance, Hart examined the social background of 1,525 rank and file members of the Munster IRA in 1920–1, but the comparable samples for Connacht, Leinster, and Ulster were only 126, 216, and 118.[172] It may be that a more extensive study of the composition of the IRA throughout Ireland would suggest rather different conclusions from those based mainly on evidence from the south-west.

A number of IRA 'engagements' in Galway appear to have been, as they were in neighbouring Clare, 'thinly disguised' land agitations.[173] The ambush of four policemen at Killacloher, near Skehana, on Sunday, 24 June 1920, is a case in point. Ostensibly, the ambush, which was carried out by members of the Cussaun, Menlough, Monivea, and Skehana IRA companies, was an attack on the RIC who were protecting James Hutcheson, a grazier, as he travelled to Monivea church with his two daughters.[174] However, local sources suggest that the real aim of the ambush was to intimidate Hutcheson, who had recently been asked to give up a 160-acre grazing farm for redistribution among local congests.[175] According

---

[168] It is also significant that the farmers' sons who were officers in the Galway IRA were drawn from farms of a similar valuation to those of the farmers' sons who were rank and filers.

[169] Fitzpatrick, *Politics and Irish life*, 204; 203.

[170] Joost Augusteijn, *From public defiance to guerilla warfare: the experience of ordinary volunteers in the Irish War of Independence, 1916–1921* (Dublin, 1996), 353, 357–364. It should be pointed out, however, that Augusteijn's assumption that members of the IRA shared the same occupation as their father is unreliable. Consequently, some of Augusteijn's conclusions regarding the occupations of Volunteers may be inaccurate.

[171] Hart, 'The social structure of the Irish Republican Army, 1916–1923', 212.

[172] Ibid. 230–1.   [173] Fitzpatrick, 'The geography of Irish nationalism', 119.

[174] Paddy King witness statement, MA BMH WS 1,727; CI monthly report, east Galway, June 1920, PRO CO 904/112.

[175] There were seventeen tenants in the two townlands who occupied holdings valued at between £1 10s. and £7. *Galway Express*, 21 Feb. 1920.

to Micky Tannian, ''Twas all about land. That's what that trouble [at Killacloher] was about—all about land.'[176]

There is a good deal of circumstantial evidence to support Tannian's assertion. On 7 February 1920, a deputation of tenants from the townlands of Doonane and Kilbeg had waited on Hutcheson and asked him to give up his grazing farm at Ballybane. However, he refused to sell his land, and 'appeared much out of sorts and intimated to the tenants that if things were pushed they (the tenants) would be playing with fire'.[177] Three members of the attacking party at Killacloher—Darby Forde, Michael Jordan, and Peter Dolly—were inhabitants of these two townlands; and, on the same day as the Hutcheson deputation, Peter Dolly and Thomas Lally (whose brother Robert also participated in the Killacloher ambush) were part of another deputation which demanded that James Smyth give up 900 acres of his ranch at Colmanstown for division among local small-holders.[178] On 15 and 16 February, just over a week after Hutcheson had received the deputation, two of his employees, Michael Keary and Michael Costello, received threatening letters demanding that they give up working for him 'until he gave up land for division'.[179] There were probably other attempts to intimidate Hutcheson, but they are not recorded because the monthly police reports for March, April, and May 1920 have not survived. The Killacloher ambush may have been a further attempt to pressurize Hutcheson into giving up his land. Paddy King, a member of the attacking party, has provided the following account of the incident:

At about 2 p.m. on the Sunday in question, four R.I.C. men accompanying Houtchinson [sic] (two in front of horse trap and two in rear) ran into the scene [of the ambush]. Fire was opened, and the R.I.C. men were called on to surrender. The driver of the trap turned the horse, and raced back home at a galloping speed, standing in the trap and whipping the horse, as fast as he could. One of the R.I.C. men, Constable McGloin, threw his rifle on the road. The other constable opened fire, and was wounded while jumping from [the] road down into the field on the other side of [the] road.

The other two constables, who were in front, seemed very anxious to surrender and held their rifles over their heads, at the same time, taking a few side steps towards the opposite side; then suddenly they jumped right down to the field below where they had safe cover. Fire from both sides continued for some time. The R.I.C. eventually retreated under safe cover.[180]

[176] Interview with Micky Tannian, Colmanstown, 24 Aug. 2003.
[177] *Galway Express*, 21 Feb. 1920.   [178] Ibid.
[179] CI monthly report, east Galway, February 1920, PRO CO 904/111.
[180] Paddy King witness statement, MA BMH WS 1,727.

Certainly, this must have been a terrifying experience for Hutcheson and his daughters and less than a month after the ambush he agreed to sell his grazing farm to the local congests.[181] Although the Killacloher incident is depicted in both contemporary police reports and the recollections of IRA men as an attack on the RIC, the guerrillas may well have had an ulterior agrarian motive.[182]

The Killacloher ambush was not the only incident during the War of Independence when members of the Galway IRA appear to have pursued agrarian objectives. A significant number of IRA men were involved in the Estates Committees established in early 1920 to petition landlords and graziers to sell their grazing farms. At a meeting of the Killimordaly and New Inn Estates Committee in February 1920, for instance, four of the delegates were prominent members of the south Galway IRA. Martin Murray, the captain of the New Inn company, was the chairman of the committee; and three of the delgates from Killimordaly—Edward Burke, Michael Hanlon, and Hubert Dilleen—were officers of the local Volunteer company.[183] At this meeting, Martin Murray expressed his view of agrarian agitation, and

said that large graziers who had made huge fortunes out of the war were now more greedy than ever for the ranches, and should be watched closely. In other parts of the county some graziers had added immensely to their territory, and it was about time the people awoke, and not alone curb the onward march of greedy landowners, but where they had encroached recently on the rights of the people, it was time the parties so aggrieved should re-organise and drive them back.[184]

Letters were then dispatched by the committee to Lord Ashtown and other landowners, demanding that they sell their grazing farms. Neither were these idle words. A month later, the *Galway Express* reported (under the headline 'Sinn Féin Sheep') that 'all the farms on the Ashtown estate were . . . cleared. The sheep and cattle were seen on Sunday parading the roads in several directions, many of the sheep wearing the tricolour on the back of their necks.' Although membership lists of the various Estates Committees do not survive, it is likely that many members of the south Galway IRA were also involved in agrarian agitation. Most importantly, it is possible that Frank Shawe-Taylor was shot dead by the Galway IRA.

181 CI monthly report, east Galway, July 1920, PRO CO 904/112.
182 CI monthly report, east Galway, June 1920, PRO CO 904/112; Paddy King witness statement, MA BMH WS 1,727; Haverty, 'Memoirs of an ordinary republican', MA BMH CD 72.
183 *Galway Express*, 21 Feb. 1920; Michael Healy witness statement, MA BMH WS 1,064; Daniel Kearns witness statement, MA BMH WS 1,124; Gilbert Morrissey witness statement, MA BMH WS 1,138.   184 *Galway Express*, 21 Feb 1920.

In an interview at Castle Lambert in August 1990, Paddy Kelly stated that Lawrence Lardner, an officer of the Galway brigade, had accompanied his father on a deputation asking Shawe-Taylor to give up his land for redistribution. After Shawe-Taylor's refusal, Kelly suggests that it was the IRA who later ambushed and shot him, and that this explains why some members of the IRA then went into hiding at Roscrea (county Tipperary) until the signing of the Truce.[185]

It is significant that the Volunteers did not engage in agrarian conflict in the name of the IRA. Presumably because GHQ was opposed to IRA participation in land disputes, Volunteers tended to either join separate land committees, or to identify targets that enabled them to promote both their political and agrarian objectives at the same time.[186] However, in north Galway, the IRA purchased estates and then let grazing land to local congests and Volunteers. Thomas Hussey, lieutenant of the Sylaun company, recalled:

There was then a big estate (Castlehackett) in Belclare parish. It belonged to an absentee landlord named Colonel Bernard who, as far as I can remember, was at that time Governor of Bermuda. Many people hoped that Castlehackett estate would be divided amongst the local smallholders. The division did, in fact, eventually take place. About the year 1920, the estate was taken over by the Volunteers and set to local farmers for grazing. The proceeds went to Sinn Féin and Volunteer funds.[187]

Similarly, at Ballyglunin, near Tuam:

a local estate named Barbersfort was then about to be sold [and] the local Volunteer Executive decided to purchase the house and estate on behalf of the Volunteers. This was done principally for the purpose of preventing a grabber from securing the estate. And so the place was purchased out of Volunteer funds . . . The estate was set for grazing to the local uneconomic landholders and local members of the Volunteers.[188]

It would seem that the Central Volunteer Executive's order that local

---

[185] *Galway Express*, 20 Mar. 1920; Finbarr O'Regan (ed.), *The Lamberts of Athenry* (Galway, 1999), 211–12.

[186] In August 1920, the IRA burned down Monatigue House, near Craughwell, claiming that they suspected the British forces were about to occupy the building. However, there was also an agitation to force the owner of the Monatigue grazing farm to sell it to local congests, and the IRA's intervention may have complemented the agrarian agitation. See *Connacht Tribune*, 10 Apr. 1920; *Galway Express*, 1 May 1920; Gilbert Morrissey witness statement, MA BMH WS 1,138; CI monthly report, east Galway, Aug. 1920, PRO CO 904/112.

[187] Thomas Hussey witness statement, MA BMH WS 1,260.

[188] Seán O'Neill witness statement, MA BMH WS 1,219.

companies should not be involved in agrarian matters fell on deaf ears in Galway.

These examples suggest that the IRA's official policy on the land question probably did not dissuade young agrarian agitators from joining the ranks of the Volunteers.[189] Indeed, local IRA activists provide a variety of other reasons for the absence of sustained military conflict in Galway during this period. Gilbert Morrissey suggests that the high level of activism in the county during the 1916 Rising, and the subsequent imprisonment of almost 500 Volunteers, may have had a negative impact on later IRA activity:

[M]any of the Volunteers in Co. Galway suffered a great deal of hardship subsequent to the Rising of 1916. At that time, a great many of them were in poor circumstances. Many of them were bread-winners for their families and, when they were imprisoned after the Rising, the families suffered. The neighbours at that time were not as sympathetic as they became as the fight progressed, and there were no funds out of which any provision could be made towards the amelioration of their conditions. Many of the interned Volunteers belonged to the farming class. At that time, they were not as well-off as they became two or three years later. They could not afford to pay hired men and their crops were left unattended until the general release in December, 1916. They and their families underwent a great deal of hardship which might have affected their later service in the Irish Volunteers and Irish Republican Army.[190]

A tradition of republican activity—evident in Galway between 1879 and 1916—did not necessarily result in continued activism, and the harsh treatment of the Galway Volunteers after 1916 may have played a part in restraining IRA activity during 1919–21. Certainly, the Loughrea and Athenry districts of county Galway, which were most active during the period between the Land War and the Easter Rising, were more or less inactive during the War of Independence.[191] Between 1919 and 1921, the location of radical republican activity shifted west to Connemara, north to the districts around Tuam, and south to the mountainous land on the border with Clare. Moreover, men from farming backgrounds had a great

189 Although it should be noted that some Volunteers who were not from agricultural backgrounds did oppose land agitation. See, for instance, Thomas Keely's witness statement, MA BMH WS 1,491. Keely was a building contractor.

190 Gilbert Morrissey witness statement, MA BMH WS 1,138.

191 See Peter Howley witness statement, MA BMH WS 1,379, and the narrative of IRA activity in Galway in Appendix II. The most serious incident during the War of Independence in the heartland of the Galway secret society was the attack on Bookeen barracks (near Dunsandle) on 2 July 1920. For an account of the attack, see Patrick Callanan witness statement, MA BMH WS 448.

deal to lose economically if they were absent from their farms, and this probably prevented many of the Galway IRA from going 'on the run'. Given that the most radical and violent phase of the War of Independence occurred when Volunteers joined flying columns,[192] this may have been a critical factor in explaining the absence of serious military activity in Galway until the early months of 1921.

The Galway IRA also appears to have been in an extremely disorganized state due to the erratic leadership of Seamus Murphy. Murphy was a veteran of the Easter Rising in Dublin, the manager of the *Galway Express*, and appointed by GHQ as the commanding officer of the Galway brigade in 1917.[193] Patrick Callanan, the brigade chief of scouts, recalls that in late 1919:

Headquarters at this time was not satisfied with the way things were going in Galway.

Several times at Brigade Council meetings, Brigade officers and Battalion O.Cs. made suggestions, submitted plans and sought permission to carry out ambushes and other attacks on enemy forces. Permission was always refused by the Brigade O.C. on the grounds that G.H.Q. did not approve of such attacks. Two attacks on enemy forces were carried out in North Galway without the knowledge or sanction of the Brigade O.C. He was very annoyed when he heard of them.[194]

Ten of the witness statements submitted to the Bureau of Military History by members of the Galway IRA testify that Murphy refused permission for various companies to carry out military engagements.[195] As a consequence, local company leaders often dissented from Murphy's dictates, as at Galway city in 1919 when

the Captain of the Company, Sean Turk protested very vigorously against the postponement of operations [by Seamus Murphy] that were due to be carried out. He said it was time to do something definite, that there were many cases of failure to put plans into operation and that if there were any more postponements he would take action himself.[196]

[192] Fitzpatrick, *Politics and Irish life*, 217–19.
[193] On Murphy, see Seán O'Neill witness statement, MA BMH WS 1,219; Patrick Callanan witness statement, MA BMH WS 448; Daniel Kearns witness statement, MA BMH WS 1,124; Peter Howley's witness statement, MA BMH WS 1,379.
[194] Patrick Callanan witness statement, MA BMH WS 448.
[195] Ibid.; Daniel Kearns witness statement, MA BMH WS 1,124; Thomas O'Mahony witness statement, MA BMH WS 1,125; Michael Newell witness statement, MA BMH WS 571; Thomas (Sweeney) Newell witness statement, MA BMH WS 698; Patrick Coy witness statement, MA BMH WS 1,203; Martin O'Regan witness statement, MA BMH WS 1,202; George Staunton witness statement, MA BMH WS 453; Martin Conneely witness statement, MA BMH WS 1,611; Peter McDonnell witness statement, MA BMH WS 1,612.
[196] Thomas O'Mahony witness statement, MA BMH WS 1,125.

And on one occasion, the Castlegar company carried out an ambush without Murphy's consent, leading to the threat of the local leaders being court-martialled.[197] Overall, the absence of strong leadership led to a great deal of in-fighting between Volunteer companies,[198] and must have had a serious impact on the number of incidents in the county. Undoubtedly, their lack of arms also meant that the Galway IRA were unable to carry out an extensive military campaign.[199]

Although the Galway IRA lacked strong leadership, they did exercise great power in the county up to the summer of 1920. The County Inspector for west Galway explained in June that

The Irish Volunteers are in control everywhere and the Police are set aside. The Police cannot go on patrol except in considerable force and on the slightest opportunity they are held up. It is difficult for them to get provisions and fuel and light in many places. Their condition of life in barracks with light and air shut out by sand bags, shell boxes, and steel shutters is very irksome and disagreeable. At night they cannot sleep during the dark hours apprehending an attack at any time. No one speaks to them in a friendly way. No one will give them any information ... The old form of Police control is practically beaten to the ropes and it is as well to recognise the situation.[200]

However, as a result of the arrival of the Black and Tans[201] and the Auxiliary division of the Royal Irish Constabulary[202] in the autumn of 1920, the position of the forces of the Crown was greatly strengthened. In October, the County Inspector acknowledged that

The increased assistance given to the Police by the military, by the Auxiliary

[197] The ambush in question was carried out at Merlinn Park on 21 August 1920. See Thomas (Sweeney) Newell witness statement, MA BMH WS 698, and Michael Newell witness statement, MA BMH WS 571.

[198] For examples of conflict between Volunteer companies, see Michael Healy witness statement, MA BMH WS 1,064, and Patrick Mahony witness statement, MA BMH WS 1,311.

[199] A large number of witness statements suggest that the absence of serious military conflict in Galway during the War of Independence was caused by the lack of arms available to members of the IRA. See, for instance, Joseph Stanford witness statement, MA BMH WS 1,334, and Thomas McInerney witness statement, MA BMH WS 1,150.

[200] CI monthly report, west Galway, June 1920, PRO CO 904/112.

[201] From January 1920, the government recruited ex-soldiers and sailors to reinforce the RIC. Due to a shortage of RIC uniforms, these recruits were issued with khaki military trousers and dark green military tunics, and this mixed dress led to their being described as 'Black and Tans'.

[202] The Auxiliary division of the RIC was recruited from demobilized officers of the British army. Recruitment began in July 1920, and by November 1921, 1,900 men had joined. Although they were nominally under RIC command, outside Dublin Auxiliary companies (usually of about 100 men) operated independently and acquired a reputation for drunkenness and brutality.

Division & by the growing increase of transport is having a very healthy effect on the moral [*sic*] of the Force . . . I am satisfied that the great majority of the people are glad that the reign of terror exercised by shop boys[,] farmers['] & labourers [']sons under the guise of Irish Volunteers is being lifted, and they are bearing very patiently, on the whole, the inevitable hardships which the campaign against the gunman entails.[203]

The disorganized Galway IRA was no match for the military campaign now waged against them, and in late 1920 the Volunteer organization in the county began to unravel. Following a spate of killings carried out, apparently, by the Crown forces, as well as the arrest of a number of local leaders, Seamus Murphy emigrated to England in the autumn of 1920.[204] The Galway IRA was left in a demoralized state. Peter Howley, the vice-commandant of the Gort battalion, recalls that 'As far as I know, no brigade meetings were held after that time and no correspondence came to my battalion from Brigade Headquarters in Galway. We were left to work on our own initiative.'[205] Similarly, at Closetoken, Patrick Connaughton remembers, 'There was great disappointment at this time because we had no Brigade O/C. and no Brigade staff officer to take any interest in us.'[206] In Galway city, the situation was even worse: 'what was left of us in Galway were sleeping out under bushes and hedges listening to the shooting.'[207] Michael Brennan, the commander of the east Clare brigade, who was called in to reorganize the county in 1921, recalls that 'My first instruction was to go at once to South Galway and endeavour to get a Volunteer organisation established there. According to G.H.Q. the old Brigades in South Galway had completely collapsed and I would find very little on which to work.'[208]

The military campaign against the republican movement in Galway reached its darkest point in November 1920 when Father Michael Griffin was shot dead, apparently by a contingent of Auxiliaries based at Taylor's Hill. Griffin, the son of Thomas George, was reared in a prominent Home Rule family in east Galway.[209] However, he had embraced republican politics after his father's death in 1914, and was a prominent Gaelic Leaguer

[203] CI monthly report, west Galway, Oct. 1920, PRO CO 904/113.
[204] See the chronology of the War of Independence in Galway in Appendix II. On arrests, see Gilbert Morrissey witness statement, MA BMH WS 1,138, and on Murphy emigrating, see Thomas Hynes witness statement, MA BMH WS 714.
[205] Peter Howley witness statement, MA BMH WS 1,379.
[206] Patrick Connaughton witness statement, MA BMH WS 1,137.
[207] Thomas Hynes (quartermaster of the Galway brigade in 1920) witness statement, MA BMH WS 714.
[208] Michael Brennan witness statement, MA BMH WS 1,068.
[209] Thomas George Griffin's obituary, *Connacht Tribune*, 4 Apr. 1914.

and Sinn Féin supporter in the city.[210] It would seem that he was shot by members of the Auxiliaries who were actually looking for Father O'Meehan, who resided with Griffin at 2 Mount Pellier Terrace. O'Meehan had provided the last rites for Patrick Joyce, a National School teacher from Barna, who was believed to be an informer and executed by the IRA on 15 October.[211] Before his death in 1923, O'Meehan told his sister that

he [had] attended to the spiritual needs of Joyce, a spy, executed by the I.R.A. Shortly after Joyce's execution a party of Black & Tans called one night at the house of Dr. O'Byrne . . . in Galway. They inquired if Father O'Meehan was there and searched the house. He had been in the house at a card party but had left before the arrival of the Black & Tans . . . When the party of R.I.C. failed to find him, when they raided Dr. O'Byrne's, it seems that they went to the Curate's house in Mount Pellier Terrace. They did not enter the house. They sent in a man dressed in civilian clothes to knock at the door. The house-keeper, whose name I forget, looked out of a window upstairs when she heard the knock and inquired who was there. The man at the door below said 'Urgent sick call'.

The housekeeper called Father Griffin and told him of the urgent sick call. She advised him not to go as the night was very bad and it was past midnight. Father Griffin went out with the man who knocked and never came back alive . . . [212]

My brother also said that it was he himself the Tans wanted to murder that night but, failing to find him, they murdered Father Griffin because he refused to tell where he (Father O'Meehan) was.[213]

A week after his disappearance on 14 November, Griffin's body was found in a shallow grave at Barna. Although an official inquiry found that he had been shot by an unknown person, Brigadier-General F. P. Crozier later confirmed that a member of the Auxiliaries had fired the fatal shot, and that Dublin Castle had asked that the results of the inquiry remain inconclusive.[214] Michael Francis Kelly-Mor's witness statement to the Bureau of Military History also suggests that the Auxiliaries were responsible for shooting Griffin. In the early 1930s, Kelly-Mor worked as a draughtsman

---

[210] O'Farrell, *Who's who in the Irish War of Independence*, 64.

[211] For an account of the IRA 'court' that tried Joyce, see Mícheál Ó Droighneáin witness statement, MA BMH WS 1,718.

[212] Joseph Togher suggests that the man who called Griffin out on the sick call was Patrick Joyce's son William, who later broadcast messages on German radio during the Second World War and became known as Lord Haw Haw, and was executed by the British in 1945. Joseph J. Togher witness statement, MA BMH WS 1,729.

[213] Mrs Mary Leech witness statement, MA BMH WS 1,034. An alternative interpretation is that Patrick Joyce's son believed (wrongly) that Griffin (and not O'Meehan) had attended his father before his execution. Thomas Hynes witness statement, MA BMH WS 714.

[214] McMahon, *Pádraig Ó Fathaigh's War of Independence*, 26; F. P Crozier, *Ireland for ever* (London, 1932), 107–8. Crozier was the commander of the Auxiliaries.

in the Land Valuation Office in Ely Place, when he had the following conversation with three of his colleages, Messrs. Reilly, Carty, and Morris:

I referred, in the course of a conversation, to the brutal murder of Rev. Fr. Griffin in Galway. Mr. Morris spoke up and said, 'That bastard got what he deserved, and there was another man there too we were looking for, and he'd have got the same if we found him' . . . .A few days after the conversation . . . I met Mr. Morris at St. Stephen's Green and offered him a ten-pound note if he would give me a detailed description of the capture and death of Fr. Griffin. he paused for a moment, blushed and said, 'The offer is very tempting and I'll consider it'. He went away rather quickly, and neither he nor I referred to the matter afterwards. It was generally known that Mr. Morris was in the Black and Tans or Auxiliaries.[215]

Morris's comment that there was 'another man there' who would have 'got the same if we found him' corroborates Mary Leech's statement that the Auxiliaries were looking for Father O'Meehan, whom they believed to have been present when Joyce was executed. Following the murder of Griffin, there was a widespread public outcry, and Thomas Kettrick, the quartermaster of the west Mayo brigade, passing through the city, found that 'Galway, at this time, was seething due to the shooting of Father Griffin'.[216] The series of murders which culminated in the killing of Father Griffin, also provoked the IRA in Galway to reorganize in late 1920 and early 1921.

The initiative for the reorganization of the Galway IRA came from local Volunteers. By December 1920, a number of members of the south Galway IRA had been forced to go on the run, and were living in a makeshift tent on the mountainside near the village of Gortacarnane.[217] In the absence of any instructions from Seamus Murphy, they decided to make contact with Michael Brennan, with the intention of either joining his east Clare brigade or asking for his help to reorganize Galway.[218] After a series of discussions with Brennan, a meeting of the south Galway IRA was held at Limepark in April 1921 at which it was decided to establish two new brigades in southeast and south-west Galway.[219] Before this meeting, Brennan had been issued with instructions from GHQ to both reorganize and take control of the south Galway IRA.[220] At this time, GHQ was keen to initiate a military campaign in the western counties which might relieve the pressure on the

[215] Michael Francis Kelly-Mor witness statement, MA BMH WS 1,126.

[216] Louis O'Dea (a prominent Sinn Féiner and solicitor in Galway city) witness statement, MA BMH WS 1,107, and Thomas Kettrick witness statement, MA BMH WS 872. I am grateful to Fergus White for bringing Kettrick's statement to my attention.

[217] Joseph Stanford witness statement, MA BMH WS 1,334.   [218] Ibid.

[219] Ibid.   [220] Michael Brennan witness statement, MA BMH WS 1,068.

TABLE 29. Number of incidents and number of persons killed or seriously wounded during the War of Independence in Galway, 1919–1921

Year	No. of incidents	No. killed or seriously wounded
1919	3	0
1920	31	24
1921	32	48
Total	66	72

Notes and sources: See Appendix II.

IRA in the south-west.[221] As a result, the single Galway brigade, which had been established in 1917, was split into six new brigades, each of which was to be in direct contact with GHQ.[222] In many cases, new leaders were appointed and 'inactive' officers were relieved of their positions.[223] Following this reorganization, IRA activity in the county greatly increased. As Table 29 indicates, almost half (48 per cent) of the total number of military incidents took place in 1921, and two-thirds (67 per cent) of the total casualties of the conflict were killed or seriously wounded in 1921.[224]

The revived Galway IRA's campaign against the forces of the Crown culminated in the Ballyturin ambush in May 1921. On Sunday afternoons, District Inspector Cecil Blake, his wife, Captain Cornwallis and Lieutenant McCreery of the 17th Lancers, and Mrs Margaret Gregory were in the habit of visiting Mr Baggot's estate, near Gort, to play tennis.[225] District Inspector Blake's visits to Baggot House had been observed by Brigid Ryan

[221] Peter McDonnell (commanding officer of the west Connemara brigade) witness statement, MA BMH WS 1,612; Augusteijn, *From public defiance*, 183.

[222] The six new brigades were in south-east Galway, south-west Galway, mid-Galway, north Galway, east Connemara, and west Connemara. See Gilbert Morrissey witness statement, MA BMH WS 1,138; Michael Newell witness statement, MA BMH WS 571; Patrick Dunlevy witness statement, MA BMH WS 1,489; Peter McDonnell witness statement, MA BMH WS 1,612.

[223] Patrick Dunlevy (commanding officer north Galway brigade) witness statement, MA BMH WS 1,489.

[224] See Appendix II for a discussion of how these figures were calculated. It is worth bearing in mind that the number of casualties in Galway is tiny in comparison to that in Cork where 1,036 persons were killed or seriously wounded between 1920 and 1921. See Peter Hart, *The IRA and its enemies: violence and community in Cork, 1916–1923* (Oxford, 1998), 87.

[225] 'Report on the Ballyturin tragedy', PRO CO 904/121. Cecil Arthur Maurice Blake (1885–1920), a native of Hampshire and formerly an officer in the Royal Horse Artillery who had been injured in the battle of the Somme, was appointed a third-class District Inspector in the Royal Irish Constabulary on 12 Jan. 1920. Margaret Gregory was the widow of Robert Gregory, and the daughter-in-law of Lady Gregory.

who told her brother Daniel, the quartermaster of the south-west Galway brigade,[226] and the local IRA began to plan an ambush of Blake outside Baggot's house.[227]

On Sunday, 15 May 1921, about twenty members of the south Galway IRA, including Captain Patrick Houlihan (a member of Michael Brennan's flying column), occupied the gate lodge at the entrance to the Baggot estate. At about one o'clock, Blake's motor car containing three men and two women drove into the Big House. The visitors spent the afternoon playing tennis until the Volunteers in the gate lodge heard the 'motor starting from the house' at about eight o'clock.[228] According to Ryan:

We had taken the precaution to close one side of the gate to prevent the car driving through our position too quickly . . . The car stopped at the gate and one man, Captain Cornwallis I believe, stepped out of the car to open the second side of the gate. They got the order 'Hands up, surrender' from Glynn and myself as arranged beforehand. Cornwallis dodged for cover very quickly and opened fire from his automatic at the men by the fallen tree. All our party then opened fire on the car and on Cornwallis, but before he was killed he had fired shots and very nearly got Stanford. Blake fell out of the car dead. McGreedy [*sic*] also fell out dead and Mrs. Blake. Lady Gregory [*sic*] was saved being hit. It looked as if Mrs. Blake tried to fire her own or Blake's gun. It was known that she always carried an automatic and at times threatened people in the town of Gort with it. Fire ceased and we approached the car.

We found Lady Gregory in a sitting position behind the car. She looked quite cool and answered 'yes' in a cool, calm voice when asked if she was alright. She said she wished to go to Baggot's and we proceeded there with her. We met one of the Miss Baggot's in the drive and handed over Lady Gregory to her. Lady Gregory was daughter-in-law of the famous Lady Gregory. Miss Baggot had heard the shooting and was hysterical.[229]

Ryan's account is, broadly speaking, similar to that of the other members of the IRA involved in the ambush. All agree that the passengers in the car were told to put their 'hands up', before fire was opened on them. Cornwallis, who was attempting to open the gate, then opened fire on the attackers, wounding Stanford several times before being shot dead by Keely. The IRA then opened fire on the passengers, who were scrambling to get out of the left side of the car, but none of them returned fire, and

[226] Daniel Ryan witness statement, MA BMH WS 1,007.
[227] Joseph Stanford witness statement, MA BMH WS 1,334.
[228] Ibid.
[229] Daniel Ryan witness statement, MA BMH WS 1,007. Cornwallis and McCreery were both officers of the 17th Lancers.

only Gregory survived the attack.[230] According to Patrick Glynn, 'We concentrated fire on the car, doing our best to save the women in it,'[231] and Stanford also claims that they gave the order 'hands up': 'as we expected they might consider the safety of their women.'[232] Keely expresses himself relieved that Mrs. Gregory was 'fortunately saved'.[233] Ryan, however, makes no mention of any attempt to avoid killing the women in the car, and instead suggests that Mrs Blake may have tried to open fire on them.[234]

The police report of this incident, based largely on Mrs Gregory's eye-witness account, suggests a rather different sequence of events. According to the police, Captain Cornwallis got out of the car to open the gate and Mrs Blake then saw a number of men coming through the trees towards the car, and realized that they were about to be ambushed:

Simultaneously one or two shots rang out from the right and the wind-screen was shattered by a bullet from the front, the shattered glass falling into the laps of Capt. Blake and Mrs. Gregory. The occupants seeing the men on the right of the car proceeded to get out as quickly as possible on the left, but the steering-wheel somewhat delayed Capt. Blake, who was followed by Mrs. Gregory. Capt. Cornwallis appears to have attempted to take shelter outside the gates behind the wall on the right, and fell . . . shot through the back by the assassins concealed in the cottage.[235]

Mrs Gregory then managed to get out of the left side of the car and hid beside the rear wheel, observing that

Capt. Blake was kneeling behind the front wheel with Mrs Blake on his right, and Mr McCreery on his left: it was then I saw for the first time men coming from the trees on the left of the drive and realized we were surrounded. Shots were fired then from the left rear and from the lodge in front spluttering up the gravel all round me. I looked at Capt. Blake and saw that he had been wounded in one arm and was trying to extricate his revolver from his pocket with the other hand: he succeeded in pulling out his revolver . . . but before he could use it, it fell from his nerveless fingers under the car as he fell mortally wounded.

For myself, I felt that death might come at any moment and hoped that the bullet might come through my head and terminate that long drawn-out agony. Mrs Blake was still kneeling, and I heard a sound like the running of water from a

230 See Joseph Stanford witness statement, MA BMH WS 1,334; Daniel Ryan witness statement, MA BMH WS 1,007; Patrick Glynn witness statement, MA BMH WS 1,033; Thomas Keely witness statement, MA BMH WS 1,491.

231 Patrick Glynn witness statement, MA BMH WS 1,033.

232 Joseph Stanford witness statement, MA BMH WS 1,334

233 Thomas Keely witness statement, MA BMH WS 1,491.

234 Daniel Ryan witness statement, MA BMH WS 1,007.

235 'Report on the Ballyturin tragedy', May, 1921, PRO CO 904/121.

tap, as the blood poured from a lacerated wound in her neck and chest. A volley was then fired at Mrs Blake: she fell side-ways pierced by eleven bullets, her head just resting on her husband's foot.

I then moved to the right rear of the car . . . and there I waited until the raiders came forward. I heard a shout of 'Hands Up' which I thought at the time was intended for me, but afterwards discovered it was addressed to Mr and Mrs Baggot who had run down the drive on hearing the firing.[236]

The police account of the ambush differs from that of the IRA in two critical respects. First, the attackers all agree that they gave their victims the opportunity to put up their hands before opening fire. However, Mrs Gregory makes no mention of this, and instead suggests that this order came later—after the shooting—and that it was directed instead to Mr and Mrs Baggot. While it is difficult to verify the truth of either version, it seems unlikely that the IRA would have given their adversaries, including three soldiers, the opportunity to return fire before the attack began. More seriously, the IRA's statements claim that they had no intention of killing any of the women in the group. Mrs Gregory's statement strongly suggests that this was not the case, and that Mrs Blake was deliberately killed by the attackers. Mrs Blake was hiding on the left-hand side of the car and could have been 'saved', as Mrs Gregory was. Instead, a volley of shots was fired at her, wounding her twelve times, and she fell dead next to her husband.[237] It would seem that Mrs Blake was deliberately shot by the IRA, perhaps because of her behaviour in the town of Gort, and that one member of the Galway IRA breached the generally accepted rules of combat by killing a pregnant woman. Nationalist accounts of this incident, and particularly that by Martin Dolan published in the *Capuchin Annual* in 1970, have attempted to justify the killing of Mrs Blake, writing that 'The ambushers called to the women to return to the house . . . but Mrs Blake declared she would die with her husband. Volleys were then fired and the three men died but Mrs Blake, a deadly shot with a revolver, picked up her husband's weapon and pinned down the attackers . . . Having no option, the ambushers killed the woman.'[238] There is no evidence in either the contemporary police reports or the later witness statements of the IRA to substantiate this implausible account of the shooting of Mrs Blake. It is more likely that Mrs Blake was deliberately shot in revenge for the killing of Mrs Ellen Quinn (who was also pregnant) at nearby Kiltartan by the

[236] Ibid.
[237] CI monthly report, west Galway, May 1921, PRO CO 904/115.
[238] Martin Dolan, 'Galway 1920–1921', *Capuchin Annual* (1970), 395.

RIC the previous November, and the brutal murder of the Loughnane brothers by the Auxiliaries in November 1920.[239]

Although there were far fewer violent incidents in Galway during the War of Independence than in, say, Cork, the Ballyturin ambush demonstrates that the county was by no means in a peaceful state during this period. Indeed, the intensification of IRA activity in Galway during 1921 suggests that the real distinction between western counties and those of the south-west may have been simply that the process of radicalization—whereby Volunteers went on the run and became involved in more violent guerrilla warfare—began later in Galway than it did in Cork. The police observed that 'Very considerable activity was shown by the Sinn Féin and I.R.A. organizations up to the morning of the Truce', suggesting that more violent incidents would have taken place in Galway had the conflict continued for a longer period.[240] While this may well be the case, it does need to be emphasized that the number of people who were either killed or seriously wounded in Galway during 1920–1 (72) was tiny in comparison to that in Cork (1,036).[241] While Cork may not have been the only place where IRA men were willing to kill for Ireland, they were much more likely to do so than their colleagues in the Galway IRA. This was probably because, unlike the Munster IRA, the Galway IRA was dominated by the sons of small farmers.[242] Farmers' sons tended to be reluctant to join armies when doing so would require them to leave their farms for long periods of time, and this probably explains why Galway farmers contributed comparatively few men to both the Great War[243] and the IRA's guerrilla war in 1919–21. To be sure, the absence of arms and effective leadership in Galway must also have restricted the number of military engagements, but the distinctive social composition of the Galway IRA probably explains why fewer of them made the transition from Volunteers to guerrilla fighters.

In 1921, the IRA's military campaign throughout Ireland was

---

[239] Mrs Quinn, who was pregnant and holding her infant son, was shot by members of the RIC from a lorry as they passed by her house at Kiltartan on 1 November 1920. See McMahon, *Pádraig Ó Fathaigh's War of Independence*, 25–6. On the murder of the Loughnane brothers, see Padraig Fahy's witness statement, MA BMH WS 1,517 and Joseph Stanford's witness statement, MA BMH WS 1,334. Cait Ni Lochlainn (a sister of the Loughnane brothers) submitted photographs of her murdered brothers to the Bureau of Military History, MA BMH Photograph (P) 39.

[240] CI monthly report, east Galway, July 1921, PRO CO 904/116.

[241] See Table 29; Hart, *The IRA and its enemies*, 87.

[242] See Hart, 'The social structure of the Irish Republican Army, 1916–1923', 230–1; and Tables 22–8.

[243] See Ch. 5.

intensifying.[244] The escalation of the violence is reflected in the numbers of casualties. In 1919, there were 18 deaths; in 1920, there were 282; and in the first six months of 1921, there were 1,086 deaths due to the conflict.[245] At the same time as the military struggle, Dáil Éireann was establishing a new counter-state on the ruins of the old. As we have seen, the Dáil courts were gradually replacing the British courts; and in June 1920, the Dáil had taken control of local government in Ireland, with the majority of county councils transferring their allegiance from the British Local Government Board to the Department of Local Government in Dublin.[246] As early as 1919, a *Daily Herald* report captured the sense that a new Irish state had already come into existence: 'This invisible republic, with its hidden courts and its prohibited volunteer troops, exists in the hearts of the men and women of Ireland, and wields a moral authority which all the tanks and machine guns of King George cannot command.'[247] By the spring of 1921, a political and military stalemate had been reached, resulting in the declaration of a Truce on 11 July. The combined impact of the IRA's military campaign, and the Dáil's establishment of an alternative government, pressurized the British into a compromise agreement; and, after six months of negotiations, the Anglo-Irish Treaty was signed on 6 December 1921. On 7 January 1922, the Treaty was approved by the Dáil, and an 'independent' Irish state was brought into existence.[248]

V

In a recent discussion of the nature of the Irish revolution, John Regan and Mike Cronin argue that

There is little evidence of a social component within the Irish revolution and less again in its settlement. Such potential as there was for social upheaval had to a great extent been defused by the transfer of land back to native ownership under a series of reforming land acts at the end of the nineteenth, and the beginning of the new century.[249]

[244] For a full account of the Anglo-Irish war, see Hopkinson, *The Irish War of Independence*.

[245] David Fitzpatrick, 'Ireland since 1870', in R. F. Foster (ed.), *The Oxford history of Ireland* (Oxford, 1992), 207.

[246] M. E. Daly, 'Local government and the first Dail', in Brian Farrell (ed.), *The creation of the Dáil* (Dublin, 1994), 125.

[247] Quoted in Arthur Mitchell, 'Alternative government: "Exit Britannia" – the formation of the Irish nation state, 1918–21', in Augusteijn (ed.), *The Irish revolution, 1913–23*, 76–7.

[248] Ibid. 83–4.

[249] J. M. Regan and Mike Cronin, 'Introduction: Ireland and the politics of independence 1922–49, new perspectives and re-considerations', in Mike Cronin and John M. Regan (eds.), *Ireland: the politics of independence, 1922–49* (Basingstoke, 2000), 1–2.

The evidence presented in this chapter suggests the limitations of this analysis. Far from being resolved, serious agrarian grievances remained unaddressed and provided the basis for renewed land agitation on a scale not seen since the days of the Land War (1879–81). Indeed, *pace* Laffan, the land agitation that erupted in the spring of 1920 threatened the 'social balance of power' in Ireland in three critical respects. First, the agitation constituted a serious threat to the primacy of private property. Throughout Connacht, hundreds of grazing farms were forcibly seized during the agitation. As the existing social order was underpinned by property rights, the agitation represented a fundamental threat to the entire basis of Irish society. This was certainly the view of Kevin O'Shiel, who described the agitation as 'a grave menace to property and life at a time of violent, revolutionary turmoil in the country'.[250] Second, the agitators implemented a radical agrarian policy, by forcibly seizing grazing land and redistributing it among the rural poor. For a few brief months in the spring of 1920 the world was turned upside down in Connacht. Landlords and graziers who had dominated the rural economy were forced to give up their land to labourers and small farmers.[251] And third, some of the agitators did envisage a radical reorganization of Irish society. In Galway, for example, there was an experiment in communal land ownership. The Creggs Land Committee established a collective farm comprising 'thousands of acres' which had been seized during the agitation. By rejecting the principle of private ownership, the committee represented a profound challenge to the social order.[252]

The success of the Dáil courts in taking control of the agitation was by no means a foregone conclusion. As O'Shiel later conceded, the agitation in Roscommon was an 'agrarian avalanche' that was 'almost impossible to cope with'.[253] Indeed, the republican movement was frequently obliged to use force to establish its control over the agitation. This was most evident in the case of *Prendergast and others* v. *Hyland and Murphy*,

250 Kevin O'Shiel, 'Fellow travellers', *Irish Times*, 17 Nov. 1966.

251 Symbolically, the authority of the propertied classes was inverted, and they were subjected to ritual humiliation by their adversaries. At Headford, for example, Mr Lynch Staunton was forced to stand on a cart, wave a tricolour, and shout 'Up Sinn Féin!' *Connacht Tribune*, 3 Apr. 1920.

252 Kevin O'Shiel, 'The Dáil land courts', *Irish Times*, 14 Nov. 1966. For a more detailed discussion of the Creggs Land Committee, see Kevin O'Shiel witness statement, MA BMH WS 1,770 (vol. viii). O'Shiel – perhaps in an attempt to discredit this experiment—suggests that the members of the Committee were 'not poor or needy men by any manner of means', and this episode deserves to be researched in more detail.

253 O'Shiel, 'On the edge of anarchy'.

heard by O'Shiel at Ballinrobe in May 1920.[254] The case concerned a 120-acre grazing farm at Fountain Hill, let by two joint tenants, both of whom also occupied 24-acre farms 3 miles away. A number of claimants, all of whom were labourers or congested tenants, demanded that the farm be redistributed among them. However, the court decided in favour of the defendants, arguing that because the land was so poor, the lessees 'could not satisfy the reasonable requirements of their families' without it.[255] The claimants were outraged, declared that this was 'worse than the British', and remained in forcible occupation of the Fountain Hill lands in defiance of the court. O'Shiel recognized that unless the ruling of the court was upheld, the case would 'annihilate our courts in a storm of ridicule'. He requested the assistance of Cathal Brugha, who sent an IRA unit to arrest the 'misdemeanants' and imprison them on an island in Lough Corrib, thereby enforcing the will of the court. As a result, 'few disaffected claimants were bold enough to defy [the courts]', and where there was dissent, it was 'effectively countered by the police arm of the IRA'.[256]

The Dáil courts did not establish absolute control over the agitation. The Roscommon agitators were 'exceptionally bad'[257] according to O'Shiel as they exhibited an 'aggressive "Bolshie" spirit'.[258] A number of Roscommon men could not be persuaded, even by the IRA, to rebuild walls that they had knocked down.[259] Most significantly, the Creggs Land Committee refused to give up its books to Eamon Casey, the local Sinn Féin courts registrar. Ultimately, Casey managed to take possession of the accounts from the committee only by 'drawing a large revolver from his pocket, [which] he aimed at them saying: "Any man that tries to get out of this hall until I get those books and papers I'll shoot dead."'[260] As these examples suggest, there was substantial resistance to the authority of the Dáil courts. Indeed, the Dáil's regulation of the conflict was achieved only after a series of contests between the radical initiatives of the agitators and the moderating reactions of the Sinn Féin courts. These contests suggest that we may need to reconsider the dynamics of the Irish revolution more generally. The agrarian agitation of 1920 was not the only radical initiative

[254] The details of this case are discussed in Varley, 'Agrarian crime and social control', 62–3.
[255] Although the Fountain Hill farm comprised 120 acres, only one-third of it was arable, the rest being stony or marshy ground of poor quality. Varley, 'Agrarian crime and social control', 62.
[256] O'Shiel, 'Dáil courts in action'; Varley, 'Agrarian crime and social control', 62.
[257] O'Shiel, 'On the edge of anarchy'.   [258] O'Shiel, 'No contempt of court'.
[259] Varley, 'Agrarian crime and social control', 63.
[260] O'Shiel, 'The Dáil land courts'.

that manifested itself during the revolution. There were a number of other radical impulses, notably the wave of strike activity that spread through Ulster, Leinster, and Munster between 1917 and 1923.[261] These radical initiatives also contained revolutionary elements, some of which aimed to abolish private property altogether.[262] Indeed, Tom Crean's recent discussion of the ITGWU's official newspaper, the *Voice of Labour*, suggests that 'for a period—both the leadership and key activists of the ITGWU believed that the revolutionary wave which had begun in Russia might topple European capitalism'.[263] The claim that the Irish revolution did not contain 'a social component', therefore, is easily disproved. Although the outcome of the revolution was the conservative Irish Free State, this was established only after a series of contests between radical initiatives and moderating or conservative reactions; and the post-revolution settlement was the result of the eventual victory by the reactionary elements among the elite of Sinn Féin.

The nature of this conservative reaction is only beginning to be examined, and the activities of the Special Infantry Corps, established in February 1923, suggest the lengths to which the conservatives in Sinn Féin (and later the Provisional Government) were prepared to go in their suppression of social radicalism. In December 1922, Patrick Hogan, the Minister for Agriculture, forwarded a memorandum on 'seizures of land' to the Minister for Defence which explained that

The Land War is very widespread and very serious even at present . . . Already people have been shot at. I have interviewed some people—stewards, owners, etc. who have been fired at, and one who has been badly wounded—who simply left their lands derelict and are afraid to return. There is the usual knocking of walls, cattle driving, and forcible occupation . . . We have explicit evidence from the letters which have been captured that the campaign is organised, but even without that evidence the general condition of affairs makes it quite clear that the Land War is coming . . . This . . . is no new thing in Ireland; the parties know every move in the game, they are prepared to do now even more than they ever did before, and unless we take advantage of the present situation to meet the case we will have a sordid and fairly bloody squabble on our hands for the next ten years.[264]

To avoid this eventuality, Hogan recommended that 'the problem can

---

261 O'Connor, *Syndicalism in Ireland*, 25, 27.

262 See, for example, the Creggs Land Committee discussed above.

263 Tom Crean, 'The *Voice of Labour* and world revolution, 1917–23', paper delivered at conference on the Irish revolution (1913–23), Department of Modern History, Queen's University, Belfast, Sept. 1999, 6.

264 Patrick Hogan, 'Memorandum: seizures of land', 22 Dec. 1922, MA A/7869.

only be dealt with by the Army'.[265] Consequently, the Special Infantry Corps was established to suppress agrarian agitation, strikes, and other offences against the law. During 1923, the Corps arrested 371 offenders, 173 of whom were alleged to have committed 'agrarian offences'.[266] The Provisional Government's use of force to 'clean up' this social radicalism suggests that the 'conservative revolutionaries' feared their authority was seriously under threat during the turbulent months of 1923.[267]

Although the republican movement has been characterized as entirely conservative, this chapter offers a more nuanced and complex interpretation of Sinn Féin (and the IRA's) policy on the land question. Historians have often argued that the Sinn Féin leadership was not committed to agrarian reform, and that it avoided becoming involved in social conflicts.[268] Laffan, for instance, suggests that 'The Sinn Féin leadership resisted all temptations to involve itself in social disputes where it would be obliged to take sides and antagonise one or another group of its supporters.'[269] While some of the leadership were keen to avoid involvement in social conflicts, Sinn Féin did favour a radical agrarian policy.[270] Although the party was opposed to unregulated and violent land seizures, land redistribution was officially sanctioned in two critical policy documents published in 1917 and 1918, and at three Land Conferences held in May 1920. The leadership of the IRA, on the other hand, appear to have taken a more dismissive view of land agitation. Sean Moylan, a senior IRA officer and later Fianna Fáil Minister for Agriculture, told the Dáil in 1946:

I know what the IRA were doing in 1920–21; they were engaged in an unselfish struggle for the freedom of this country. An attempt was made by many selfish people in many areas to cash in on the work of the IRA, and in Mayo and in many

---

[265] Ibid.
[266] Anthony Kinsella, 'The special infantry corps', *Irish Sword*, 20/82 (Winter 1997), 343.
[267] Ibid. 342.
[268] See, for instance, Fitzpatrick, *Politics and Irish life*, 158.
[269] Laffan, *The resurrection of Ireland*, 258.
[270] Paul Bew has argued that graziers supported Sinn Féin in north Longford during the by-election campaign in 1917, leading him to suggest that 'Sinn Fein was able to outflank the [Irish parliamentary] party on the agrarian left, but perhaps more suggestively also on the right . . . Sinn Fein, in other words, played both cards.' Bew, *Conflict and conciliation*, 214. However, recent research has demonstrated that Bew incorrectly identified the McCanns, who were prominent graziers in the region, as Sinn Féin supporters, and that there is no evidence that graziers in north Longford supported (or were supported by) Sinn Féin. Communication to the author from Dr Mike Wheatley (Nov. 2000). Laffan also uses the erroneous example of the McCanns in Longford to illustrate his point that 'when social issues emerged in the course of [Sinn Féin's] . . . campaigns . . . consistency was not highly prized . . . Such flexibility revealed the party's opportunistic lack of a policy.' Laffan, *The resurrection of Ireland*, 258.

parts of the west attempts were made to cover up under the idea that it was IRA activity, the work of people who wanted something for themselves and did not give a damn about the nation. I remember very well a discussion by IRA headquarters officers on the question of cleaning up the cattle drivers in Co. Mayo—and they were cleaned up by the IRA and by the County Mayo IRA.[271]

However, Cathal Brugha and Austin Stack had both attended the Land Conference held in Dublin on 29 May 1920, at which a policy of regulated land redistribution was advocated. Furthermore, many members of the Galway IRA probably joined the movement in the hope that they might gain land as a reward for their activism. The members of the Galway IRA were not drawn from every walk of life, but tended to be labourers and the sons of small farmers. These men required additional land if they were to avoid emigrating, and a number of IRA engagements in Galway appear to have been—as they were in Clare—thinly veiled agrarian agitations. Although subsequent accounts often paint the IRA as a movement that aimed for the pure goal of national independence, there were clearly strong social impulses beneath the surface of the republican movement and these have been airbrushed out of history, not least by republicans themselves.[272]

The revolution in Ireland resulted in the formation of a conservative state, but not all Irish revolutionaries were conservatives. If we are to gain a fuller and more nuanced understanding of the Irish revolution than that currently available, it is necessary to acknowledge that there were both radical and conservative currents, even if the forces of reaction ultimately prevailed. Even so, Irish society was transformed in the years between 1918 and 1921. During 1920, a great deal of grazing land was redistributed among the rural poor, as a result of both the activities of the agrarian agitators and the radical agrarian policy of Sinn Féin. As a result, the lives of many small farmers and landless labourers' were improved, as they now had sufficient land to achieve at least a reasonable standard of living. Similarly, the leaders of the labour movement may have failed to establish a workers' republic, but serious gains were made by labourers and other workers in terms of wages, representation on local councils, and overcoming deference to the farming and business classes.[273] A social revolution may have been averted, but the position of workers in Irish society would never be

---

[271] Quoted in Paul Bew, 'Sinn Fein, agrarian radicalism and the war of independence, 1919–21', 232.

[272] The speech by Seán Moylan to the Dáil in 1946 (and quoted above) is a case in point.

[273] See T. N. Crean, 'The Labour movement in Kerry and Limerick, 1914–1921' (Trinity College, Dublin, Ph.D., 1995), Ch. 4.

the same as it had been in the pre-Great War period. Furthermore, the 1918 general election inaugurated a revolution in the social composition of the nationalist movement. For the first time, the popular classes and the young took their place among the leadership of nationalist Ireland, and this new generation dominated Irish political life after independence. To be sure, there were important continuities between the 'old' and the 'new' Irelands, but there were some sharp discontinuities, and the path to a conservative revolution was not always a smooth one.

Broadly speaking, the evidence presented here endorses Hart's view of the Irish revolution. Although there were significant social changes, the political revolution was not accompanied by the transformation of class structures. This may explain why the historiography of the Irish revolution has tended to focus on the IRA's successful military campaign against British rule, and to ignore the various unsuccessful attempts to transform Irish society during this period. This tendency has seriously skewed the historical record. In Galway, there were only a few hundred IRA activists involved in the War of Independence,[274] while the extensive agrarian agitation of 1920—characterized by O'Shiel as 'a revolution within a revolution'—was enthusiastically promoted by thousands of young men.[275] Yet the agrarian conflict of 1920 has received very little attention from historians in comparison to the legion of accounts of IRA activities during the War of Independence. History-writing in independent Ireland has—in general—emphasized the unity of the cross-class nationalist struggle against the British state,[276] and conveniently ignored those social conflicts that threatened to fragment the nationalist movement. This chapter, on the other hand, attempts to restore those conflicts to their rightful place in the history of the Irish revolution, and to demonstrate that even in failure they were a part of the revolutionary firmament and deserve to be rescued from 'the enormous condescension of posterity'.[277]

---

[274] In December 1920, there were 3,086 Irish Volunteers (IRA) in Galway. CI monthly reports, east and west Galway, Dec. 1920, PRO CO 904/113. However, Hart estimates that 'less than 20 per cent' of the total IRA membership were likely to be involved in military activity. Hart, 'The social structure of the Irish Republican Army, 1916–1923', 209.

[275] Kevin O'Shiel witness statement, MA BMH WS 1,770 (vol. viii).

[276] See, for instance, Richard English, *Radicals and the republic: socialist republicanism in the Irish Free State, 1925–1937* (Oxford, 1994), 40.

[277] E. P. Thompson, *The making of the English working class* (London, 1963), 13.

Conclusion

By 1921, the lives of smallholders in the west of Ireland had been transformed by a series of land reforms. Under the terms of the Wyndham and the Birrell Land Acts, many of them had purchased their landholdings, and become owner-occupiers rather than tenants. As a result of the activities of the Congested Districts Board and the Sinn Féin courts, as well as the land seizures of 1920, over one million acres of grazing land had been redistributed in the region.[1] Moreover, the Irish Free State introduced a new Land Act in 1923, which completed the transfer of land from the landlord to the tenant; and, a decade later, the Aiken Act of 1933 facilitated the further redistribution of grazing land.[2] As a result of both British and Irish land legislation between 1881 and 1933, a revolution in land tenure in Ireland was implemented, with the tenant farmer becoming the owner of his property, and many congested tenants gaining sufficient additional acres to provide a decent standard of living.

This book suggests that the 1903 and 1909 Land Acts were introduced largely as a result of the extensive agrarian agitation organized by the United Irish League. Wyndham could not have introduced his Land Act (1903) without the United Irish League's extensive agitation for compulsory land purchase between 1901 and 1903, which forced the Government to acknowledge the necessity for revolutionary land legislation in Ireland.[3] Similarly, the Ranch War played a critical role in persuading the Government to introduce the Birrell Land Act in 1909.[4] Popular agitation was also responsible for persuading nationalist leaders to promote more radical agrarian policies than they would otherwise have been inclined to adopt. The agitation for better terms of land purchase which spread throughout Connacht, Munster, and the midlands between 1904 and 1908 caused John Redmond to support the agitators in June 1907, although he was personally more inclined to promote a conciliatory policy towards the Irish landlords.[5] Similarly, the conservatives among the leadership of Sinn Féin were obliged to adopt a radical agrarian policy when they were

---

[1] See Ch. 6.   [2] Kolbert and O'Brien, *Land reform in Ireland*, 46–55.
[3] See Ch. 2.   [4] See Ch. 3.   [5] See Ch. 3.

confronted by an agitation for land redistribution which swept across the west of Ireland like a 'prairie fire' in the spring of 1920.[6] As these examples indicate, the ordinary people of the west of Ireland were collectively able to influence the nature and outcome of the Irish revolution, and thereby to transform their own living conditions. Political leaders do not operate in a vacuum, and they are occasionally forced to respond to the ideas of the ordinary people. This was particularly the case in late nineteenth- and early twentieth-century Ireland when events in the 'bogs of Connaught'[7] were often as important as discussions in political committee rooms in determining the 'high' politics of both the British Government and the Irish nationalist leadership. The discussion of popular political activity presented in this book suggests that a number of critical episodes in late modern Irish history require some revision, and, in conclusion, I will consider the contribution which this book makes to ongoing debates in Irish historiography.

I

The historical 'revisionism' of the 1970s and 1980s reinterpreted the Irish land question in a number of fundamental respects.[8] According to nationalist historians, and particularly the work of J. E. Pomfret, the Land War was a conflict between pro-British Protestant landowners and a united class of Catholic nationalist tenant farmers.[9] In addition, the landlords were depicted as parasitic exploiters of their tenants, who extracted cripplingly high rents from their estates, and implemented mass evictions at will.[10] As E. D. Steele has pointed out, 'the entry under landlords in the index of P. S. O'Hegarty's *History of Ireland under the union* reads simply: "Landlords, iniquity of... increased iniquity of... "'.[11] These caricatures did not reflect the reality of landlord–tenant relations. William Vaughan has demonstrated that evictions were comparatively rare after the 1850s,

---

[6] See Ch. 6.

[7] Hansard, 4th series, 28 Feb. 1902, vol. civ, col. 95.

[8] Roy Foster correctly points out that 'you are a revisionist if you are a historian. The use of the word to mean pro-British or anti-nationalist is improper.' 'Our man at Oxford', *History Ireland*, 1/3 (Autumn 1993), 11.

[9] J. E. Pomfret, *The struggle for land in Ireland, 1800–1923* (Princeton, 1930). For a discussion of Pomfret, see Vaughan, *Landlords and tenants in mid-Victorian Ireland*, pp. v–viii.

[10] Vaughan, *Landlords and tenants in mid-Victorian Ireland*, p. v.

[11] E. D. Steele, 'Ireland for the Irish', *History*, 57/190 (June 1972), 240. P. S. O'Hegarty's *A history of Ireland under the Union, 1801 to 1922* (London, 1952) is a classic of nationalist historiography (written from the pro-Treaty perspective).

and suggested that landlords' rents did not keep pace with inflation: 'An examination of the rentals of over fifty estates, covering the period between the famine and the land war, made it clear that rents had not increased frequently; that rent increases had been about 20 per cent; [and] that evictions had not been common.'[12] Furthermore, landlords were by no means exclusively Protestant. In 1861, less than half of the landlords in Ireland were Church of Ireland (48 per cent) while 43 per cent were Roman Catholic.[13] The myth that the Catholic tenant farmers were a united and homogeneous group was also challenged. While O'Hegarty could view the Land War (1879–81) as 'a war coming from the root of things, from the Irish national consciousness that if the nation was to survive it must stay on the land', Bew has shown that the tenant farmer class was deeply divided, notably between graziers and small farmers.[14]

In *Conflict and conciliation*, Bew applies these insights to the later period:

The difficulties posed by the land question—the source of both vitality and division within popular Nationalism—did not diminish for Parnell's successor, John Redmond. At least in 1881 the Land League had a unifying object of hostility: the 'alien' landlords. In the period of the United Irish League (1898–1918) divisions within the tenantry became much more visible: after the massive land purchase reform embodied in the Wyndham Act of 1903, the likelihood of a *united* movement of the Irish farmers receded even further. The continuation of agrarian militancy after 1903 generated considerable disunity within the Nationalist bloc; Catholic Nationalist was set against Catholic Nationalist—it was not simply or even, in many places, mainly the now increasingly marginalized landlord stratum who felt the heat.[15]

Although there were tensions between large and small tenant farmers in the Land League, the Land War (1879–81) was primarily an anti-landlord

---

[12] Vaughan, *Landlords and tenants in mid-Victorian Ireland*, pp. viii, 23.

[13] Ibid. 11. Although it should be emphasized that the majority of landlords with estates larger than 10,000 acres were Protestant. Of the 290 landlords who owned estates of over 10,000 acres in 1881, 90 % were members of the Church of Ireland 4 % were members of the Church of England, and only 6 % were Roman Catholics. See Fergus Campbell, 'Elites, power and society in Ireland, 1879–1914', paper delivered to the American Conference of Irish Studies, New York, June 2001.

[14] O'Hegarty, *A history of Ireland under the Union, 1801 to 1922*, 462; see Bew, *Land and the national question*, 55, 223–4.

[15] Paul Bew, 'The national question, land and "revisionism": some reflections', in D. G. Boyce and Alan O'Day, (eds.), *The making of modern Irish history: revisionism and the revisionist controversy* (London, 1996), 96. In this article, Bew summarizes the main arguments in *Conflict and conciliation*.

agitation, and involved very little intra-tenant conflict.[16] However, following the revolutionary land legislation of 1881 and 1903, according to Bew, conflict between small farmers and graziers became the dominant dynamic of agrarian agitation, with anti-landlord activity relegated to a minor role.

Yet the findings of this book suggest that this interpretation of agrarian conflict during the first decade of the twentieth century requires modification. The discovery of a neglected source, unavailable to Bew, has provided new material on the dynamics of the Ranch War (1904–8).[17] As Chapter 3 demonstrates, the Ranch War consisted of two interlinked agitations. First, a land purchase agitation, in which rent combinations were organized to pressurize landlords into selling their estates at prices dictated by the tenants. And second, an agitation to intimidate graziers into giving up their eleven-month lettings of untenanted land, so that the landlords (who owned the untenanted land) would sell it to the Estates Commissioners. In both cases, the ultimate target of the agitation was the landlord, who owned both the tenanted and the untenanted land. Certainly, tension between small farmers and graziers was more significant than during the Land War, and there was a great deal of intra-tenant conflict, but the underlying dynamic of the Ranch War agitation remained anti-landlord.

These contrasting interpretations originate from different views of the impact of the Wyndham Land Act on Irish society. For Bew, the implementation of the Act caused 'social relations in the countryside . . . to change rapidly'.[18] As well-to-do tenants became peasant proprietors, they had no reason to continue agitating against landlords, and the once united tenant movement dissolved into a series of competing subgroups (graziers and congestees, purchased and unpurchased).[19] The transformation of rural social relationships, inaugurated by the Wyndham Land Act, thus changed the basis for agrarian collective action in Ireland. Rather than agitating against the landlords (for land purchase), farmers began to agitate against each other (for land redistribution).

[16] Samuel Clark analysed the resolutions passed at 153 land meetings reported in the *Nation* between June 1879 and August 1881, and did not find one demand for the division of grazing farms. See Samuel Clark, 'The importance of agrarian classes: agrarian class structure and collective action in nineteenth-century Ireland', in Drudy (ed.), *Ireland: land, politics and people*, 24, 26, 36 n. 36.

[17] Inspector General's and County Inspector's monthly reports (for each county), Jan. 1903–Dec. 1908, NA IGCI/1–15. These reports are missing from the sequence of monthly reports between 1898 and 1921 contained in the CO 904 series in the Public Record Office, London.

[18] Bew, 'Sinn Fein, agrarian radicalism and the war of independence, 1919–1921', 221.

[19] Ibid.

While elements of this argument are convincing, the process by which tenants were converted into proprietors was a good deal slower than Bew suggests. Although 53 per cent of holdings had either been sold or agreed to be sold,[20] only 30 per cent of tenanted land had actually been sold by 1908, so that even at the end of the Ranch War, more than two-thirds (70 per cent) of tenanted land had not been purchased.[21] In part, this was because the Wyndham Land Act created the circumstances for continued agrarian agitation. Serious conflicts arose between landlord and tenant over the terms of land purchase, and these disputes provided the basis for the Ranch War (1904–8).[22] Although Bew claims that resistance to rent payment 'played an inessential role' in the Ranch War,[23] there were an average of thirty-five combinations against the payment of rent each month between January 1907 and June 1908, all of which aimed to force the landlords to sell their estates on terms dictated by the tenants. It would be some time before the land tenure issue was removed from the centre of Irish politics, and anti-landlord agitation remained significant well into the second decade of the twentieth century.

The Ranch War agitation was probably more likely to unite than to fragment the nationalist movement. Even if we accepted the view that the Ranch War was a predominantly anti-grazier conflict, graziers were by no means exclusively Catholic nationalists. They were often Protestants, and, just as often, they were Catholics who were not subscribing nationalists.[24] When the police compiled statistics on the number of eleven-month lease-holders who were officials of the United Irish League in 1903, they found that 166 Leaguers held such a lease (0.12 per cent of the total membership of the UIL) and that 91 per cent of UIL branch committees contained no eleven-month leaseholders whatsoever.[25] Indeed, there is evidence that graziers rarely participated in nationalist politics, preferring to affiliate themselves with the political and cultural activities of the landlord class.[26] An anti-grazier conflict, then, would not seriously deplete the ranks of the

---

[20] Ibid.   [21] See Table 3.

[22] See Ch. 3.

[23] Bew, *Conflict and conciliation*, 42.

[24] See Ch. 1. The Smiths of Colmanstown were Catholic graziers who did not subscribe to nationalist politics. See Ch. 4.

[25] 'U. I. League officials holding grazing and evicted farms on 1st February, 1903', the confidential print, 1903, PRO CO 903/10/77; UIL membership figures, 31 Dec. 1902, PRO CO 904/20/2. If we assume that there were twenty officials in each UIL branch (see Appendix I), less than 1 % of the total number of officials in Ireland held eleven-month grazing farms.

[26] James Smith of Colmanstown hunted with the Galway Blazers. Interview with Annie Jordan (Smith's housekeeper in the 1930s), at Pollacrossaun, 17 May 1993. On the Galway Blazers, see Edmund Mahony, *The Galway Blazers* (Galway, 1979).

nationalist movement. Furthermore, the use of rent combinations during the Ranch War tended to unite the Irish farmers. All tenants, whether large or small, wanted to purchase their land as cheaply as possible, and the United Irish League's agitation for reasonable terms of purchase was as relevant to the large tenant farmer as it was to the congested tenant. Rather than generating disunity within the nationalist movement, the Irish Party's support for the Ranch War strengthened the position of the United Irish League *vis-à-vis* the Sinn Féin threat.[27]

It is necessary, of course, to distinguish between resident graziers, or large tenant farmers, and non-resident graziers, and eleven-month lease-holders, against whom the bulk of anti-grazier agitation was directed. Large tenant farmers played a significant role in the Land League and the United Irish League. Hoppen's study of the social composition of Land League branches in Cork and Queen's county indicates that the proportion of large tenant farmers in Land League branches was broadly similar to the proportion of large tenant farmers in the wider rural area in which the branch existed.[28] Similarly, my study of the composition of the United Irish League in east Galway indicates that large farmers constituted 11 per cent of the UIL membership,[29] and that large holdings (in excess of 50 acres) accounted for 18 per cent of holdings in the Loughrea Poor Law Union.[30] Most anti-grazier agitation was not directed against these large tenant farmers, but against the eleven-month leaseholders, very few of whom were actually members of the UIL. Consequently, the anti-grazier agitation during the Ranch War did not seriously divide the membership of the United Irish League. Interestingly, my study of the social composition of Sinn Féin in Galway indicates there were neither resident nor non-resident graziers in Sinn Féin in the county.[31] There was one case of a Sinn Féiner attempting to purchase a grazing farm at Clifden in 1918, but the opposition which he encountered from within the Sinn Féin movement forced him to give it up.[32] This suggests that grazier involvement in nationalist politics gradually declined between 1879 and 1918, and that the republican movement in Connacht was not fraught with

[27] See Ch. 3.
[28] K. T. Hoppen, *Elections, politics, and society in Ireland 1832–1885* (Oxford, 1984), 477–8.
[29] See Table 18.
[30] *Royal Commission on Congestion: appendix to the tenth report*, HC (1908), [Cd. 4007], xlii. 437–8.   [31] See Table 18.
[32] J. B. Joyce, a Clifden butcher and Sinn Féiner, attempted to purchase the Clifden demesne lands (comprising 220 acres) in February 1918 but opposition from the local Sinn Féin club (and others) forced him to withdraw and allow the Congested Districts Board to purchase the demesne. CI monthly report, west Galway, Feb. and Aug. 1918, CO 904/105–6.

inter-class tension, as has been suggested by Bew, Fitzpatrick, and Laffan.[33]

The historiographical debates on the Irish land question were unusually vibrant (and productive) during the two decades between 1968 and 1988, when a wealth of innovative new studies were completed. However, since the late 1980s, the conclusions of historians have tended to harden into a consensus which may now require revision. The evidence presented in this book suggests the necessity for renewed discussion of a number of central issues, particularly regarding the impact of the 1881 and 1903 Land Acts on the nature of agrarian agitation, and the involvement of graziers in nationalist politics. As Vaughan has pointed out, the new interpretations of the land question put forward in the 1970s and 1980s do not constitute a new orthodoxy: 'They are based on empirical methods and not on a priori assumptions; they are tinged with scepticism and purged of faith; they have not been received as dogmatic by all the faithful; they open rather than conceal the subject; they offer no comfort to those who like certainty.'[34]

II

A recent survey of history-writing in Ireland argues that historians have tended to be preoccupied with 'high' politics, and have neglected the study of popular political activity.[35] This is not to suggest that Irish historians have ignored popular politics. There are at least three major collections of essays which discuss popular political activity in Ireland since 1800, and there are also a number of impressive individual contributions.[36] However, there has been no systematic investigation of the ideas

[33] Bew, *Conflict and conciliation*, 214; Fitzpatrick, *Politics and Irish life*, 267; Laffan, *The resurrection of Ireland*, 258.

[34] Vaughan, *Landlords and tenants in mid-Victorian Ireland*, p. x. Some of Vaughan's own arguments have recently been challenged. See K. T. Hoppen, *Ireland since 1800: conflict and conformity* (2nd edn., London, 1999), 97–8.

[35] Margaret MacCurtain and Mary O'Dowd, 'An agenda for women's history in Ireland, 1500–1900: part I: 1500–1800', *Irish Historical Studies*, 28/109 (May 1992), 4.

[36] See Drudy (ed.), *Ireland: land, politics and people*; Clark and Donnelly, *Irish peasants*; C. H. E. Philpin (ed.), *Nationalism and popular protest in Ireland* (Cambridge, 1987); M. R. Beames, *Peasants and power: the Whiteboy movements and their control in pre-Famine Ireland* (Brighton, 1983); Samuel Clark, *Social origins of the Irish Land War* (Princeton, 1979); Bew, *Land and the national question*; Bew, *Conflict and conciliation*; R. V. Comerford, *The Fenians in context: Irish politics and society, 1848–82* (Dublin, 1985); Fitzpatrick, *Politics and Irish life*; and Hart, *The IRA and its enemies*. I confine my remarks to the literature on popular politics in the nineteenth and twentieth centuries.

and activities of ordinary Irish people as there has been, for example, in French and English historiography. While historians have considered the impact of social and economic change on Irish agrarian class structure, and described the ideas of national and local nationalist elites, they have not—by and large—reconstructed the systems of thought and behaviour of ordinary peasants or workers in the manner of (for instance) Eric Hobsbawm or E. P. Thompson. Bew's study of nationalist politics between 1890 and 1910, for example, focuses on the different views of the land question among the leaders of the Irish Parliamentary Party rather than exploring the dynamics of the Ranch War.[37] And while Fitzpatrick's study of revolutionary Clare does consider popular political activity, it does so from above, from the perspective of the local nationalist leadership, rather than that of the rank and file activist.[38] We look in vain for an account of a cattle drive or a rent combination which attempts 'to penetrate behind the actions of peasants to the social and political assumptions and the strategic thinking which underlie them', or for a discussion of the ways in which 'rough music' was employed by agrarian agitators to enforce alternative agrarian codes.[39] As Cormac Ó Gráda has pointed out, 'Irish historians are a rather conservative bunch. There are no Irish E. P. Thompsons or Eugene Genoveses.'[40] This book has explored the nature and dynamics of popular political activity in Ireland; and the adoption of this approach has provided new interpretations of key developments in Irish political and agrarian history.

Andrew Gailey's account of the origins of the Wyndham Land Act claims that it was solely the product of Wyndham's statesmanship and his canny appreciation of the realities of Irish politics, rather than a response to civil disobedience.[41] An alternative reading of the origins of the Wyndham Land Act is outlined in Chapter 2. When he became Chief Secretary in November 1900, Wyndham was firmly committed to

[37] See Bew, *Conflict and conciliation.*

[38] For instance, Fitzpatrick's examination of the Sinn Féin movement in Clare is largely based on newspaper reports and on the diary of Edward Lysaght (later MacLysaght), a leading cultural nationalist in the region. See Fitzpatrick, *Politics and Irish life*, 127–64. Peter Murray described *Politics and Irish life* as a 'history of popular politics from above' in his review of the book published in *Saothar*, 5 (May 1979), 67.

[39] E.J. Hobsbawm, 'Peasant land occupations', *Past and Present*, 62 (Feb. 1974), 120; on 'rough music', see E. P. Thompson, *Customs in common* (London, 1991), 467–538.

[40] Cormac Ó Gráda, *Ireland before and after the Famine: explorations in economic history* (2nd edn., Manchester, 1993), 101. A similar point was made by A. C. Hepburn in 1968, which more or less continues to apply: 'The Irish revolution awaits its Georges Lefebvre'; A. C. Hepburn, 'Liberal policies and nationalist politics in Ireland, 1905–10' (University of Kent, Ph.D., 1968), 825.

[41] Gailey, *Ireland and the death of kindness*, 190, 192.

introducing a substantial reform of the land question. However, there was substantial opposition in both the cabinet and the Irish office to his proposed scheme of Government-subsidized land purchase. During the spring of 1902, he even considered resigning when the coercionists in the cabinet gained the upper hand and proclaimed nine counties and two county boroughs under the Crimes Act. In the event, however, it was the United Irish League's extensive agitation on behalf of compulsory land purchase that enabled Wyndham to regain the initiative in the cabinet. The Prime Minister and the Chancellor of the Exchequer were persuaded to sanction a 'great measure' only when Wyndham warned them that if they did not do so an extensive agitation might ensue.[42] Wyndham's Land Act, then, was as much the product of the United Irish League's agitation as it was the result of the Chief Secretary's imaginative statesmanship.

The reinterpretation of the dynamics of the Ranch War agitation, discussed in Chapter 3, also provides scope for a reassessment of our understanding of political developments in the first decade of the new century. In an influential analysis, Philip Bull has suggested that the period following the introduction of the Wyndham Land Act created the opportunity for the Irish Parliamentary Party to adopt a more conciliatory policy towards the landlords, which might have resulted in the evolution of a more plural and less sectarian nationalist movement. According to Bull, after 1903 'it was . . . for the first time possible to remove the land tenure issue from the centre of Irish politics' because 'Ireland was now dominated by small capitalist peasant proprietors, their interests distinctly different from when they had been tenants'.[43] As the land question had been solved, it was possible for the conciliatory policy advocated by—among others—Charles Stewart Parnell and John Shawe-Taylor to be adopted by the leadership of the Irish Party. The policy of conciliation was based on the assumption that once the land difficulty was solved, landlord and tenant, and Protestant and Catholic, could unite in the demand for an independent Ireland. However, after 1903, the leaders of the Irish Party rejected conciliation and instead promoted a militant, anti-landlord policy. For Bull, this represented a failure of nerve and imagination, which resulted in the possibility of a broader *rapprochement* between Protestant and Catholic being lost for almost a century. The truculent militancy of the Dillonite wing of the party prevented Redmond from pursuing the conciliatory policy which, as a landlord and a Parnellite, he supported: 'For the first time [after 1903] the broader nationalism to which Parnell

---

[42] See Ch. 2.
[43] Bull, *Land, politics and nationalism*, 168, 173.

... had aspired was a possibility in the real world of politics ... However, with the reversion under Dillon to redundant political strategies, the parliamentary nationalist movement missed the chance to realize this new potential.'[44]

The discussion of nationalist politics between 1903 and 1910 presented in Chapter 3, suggests a number of problems with this analysis. Rather than resolving the land question, the Wyndham Land Act created the rationale for a new conflict between landlord and tenant over the terms of land purchase, which provided the basis for the Ranch War (1904–8). Furthermore, the leadership of the Irish Parliamentary Party did not actively support the Ranch War agitation until it was forced to do so. In the aftermath of the Land Conference, Redmond did promote a conciliatory policy, advising tenants to conduct purchase negotiations in a friendly manner. However, when it became clear that the Irish landlords were not reciprocating with a conciliatory attitude to tenant purchasers, the Party withdrew its support for conciliation, and avoided making any pronouncements whatsoever on the question of agrarian conflict. Indeed, between 1904 and 1907, the Irish Parliamentary Party was characterized by the police as having no agrarian policy. In the vacuum created by the Party's silence, an unofficial agitation was initiated in the west of Ireland, and gradually this agitation spread throughout Connacht, Munster, and the midlands.[45] The Ranch War, therefore, was a popular movement from below, not supported initially by the leaders of the Irish Parliamentary Party.

In fact, Redmond's support for the Ranch War (first expressed in July 1907) was a strategic manoeuvre designed to restore popular confidence in the Irish Party after the Irish Council Bill debacle. The rise of Sinn Féin, particularly in 1907–8, posed a serious ideological threat to the Party. Following the introduction of the Irish Council Bill, there was a concern that the Liberal Party might not deliver its pledge to introduce Home Rule. In this context, the Sinn Féin policy of abstention from Westminster became increasingly attractive to a significant number of nationalists. Moreover, Sinn Féin's support for agrarian agitation in parts of the west of Ireland threatened to undermine the Irish Parliamentary Party's identification with a radical agrarian policy. Redmond's support for the pre-existing Ranch War agitation, then, was designed to restore nationalist faith in the Liberal alliance (by pressurizing the Liberal Government into introducing a new Land Act), and to re-establish the Irish Party as the radical agrarian party.[46]

[44] Ibid. 168.   [45] See Ch. 3.   [46] See Ch. 3.

The Irish Parliamentary Party's support for the Ranch War, when considered in the wider context of popular politics, does not appear as paradoxical and self-defeating as Bull suggests. Redmond remained committed to conciliation, but he was forced to advocate a radical agrarian policy by the groundswell of support for agrarian agitation after 1904. If anything was to blame for the failure of conciliation after 1903, it was the continued conflict between landlord and tenant, which undermined the conciliatory spirit of the Land Conference. And for this failure, perhaps both landlord and tenant should share the responsibility, as both parties campaigned for terms of land purchase that would best suit themselves.

III

Historians generally agree that the Irish revolution was characterized more by continuity than by change. 'If revolutions are what happen to wheels', as Fitzpatrick pithily summarizes in *Politics and Irish life*, 'then Ireland underwent revolution between 1916 and 1922.'[47] According to this view, the revolution changed very little, and the new Ireland that emerged in 1922 was not radically dissimilar to the old Ireland which it replaced. This interpretation of the nature of the Irish revolution is an important corrective to the once widely held view that the 1916 Easter Rising transformed both Irish society and nationalist politics irrevocably. The nationalist historians of the Irish revolution viewed the Easter Rising as constituting a decisive turning point in Irish political history. P. S. O'Hegarty, for example, described the insurrection in quasi-mythological terms:

Like King Argimenes, who found a sword in the sand, and at once forgot that he was a slave and remembered that he was a King, Ireland found in 1916, in the men who fought for her and the men who died for her, a sword for her spirit. Home Rule, and the men of Home Rule, began to recede. In the unforgettable words of Yeats:—

> All changed, changed utterly:
> A terrible beauty is born.[48]

The Rising was thus depicted as transforming nationalist politics (with the victory of republicans over Home Rulers), and inaugurating a military struggle that would result in political independence. As we have seen, Fitzpatrick found that the impact of the Rising on provincial nationalist

---

47 Fitzpatrick, *Politics and Irish life*, 232.
48 O'Hegarty, *A history of Ireland under the Union*, 1800–1922, 710.

politics was more complex than O'Hegarty allowed. Far from signalling a decisive transformation, there were important continuities of both personnel and organizational technique between the pre-Rising Home Rule party and the post-Rising Sinn Féin movement in Clare. Sinn Féin was based on the same organizational structure as the United Irish League, and a significant minority of the Sinn Féin leadership in the county (13 per cent) were former Home Rulers.[49] Nationalist politics might have changed, but Fitzpatrick demonstrated that it had not changed utterly.

Fitzpatrick's revision of the nationalist interpretation of the Rising has influenced a generation of Irish historians. According to Charles Townshend, *Politics and Irish life*

demonstrates above all the continuities which underlay the dramatic period of political revolution. The 'drama of Sinn Féin', as it was once called, is shown to have had fairly conventional sources ... The shift from Home Rule to Sinn Féin was not accompanied by radical change in the countryside. Political bosses changed their banners, but there was no real revolution in Irish minds. The older order, which Fitzpatrick analyses with superb panache ... certainly fell; but the new order was not novel, and as his final chapter indicates, the 'underlying assumptions of communal life' were barely beginning to alter.[50]

Those historians who have written syntheses of Irish history in the nineteenth and twentieth centuries have also been influenced by Fitzpatrick's thesis. K. T. Hoppen, for instance, suggests that during the Irish revolution:

[P]olitical life at the local level remained far less dramatically altered than national events alone would seem to indicate . . . many old Home Rulers were happy to find refuge in the potentially capacious portmanteau of Sinn Fein . . . Over the whole period from the outbreak of the Great War a strong element of continuity survived in local political leadership with all the continuities in the primacy of the immediate and the tangible which that implied.[51]

Fitzpatrick's contention that 1916 did not transform provincial nationalist politics, and that the 'men of Home Rule' did not recede (as O'Hegarty suggested), has thus been broadly accepted as the new historiographical orthodoxy of the revolution.

However, Fitzpatrick tends to overstate the case for continuity between the Home Rule and Sinn Féin movements. While a significant minority of Sinn Féiners had been Home Rulers, the vast majority (87 per cent) were

[49] See Ch. 5.
[50] Charles Townshend, 'Modernization and nationalism: perspectives in recent Irish history', *History*, 66/217 (June 1981), 241.
[51] Hoppen, *Ireland since 1800*, (2nd edn.), 154–5.

not veterans of the Home Rule movement. Indeed, as Chapter 5 suggests, Sinn Féin in Galway was based not on the Home Rule tradition, but on a radical agrarian and republican political culture that had existed in the county since at least the 1880s.[52] Although Sinn Féin undoubtedly inherited the UIL's organizational structure of parish branches, and constituency, provincial, and national executives, the new party did not fully adopt the Home Rule movement's 'over-riding organisational principle—the desire to unite all Irishmen under one banner'.[53] Certainly, elements of the Sinn Féin leadership did advocate the avoidance of social struggles which might fragment a cross-class alliance. But there were also strong supporters of a radical agrarian policy in Sinn Féin, and this policy would not be popular with either landlords or graziers. As Chapter 6 shows, the republican leadership supported the radical agrarian policy of land redistribution, although it was opposed to unregulated and violent land seizures. The claim that Sinn Féin and latterly Dáil Éireann's land policy sought to unite all Irishmen (and women) is, therefore, not sustainable. Overall, Fitzpatrick was correct to stress the limitations of the O'Hegarty model, but at the same time, he tended to overemphasize the continuities between Home Rule and Sinn Féin in the provinces.

The discussion of the 1916 Rising in Galway (in Chapter 5) suggests that the insurrection was intended as a serious attempt to defeat the British military forces in Ireland. It is assumed by most historians that the aim of the insurrection was not a successful military victory, but a blood sacrifice.[54] According to this view, the rebels knew that the Rising would fail, but they carried out the insurrection in the knowledge that British repression of the rebellion would radicalize popular nationalist opinion, and therefore increase support for republicanism. However, a study of events on the ground suggests that the rebels did envisage a serious military confrontation. Chapter 5 demonstrates that extensive preparations had been made for a rebellion in the west, and that a large-scale provincial insurrection was prevented only by the capture of the *Aud* (carrying 20,000 rifles), and Eoin MacNeill's countermanding order, which undermined the rebel mobilization. After the Galway Rising, the County Inspector for west Galway stated that if MacNeill had not issued his countermand, the rebels would have taken control of the county: 'It is pretty plain now that the rebellion was precipitated and if it had been deferred until later when

---

[52] See Ch. 5.

[53] David Fitzpatrick, 'Irish people and politics: the development of political beliefs and patterns of political conduct among Irishmen from 1913 to 1921, with particular reference to county Clare' (University of Cambridge, Ph.D, 1975), 202.

[54] Townshend, *Political violence*, 299.

all was ready it would not have been confined to the Districts of Galway and Gort but would have embraced the whole County and we could not have held it.'[55] Furthermore, the fact that 500 rebels in Galway, armed with less than 50 rifles, were able to take control of a substantial proportion of the county for almost a week suggests that if similar risings had taken place in other counties, a serious provincial insurrection was a possibility.

In most of provincial Ireland, the confusion created by the countermand prevented any form of rebellion from taking place. However, the Galway evidence suggests that, without impediments, the Irish Volunteers could have staged a country-wide rebellion. This was certainly the view of the Inspector General who observed in May 1916:

> That the Sinn Fein insurrection was so quickly put down and that it was confined to so few districts outside the Metropolitan area, must be ascribed to the fortunate arrest of Sir R. Casement and the failure of the German ship to land the required arms and ammunition. There is no reason whatever to believe that if these arrangements had not miscarried the Irish Volunteers in any County would have held back. In fact the evidence is all the other way.[56]

In the event, however, the capture of the *Aud* and MacNeill's countermand reduced the insurrection to a comparatively minor military protest.

IV

The debate on the continuities (or discontinuities) underpinning the Irish revolution hinges on the question of whether there was a genuine attempt to radically transform Irish society during this period. Recent accounts have tended to suggest that neither the events of the revolution, nor the revolutionary settlement, contained a serious attempt to change the social balance of power.[57] However, this is not the view presented in earlier studies, which suggested that there was a substantial amount of social conflict during the revolution, even if the forces of conservatism ultimately prevailed.[58] As Crean, Fitzpatrick, and O'Connor have shown, a wave of strike activity spread across Ireland between 1917 and 1921: there were 894

[55] CI monthly report, west Galway, May 1916, PRO CO 904/100.

[56] IG monthly report, Apr. and May 1916, PRO CO 904/100.

[57] Laffan, *The resurrection of Ireland*, 315; Regan and Cronin, 'Introduction: Ireland and the politics of independence, 1922–49', 1–2.

[58] See Bew, 'Sinn Fein, agrarian radicalism and the war of independence, 1919–1921'; Crean, 'The Labour movement in Kerry and Limerick'; Fitzpatrick, *Politics and Irish life*; O'Connor, *Syndicalism in Ireland*; and Varley, 'The politics of agrarian reform'.

strikes during this period, 28 of which involved over 1,000 workers each.[59] This period of intense industrial conflict also witnessed the rapid expansion of the ITGWU, which by December 1920 had become a mass movement with 501 branches and 83,000 members.[60] The new membership of the ITGWU came from both urban and rural backgrounds, and the union campaigned for better wages and improved working conditions for both industrial and agricultural labourers.[61]

For Fitzpatrick, the struggle of Irish labourers for better wages and working conditions represented the only serious attempt to 'revise the underlying assumptions of communal life' during the Irish revolution.[62] In his study of the development of the provincial labour movement in Clare, he focuses on agricultural labourers' conflict with farmers over the question of wages and working conditions. This 'radical urge' was, however, opposed by the 'conservative resurgence' of the Irish farmers who 'organised themselves in defensive alliance to protect their wealth and social status'.[63] Increasingly, farmers' opposition to the radical demands of agricultural labourers was expressed through their membership of the Irish Farmers' Union, which, after the Rising, 'became more representative of Irish farmers as a class and less the preserve of paternalist landowners and large employers'.[64] By the spring of 1920, the IFU and the ITGWU were engaged in serious conflict over labourers' wages and working conditions in a number of (mainly) Leinster and Munster counties.[65] However, both the numerical dominance and the socially conservative nature of the farmers ensured that the labourers' radical initiative was successfully resisted and, as Fitzpatrick concludes, 'the few voices crying for a new social order were quickly, and it may be finally, submerged'.[66]

This compelling analysis of social conflict during the revolution demonstrates the weaknesses in Cronin, Laffan, and Regan's accounts. Clearly, there were serious attempts to change the social balance of power in Ireland, but they were (as I have argued in Chapter 6) resisted by conservative reactions, which ultimately dictated the outcome of the Irish revolution. Even so, Fitzpatrick's analysis applies more to the provinces of Leinster and Munster than it does to the western province of Connacht. The social structure of Connacht was quite different from that of the east and the south-west. Whereas the ratio of labourers to farmers in Leinster

---

[59] O'Connor, *Syndicalism in Ireland*, 25, 27.
[60] Fitzpatrick, *Politics and Irish life*, 246.
[61] Crean, 'The Labour movement in Kerry and Limerick', Ch. 4
[62] Fitzpatrick, *Politics and Irish life*, 234–5.   [63] Ibid. 235, 267, 235.
[64] Ibid. 270.   [65] Ibid. 272.   [66] Ibid. 279, 280.

(1.91:1) and Munster (1.59:1) was almost two to one, in Connacht, there were more farmers than labourers (1:0.92).[67] Moreover, farms in Connacht were generally smaller than those in Leinster and Munster. Consequently, the dominant form of social conflict in the west of Ireland during the revolution was that carried out by small farmers and landless labourers against graziers and landlords, for the redistribution of untenanted grazing land. This raises a number of questions regarding Fitzpatrick's Clare model. First, large and small farmers in Connacht did not tend to unite in the Irish Farmers' Union, as they appear to have done in Clare.[68] In the west, the farming class was clearly divided between poor small farmers and well-to-do large farmers, as it had been throughout the period since the Land War. And second, the involvement of small farmers in agrarian conflict suggests that the farming class as a whole was not unanimously conservative in outlook. Although the larger farmers may have been innately conservative, many small farmers supported the radical agrarian policy of land redistribution, and contributed to the 'radical urge' rather than the 'conservative resurgence' in Connacht.

In an important essay, Bew provides a useful discussion of agrarian conflict during the Anglo-Irish war.[69] His account recognizes that significant agrarian grievances remained in 1920 which generated conflict particularly between small farmers and graziers over the question of land redistribution. However, Bew points out that agrarian radicalism tended to be quashed by the leaders of the republican movement, who took a dim view of attempts to distract attention from the national struggle against the British forces in Ireland. Indeed, Bew suggests that Sinn Féin's agrarian policy was 'clearly . . . on the side of the rural conservatives'.[70] A more nuanced reading of Sinn Féin's policy on the land question is presented in Chapter 6. Building on Tony Varley's analysis of the republican response to agrarian agitation, I argue that Sinn Féin did support the radical agrarian policy of land redistribution, although it was opposed to unregulated and violent land seizures.[71] Furthermore, it is clear that there were both radical agrarians and conservatives in the republican movement (among the leadership and the rank and file), and that the Sinn Féin response to

---

[67] O'Connor, *Syndicalism in Ireland*, 34

[68] The small farmers who were members of the UIL and Sinn Féin in east Galway do not appear to have joined the Irish Farmers' Union. See *Irish Farmer*, 21 Feb., 26 June, 10 July, 2 Oct. 1920; and 5 Mar. 1921.

[69] Bew, 'Sinn Fein, agrarian radicalism and the war of independence, 1919–1921'.

[70] Ibid. 232, 229.

[71] Varley, 'The politics of agrarian reform'. Varley's work has not received the attention that it deserves.

agrarian conflict was not as unambiguously reactionary as has been suggested.[72]

Since the 1920s, left republicans have claimed that the Anglo-Irish war was a period of radical potential, but that this potential was restrained by socially conservative leaders. This was the view of Peader O'Donnell, who believed that 'Radical demands that could have moved whole counties into action were frowned on. All the leadership wanted was a change from British to Irish government: they wanted no change in the basis of society.'[73] For O'Donnell, the republican movement emerged from 'the ranks of workers and peasants', and the struggle against England was but 'a preliminary to freeing the Ireland of the poor from hardship'.[74]

Richard English has provided a subtle and careful critique of these claims in *Radicals and the republic*, and, in so doing, he has identified a number of critical elisions in O'Donnell's retrospective view of the War of Independence. In particular, English rightly points out that O'Donnell's claim that the driving force of the nationalist movement was provided by small farmers and the urban working class failed to acknowledge the enormous influence of the Catholic middle class on the evolution of Irish nationalist politics.[75] However, O'Donnell's suggestion that there was at least the possibility of social revolution during the Anglo-Irish war may be more useful than English suggests. As Chapter 6 demonstrates, the agrarian agitation of 1920 involved the forcible seizure of thousands of acres of grazing land, and constituted a serious threat to the law of private property in the west of Ireland. Moreover, many members of the Irish Republican Army in the west of Ireland were also smallholders and labourers who agitated for additional acres under the guise of IRA 'engagements'.[76] According to Padraic Fallon, 'the War of Independence [in Galway was] . . . a land war and a class struggle, fought primarily against the Anglo-Irish ruling and landowning class rather than against England'.[77] If the

---

[72] See, for instance, Fitzpatrick, *Politics and Irish life*, 265.

[73] Quoted in English, *Radicals and the republic*, 31.

[74] Ibid. 30.

[75] Ibid. 38.

[76] The efforts of former IRA activists in independent Ireland to gain special concessions from the Land Commission also suggests that the motivation for many Volunteers to take part in the War of Independence may have been land. See Terence Dooley, 'IRA veterans and land division in independent Ireland, 1923–48', in Fearghal McGarry (ed.), *Republicanism in modern Ireland* (Dublin, 2003).

[77] Padraic Fallon (1905–74) was born at Athenry, the son of a cattle dealer and hotel owner, and became one of Galway's most celebrated poets. Patrick O'Brien (ed.), *Erect me a monument of broken wings: an anthology of writings by and on Padraic Fallon* (Athenry, 1992), 17.

republican leadership had encouraged this agitation, rather than attempting to regulate it, then the revolutionary settlement might have been quite different. At the very least, republican support for agrarian agitation would have resulted in a thoroughgoing and rapid redistribution of grazing land among smallholders and labourers, thereby transforming the rural social structure. The O'Donnellite reading of the War of Independence may, then, have more to offer than has been supposed: the revolution did contain radical potential that was restrained by the republican elite. English's contention that 'vast numbers of the . . . rank and file' of the republican movement viewed 'social conflict between Irish classes . . . as a disruptive distraction',[78] and that popular support for republicanism was not motivated by social radicalism,[79] are based on the comments of members of the republican leadership.[80] To test the wider validity of both O'Donnell's and English's views, the systematic examination of popular political activity throughout the provinces during the revolution is required.

IV

Between 1879 and 1923, Ireland experienced two revolutions. The first—beginning with the Land War in 1879 and arguably not completed until 1984 when the Land Commission suspended its activities[81]—constituted a social revolution. In effect, the ownership of the land was transferred from the landlord to the tenant, and the class structure was, therefore, transformed. The second—beginning in 1916 and ending in 1923—was a political revolution, involving the transfer of state power from one elite to another. This book has examined the critical phase of the first revolution—that of the impact of the Wyndham Land Act on Irish society (1903–21)—and has also considered the influence of the unfinished elements of the first revolution (those aspects of the land question that remained unsolved in 1916) on the nationalist politics and military struggle that resulted in the second (political) revolution. Land played a critical

---

[78] English, *Radicals and the republic*, 40.

[79] Ibid. 37–8.

[80] English's interpretation is based on the views of the republican elite outlined in Garvin, *Nationalist revolutionaries*; J. P. McHugh, 'Voices of the rearguard: a study of *An Phoblacht* – Irish republican thought in the post-revolutionary era, 1923–37' (University College, Dublin, MA, 1983); and the *Prison letters of Countess Markievicz* (London, 1987; 1st edn., 1934). English, *Radicals and the republic*, 40.

[81] In 1984, the range of the Land Commission's activities was dramatically reduced, and the Land Commission (Dissolution) Act of 1992 effectively ended its 111-year history.

role in both revolutions; and in the absence of the first, the second would undoubtedly have been accompanied by an extensive (and probably violent) redistribution of property. Even after the implementation of Gladstone, Wyndham, and Birrell's land legislation, agrarian conflict was very nearly responsible for shattering the 'unity' of Irish nationalism between 1919 and 1921. There would be further bouts of land agitation,[82] and some grievances remained unaddressed after 1923, but the combined result of these revolutions was to create a class of sturdy smallholders who would dominate Irish society for most of the twentieth century.

[82] In particular, the land annuities agitation of the 1920s, and the agitation organized by Clann na Talmhan in the late 1930s and early 1940s. See Peader O'Donnell, *There will be another day* (Dublin, 1963), and Tony Varley, 'Farmers against nationalists: the rise and fall of Clann na Talmhan in Galway', in Gerard Moran and Raymond Gillespie (eds.), *Galway history and society: interdisciplinary essays on the history of an Irish county* (Dublin, 1996).

Methodology and Sources Used to Identify the Social Background of Nationalist Activists in Galway, 1899–1921

Throughout this book, I have examined the social composition of various nationalist political movements—the Kennyite and Hallinanite factions in Craughwell (Chapter 4), the members of the Galway secret society and the 1916 rebels (Chapter 5), the United Irish Leaguers and Sinn Féiners in east Galway (Chapter 6), and the south-east Galway IRA (Chapter 6)—and in this appendix I will briefly describe the methodology and sources used to compile these studies. Broadly speaking, when the names of the members of these movements were identified, a search was made of the manuscript census returns (in 1901 and 1911) and cancelled land valuation books for the relevant district electoral divisions to find information on the social background of political and agrarian activists. In cases where there were two or more persons of the same name in the one electoral division, they were discounted from my study (except in cases where local information could confirm which person was involved in nationalist politics).[1] While the personal details of each individual were obtained from censal and land records, the various other political and social affiliations of members of the United Irish League, Sinn Féin, and the Irish Republican Army were also identified from the systematic examination of the local press, police reports, intelligence notes, and private papers.[2]

---

[1] I conducted interviews with the late J. B. Donohoe at Loughrea (22 Nov. 1997), the late Mattie Finnerty at Galway (30 Jan. 1998), Gerry Cloonan at Craughwell (23 Nov. 1997) and Martin Dolphin at Ballinasloe (24 Nov. 1997) to verify local membership lists.

[2] To identify the political and social involvements of each individual, the following sources were systematically examined: the *Connacht Tribune*, 1909–21; the *Galway Express*, 1917–18; the County Inspector's monthly police reports for east and west Galway, 1898–1921, PRO CO 904/68–116 and NA IGCI/1–15; the confidential print, 1898–1919, PRO CO 903/8–19; the eighty-nine witness statements and eleven collections of contemporary documents and other ephemera relating to county Galway collected by the Bureau of Military History and held in the Military Archives, Dublin; the Martin Finnerty papers (in possession of Mattie Finnerty, Galway), the William Duffy papers (in possession of Mary Duffy, Loughrea), and the Martin O'Regan papers (in the possession of Patrick Barrett, Loughrea).

I

In Chapter 4, I examined the social composition of the 'Kennyites', or supporters of Tom Kenny, and the 'Hallinanites', who were supporters of Martin Hallinan in Craughwell. I identified the supporters of Tom Kenny from a variety of sources: the members of the Craughwell hurling team, of which Kenny was the captain and leading member;[3] the names of persons who were attacked by the Hallinanites between November 1910 and November 1911, according to Martin Finnerty's 'Craughwell diary';[4] the names of persons who were attacked by the Hallinanites, according to the local police;[5] and interviews with Gerry Cloonan, a local historian at Craughwell.[6] Only those persons who could be identified as Kenny's supporters in at least two of these sources were used to compile this sample of thirty-six. The members of the Hallinanite faction were also identified from a number of sources: a membership list of the reorganized Craughwell United Irish League;[7] a membership list of the Craughwell Ratepayers' Association;[8] a list of the Craughwell delegates to the south Galway United Irish League executive;[9] and interviews with Gerry Cloonan at Craughwell.[10] Again, only the twenty-nine persons who could be identified in at least two of these sources were assumed to have been supporters of Martin Hallinan. The population of the Craughwell district electoral division in 1901 was 641,[11] and, between 1909 and 1918, 149 persons were reported to be involved in political organizations in the parish, including the UIL, Sinn Féin, the GAA, the Gaelic League, and the Ratepayers' Association.[12] This sample of twenty-nine Hallinanites, together with the sample of thirty-six Kennyites, therefore, represents a substantial proportion (44 per cent) of the total number of political activists (149) in Craughwell between 1909 and 1918.

II

The Galway rebels in 1916 were identified by the police as also being members of the 'Major MacBride' secret society, and I have used the same sources to examine the social composition of these two movements. 'While this Riding has for years been the seat of agrarian crime', the County Inspector for west Galway reported, 'there was none of it to any extent during the year 1916. This is due to the fact

---

[3] *Connacht Tribune*, 24 Dec. 1910.

[4] *Connacht Tribune*, 6 Jan. 1912.

[5] CI monthly reports, east Galway, Nov. 1910–Nov. 1911, PRO CO 904/82–5.

[6] Interviews with Gerry Cloonan at Craughwell, 25 Apr., 6 June 1995 and 16 May 1996.

[7] *Connacht Tribune*, 26 Nov. 1910.

[8] *Connacht Tribune*, 26 Nov. 1910.

[9] *Connacht Tribune*, 27 Jan. 1912.

[10] Interviews with Gerry Cloonan at Craughwell, 25 Apr., 6 June 1995 and 16 May 1996.

[11] *Census of Ireland, 1901 . . . vol. iv: province of Connaught: no. 1. County of Galway*, HC (1902), [Cd. 1059], cxxviii. 232.

[12] Calculated from the membership lists of these organizations in the *Connacht Tribune*, 1909–18.

that most of the persons who organised and committed agrarian crimes in the past were interned [after the Rising].'[13] As far as the police were concerned, 'The Galway Secret Society . . . [with its] headquarters . . . at Craughwell . . . was at the back of the recent rebellion.'[14] If Patrick Callanan is to be believed, police information on the membership of the Galway secret society was also extremely accurate. He told the Bureau of Military History that after agrarian incidents the police only questioned members of the IRB.[15] Although there was a great deal of overlap between the members of the secret society and the 1916 rebels, some of the insurgents were probably not involved in the earlier movement, and so my study should be regarded as providing no more than an impression of the membership of the secret society.

After the Rising in Galway, 494 men were arrested and interned for their alleged involvement in the insurrection, and their names were published in the *Sinn Féin rebellion handbook* (Dublin, 1917).[16] More detailed information on the townland addresses of some of them is also contained in the *Blazer* (Christmas 1987). I identified 211 (43 per cent) of the rebels in the manuscript census returns and land valuation records. It is probable that all of the men who were arrested had been involved in the Rising, since the insurgents mobilized in full view of the police at Athenry, Clarinbridge, and Oranmore, and many of them were proud of their involvement in the insurrection. Martin Newell, for instance, recalled:

When I appeared before the [Royal] Commission [on the Rebellion] I was asked if I took part in the rebellion in Galway. I said 'Yes'. I was asked if I was armed. I said 'Yes'. I was then asked who was the leader. I said 'Liam Mellows'. I was also asked why I had taken up arms. I replied that I thought that my country had a right to be free.[17]

The police were also confident that they had arrested all of the participants in the Galway rebellion. The County Inspector for west Galway, for instance, observed that 'All the persons belonging to this Riding known to have taken part in the rebellion (with the exception of two who absconded and could not since be traced) were arrested and conveyed under military escort to Richmond barracks, Dublin.'[18] The fact that the number of arrests (494) bears a close resemblance to the rebels' own estimate that there were 'over 500 men' at the Department of Agriculture farm near Athenry suggests that most of the internees probably had been 'out' in 1916.[19]

[13] Report on west Galway in 1916, PRO CO 904/120.
[14] CI monthly report, west Galway, July 1916, PRO CO 904/100.
[15] Patrick Callanan witness statement, MA BMH WS 347.
[16] CI monthly reports, east and west Galway, May 1916, PRO CO 904/100.
[17] Martin Newell witness statement, MA BMH WS 1,562.
[18] Report on west Galway in 1916, PRO CO 904/120.
[19] 'Document from Ailbhe O'Monachain, January 1939', DGAD.

III

In order to assess the level of continuity between the United Irish League and Sinn Féin in Galway, the names of members of the United Irish League (reported in the *Connacht Tribune* in 1914) were compared with those of Sinn Féiners (named in the *Galway Express* between October 1917 and October 1918). The *Connacht Tribune* reported 85 meetings of UIL branches in 61 localities in County Galway in 1914, and named 493 persons who attended those meetings. Between October 1917 and October 1918, the Sinn Féin newspaper in the county, the *Galway Express* reported 143 meetings of Sinn Féin clubs in 49 localities in the county, and named 339 persons who attended these meetings. Only 11 (3 per cent) of the members of Sinn Féin in 1917–18 had been members of the UIL in 1914.

Whereas Fitzpatrick defines Home Rulers in Clare as the members of both the UIL and the Ancient Order of Hibernians, my study of Home Rulers in Galway focuses on the members of the United Irish League. This methodology has been adopted for three reasons. First, the United Irish League (and not the AOH) was the recognized constituency organization of the IPP in the Irish countryside. Second, the AOH did not advance as rapidly in Connacht as it did elsewhere, primarily due to the opposition of the Roman Catholic hierarchy; and at its height the membership of the AOH was only about one-seventh (15 per cent) of that of the United Irish League in Galway.[20] Third, and due to its small membership, AOH meetings were not regularly reported in the nationalist press in Galway, so that it was impossible to examine systematically the continuities between the AOH and Sinn Féin. Even so, there is evidence that there is unlikely to have been a high level of continuity between the members of the AOH and Sinn Féin in Galway. There was great antipathy between the two organizations and where the members of the AOH can be identified, as at Loughrea, they tended to be hard-line Home Rulers who continued to oppose Sinn Féin even after the 1918 general election.[21] This suggests that even if the members of the AOH in Galway were included, it is unlikely that they would make a great deal of difference to the amount of continuity between Home Rulers and Sinn Féiners.

Finally, Fitzpatrick also defines the Irish Volunteers (before the split of November 1914) as Home Rulers. I have not, however, included the Irish Volunteers in the ranks of the Home Rule movement in Galway for three reasons. First, most of the founding members of the Irish Volunteers in Galway were prominent Sinn Féiners. Second, the so-called Redmondite takeover of the Irish Volunteers in June 1914 was more cosmetic than real, and in Galway separatists often remained the leading figures in the Volunteers. Third, even if the majority of Irish Volunteers after the Redmondite takeover can be described as Home Rulers, many of

[20] In January 1916, there were 97 branches of the United Irish League in Galway with 10,107 members, and 27 branches of the Ancient Order of Hibernians with 1,483 members, CI monthly reports, east and west Galway, Jan. 1916, PRO CO 904/99.
[21] William Duffy and Martin Ward were both members of the AOH. *Connacht Tribune*, 22 Mar. 1919.

these men did not continue to support Redmond after his pro-recruiting speech at Woodenbridge on 20 September. Between the beginning of the Great War and the Easter Rising, the membership of the Irish Volunteers (after November 1914, the National Volunteers) declined rapidly and became inactive primarily because of the Volunteers' fear of being conscripted.[22] If these men were Redmondites before September 1914, their response to the Woodenbridge speech revealed the limitations of their Redmondism. For these reasons, it is problematic to assume that the Irish Volunteers were unambiguous supporters of Redmond who strengthened the provincial Home Rule movement in 1914.

Although Fitzpatrick first makes the argument for continuity in his chapter on 'Sinn Féiners', the statistical evidence used to substantiate this argument is based on continuities between Home Rulers and the more broadly defined 'Separatists'. While I have examined the continuity between the Home Rule movement and Sinn Féin in Galway, Fitzpatrick analyses the overlap between Home Rulers and 'Separatists' or 'Sinn Féiners, supporters of Count Plunkett or de Valera in 1917, militant critics of the Irish Party, agents of the Irish National Assurance Company, Republican justices and officers of the Irish Volunteers and Fianna Éireann . . . and those arrested for political offences, April 1916–1921'.[23] It may be that the statistical evidence for continuity between the Home Rule movement and Sinn Féin is stronger than that between Home Rulers and 'Separatists', but this evidence is not presented in *Politics and Irish life*. I have confined my analysis to Sinn Féin because I am primarily interested in the continuities between the two political movements, rather than continuities between Home Rulers and the paramilitary Irish Volunteers/Irish Republican Army.

The names of members of the United Irish League[24] and Sinn Féin[25] in eleven localities in east Galway (Loughrea, Athenry, Ballinasloe, Galway city, Craughwell, Gurteen, New Inn, Kilmeen, Kilchreest, Ardrahan, and Woodford) were identified in the local press and other sources, and then traced in manuscript census returns and cancelled land valuation books. Altogether, ninety-four Sinn Féiners and ninety-nine United Irish Leaguers from these localities were satisfactorily identified in the manuscript census returns of 1901 and 1911, and in the cancelled

---

[22] See Ch. 5.

[23] Fitzpatrick, *Politics and Irish life*, 291.

[24] The following sources were used to identify the names of members of the United Irish League in Galway: *Connacht Tribune*, 19 June, 18 Sept. 1909; 10 Feb., 18 May 1912; 8 Mar., 19 Apr., 7 June, 15 Nov. 1913; 7, 14 Feb., 19 Dec. 1914; 9 Nov., 7 Dec. 1918; and list of names and addresses of the members of the Craughwell United Irish League branch (in 1899), compiled by the police, file on 'The Craughwell conspiracy', NA CBS, 1901, 24770/S box 19.

[25] The following sources were used to identify the names of members of Sinn Féin in Galway: *Galway Express*, 24 Nov., 1 Dec. 1917; 19 Jan., 6, 27 Apr., 22 June, 20 Oct. 1918; *Connacht Tribune*, 3 Nov. 1917; 23 Mar. 1918; photograph of the members of Loughrea Sinn Féin club (in 1917), including names, Frank Fahy papers (in possession of Michael Fahy, Loughrea); files on interned (1916) rebels, NA CSORP 16627/18; General Prison Board files on men arrested under the Defence of the Realm Act NA GPB DORA, 1917–20, boxes 1–5; Home Office files on internees, 1918–19, PRO HO 144/1496/362269.

land valuation books. In addition, a further twenty-eight east Galway Sinn Féiners were identified from other sources so that the total quota of Sinn Féiners in the sample is 122.[26]

As all of the activists contained in this study were the officials (committee members and officers) of United Irish League branches and Sinn Féin clubs, these samples constitute a significant proportion of the total number of nationalist officials in east Galway during this period. In general, both UIL and Sinn Féin branches had five officers (president, vice-president, treasurer, secretary, and honorary secretary) and fifteen committee members. As there were 43 Sinn Fein branches in east Galway in January 1919, we can assume that there were about 860 officials, so that my sample of 122 represents 14 per cent of the total in the region.[27] Similarly, there were 51 United Irish League branches in east Galway in March 1916, and therefore about 1,020 officials, so that my sample of 99 represents 10 per cent of the total.[28] The size of my samples suggests that the conclusions presented here are probably applicable to nationalist officials throughout the county.[29]

IV

In order to examine the social background of Galway IRA members, I used the Bureau of Military History witness statements to compile membership lists of ten IRA companies in the south-east of the county (Athenry, Bullaun, Craughwell, Kilbeacanty, Killeenadeema, Kilmeen, Kinvara, Loughrea, Mullagh, and Skehana) and then searched the 1911 census and land valuation books for these names. As a result, I was able to compile a detailed analysis of the social background of 127 members of the south Galway IRA from a variety of urban and rural backgrounds. This constitutes a significant proportion (18 per cent) of the total membership of the IRA in the east of the county (there were 698 Irish Volunteers or IRA in east Galway in January 1920).[30]

V

In my examination of activists from farming backgrounds, I have distinguished between four different types of farm: a congested farm, valued at £10 or under; a small farm, valued at between £10 and £20; a middle-sized farm, valued at between £20 and £50; and a large farm, valued at £50 and above. Two of these categories

26 Home Office files on internees, 1918–19, PRO HO 144/1496/362269; files on interned 1916 rebels, NA CSORP 16627/18; General Prison Board files on men arrested under the Defence of the Realm Act, NA GPB DORA, 1917–20, boxes 1–5.
27 CI monthly report, east Galway, Jan. 1919, PRO CO 904/108.
28 CI monthly report, east Galway, Mar. 1916, PRO CO 904/99.
29 The figures on occupational groups in Galway in 1911 were calculated from 'Table XX – Occupations of Males by Ages, Religious Professions, and Education, in the County of Galway', *Census of Ireland, 1911 . . . county of Galway*, HC (1912–13), [Cd. 6052] cxvii. 130–5.
30 CI monthly report, east Galway, Jan. 1920, PRO CO 904/111.

were used by contemporaries: the Congested Districts Board defined a farmer with a landholding valued at £10 or under as a congested tenant, and the United Irish League defined a farmer with a landholding valued at over £50 as a grazier (or large farmer).[31] I have divided those farmers with more land than congested tenants and less land than graziers into two groups—the small farmers and middle-sized farmers—because they occupied different positions in the agricultural economy.

[31] See Ch. 1.

Chronology of the War of Independence in Galway, 1919–1921[1]

1919

May	(25 May) Attack on Loughgeorge barracks.
November	(7 Nov.) Attack on Maam barracks.
December	(25 Dec.) Bomb exploded outside Menlough barracks.

1920

January	(6 Jan.) Attack on Roundstone barracks.
	(9 Jan.) Attack on Castlehackett barracks. One RIC wounded.
April	(n.d.) Attack on Castlegrove barracks.
May	(27 May) Four RIC held up at gunpoint at Lackagh, Turloughmore.
	(28 May) RIC lorry shot at near Galway city. Two RIC wounded.
June	(24 June) Four RIC ambushed at Killacloher, near Monivea. One RIC wounded. (29 June) Shooting of Head Constable William Elliott at Castletaylor, Ardrahan. Elliott is seriously wounded.
July	(2 July) Attack on RIC barracks at Bookeen. (4 July) Two RIC held up at a holiday resort (the Punchbowl), near Gort. (5 July) RIC patrol ambushed at Kilcolgan. (11 July) Shots fired at RIC at Gort. (14 July) Shots fired at RIC at Caltra. One RIC wounded. (19 July) RIC lorry ambushed at Gallagh, near Dunmore. Two RIC shot dead. That night 'the town of Tuam was sacked'.[2] The Town Hall and many other buildings in Tuam were burned down by the forces of the Crown, apparently in reprisal for the ambush.

---

[1] This chronology has been compiled from the monthly police reports for east and west Galway between January 1919 and July 1921, and the eighty-nine witness statements and eleven collections of contemporary documents relating to county Galway compiled by the Bureau of Military History. In the chronology, I have included only attacks on occupied barracks, ambushes, executions of spies, and serious attacks using firearms. Raids for arms, raids on mails, the destruction of vacated barracks, and the burning of individual houses have not been included. I have also used this chronology to calculate the number of incidents and the number of persons killed or seriously wounded during the War of Independence in Galway (see Table 29). This chronology is intended to provide a guide to the main military events in Galway during the Anglo-Irish war until a full-scale local study of the IRA in Galway between 1916 and 1923 is undertaken.

[2] Michael J. Ryan witness statement, MA BMH WS 1,320.

August   (12 Aug.) A sentry at Tuam court house shot at. (13 Aug.) Two sentries at Tuam court house shot at. (21 Aug.) A party of RIC ambushed at Merlinn Park, near Galway city. One shot dead. (21 Aug.) RIC patrol fired at from Mrs Keane's public house at Oranmore. RIC returned fire and subsequently the public house was burned down. This incident is believed by the IRA to be a reprisal for the Merlinn Park ambush.

September   (9 Sept.) Detective Crumm shot dead at Galway railway station. In reprisal, two IRA members are shot dead and two are wounded. (23 Sept.) RIC surprise an ambush party near Ardrahan and open fire.

October   (n.d.) Michael Howley severely beaten by Black and Tans at Gort. Still in doctor's care in 1956 as a consequence.[3] (15 Oct.) Patrick Joyce, a National School teacher at Barna—believed by the IRA to be an informer—kidnapped and executed by the IRA. (15 Oct.) Armed men—believed to be the Black and Tans—fire shots at members of the King and Furey families at Oranmore. (17 Oct.) Shots fired at RIC sentry at Earl's Island, Galway city (where the 6th Dragoon Guards were stationed). (19 Oct.) Michael Walsh, the proprietor of the Old Malt House, High Street, Galway city, and a Sinn Féin member of the urban council, shot dead and his body washed up at the mouth of the Corrib. (30 Oct.) Ambush of RIC at Castledaly. One RIC shot dead and one wounded.

November   (n.d.) Michael Moran, commandant of the Tuam battalion, whom the police believed to be responsible for the Gallagh ambush, shot dead—allegedly—by the RIC in Earl's Island barracks. (1 Nov.) Mrs Ellen Quinn of Kiltartan, who was pregnant, shot dead by the RIC. (26 Nov.) Two members of the Beagh company of the IRA—Patrick and Harry Loughnane—were arrested. On 5 December, their bodies were found near Kinvara. (21 Nov.) Father Michael Griffin's body found at Barna. He had left his home at 2 Montpelier Terrace on the night of Sunday, 14 November, apparently on a sick call. Believed to have been murdered by the Auxiliaries based at Lenaboy Castle.

December   (3 Dec.) Galway county council pass a resolution calling for a truce.

1921

January   (12 Jan.) Shots fired at two RIC as they leave Blake's pub at Kilconly. One RIC wounded. Apparently, the forces of the Crown later fired indiscriminately on civilians near Kilconly, wounding Messrs. Banks and Kelly. (18 Jan.) Ambush of nine Auxiliaries at Kilroe, Headford. Four Auxiliaries seriously wounded and one IRA wounded. (18 Jan.) As a reprisal for the Kilroe ambush, three men whom the police believed to be members of the IRA were 'shot dead when

---

[3] Peter Howley witness statement, MA BMH WS 1,379.

attempting to escape from custody'. Although two (Michael Hoade and William Walsh) were members of the IRA, one (John Kirwan) was not. (4 Jan.) Shots fired at RIC and Auxiliaries at Loughrea.

February   (20 Feb.) John Geoghegan, quartermaster of the east Connemara brigade, shot dead by the Black and Tans at Moycullen.

March   (16 Mar.) Four RIC ambushed at Clifden. Two shot dead. As a reprisal, fourteen houses were burned down in the town, one civilian (a former Connaught Ranger) was shot dead and another seriously wounded. (23 Mar.) Commandant Louis Darcy of the Headford battalion arrested at Oranmore railway station and the following day (24 March)—according to the police—was shot dead while trying to escape.

April   (2 Apr.) James Morris—believed to be an informer—shot dead by IRA at Kinvara. (6 Apr.) Attack on a four-man RIC cycling patrol at Screebe. One wounded. (6 Apr.) Volunteer Patrick Cloonan shot dead at Oranmore, apparently by the forces of the Crown. (16 Apr.) Shots fired at RIC at Milltown. Two RIC wounded. (23 Apr.) An eleven-hour engagement took place between the IRA based at Mounterowen House, Maam, and fourteen RIC under DI Sugrue. One RIC killed and two wounded. RIC believe that two IRA were wounded during this conflict. (26 Apr.) Thomas Hannon— believed to be an informer—shot dead by the IRA at Clonberne. (30 Apr.) Shots fired at six RIC near Dunmore. (30 Apr.) Attack on RIC barracks at Headford.

May   (12 May) Christy and Joseph Folan, whose brother James was a member of the IRA, shot by forces of the Crown in Galway city. One wounded and one killed. On the same night, Hugh Tully, the IRA's contact at Galway railway station, was also shot dead. (13 May) Shots fired at a six-man police patrol at Spiddal. (15 May) District Inspector Cecil Blake, Mrs Blake (who was pregnant), Captain Cornwallis, Lieutenant McCreery, and Mrs Margaret Gregory ambushed by the IRA as they departed a tennis party at Ballyturin, near Gort. All shot dead except Mrs Gregory. (15 May) Constable John Kearney—believed to be assisting the IRA—appears to have been shot dead by the Black and Tans. (15 May) A medical student named Greene shot and wounded at Galway city, apparently by the Black and Tans. (20 May) Thomas McKeever shot dead at Dunmore. According to the RIC, he was shot by the IRA, but the IRA allege that he was shot by the RIC. (28 May) Shots fired at five RIC in a motor car at Coorheen cross, near Loughrea. (30 May) P. Molloy—believed to be an informer—shot by the IRA.

June   (5 June) Shots fired at RIC at Moylough. One RIC shot dead and one wounded. (5 June) Ambush of two RIC lorries *en route* from

Moylough to Mount Bellew. (27 June) IRA ambush a four-man police patrol at Milltown. Two RIC shot dead and one wounded. RIC believe two IRA are wounded or killled.

July   (1 July) Shots fired at RIC at Ballygar. Two wounded. (5 July) RIC open fire on IRA waiting in ambush at Ballygar. (11 July) Attack on RIC patrol at Fishpond, near Kilchreest, in breach of the Truce declared the previous day. One RIC wounded.

Bibliography

1. MANUSCRIPT COLLECTIONS

DUBLIN

Irish Military Archives

Bureau of Military History witness statements and contemporary documents.
Special Infantry Corps papers.

National Archives

Chief Secretary's Office Registered Papers.
General Prisons Board records.
Manuscript census returns, 1901 and 1911.
Dáil Éireann Local Government Department records.
Sinn Féin papers.
RIC Inspector General and County Inspectors' monthly reports.
Crime Branch Special 'S' files.
Protection of Person and Property Act files.

National Library of Ireland

John Redmond papers.
Lord Clonbrock papers.
United Irish League records.
James O'Meara papers.
James Bryce papers.
Pádraig Ó Fathaigh papers.
Hicks Beach papers [copies of those held in Gloucestershire Records Office].

Trinity College

John Dillon papers.
Congested Districts Board, *Baseline reports* (Dublin, 1892–8).

Department of Irish Folklore

Schools manuscripts collection, co. Galway.
Mhiceáil Uí Coincheannain, Móinteach, baile Chlár na Gaillimhe, 'Eirghe amach na Cásca 1916 i mbaile Chlár na Gaillimhe [The 1916 Easter Rising in Claregalway]'.

Land Valuation Office

Cancelled valuation books.

CORK

University College, Cork

William O'Brien papers.

GALWAY

Galway county council offices

Galway county council minutes, 1899–1921.

OTHER

In private possession

Martin Finnerty papers.
Martin Ward papers.
William J. Duffy papers.
Martin O'Regan papers.
Frank Fahy papers.
Lawrence Lardner papers.

C. D. Greaves Archive

(c/o Dr Anthony Coughlan, Dept. of Sociology, Trinity College, Dublin)
Ailbhe O'Monachain papers.

LONDON

British Library

Arthur Balfour papers.
Campbell-Bannerman papers.

Public Record Office

Colonial Office

The confidential print, 1898–1919.
RIC Inspector General and County Inspectors' monthly reports, 1898–1921.
Illegal drilling reports.
Précis of information and reports on secret societies.
Précis of information received by Crime Special Branch.
Report on Ballyturin ambush.

Returns of agrarian outrages, 1903–8.
United Irish League membership figures.

War Office
Files on military response to Easter Rising.
Files on Sinn Féin activists.

Home Office
RIC officers' register.
Files on prisoners' correspondence, 1918–19.

Cabinet Office
Cabinet papers.

Other
Carnarvon papers.

MANCHESTER

John Rylands Library, University of Manchester
C. P. Scott papers.

2. GOVERNMENT PUBLICATIONS

GREAT BRITAIN

Agricultural statistics of Ireland . . . for the year 1901, HC (1902), [Cd. 1170], cxvi, part one, 319.

Agricultural statistics of Ireland . . . for the year 1908, HC (1909), [Cd. 1940], cii. 355.

Agricultural statistics of Ireland . . . for the year 1917, HC (1921), [Cmd. 1316], vol. xli. 135.

Census of Ireland, 1881 . . . vol. iv: province of Connaught. No. 1. County of Galway, HC (1882), [C. 3268–1], lxxix. 3

Census of Ireland, 1901 . . . vol. iv: province of Connaught. No. 1. County of Galway, HC (1902), [Cd. 1059] cxxviii. 1.

Census of Ireland, 1911 . . . province of Connaught. County of Galway, HC (1912–13), [Cd. 6052], cxvii. 1.

Royal Commission on Congestion in Ireland: appendices to the first report, HC (1906), [Cd. 3267], xxxii. 621.

Royal Commission on Congestion in Ireland: appendix to the third report, HC (1907), [Cd. 3414], xxxv. 337.

Royal Commission on Congestion in Ireland: appendix to the tenth report, HC (1908), [Cd. 4007], xlii. 5.

Royal Commission on Congestion in Ireland: final report, HC (1908), [Cd. 4097], xlii. 729.
The Royal Commission on the Rebellion in Ireland: minutes of evidence and appendix of documents, HC (1916), [Cd. 8311] xi. 185.

IRELAND

Report of the Irish Land Commissioners for the period from 1st April, 1923, to 31st March, 1928, and for the prior period ended 31st March, 1923 (Dublin, 1928).
Report of the Irish Land Commissioners for the year from 1st April, 1970, to 31st March, 1971, and for the period ended 31st March, 1971 (Dublin, 1971).

3. NEWSPAPERS AND JOURNALS

An t-Óglach.
Blazer [Craughwell Parish Magazine].
Connaught Champion.
Connaught Leader.
Connaught Telegraph.
Connacht Tribune.
Freeman's Journal.
Gaelic American.
Galway Express.
Galway Vindicator.
Irish Law Times and Solicitor's Journal.
Irish People.
Irish Times.
Mayo News.
Sinn Féin.
Weekly Freeman.
Western News.

4. CONTEMPORARY PUBLICATIONS

ANDREWS, C. S., *Dublin made me* (Dublin, 1979).
——, *Men of no property* (Dublin, 1982).
BAKER, JOE, *My stand for freedom: autobiography of an Irish republican soldier* (Westport, 1988).
BARRY, TOM, *Guerilla days in Ireland* (Dublin, 1949).
BECKER, B. H., *Disturbed Ireland: being the letters written during the winter of 1880–81* (London, 1881).

BIRMINGHAM, GEORGE, *Irishmen all* (New York, 1913).

BLUNT, W. S., *My diaries: being a personal narrative of events, 1888–1914* (London, 1932).

—— *The land war in Ireland* (London, 1912).

BREEN, DAN, *My fight for Irish freedom* (2nd edn., Dublin, 1981).

BRENNAN, MICHAEL, *The war in Clare 1911–21* (Dublin, 1980).

BRENNAN, ROBERT, *Allegiance* (Dublin, 1950).

BULFIN, WILLIAM, *Rambles in Éirinn* (Dublin, 1927).

CAWLEY, THOMAS, *An Irish parish: its sunshine and shadows* (Boston, 1911).

CHILDERS, ERSKINE, *Constructive work of Dáil Éireann* (Dublin, 1921).

COLUM, PADRAIC, *The land* (Dublin, 1905).

CROZIER, F. P., *Ireland for ever* (London, 1932).

DAVITT, MICHAEL, *The fall of feudalism in Ireland* (London, 1904).

DEVOY, JOHN, *Recollections of an Irish rebel* (Shannon, 1969).

DUNRAVEN, EARL of, *Past times and pastimes* (2 vols., London, 1922).

FIGGIS, DARRELL, *Recollections of the Irish war* (London, 1927).

GINNELL, LAURENCE, *Land and liberty* (Dublin, 1908).

—— 'The land question' (Dublin, n.d. [1917?]).

GWYNN, STEPHEN, *A holiday in Connemara* (London, 1909).

—— *Memories of enjoyment* (Tralee, 1946).

Land Conference: report of a conference held at the Mansion House, Dublin, 1902–1903 (Dublin, 1903).

LEECH, H. B., *1848 and 1912: the continuity of the Irish revolutionary movement* (London, 1912).

LEWIS, G. C., *Local disturbances in Ireland* (London, 1836).

MAC GIOLLA CHOILLE, BREANDÁN, *Intelligence notes, 1913–16* (Dublin, 1966).

MACKAIL, J. W., and WYNDHAM, GUY, *Life and letters of George Wyndham* (London, 1925).

MARKIEVICZ, CONSTANCE, *Prison Letters of Countess Markievicz* (2nd end. London, 1987)

MICKS, W. L., *An account of the constitution, administration and dissolution of the Congested Districts Board for Ireland from 1891 to 1923* (Dublin, 1925).

O'BRIEN, WILLIAM, *An olive branch in Ireland and its history* (London, 1910).

O'DONNELL, PEADER, *There will be another day* (Dublin, 1963).

O'MALLEY, ERNIE, *On another man's wound* (London, 1936).

O'MALLEY, WILLIAM, *Glancing back* (London, 1933).

O'SHIEL, KEVIN, 'The Dáil courts driven underground', *Irish Times*, 11 Nov. 1966.

—— 'The Dáil land courts', *Irish Times*, 14 Nov. 1966.

—— 'Years of violence', *Irish Times*, 15 Nov. 1966.

—— 'Fellow travellers', *Irish Times*, 17 Nov. 1966.

—— 'Dáil courts in action', *Irish Times*, 18 Nov. 1966.

—— 'No contempt of court', *Irish Times*, 21 Nov. 1966.

—— 'The last land war', *Irish Times*, 22 Nov. 1966.

—— 'On the edge of anarchy', *Irish Times*, 23 Nov. 1966.

PAUL-DUBOIS, LOUIS, *Contemporary Ireland* (Dublin, 1908).

PLUNKETT, H. C., *Ireland in the new century* (London, 1904).

ROBINSON, HENRY, *Memories: wise and otherwise* (London, 1924).

—— *Further memories of Irish life* (London, 1924).

SULLIVAN, A. M., *The last serjeant: the memoirs of Serjeant A. M. Sullivan* (London, 1952).

TYNAN, P. J., *The Irish national Invincibles and their times* (London, 1894).

United Irish League: constitution and rules adopted by the Irish National Convention, 19th and 20th June, 1900 (Dublin, 1900).

Weekly Irish Times, *Sinn Féin rebellion handbook* (Dublin, 1917).

5. PUBLISHED WORKS: GALWAY

BURKE, O. J., *The south isles of Aran* (London, 1887).

CLAFFEY, J. A. (ed.), *Glimpses of Tuam since the Famine* (Tuam, 1997).

DEUTSCH-BRADY, CHANTAL, 'The cattle drive of Tulira', *Journal of the Galway Archaeological and Historical Society*, 34 (1974–5).

DOLAN, MARTIN, 'Galway 1920–1921', *Capuchin Annual* (1970).

EGAN, P. K., *The parish of Ballinasloe: its history from the earliest times to the present century* (2nd edn., Galway, 1994).

FLYNN, J. S., *Ballymacward: the story of an east Galway parish* (Ballymacward, 1991).

FORDE, JOSEPH, CASSIDY, CHRISTINA, MANZOR, PAUL, and RYAN, DAVID (eds.) *The district of Loughrea*, i: *History, 1791–1918* (Galway, 2003).

—— *The district of Loughrea*, ii: *Folklore, 1860–1960* (Galway, 2003).

FUREY, BRENDA, *The history of Oranmore Maree* (Oranmore, 1991).

HARDIMAN, JAMES, *The history of the town and county of the town of Galway* (Dublin, 1820).

JORDAN, KIERAN, *Kiltullagh/Killimoredaly as the centuries passed: a history from 1500–1900* (Kiltullagh, 2000).

KAVANAGH, MARY, *A bibliography of the county Galway* (Galway, 1965).

LANE, P. G., 'On the general impact of the Encumbered Estates Act of 1849 on counties Galway and Mayo', *Journal of the Galway Archaeological and Historical Society*, 32 (1972–3).

—— 'The impact of the Encumbered Estates Court upon the landlords of Galway and Mayo', *Journal of the Galway Archaeological and Historical Society*, 38 (1981–2).

LANGAN-EGAN, MAUREEN, *Galway women in the nineteenth century* (Dublin, 1999).

MCHALE, BERNARD (ed.), *Menlough looking back: a parish and sporting history* (Menlough, 1991).

McMahon, T. G. (ed.), *Pádraig Ó Fathaigh's War of Independence: recollections of a Galway Gaelic Leaguer* (Cork, 2000).

Mahony, Edmund, *The Galway Blazers* (Galway, 1979).

Moran, Gerard, and Gillespie, Raymond (eds.), *Galway history and society: interdisciplinary essays on the history of an Irish county* (Dublin, 1996).

Murphy, Joseph, *The Redingtons of Clarinbridge: leading Catholic landlords in the nineteenth century* (Dublin, 1999).

O'Brien, Patrick (ed.), *Erect me a monument of broken wings: an anthology of writings by and on Padraic Fallon* (Athenry, 1992).

Ó Cadhain, Máirtín, *The road to bright city* (Dublin, 1981).

O'Connor, Gabriel, *A history of Galway county council: stair chomhairle chontae na Gaillimhe* (Galway, 1999).

O'Donoghue, Noel, *Proud and upright men* (Tuam, 1987).

Ó Gaora, Colm, *Mise* (Dublin, 1943).

Ó Laoi, Padraic, *Annals of the G.A.A. in Galway, 1884–1901* (Galway, 1983).

—— *Annals of the G.A.A. in Galway, 1902–1934* (Galway, 1992).

—— *History of Castlegar parish* (Galway, n.d. [probably 1999]).

O'Regan, Finbarr (ed.), *The Lamberts of Athenry* (Galway, 1999).

Pethica, J. L., and Roy, J. C., '*To the land of the free from this island of slaves': Henry Stratford Persse's letters from Galway to America, 1821–1832* (Cork, 1998).

Qualter, Aggie, *Athenry: a history* (Galway, 1974).

Robinson, Tim, *Stones of Aran: labyrinth* (Dublin, 1995).

Ryan, David, 'The trial and execution of Anthony Daly' in Joseph Forde, Christina Cassidy, Paul Manzor, and David Ryan (eds.), *The district of Loughrea*, i: *History 1791–1918* (Galway, 2003).

Spellissy, Seán, *The history of Galway: city and county* (Limerick, 1999).

Stanley, Cathal (ed.), *Castles and demesnes: gleanings from Kilconieron and Clostoken* (Loughrea, 2000).

Synge, J. M., *The Aran islands* (London, 1907).

Thomas, Conal, *The land for the people: the United Irish League and land reform in north Galway, 1898–1912* (Corrandulla, 1999).

Villiers-Tuthill, Kathleen, *Beyond the Twelve Bens: a history of Clifden and district, 1860–1923* (Galway, 1986).

Waldron, Jarlath, *Maamtrasna: the murders and the mystery* (Dublin, 1992).

Woodford Heritage Group, *A forgotten campaign: aspects of the heritage of south-east Galway* (Woodford, 1986).

—— *Clanricarde country and the land campaign* (Woodford, 1987).

6. OTHER BOOKS AND ARTICLES

AGULHON, MAURICE, *The republic in the village: the people of the Var from the French Revolution to the Second Republic* (Cambridge, 1982).

ANDERSON, BENEDICT, *Imagined communities: reflections on the origin and spread of nationalism* (London, 1983).

ARENSBERG. C. M., *The Irish countryman: an anthropological study* (London, 1937).

—— and KIMBALL, S. T. *Family and community in Ireland* (3rd edn., Ennis, 2001).

ARNOLD, BRUCE, 'An old dog for a hard road: Synge and Jack Yeats in the congested districts', *Times Literary Supplement*, 4785 (16 Dec. 1994).

AUGUSTEIJN, JOOST, *From public defiance to guerilla warfare* (Dublin, 1996).

—— (ed.), *The Irish revolution, 1913–1923* (Basingstoke, 2002).

BEAMES, M. R., *Peasants and power: the Whiteboy movements and their control in pre-Famine Ireland* (Brighton, 1983).

BEW, PAUL, *Land and the national question in Ireland 1858–82* (Dublin, 1978).

—— 'The Land League ideal: achievements and contradictions', in P. J. Drudy (ed.), *Ireland: land, politics and people* (Cambridge, 1982).

—— *Conflict and conciliation in Ireland, 1890–1910: Parnellites and radical agrarians* (Oxford, 1987).

—— 'Sinn Fein, agrarian radicalism and the war of independence, 1919–1921', in D. G. Boyce (ed.), *The revolution in Ireland, 1879–1923* (London, 1988).

—— *Ideology and the Irish question: Ulster unionism and Irish nationalism, 1912–1916* (Oxford, 1994).

—— *John Redmond* (Dundalk, 1996).

—— 'The national question, land and "revisionism": some reflections', in D. G. Boyce and Alan O'Day, (eds.), *The making of modern Irish history: revisionism and the revisionist controversy* (London, 1996).

BOYCE, D. G., *Nationalism in Ireland* (3rd edn., London, 1995).

—— (ed.), *The revolution in Ireland, 1879–1923* (London, 1988).

BREWER, J. D., *The Royal Irish Constabulary: an oral history* (Belfast, 1990).

BRODY, HUGH, *Inishkillane: change and decline in the west of Ireland* (London, 1973).

BROWN, TERENCE, *Ireland: a social and cultural history, 1922–79* (London, 1981).

BUCKLAND, P. J., *Irish unionism: the Anglo-Irish and the new Ireland, 1855–1922* (Dublin, 1973).

BULL, PHILIP, 'The United Irish League and the reunification of the Irish Parliamentary Party, 1898–1900', *Irish Historical Studies*, 26/1 (May 1988).

—— *Land, politics and nationalism: a study of the Irish land question* (Dublin, 1996).

CALLANAN, FRANK, *The Parnell split, 1890–91* (Cork, 1992).

CAMPBELL, FERGUS, 'The hidden history of the Irish land war: a guide to local sources', in Carla King (ed.), *Famine, land and culture in Ireland* (Dublin, 2000).

CAMPBELL, FERGUS,

—— 'Irish popular politics and the making of the Wyndham Land Act, 1901–3', *Historical Journal*, 45/4 (2002).

—— 'The last land war? Kevin O'Shiel's memoir of the Irish revolution (1916–1921)', *Archivium Hibernicum*, 57, (2003).

—— 'Elites, power and society in Ireland, 1879–1914', paper delivered to the American Conference of Irish Studies, New York, June 2001.

CARROLL, DENIS, *'They have fooled you again': Michael O'Flanagan, 1876–1942: priest, republican, social critic* (Dublin, 1993).

CLARK, SAMUEL, 'The social composition of the Land League', *Irish Historical Studies*, 17 (1971).

—— 'The political mobilisation of Irish farmers', *Canadian Review of Sociology and Anthropology*, 12 (1975).

—— *Social origins of the Irish Land War* (Princeton, 1979).

—— 'The importance of agrarian classes: agrarian class structure and collective action in nineteenth-century Ireland', in P. J. Drudy (ed.), *Ireland: land, politics and people* (Cambridge, 1982).

—— and J. S. DONNELLY, (eds.), *Irish peasants: violence and political unrest 1780–1914* (Manchester, 1983).

COLEMAN, MARIE, *County Longford and the Irish revolution, 1910–1923* (Dublin, 2003).

COMERFORD, R. V., *The Fenians in context: Irish politics and society, 1848–82* (Dublin, 1985).

—— 'Patriotism as pastime: the appeal of Fenianism in the mid-1860s', *Irish Historical Studies*, 22/87 (Mar. 1981).

COOGAN, OLIVER, *The war in Meath, 1913–23* (Dublin, 1983).

CRAWFORD, E. M. (ed.), *Famine, the Irish experience 900–1900: subsistence crises and Famine in Ireland* (Edinburgh, 1989).

CREAN, TOM, 'From Petrograd to Bruree', in David Fitzpatrick (ed.), *Revolution? Ireland, 1917–1923* (Dublin, 1990).

—— 'The *Voice of Labour* and world revolution, 1917–23', paper delivered at conference on the Irish revolution (1913–23), Department of Modern History, Queen's University, Belfast, Sept. 1999.

—— 'Crowds and the Labour movement in the southwest, 1914–23', in Peter Jupp and Eoin Magennis, *Crowds in Ireland, c.1720–1920* (Basingstoke, 2000).

CRONIN, MAURA, *Country, class or craft? The politicisation of the skilled artisan in nineteenth-century Cork* (Cork, 1994).

CRONIN, MIKE, and REGAN, J. M. (eds.), *Ireland: the politics of independence, 1922–49* (Basingstoke, 2000).

CROTTY, RAYMOND, *Irish agricultural production: its volume and structure* (Cork, 1966).

CULLEN, L. M., *The emergence of modern Ireland, 1600–1900* (London, 1981).

CUNNINGHAM, JOHN, *Labour in the west of Ireland: working life and struggle, 1890–1914* (Belfast, 1995).

CURRAN, J. M., *The birth of the Irish Free State, 1921–23* (London, 1980).

CURTIN, CHRIS, and WILSON, T. M., *Ireland from below: social change and local communities* (Galway, n.d. [probably 1988]).

CURTIS, L. P., *Coercion and conciliation in Ireland, 1880–1892* (Princeton, 1963).

—— 'Incumbered wealth: landed indebtedness in post-Famine Ireland', *American Historical Review*, 85 (1980).

—— 'Landlord responses to the Irish Land War, 1879–87' *Éire/Ireland*, 38/3–4 (2003).

DALY, M. E., *Social and economic history of Ireland since 1800* (Dublin, 1981).

—— 'Local government and the first Dáil' in Brian Farrell (ed.), *The creation of the Dáil*, (Dublin, 1994).

DAVIS, RICHARD, *Arthur Griffith and non-violent Sinn Fein* (Dublin, 1974).

DONNELLY, J. S., *The land and the people of nineteenth-century Cork: the rural economy and the land question* (London, 1975).

DOOLEY, TERENCE, *The decline of the big house in Ireland: a study of Irish landed families, 1860–1960* (Dublin, 2001).

—— 'IRA veterans and land division in independent Ireland, 1923–48', in Fearghal McGarry (ed.), *Republicanism in modern Ireland* (Dublin, 2003).

DRUDY, P. J. (ed.), *Ireland: land, politics and people* (Cambridge, 1982).

EDWARDS, O. D., and Pyle, Fergus (eds.), *1916: the Easter Rising* (Dublin, 1968).

EDWARDS, R. D., *Patrick Pearse: the triumph of failure* (London, 1977).

ENGLISH, RICHARD, *Radicals and the republic: socialist republicanism in the Irish Free State, 1925–1937* (Oxford, 1994).

—— *Ernie O'Malley: IRA intellectual* (Oxford, 1998).

FANNING, RONAN, *Independent Ireland* (Dublin, 1983).

—— "The great enchantment": uses and abuses of modern Irish history', in J. Dooge (ed.), *Ireland in the contemporary world: essays in honour of Garret FitzGerald* (Dublin, 1986).

FARRELL, BRIAN, *The creation of the Dáil* (Dublin, 1994).

FARRY, MICHAEL, *Sligo, 1914–1921: a chronicle of conflict* (Trim, 1992).

—— *The aftermath of revolution: Sligo, 1921–23* (Dublin, 2000).

FEINGOLD, W. L., *The revolt of the tenantry: the transformation of local government in Ireland, 1872–1886* (Boston, 1984).

FERRITER, DIARMAID, 'In such deadly earnest', *Dublin Review*, 12 (Autumn 2003).

FITZPATRICK, DAVID, *Politics and Irish life, 1913–1921: provincial experience of war and revolution* (Dublin, 1977).

—— 'The geography of Irish nationalism, 1910–1921', *Past and Present*, 78 (1978).

—— 'The disappearance of the Irish agricultural labourer, 1841–1912', *Irish Economic and Social History*, 7 (1980).

—— 'Class, family and rural unrest in nineteenth century Ireland', in P. J. Drudy (ed.), *Ireland: land, politics and people* (Cambridge, 1982).

—— 'Unrest in rural Ireland', *Irish Social and Economic History*, 12 (1985).

—— (ed.), *Ireland and the First World War* (Dublin, 1986).

FITZPATRICK, DAVID,

—— 'Ireland since 1870', in R. F. Foster (ed.), *The Oxford history of Ireland* (Oxford, 1992).

—— (ed.), *Revolution? Ireland, 1917–1923* (Dublin, 1990).

—— 'The logic of collective sacrifice: Ireland and the British army, 1914–1918', *Historical Journal*, 38/4 (Dec. 1995).

—— *The two Irelands, 1912–1939* (Oxford, 1998).

FOSTER, R. F., *Modern Ireland, 1600–1972* (London, 1988).

—— (ed.), *The Oxford history of Ireland* (Oxford, 1992).

—— *Paddy and Mr. Punch: connections in Irish and English history* (London, 1993).

FREEMAN, T. W., *Ireland: a general and regional geography* (4th edn., London, 1969).

GAILEY, ANDREW, *Ireland and the death of kindness: the experience of constructive unionism, 1890–1905* (Cork, 1987).

GARVIN, TOM, *The evolution of Irish nationalist politics* (Dublin, 1981).

—— *Nationalist revolutionaries in Ireland, 1858–1928* (Oxford, 1987).

GAUGHAN, J. A., *Austin Stack: portrait of a separatist* (Dublin, 1977).

GEARY, LAWRENCE, *The Plan of Campaign, 1886–91* (Cork, 1986).

GIBBON, PETER, 'Arensberg and Kimball revisited', *Economy and Society*, 2/4 (1973).

GILLESPIE, RAYMOND, and HILL, MYRTLE (eds.), *Doing Irish local history: pursuit and practice* (Belfast, 1998).

—— and MORAN, GERARD, *'A various country': essays in Mayo history, 1500–1900* (Mayo, 1987).

GOLDRING, MAURICE, *Pleasant the scholar's life: Irish intellectuals and the construction of the nation state* (London, 1993).

GREAVES, C. D., *Liam Mellows and the Irish revolution* (2nd edn., London, 1987).

GWYNN, D. R., *Life of John Redmond* (London, 1932).

HANLEY, BRIAN, *The IRA, 1926–1936* (Dublin, 2002).

HART, PETER, 'The geography of revolution in Ireland, 1917–1923', *Past and Present*, 155 (May, 1997).

—— *The IRA and its enemies: violence and community in Cork, 1916–1923* (Oxford, 1998).

—— 'The social structure of the Irish Republican Army, 1916–1923', *Historical Journal*, 42/1 (Mar. 1999).

—— 'Definition: defining the Irish revolution', in Joost Augusteijn, *The Irish revolution, 1913–1923* (Basingstoke, 2002).

—— (ed.), *British intelligence in Ireland, 1920–21: the final reports* (Cork, 2002).

HEPBURN, A. C., 'The Irish Council Bill and the fall of Sir Anthony MacDonnell, 1906–7', *Irish Historical Studies*, 17/68 (Sept. 1971).

—— (ed.), *The conflict of nationality in modern Ireland* (London, 1980).

HIGGINS, M. D., and GIBBONS, J. P., 'Shopkeeper-graziers and land agitation in Ireland, 1895–1900', in P. J. Drudy (ed.), *Ireland: land, politics and people* (Cambridge, 1982).

Hobsbawm, E. J., *Primitive rebels: studies in archaic forms of social movement in the 19th and 20th centuries* (Manchester, 1959).

—— 'Peasant land occupations', *Past and Present*, 62 (Feb. 1974).

—— *Nations and nationalism since 1780: Programme, myth, reality* (Cambridge, 1990).

Hopkinson, Michael, *Green against green: the Irish Civil War* (Dublin, 1988).

—— *The Irish War of Independence* (Dublin, 2002).

Hoppen, K. T., *Elections, politics, and society in Ireland 1832–1885* (Oxford, 1984).

—— *Ireland since 1800: conflict and conformity* (London, 1989).

—— *Ireland since 1800: conflict and conformity* (2nd edn., London, 1999).

Hroch, Miroslav, *Social preconditions of national revival in Europe* (Cambridge, 1985).

Hutchinson, John, *The dynamics of cultural nationalism* (London, 1987).

Jalland, Patricia, *The Liberals and Ireland: the Ulster question in British politics to 1914* (Brighton, 1980).

Jones, D. S., 'The cleavage between graziers and peasants in the land struggle, 1890–1910', in Samuel Clark and J. S. Donnelly (eds.), *Irish peasants: violence and political unrest, 1780–1914* (Manchester, 1983).

—— *Graziers, land reform and political conflict in Ireland* (Washington, 1995).

Jordan, D. E., *Land and popular politics in Ireland: county Mayo from the Plantation to the Land War* (Cambridge, 1994).

—— 'The Irish National League and the "unwritten law": rural protest and nation-building in Ireland 1882–1890', *Past and Present*, 158 (Feb. 1998).

Kavanagh, Patrick, *Collected poems* (London, 1964).

Kee, Robert, *The green flag: a history of Irish nationalism* (London, 1972).

Kennedy, Liam, 'Farmers, traders, and agricultural politics in pre-independence Ireland', in Samuel Clark and J. S. Donnelly (eds.), *Irish peasants: violence and political unrest, 1780–1914* (Manchester, 1983).

—— 'Farm succession in modern Ireland: elements of a theory of inheritance', *Economic History Review*, 44/3 (1991).

King, Carla, *Michael Davitt* (Dundalk, 1999).

Kinsella, Anthony, 'The special infantry corps', *Irish Sword*, 20/82 (Winter 1997).

Kolbert, C. F., and O'Brien, T., *Land reform in Ireland: a legal history of the Irish land problem and its settlement* (Cambridge, 1975).

Kotsonouris, Mary, *Retreat from revolution: the Dáil courts, 1920–24* (Dublin, 1994).

Laffan, Michael, 'The unification of Sinn Féin', *Irish Historical Studies*, 17 (1971).

—— '"Labour must wait": Ireland's conservative revolution', in P. J. Corish (ed.), *Radicals, rebels and establishments: historical studies XV* (Belfast, 1985).

LAFFAN, MICHAEL,
—— *The resurrection of Ireland: the Sinn Féin party, 1916–1923* (Cambridge, 1999).

LAVELLE, PATRICIA, *James O'Mara: a staunch Sinn Féiner, 1873–1948* (Dublin, 1961).

LAWLOR, SHEILA, *Britain and Ireland, 1914–23* (Dublin, 1983).

LEE, J. J., *The modernisation of Irish society, 1848–1918* (Dublin, 1973).

—— 'Patterns of rural unrest in nineteenth century Ireland: a preliminary survey', in L. M. Cullen and François Furet (eds.), *Ireland and France, 17th–20th centuries: towards a comparative study of rural history* (Paris, 1980).

—— (ed.), *Irish historiography, 1970–79* (Cork, 1981).

—— *Ireland, 1912–1985: politics and society* (Cambridge, 1989).

LUCEY, D. S., *The Irish National League in Dingle, county Kerry, 1885–1892* (Dublin, 2003).

LYNCH, PATRICK, 'The social revolution that never was', in T. D. Williams (ed.), *The Irish struggle, 1916–1926* (London, 1966).

LYONS, F. S. L., *The Irish Parliamentary Party, 1890–1910* (London, 1951).

—— *John Dillon: a biography* (London, 1968).

—— *Ireland since the Famine* (London, 1971).

—— *Culture and anarchy in Ireland, 1890–1939* (Oxford, 1979).

—— and Hawkins, R. A. J. (eds.), *Ireland under the union: varieties of tension* (Oxford, 1980).

MACCURTAIN, MARGARET, and O'DOWD, MARY, 'An agenda for women's history in Ireland, 1500–1900: part i: 1500–1800', *Irish Historical Studies*, 28/109 (May 1992)

MACDONAGH, OLIVER, *States of mind: a study of Anglo-Irish conflict, 1780–1980* (London, 1983).

MANDLE, W. F., 'The IRB and the beginnings of the Gaelic Athletic Association', *Irish Historical Studies*, 20 (1977).

—— *The Gaelic Athletic Association and Irish nationalist politics, 1884–1924* (Dublin, 1987).

MANSERGH, NICHOLAS, *The Irish question, 1840–1921* (London, 1965).

MARTIN, F. X. (ed.), *Leaders and men of the Easter Rising: Dublin 1916* (London, 1967).

—— '1916: myth, fact, and mystery', *Studia Hibernica*, 7 (1967).

—— 'The 1916 Rising—a *coup d'état* or a "bloody protest"?', *Studia Hibernica*, 8 (1968).

MAUME, PATRICK, *The long gestation: Irish nationalist life, 1891–1918* (Dublin, 1999).

MILLER, D. W., *Church, state and nation in Ireland, 1898–1921* (Dublin, 1973).

MITCHELL, ARTHUR, 'Alternative government: "Exit Britannia"—the formation of the Irish nation state, 1918–21', in Joost Augusteijn, *The Irish revolution, 1913–23* (Basingstoke, 2002).

MURPHY, J. A., *Ireland in the twentieth century* (Dublin, 1975).

NEESON, EOIN, *The Civil War in Ireland, 1922–23* (Cork, 1966).

NÍ DHONNCHADHA, MÁIRÍN, and DORGAN, THEO, *Revising the Rising* (Derry, 1991).

NOVICK, BEN, *Conceiving revolution: Irish nationalist propaganda during the First World War* (Dublin, 2001).

NOWLAN, K. B. (ed.), *The making of 1916* (Dublin, 1969).

O'BRIEN, J. V., *William O'Brien and the course of Irish politics, 1881–1918* (Berkeley, 1976).

Ó BROIN, LEON, *Revolutionary underground: the story of the Irish Republican Brotherhood, 1858–1924* (Dublin, 1976).

—— 'The Invincibles', in T. D. Williams (ed.), *Secret societies in Ireland* (Dublin, 1973).

O'CONNOR, EMMET, *Syndicalism in Ireland, 1917–1923* (Cork, 1988).

Ó CORRAIN, DONNCHADH (ed.), *James Hogan: revolutionary, historian and political scientist* (Dublin, 2001).

O'DAY, ALAN (ed.), *Reactions to Irish nationalism, 1865–1914* (Dublin, 1987).

Ó DUIBHIR, CIARÁN, *Sinn Féin: the first election, 1908* (Manorhamilton, 1993).

O'FARRELL, PADRAIC, *Who's who in the Irish War of Independence, 1916–1921* (Dublin, 1980).

Ó GRÁDA, CORMAC, *Ireland before and after the Famine: explorations in economic history, 1800–1925* (Manchester, 1984).

—— *Ireland: a new economic history, 1780–1939* (Oxford, 1994).

O'HEGARTY, P. S., *A History of Ireland under the Union, 1801 to 1922* (London, 1952).

O MAHONY, SEAN, *Frongoch: university of revolution* (Dublin, 1987).

O'NEILL, T. P., 'The food crisis of the 1890s', in E. M. Crawford (ed.), *Famine, the Irish experience 900–1900: subsistence crises and Famine in Ireland* (Edinburgh, 1989).

Ó TUATHAIGH, GEARÓID, 'The land question: politics and Irish society, 1922–1960', in P. J. Drudy (ed.), *Ireland: land, politics and people* (Cambridge, 1982).

—— 'Ireland's land questions: a historical perspective', in John Davis (ed.), *Rural change in Ireland* (Belfast 1999).

'Our man at Oxford', *History Ireland*, 1/3 (Autumn 1993).

PATTERSON, HENRY, *The politics of illusion: republicanism and socialism in modern Ireland* (London, 1989).

PHILPIN, C. H. E. (ed.), *Nationalism and popular protest in Ireland* (Cambridge, 1987).

POMFRET, J. E., *The struggle for land in Ireland, 1800–1923* (Princeton, 1930).

PRICE, ALAN (ed.), *J. M. Synge collected works, ii: Prose* (Oxford, 1966).

PYLE, HILARY, *Jack Yeats: a biography* (London, 1970).

REGAN, J. M., and CRONIN, MIKE, 'Introduction: Ireland and the politics of independence 1922–49, new perspectives and re-considerations', in Mike Cronin and J. M. Regan (eds.), *Ireland: the politics of independence, 1922–49* (Basingstoke, 2000).

ROCHE, DESMOND, *Local government in Ireland* (Dublin, 1982).

RUMPF, ERHARD, and HEPBURN, A. C., *Nationalism and socialism in twentieth-century Ireland* (Liverpool, 1977).

SKOCPOL, THEDA, *States and social revolutions: a comparative analysis of France, Russia and China* (Cambridge, 1979).

SMYTH, WILLIE, and WHELAN, KEVIN (eds.), *Common ground: essays on the historical geography of Ireland* (Cork, 1988).

SOLOW, B. L., *The land question and the Irish economy 1870–1903* (Cambridge, Mass., 1971).

STRAUSS, ERICH, *Irish nationalism and British democracy* (London, 1951).

STEELE, E. D., 'Ireland for the Irish', *History*, 57/190 (June 1972).

THOMPSON, E. P., *The making of the English working class* (London, 1963).

—— *Customs in common* (London, 1991).

TOWNSHEND, CHARLES, *The British campaign in Ireland, 1919–1921: the development of political and military policies* (Oxford, 1975).

—— 'Modernization and nationalism: perspectives in recent Irish history', *History*, 66/217 (June 1981).

—— 'The Irish Republican Army and the development of guerrilla warfare, 1916–21', *English Historical Review*, 94 (1979).

—— 'The Irish railway strike of 1920: industrial action and civil resistance in the struggle for independence', *Irish Historical Studies*, 12 (1979).

—— *Political violence in Ireland: government and resistance since 1848* (Oxford, 1983).

VARLEY, TONY, 'Agrarian crime and social control: Sinn Féin and the land question in the west of Ireland in 1920', in Ciaran McCullagh, Mike Tomilson, and Tony Varley (eds.), *Whose law and order? Aspects of crime and social control in Irish society* (Belfast, 1988).

—— 'Farmers against nationalists: the rise and fall of Clann na Talmhan in Galway', in Gerard Moran and Raymond Gillespie (eds.), *Galway history and society: interdisciplinary essays on the history of an Irish county* (Dublin, 1996).

—— 'A region of sturdy smallholders? Western nationalists and agrarian politics during the first world war', *Journal of the Galway Archaeological and Historical Society*, 55 (2003).

VAUGHAN, W. E., *Landlords and tenants in Ireland 1848–1904* (Dublin, 1984).

—— *Landlords and tenants in mid-Victorian Ireland* (Oxford, 1994).

—— and Fitzpatrick, A. J. (eds.), *Irish historical statistics: population, 1821–1971* (Dublin, 1978).

WALKER, B. M. (ed.), *Parliamentary election results in Ireland 1801–1922* (Dublin, 1978).

WARWICK-HALLER, SALLY, *William O'Brien and the Irish land war* (Dublin, 1990).

WEBER, EUGEN, *Peasants into Frenchmen* (London, 1971).

WHELAN, KEVIN, 'The bases of regionalism', in Proinsias Ó Drisceoil, (ed.), *Culture in Ireland: regions: identity and power* (Belfast, 1993).

WILLIAMS, T. D. (ed.), *The Irish struggle, 1916–1926* (London, 1966).
—— (ed.), *Secret societies in Ireland* (Dublin, 1973).
WINSTANLEY, M. J., *Ireland and the land question 1800–1922* (London, 1984).
WOLF, E. R., *Peasant wars of the twentieth century* (New York, 1969).
YOUNGER, CARLTON, *Ireland's Civil War* (London, 1970).

7. ORAL SOURCES

CLOONAN, GERRY, Caherfurvaus, Craughwell, 25 Apr. 1995, 6 June 1995, 16 May
1996, 23 Nov.1997. Transcript.
COEN, Father MARTIN, Athenry, 15 May 1994. Transcript.
DOLPHIN, MARTIN, Ballinasloe, 24 Nov. 1997. Transcript.
DONOHOE, J. B., Loughrea, 16 May 1996, 22 Nov. 1997. Transcript.
FINNERTY, MATTIE, Galway, 15 Dec. 1994, 24 Nov. 1997, 30 Jan. 1998. Transcript.
JORDAN, ANNIE, Pollacrossaun, Colmanstown, 17 May 1993. Tape.
KELLY, TOM, Maynooth, 13 Sept. 2003. Transcript.
LAFFY, TOMMY, Cloonkeenabbert, Abbeyknockmoy, 24 Aug. 1992. Tape.
MCELWAIN, MICHAEL, Mount Bellew, 21 Aug. 1992. Tape.
NEWELL, NED, Craughwell, 15 Dec. 1994. Transcript.
ROHAN, KEVIN, Colmanstown, 24 Dec. 2003. Transcript.
RUANE, BRIAN, Colmanstown, 23 Aug. 1992. Tape.
TANNIAN, MICKY, Colmanstown, 24 Aug. 2003. Transcript.

8. UNPUBLISHED THESES

AUGUSTEIJN, JOOST, 'From public defiance to guerilla warfare: the radicalisation
of the Irish Republican Army, a comparative analysis, 1916–1921' (University of
Amsterdam, Ph.D., 1994).
BALL, S. A., 'Policing the Land War: official responses to political protest and
agrarian crime in Ireland, 1879–91' (University of London, Ph.D., 2000).
BORAN, MARIE, 'Manifestations of Irish nationalism' (University College, Galway,
M.Ed., 1989).
BULL, P. J., 'The reconstruction of the Irish parliamentary movement, 1895–1903:
an analysis with special reference to William O'Brien' (University of Cambridge,
Ph.D., 1972).
CAMPBELL, FERGUS, 'Land and politics in Connacht, 1898–1909' (University of
Bristol, Ph.D., 1997).
CREAN, T. N., 'The Labour movement in Kerry and Limerick, 1914–1921' (Trinity
College, Dublin, Ph.D., 1995).
DAY, CHRIS, 'Problems of poverty in the congested districts, 1890–1914' (University
College, Galway, MA, 1986).

FEINGOLD, W. L., 'The Irish boards of poor law guardians, 1872–86: a revolution in local government' (University of Chicago, Ph.D., 1974).

FINNEGAN, ANN, 'The land war in south-east Galway, 1879–90' (University College, Galway, MA, 1974).

FITZPATRICK, DAVID, 'Irish people and politics: the development of political beliefs and patterns of political conduct among Irishmen from 1913 to 1921, with particular reference to county Clare' (University of Cambridge, Ph.D., 1975).

GIBBONS, J. P., 'Local politics and power in county Mayo, 1895–1900' (University College, Galway, MA, 1980).

GRIFFIN, BRIAN, 'The Irish police, 1836–1914: a social history' (Loyola University of Chicago, Ph.D., 1991).

HART, PETER, 'The Irish Republican Army and its enemies: violence and community in county Cork, 1917–23' (Trinity College, Dublin, Ph.D., 1993).

HEPBURN, A. C., 'Liberal policies and nationalist politics in Ireland, 1905–10' (University of Kent, Ph.D., 1968).

MCEVOY, J. N., 'A study of the United Irish League in the King's county, 1899–1918' (National University of Ireland, Maynooth, MA, 1992).

MCHUGH, J. P., 'Voices of the rearguard: a study of *An Phoblacht*—Irish republican thought in the post-revolutionary era, 1923–37' (University College, Dublin, MA, 1983).

MAUME, PATRICK, 'Aspects of Irish nationalist political culture, c.1900–18' (Queen's University, Belfast, Ph.D., 1993).

MELVIN, PATRICK, 'The landed gentry of Galway, 1820–80' (Trinity College, Dublin, Ph.D. 1991).

MULLEN, R. G., 'The origins and passing of the Irish Land Act of 1909' (Queen's University, Belfast, MA, 1978).

SHEEHAN, J. T., 'Land purchase policy in Ireland, 1917–23' (National University of Ireland, Maynooth, MA, 1993).

VARLEY, ANTHONY, 'The politics of agrarian reform: the state, nationalists and the agrarian question in the west of Ireland' (Southern Illinois University, Ph.D., 1994).

Index

NOTE: References to tables are indicated by the page number followed by (t)

Abbey, county Galway 244
Abercorn, Duke of 50, 76
abstention 110, 117, 190, 295
 pressure on IPP 112, 115–16
Act of Union 230, 236
 repeal sought 168–9
agrarian agitation 2, 64–9, 74, 96
 Connacht (1920) 3, 205, 246–53, 287;
 agreement, 254; methods of, 249–
 53
 Connacht (1891–9) 8–41
 Dáil control of 279–85
 and Easter Rising 219–20
 effects of 286–7
 effects of legislation 53
 Galway secret society 174–7, 178–9,
 182–4
 historiography of 287–304
 IPP policy 29, 30, 86–7, 104–5, 119–
 20
 and nationalism 3, 5, 145–8, 286–7,
 302–4
 and revolution (1918–21) 226–85
 Sinn Féin policy 114–18, 221, 223–4,
 237, 240–6
 and social structure 279–85, 288–92
 UEC 183–4
 UIL policy 57–63, 106, 141–5, 184–5,
 286–7
 violence 128; legitimate targets 240–
 1; murders 147, 156–60, 175–6,
 252–3, 266–7; threat to property
 280, 302

War of Independence 264–8, 301–3
 see also Ranch War
Agricultural College, Athenry 211–12,
 213
agriculture 13, 169
 prices 247–8
Agriculture, Dáil Department of 256
Agriculture and Technical Instruction,
 Department of 107–8
Ahascragh, county Galway 87 n, 179,
 253
Aiken Act (1933) 286
Alcorn, James G. 248, 252
Allen, Richard 67, 68
Ancient Order of Hibernians (AOH)
 110 n, 153, 167
Anglo-Irish Treaty (1921) 6, 226, 279
Anglo-Irish war, see War of
 Independence
Annaghdown, county Galway 238
anti-recruitment campaign 115, 196–7,
 199, 203, 221, 223–4
 literature 117–18
Ard, county Galway 250
Ardagh, county Limerick 134, 135
Ardcumber, county Sligo 174
Ardrahan, county Galway 76, 77, 172,
 174 n, 188, 193
 Volunteers 198, 208
Armstrong, Captain Sir Andrew 211
artisans 230, 232, 233
 in IRA 260(t), 261(t), 262, 263
 in UIL 234

Ashbourne Act 89, 151 n
Ashtown, Lord 4, 13, 17, 76, 148, 266
Athea, county Limerick 138
Athenry, county Galway 67–8, 115–16,
    147, 152, 155, 188, 189
  agrarian agitation 64–9
  anti-conscription meeting 203–4
  Easter Rising 205, 206, 207, 211–12,
    213, 221
  Galway secret society 191
  IRB activity 182
  Land League court 132
  MacBride in 176–7
  Sinn Féin activity 171, 173
  TTL activity 182–3
  Volunteers 194, 195, 199–200, 200,
    202
  War of Independence 268
Athlone Poor Law Union 14
Attymon, county Galway 216
Aud (submarine) 205, 206, 298, 299
Aughrim, county Wicklow 86
Augusteijn, Joost 264
Australia 10, 110 n
Austria 168
Auxiliaries 270, 271–3, 278

Baggot, Miss 275
Baggot, Mr 245, 274, 277
Baggot, Mrs 277
Baggot House ambush 274–7
Baggott, J. C. 251
Baker, Widow 138
Balfour, Arthur, PM 26, 47, 56, 59, 71,
    72, 80, 81–2, 146
Balfour, Gerald 56, 59, 129
Ballaghaderreen, county Mayo 43
Ballinakill, county Galway 244
Ballinasloe, county Galway 4, 14, 206,
    253, 254
  Convention 153
  Easter Rising 214
  Poor Law Union 18

Ballinderreen, county Galway 179, 208,
    242
Ballingrane, county Limerick 138
Ballinrobe, county Mayo 16, 281
Ballybane, county Galway 265
Ballycahalan, county Galway 208
Ballygar, county Galway 65
Ballyglunin, county Galway 267
Ballylongford, county Kerry 45, 47
Ballymacward, county Galway 248
Ballymore, county Galway 250
Ballyturin, county Galway 251, 274–8
Banagher, King's county 106
Bangor, county Down 62
Barbersfort, county Galway 267
Barna, county Galway 272
Barrett, James 199, 207, 216
Barry, Edward 110, 112
Barry, Redmond 161
Barrymore, Lord 79
basket-weaving 28
Beard, C. J. 99, 120
Becker, Bernard 15
bee-keeping 27
Beirne, Mr 102
Belcarra, county Mayo 150
Belclare, county Galway 243, 267
Belfast 114, 169, 258
Belmullet Poor Law Union 14
Bernard, Colonel 267
Berridge estate 4
Bew, Paul 17–18, 85, 124, 283 n, 288–9,
    292, 293
  Anglo-Irish war 301–2
Birmingham, George 20, 23
Birrell, Augustine 28, 107, 108, 112, 120
  Land Bill 1913, 238
Birrell Land Act (1909) 120–2, 184–5,
    286, 304
  sales under 238–9
Black and Tans 270, 273
Blake, DI Cecil 274–7
Blake, John 148 n

Blake, Mr 177 n
Blake, Mrs 274–7
Boer war 51
Bookeen barracks, county Galway
    268 n
Bourke, Father 245–6
Bourke, Walter 77–8, 147, 175–6, 219
Bowes, Reverend 164
boycotting 38, 39, 76, 104, 124, 155–6,
    164
  anti-Wyndham Bill 75–6
  compulsory purchase campaign 58–
    9, 60–1
  effects of 140–1
  persons boycotted 128, 138–9
  proclamations 71–2, 82
  prosecutions for 66, 74
  Sinn Féin policy 243, 245
  UIL strategy 33, 128, 130–1, 139–43
Bradley, Ned 22
Brennan, Michael 271, 273, 275
Brett, Father 32
Britain, *see* England; Scotland; Wales
British army 221, 270 n
  Easter Rising 206, 211, 216, 217
  see also anti-recruitment campaign
British Government 6
  Birrell Land Act 120–1
  coercion policy 58–9, 73–4, 76
  and land reform 3, 70–2, 81–3;
    Wyndham Act 79–80, 294
  law and order 71–2
Broderick, John 206
Brown, Thomas 151
Brugha, Cathal 245–6, 255, 256, 281, 284
Bryce, James 99, 111, 119, 120
Bull, Philip 30, 35, 294–5, 296
Bullaun, county Galway 158 n, 188
Burke, Edward 266
Burke, Haviland 19–20
Burke, T. H. 175
Burke, Walter 178
Burke, William 252 n

Burke estate 125
businessmen:
  in IRA 260(t), 261(t), 263
  in Sinn Féin 228(t), 230, 233–4, 236

Cadogan, Lord 71–2, 81–2, 125
Cahalan, Father 94–5
Caheroyan, county Galway 116
Cahir, Frank 144
Callanan, Michael 160 n, 209
Callanan, Patrick 160 n, 193, 203, 255
  Easter Rising 208, 209, 218
  on IRB 162, 178, 180–1, 182
  War of Independence 269
Caltra, county Galway 164, 242
Campbell-Bannerman, Sir Henry, PM
    108, 120
Capuchin Annual 277
Carlow, county 247 n
Carna, county Galway 28
Carnaglough, county Galway 251
Carnmore, county Galway 212
Carr, Patrick 94
Carron, county Clare 115
Carrownamorrissey, county Galway
    244–5
Carter, Mrs 138
Carter, Volunteer 221–2
Carty, Mr 273
Casement, Roger 193, 299
Casey, Eamon 281
Casserly, Volunteer 212
Castle Lambert, county Galway 267
Castle Pinch, county Galway 244
Castlebar, county Mayo 21, 24, 30, 36
Castledaly, county Galway 147, 175–6
Castlegar, county Galway 182, 199, 204,
    270
  Easter Rising 208, 212–13
Castlegrove, county Galway 251
Castlehackett, county Galway 267
Catholic church:
  support for Volunteers 195–6

Catholic clergy 164
  and RIC 180–1
  Sinn Féin support 223, 224
  support for Volunteers 204–5
  and UIL 36
Catholic hierarchy 70, 253
  opposes Galway secret society 179–
    82
Catholics 4, 234
  employment of 231
  as graziers 19, 290
  as landlords 4, 288
cattle driving 101–2, 106–7, 116, 124, 142,
    182, 237, 284, 293
  agitation (1920) 249, 251, 253
  crowd fired on 174
  Easter Rising 215–16
  Galway secret society 178
  and IRA 266
  SF policy 240–1, 243, 244
  TTL 183
  used by UIL 143–4
cattle production 12–13, 18, 54
Cavan, county 62, 171, 185 n, 247 n
Cavendish, Lord Frederick 175
Cawley, Bartholomew 164
Cawley, Thomas 149
Ceannt, Eamon 193
census returns 6, 17, 233
Chamberlain, Neville 63–4, 69, 72, 75
Chartism 18
Church of Ireland 288
Civil War 2 n, 226
Clan na Gael 192
Clancy, J. J. 110
Clann na Talmhan 94 n, 304 n
Clanricarde, Lord 4, 136, 154
Clanricarde estate 19, 35, 64, 106
Clare, county 3, 167, 168, 273, 293, 297
  agrarian agitation 20, 70, 184 n,
    185 n, 247 n, 284; Ranch War 102,
    107
  Easter Rising 216

Galway secret society 188
IRA activity 264
labour movement 300–1
Sinn Féin activity 224–5
untenanted land 14
War of Independence 258, 259, 268,
  271
Clare Island, county Mayo 20
Claregalway, county Galway 208, 212–
  13
Clareman 60 n
Claremorris, county Mayo 9, 24–5,
  127–8, 146, 251
Clarinbridge, county Galway 175, 182,
  204
  Easter Rising 207–11, 216–17
  Volunteers 193, 194, 195, 199
Clarke, Thomas 186, 207
Clasby, Michael 164
Clayton, County Inspector 211
clerks 228, 231, 232
Clifden, county Galway 23, 291
  Poor Law Union 18
Cloghan's Hill, county Galway 251
Clogher, county Mayo 47, 48
Clonbrock, Lord 4, 76, 129
Clonbrock estate 242
Clondra, county Longford 143
Clonfert, Bishop of 14 n
Clontuskert, county Galway 14,
  134–5
Cloonkeenkerrill, county Galway 151
Cloonturbrit, county Mayo 21
Closetoken, county Galway 198, 271
Coady, Patrick 156, 157
Coen, Father Martin 149 n, 153 n
coercion 58–9, 73–4, 76
Cogan, Mr 106
Colberts 138
Coleman, Marie 225 n
collective farm 280, 281
Colmanstown, county Galway 151–2,
  265

Colum, Padraic 80
Commins, Michael 211
communal farming 280, 281
conacre 128, 242
Concannon, Thomas 172, 191
congested districts 9, 92, 131, 233 n, 259,
    286
    agitation (1920) 249
    effects of 1881 Act 53–4, 56
    extent of 1913, 239
    improvement sought 55–6, 57
    land prices 51–2
    needs overlooked by Leagues 25–6
    UIL activity 237
    untouched by Wyndham Act 177,
       247
    and Wyndham Bill 69
Congested Districts Board (CDB) 9 n,
    107–8, 244, 256, 286, 291 n
    agitation against 248
    aims of 26–8
    difficulties of 92
    established 55, 59
    forced sales to 129
    land prices 257
    leases to graziers 239–40, 243, 248
    pressure on 183–4
    redistribution by 23–4, 238–9
    reform 121–2
    reports 10, 12
    small farms definition 229–30
    and UIL 31–3, 38–9
Congestion, Royal Commission on 7,
    12, 13, 14 n, 16, 92, 95
    evidence on shopkeepers 20–1, 23,
       148
    reform of CDB 121–2
Connacht 3, 57, 173, 185 n, 189, 232, 286,
    295
    agrarian agitation 280; 1891–99, 8–
      41; land war 1920, 246–53; no-rent
      campaign 62, 63; Ranch War 102,
      104; rent combinations 97

compulsory purchase 48–9
IRA activity 264
labour movement 300–1
land redistribution 5, 24–5
Sinn Féin activity 170, 243
social structure 291–2
UIL activity 36, 39, 131, 145; branches
    45, 46–7; councillors 61; courts
    125, 128
untenanted land 15(t), 129
War of Independence 258
Wyndham Act 90
Connacht Tribune 115 n, 116, 172 n, 174,
    247 n, 248, 250, 252, 254
Connaught Leader 8, 134–5, 136, 137, 138
Connaught Rangers 211
Connaught Telegraph 150
Connaughton, Patrick 198, 271
Connemara 4, 18, 268
    poverty 8–12
Connolly, Father 206
Connolly, Mr 164
Conroy, Mr 254
conscription 197, 203–4, 221, 223–4, 235
Considine, Tim 240
Corbett, Captain Eamon 205, 213, 218
Cork, county 10 n, 102, 171, 291
    rent combinations 97–8
    War of Independence 258, 278
Cork city 28, 93, 200
Cork Examiner 60 n
Cornwallis, Captain 274–7
Cosgrave, W. T. 241
Costello, Michael 265
Costello, Sergeant 67
Costelloe, Michael 244, 245
county councils 21, 231, 279, 284
County Inspector, Galway, reports of
    67, 69, 111, 249
    Easter Rising 298–9
    Galway secret society 176, 180
    Kenny 191–2
    Sinn Féin 166, 172, 242–3

County Inspector, Galway, reports of (*cont.*):
Volunteers 195, 203, 218
War of Independence 270–1
County Inspector, Mayo, reports of 128–9
Craughwell, county Galway 5, 94, 188, 189, 234, 267 n
faction fighting 161–2
Galway secret society 188, 190–1
Goldrick murder 178
IRB activity 147
MacBride in 176–7
Sinn Féin activity 166, 171, 172–6, 179, 194, 225, 244–5
split 153–64
UIL branch 66–9, 77, 191, 192
Volunteers 195, 215, 216
War of Independence 258
Craughwell Ratepayers' Association 160
Crean, Tom 282, 299–300
Creggs, county Galway 251, 280, 281
Crimes Act 71, 72, 76, 82, 294
reintroduced (1902) 73–4
UIL protests 74–5
Crimes Act (1887) 59
criminal justice reforms 74
Crinnage, county Galway 181
Cronin, Mike 279, 300
Croom Board of Guardians 134
Crossna, county Roscommon 241
Crozier, Brigadier-General F. P. 272
Cumann na mBan 211, 231 n
Cumann na nGaedheal 169–70, 171
Cummer, county Galway 179, 188
Cusack, Bryan, 204 n, 232
Cussaun, county Galway 211, 264

Dáil courts 255, 280–1
Dáil Éireann 231 n, 243, 246, 259
and agrarian agitation 255, 256–7, 298

established 166–7
War of Independence 279
Daily Herald 279
Daily News 15, 36
Daly, Anthony 189
Daly, Charles 150
Daly, James 150, 231
Daly, William 94–5, 150
Daly family 216
Daniher, John H. 138
Davidson, Mr 254
Davies, Mr 144
Davoren, Father 179
de Valera, Éamon 241
Deák, Ferenc 168
Deely, Darby 215
Deely, Mr 132
Dempsey, W. 151
deputations 249–50, 265
Dermody, Michael 157–60, 190–1
Derrydonnell, county Galway 211
Derrylaur, county Galway 27
Devine, Constable 181
Devlin, Joseph 106, 107, 116, 118
Leitrim by-election 113–14
Dilleen, Hubert 266
Dillon, John 6, 37, 40, 42, 107, 112, 120, 294–5
Gurteen dispute 153
Irish Council Bill 108, 109
and land purchase 31, 60, 89
Shawe-Taylor letter 76–7
and UIL 42, 43–4, 45
Dillon, John Blake 43
Dillon estate 38
dissenters 4
Dolan, Charles 110, 112, 113–14
Dolan, Martin 174–5, 220, 277
Dolly, Peter 265
Donegal, county 10 n, 51, 247 n
Donohoe, J. B. 236
Doolin, county Clare 144
Doonane, county Galway 265

Doran, Sir Henry 92
Doris, William 34–5
Douglas estate 143
Drew, Massy 138
Drumkeerin, county Leitrim 114
Drummin, county Mayo 24
'drumming parties' 65, 142, 143, 151
Dublin 114, 170
   Craughwell murder trial 158–60
   Easter Rising 207, 216, 217
   Land Conference 1920, 256, 284
   lock-out 1913, 246
   Sinn Féin activity 171, 173
   War of Independence 258
Dublin, county 43, 46, 264
Dublin Metropolitan Police (DMP)
   175 n
Dudley, Lord 92
Duffy, William 65, 116, 132, 137, 148, 152,
   191, 233, 238
   election defeat 235–6
Dungannon clubs 169–70
Dunkellin, county Galway 175
Dunmore, county Galway 14
Dunraven, Earl of 56, 79, 96–7
Dunsandle, county Galway 150, 216,
   268 n
Dunsandle, Lord 4
   estate 65, 94–5, 96, 97
Dunworth, Robert and Jeremiah
   138
Durkan, John, accounts of 21–2

Easter Rising (1916) 2 n, 197, 207–20,
   226, 269, 300
   aftermath 220–5
   aims of 220
   cattle seizures 215–16
   Galway 168, 172 n, 205–20, 230, 262,
      268, 298–9
   historiography of 296–9
   and IPP 122
   plans 200–3

   prelude 205–7
Education Board 107–8
education levels 231, 233
Edward VII, King 169
eleven-months system 17, 19–20, 52,
   53, 244
   auctions boycotted 33
   campaign against 65, 248, 289, 291;
      boycotting 128
   cattle driving 102
   CDB leases to graziers 239–40
   growth of 55
   prices 90–2
   UIL courts 125, 135
   UIL leaseholders 290
Elphin, county Roscommon 106, 241
emigration 4, 10, 175, 228
   fear of conscription 203 n
   wartime restrictions 247
Encumbered Estates Act (1849) 14
England:
   cattle trade 12, 13
   internment 218
   investors 19
   labourers to 11
   tenants from 15–16, 31
   UIL in 110 n
English, Richard 302, 303
Episcopalians 4
Errismore, county Mayo 32
Esmonde, Sir Thomas 109, 110, 112
Estates Commissioners 88, 106, 244
   attempts to force sales to 86, 99, 102,
      136, 178, 289
Estates Committees 266
Evicted Tenants' Fund 35
evictions 13–15, 19, 29, 154, 256
   compensation for 61, 75
   reinstatement campaign 46, 127
Eyrecourt, county Galway 245, 250

faction fighting 161–2
Fahy, Frank 232

Fahy, Michael 262
Fahy, Pádraig 154, 201, 202 n
Fahy, Father Tom 216
Fallon, Father 94
Fallon, Joe 132–3
Fallon, Kathleen 237
Fallon, Padraic 302
farmers, *see* large farmers; small
    farmers
Farmers' Party 94 n
farmers' sons 227–9, 232, 260(t), 261(t),
    263–4
  in IRA 260(t), 261(t), 263–4, 278
Farrell, J. P. 106, 110
Farrelly, Miss 207
Feakle, county Clare 240
Feeney, Fr Henry 204, 207, 211, 214, 217,
    218
Feingold, William 17
Fenianism 18, 43, 148, 170, 175, 193, 263
  church attitude to 180
  and IRB 145, 169, 189
  social composition 230
  and UIL 153, 222
Fianna Fáil 94 n, 283–4
Figgis, Darrell 241 n
Finlay, T. A., SJ 12
Finnerty, Martin 13, 95, 158 n
  on IRB 176, 177
  on rent combinations 94, 96
  on Sinn Féin 222
  on UEC 183–4
  on UIL factions 151–3, 164
First World War 196, 197, 198, 234 n,
    237–8, 278
  CDB leases to graziers 239–40, 243,
    248
  effects on nationalism 200
  emigration restrictions 247
  food crisis (1917–18) 242
  land purchase suspended 239, 243
fisheries 10, 27, 31
Fitzgerald, Dick 186

Fitzgerald, Lord Edward 56
FitzGibbon, Sean 193 n
Fitzpatrick, David 249, 264, 292, 299–
    300, 300–1
  Clare study 224, 259, 293
  on Easter Rising 296–9
  on Sinn Féin 167–8
Flatley, Reverend John 20–1
Flavin, M. J. 110
Fleming, George 175
Fleming, Volunteer 207
flying columns 269
food crisis (1917–18) 242
Ford, Richard 231
Forde, Darby 265
Forde, Martin 244
Forde, Michael 136, 137
Fountain Hill, county Mayo 281
Freeman's Journal 25, 29, 34, 62, 88, 108,
    109, 130
Frongoch camp, Wales 218

Gaelic Athletic Association (GAA) 115,
    117, 164, 172, 173, 176, 185
  Kenny in 179, 188
Gaelic League 115, 169, 219, 233, 271–2
Gaelic revival 188
Gailey, Andrew 83, 293
Galway, county 1, 17, 111, 141
  agrarian agitation 77–8, 145, 247 n,
    249; intimidation 250–3; Ranch
    War 94, 100, 102, 103, 107; rent
    combinations 95, 97–8
  description of 3–5, 10, 27
  east Galway case study 64–9
  Easter Rising 268, 298–9; aftermath
    221–5; events 207–20; plans 200–3;
    prelude 205–7; Volunteer
    membership 218–19
  IRA activity: Ballyturin ambush
    274–8; 'land agitations' 264–8;
    under Murphy 269–71;
    reorganization 273–5; social

composition 284
population 3–4
poverty 10, 27
rents 90
Sinn Féin activity 114–15, 171, 190, 242–3, 243–6, 298, 301 n; evolution (1905–18) 166–225; Land Conference 256; social composition 227–33, 291
trials 158, 160
UIL activity 35, 128, 131, 291, 301 n
valuations 18
Volunteers 193–5, 197–200, 202–4
War of Independence 257–99
Galway Blazers 290 n
Galway city 4, 224
  Easter Rising 205, 206, 214, 216, 221–2
  Sinn Féin activity 171, 231 n
  UIL activity 75, 234, 236
  Volunteers 198
  War of Independence 271–3
Galway county council 23 n, 221, 232
Galway Express 224 n, 248–9, 253, 266, 269
Galway secret society 174–7
  and Easter Rising 200–1, 215, 219–20, 222
  intimidation 178–9, 182–4
  IRA links 262–3
  and IRB 185–8
  membership of 185, 188–9
  relations with church 179–82
  and Sinn Féin 185–8, 224–5, 244–6
  strength of 188–9, 190–2
  and Volunteers 193–5
Galway Woollen Manufacturing Company 234
Ganly, William 112
Garbally College, Ballinasloe 206
Garrankyle, county Galway 244–5
Garvin, Tom 230, 231
Gaskell, Major W. P. 27

General Council of County Councils 169
general elections:
  (1900) 47
  (1906) 170
  (1910) 123
  (1918) 166–7, 220, 227, 235–6, 237, 238
Genovese, Eugene 293
Gibbons, John Patrick 21
Gibson, Justice 37
Gilligan, Patrick 154, 155
Ginnell, Laurence 92, 101, 102, 106–7, 110, 150, 202
  agrarian policy 240, 241, 246
Gladstone, W. E. 50, 59, 304
Globe 71
Glynn, Patrick 275, 276
Goldrick, Constable Martin, murder of 156–60, 173–4, 178, 181, 190–1, 244
'gombeenmen' 24, 29
Gort, county Galway 27, 176, 271, 277
  Easter Rising 206, 208, 299
  secret society 166, 188, 224, 245, 251
Gortacarnane, county Galway 273
'grabbers' 20, 31, 32, 59, 60, 115, 267
  boycotting 128, 130–1, 138–9
  compensation paid by 61, 75
  UIL opposition to 38, 129, 135
Grand Juries 39, 40
graziers 2, 8, 9, 12, 15, 16–17, 59, 280, 288
  agitation against 45–6, 61, 254
  cattle driving 101–2, 144; UIL victories 37–8; boycotted 128, 130–1; Craughwell campaign 66–9; deputations to 249–50; intimidation 32, 39, 65, 289
  block redistribution 23–4, 29
  Catholic 19, 290
  CDB lets land to 239–40, 243, 248
  definitions 17–18
  Galway 4–5

graziers (*cont.*):
  and Land Acts 16–17
  land prices 247–8
  and landlords 19–20
  political interests 290–2
  Protestant 290
  Ranch War 85–6
  shopkeepers as 149–50
  Sinn Féin opposition to 115, 241–3,
    246, 257
  in tenants' movement 25
  types of 15–19
  in UIL 233, 236
  UIL opposition to 125, 127, 129,
    135–6
grazing system 247–8
  abolition sought 127
  Ranch War 99–102
  redistribution sought 146–7, 169,
    177–8, 243–5
  scarcity of 55–6
  seizures of 280
  see also untenanted land
Great Famine 13–14, 19, 25–6, 29
Great Southern and Western Railway
    162
Great War, *see* First World War
Greene, Gerard 77
Greene, William 77 n
Gregory, Augusta Lady 76, 274 n, 275
Gregory, Margaret 274–8
Gregory, Robert 274 n
Griffin, John 234
Griffin, Father Michael 271–3
Griffin, Thomas George 149–50, 151–3,
    164, 271
Griffith, Arthur 168–9, 173, 190
  agrarian policy 240–1, 246, 254–5
  and physical force 170
Gurteen, county Galway 13, 94 n, 149–
    50, 176, 231
  secret society 179, 188
  UIL factions 151–3, 164

Gurtymadden, county Galway 188
Gwynn, Stephen 234

Habeas Corpus Suspension Act 230
Hallinan, Martin 155–64
Hanlon, Michael 266
Hannay, J. O. 20 n
Hardiman, Volunteer 221–2
Harrel, David 60 n, 72
Harrington, Tim 43
Harris, Matthew 18, 24–5, 43–4, 147, 189
Hart, Peter 226, 232, 257–8, 263, 264,
    285
Hartnett, John 138
Hastings, William 65
Hastings Jones, Captain Henry 90–1
Haverty, James 180, 194
Hayden, J. P. 106, 110
Headford, county Galway 248, 252, 280 n
Healy, Morgan 194
Healy, Tim 40, 110
Hegarty, T. 16
Hepburn, A. C. 109, 293 n
Herd, District Inspector 212
Hession, Mr 134–5
Hicks Beach, Michael 70, 72–3, 82
historiography 287–304
  Land War 287–9
Hobsbawm, Eric 2, 293
Hobson, Bulmer 122, 169–70, 186,
    192–3
Hogan, James 258
Hogan, Martin 138
Hogan, Patrick 232, 258, 282–3
Holland, P. J. 182 n
Hollypark, county Galway 177 n
Holycross, county Tipperary 115
Home Rule Bill 1912, 192, 198, 221,
    237–8
Home Rule movement 40, 123, 189,
    225, 227, 271
  and agrarian campaign 43–4
  Bill (1893) 108

constructive unionism against 83–4
and Irish Council Bill 109–10, 295
Liberal failure 107, 110–11, 170
and Sinn Féin 113, 118, 166, 167–8,
    297–8
and UIL 235–6, 237
Hoppen, K. T. 297
Hosty, John 205
Houlihan, Captain Patrick 275
House of Commons 44, 72–3, 84, 189–
    90
    IPP obstruction 73
    IPP withdrawal sought 168–9
    Wyndham Bill opposed 75
    see also abstention
House of Lords veto 123, 189
housing 11–12
Houston, Captain 23–4, 29
Howard, Henry 250
Howard, James 250–1
Howley, Joe 210
Howley, Peter 193, 198, 208, 271
Howley, William 193, 194
Hue and Cry 172 n
Hughes, grazier 65
Hungary 168
Hussey, Thomas 243, 267
Hutcheson, James 264–6
Hynes, Frank 201, 207, 213–14
Hynes, Thomas 157–60, 190–1, 199

industry 27–8, 230, 236
Inspector General, RIC, reports of 67,
    106
    boycotting 139–40
    Easter Rising 299
    intimidation 141–2, 145
    no-rent campaigns 93
    Ranch War 97, 100, 103, 107
    recruitment 196, 197
    rent combinations 97–8
    Sinn Féin 117, 118, 171
    UIL 104, 124, 132

Volunteers 195, 200
Wyndham Land Act 86, 87, 89–90
Intelligence Notes 6, 223–4
intimidation 38, 39, 65, 76, 80, 106, 124,
    139
    1920 campaign 249–53
    Craughwell 155–6
    Galway secret society 178–9, 182–4
    of grabbers 60
    of graziers 289
    proclamation 71–2, 82
    prosecutions 66–9, 74
    serious violence 251–3
    of Sinn Féin 114
    by UEC 183–4
    by UIL 32–3, 141–5
    War of Independence 264–8
Invincibles 166, 175, 176
Irish Council Bill 1906, 107–12, 118, 122,
    170, 171 n, 190, 295
Irish Farmers' Union 300, 301
Irish Free State 6, 232, 282–3, 286
Irish Freedom 176
Irish Independent 36
Irish Land Trust 76
Irish Landlords' Convention 13 n
Irish language 4, 201 n, 219, 233, 235
Irish Law Times and Solicitor's Journal
    73, 79
Irish National Federation (INF) 29–30,
    31, 35
Irish National Foresters 110 n
Irish National Land League, *see* Land
    League
Irish National League, *see* National
    League
Irish Office 62, 63, 64, 72, 120, 294
    coercion 73–4
    and land reform 81–3
    and Wyndham 70–2
Irish Parliamentary Party (IPP) 5, 63,
    192
    abstention sought 115–16, 168–9

Irish Parliamentary Party (IPP) (*cont.*):
  agrarian policy 96, 106–7, 116, 117,
    118, 119–20; during Great War
    237–8; opposes agitation 86–7;
    split 104–5
  compulsory purchase campaign 59
  conciliation policy 294–6
  and Easter Rising 221
  elections: (1918) 166; Leitrim by-
    election 113–14
  funding 44, 45
  historiography of 293
  and Irish Council Bill 108–12, 170;
    resignations 112–13
  and Land Acts 75; 1909, 122–3, 185,
    189; Wyndham Act 69–70, 73, 80,
    92–3
  membership 35
  Parnell split 28–9, 30, 40, 42, 45
  Sinn Féin threat to 116–19, 122–3,
    223, 295
  and UIL 42–5, 75, 129–30, 235–6, 236
  and Volunteers 195–6
Irish People 42, 58, 60, 62
Irish Republican Army (IRA) 248, 249,
    255, 256
  agrarian agitation 258–9, 281, 283–4,
    302–3
  Connacht 3
  Galway: under Murphy 269–71;
    reorganization 273–5
  informers shot 272
  membership 7, 259–62; age 261(t),
    262; cross-class appeal 263; social
    composition 262–4, 278, 284
  War of Independence 257–79, 285
Irish Republican Brotherhood (IRB)
    35, 94 n, 115, 117, 180, 222, 230, 245
  Craughwell 155, 157–60, 162, 219
  and Cumann na nGaedheal 169
  and Galway secret society 182, 185–8
  Kenny in 173–7
  physical force 170

rebellion plans 200–3
  in Sinn Féin 171–2
  Supreme Council 172, 173, 186, 231 n
  and UIL 35–6, 145–8, 164
  and Volunteers 192–3, 194, 199
  see also Easter Rising (1916)
Irish Times 50–1, 156
Irish Transport and General Workers'
    Union (ITGWU) 282, 300
Irish Unionist Alliance 72
Irish Unionist Press 73
Irish Volunteers 200–3, 242, 255, 258–9,
    267, 268
  clerical support of 204–5
  established 192–3
  flying columns 269
  in Galway 193–5
  in-fighting 270
  internment 218, 222
  and IPP 195–6
  membership 7, 192, 218–19
  numbers in Galway 203
  social composition 230
  split 196–200
  see also Easter Rising (1916); IRA
Island townland, county Mayo 9

Jackson, Mr 250
Johnston, Robert 169 n
Johnstone, Denis 109, 114
Jones, David 14, 124
Jordan, Michael 265
Jordan, Patrick 194
Jordan, Stephen 115, 182 n, 183, 194, 203,
    237
Joyce, Father 152 n
Joyce, J. B., 291 n
Joyce, Michael 110
Joyce, Patrick 272
Joyce, Walter 141
Joyce, William 272 n
Joyce family 4
juries 74

Keary, Michael 265
Keely, Thomas 275, 276
Kells Poor Law Union 14
Kelly, James 66–7, 68
Kelly, Laurence 263
Kelly, Michael 194, 208, 209, 216–17, 220
Kelly, Paddy 267
Kelly, P. J. 22, 147–8, 173, 263
Kelly, Rev 23
Kelly-Mor, Michael Francis 272–3
Kenny, Mr, of Eyrecourt 245
Kenny, Thomas J. 115 n, 116
Kenny, Tom 245
    and Catholic church 179, 181–2
    Craughwell faction 155–64; Goldrick murder trial 190–1
    Easter Rising 200–1, 207, 214, 215, 218, 219–20
    Galway secret society 174–6, 179–82, 190–2, 222, 224, 225, 244
    and Mellows 201–2
    in Sinn Féin 172–6, 185–8
    in Volunteers 194–5, 205
Kerry, county 10 n, 171, 247 n, 254, 258
Kettle, Tom 110
Kettrick, Thomas 273
Kilbeacanty, county Galway 132, 245, 262
Kilbeg, county Galway 265
Kilchreest, county Galway 136, 137, 188, 244
Kilclooney, county Galway 14
Kilcolgan, county Galway 188, 208 n
Kilconieron, county Galway 177 n, 211
Kilconnell, county Galway 253
Kildare, county 12, 43, 46, 107
Kileelly, county Galway 160
Kilfenora, county Clare 144
Kilkenny, county 185 n
Kilkenny People 60 n
Killacloher, county Galway 264–5
Killeen, county Longford 143

Killeen, Thomas 151
Killeenadeema, county Galway 147–8, 173, 263
Killeeneen, county Galway 205, 207, 208, 209
Killimordaly, county Galway 266
Kilmaclasser, county Mayo 33–4
Kilmaine, county Mayo 60, 251
Kilmainham jail 36
Kilmeen, county Galway 250
Kilmeena, county Mayo 35
Kilmorey, Lord 50
Kilreekle, county Galway 125, 135, 171, 188 n, 189
Kiltartan, county Galway 277–8
Kiltormer, county Galway 164
Kiltulla, county Galway 188
Kiltullagh, county Galway 212
King, Paddy 265
King, Sheila 212
King's county (Offaly) 3, 102, 107, 115, 185 n, 189 n
Kinvara, county Galway 158 n, 179, 204, 205, 208
Kirby, Mr 128 n
Knappogue, county Longford 143

Labasheeda, county Clare 20
labour movement 284, 299–301
labourers 233, 247–9, 249, 300
    in IRA 259, 260(t), 261(t), 263
    in Sinn Féin 227–30
Labourers' Act 106 n
lace school 28
Laffan, Michael 227, 280, 283, 292, 300
Lally, Robert 265
Lally, Thomas 265
Lambert estate 116
Land Act (1881) 16–17, 59, 92, 289, 292
    effects of 48, 50–6
Land Act (1891) 26
Land Act (1896) 93

Land Act (1903), *see* Wyndham Land
    Act
Land Act (1923) 90, 286
Land Act (1933) 286
Land Act (1909) (Birrell Act) 10 n,
    120–2, 184–5, 189, 238–9, 286, 304
Land Acts 1, 2, 220
land annuities 304 n
Land Bill (1913) 238
Land Bill (1920) 247 n
land clearance 13–15
Land Commission 26, 48, 51, 55, 99,
    302 n
    dissolved 303
Land Conference (1880) 25
Land Conference (1902) 78, 83, 87, 89,
    92, 96, 295, 296
Land Conferences (1920) 255–7, 283,
    284
land courts 16–17, 48, 54
    Sinn Féin 255–7
    in Wyndham Bill 73
    see also UIL, courts
Land League 3, 5, 18, 30, 61, 176, 193,
    204, 253, 288
    and bourgeoisie 149
    courts 126, 132, 135
    eviction aid 35
    influence on UIL 37
    intimidation 142
    and IRB 145–6, 147
    redistribution sought 24–5
land purchase, compulsory 41, 44, 106,
    116, 286, 290–1
    agitation 3, 57–63, 75, 289; east
        Galway 64–9
    CDB powers 121–2
    under Land Acts 54–5, 121;
        Wyndham Act 69–79, 80, 81, 82–
        4, 87–90, 90, 103–4, 295
    and landlords 77
    no-rent agitation 95–9
    prices 88–90, 103–4

and Ranch War 102–4
    slow pace of 238–9
    UIL campaign 47–50, 127, 130–1
Land Purchase Acts 51, 53, 130
land purchase agencies (Sinn Féin)
    243–4
land redistribution 1–2, 5, 24–6, 43,
    280, 284
    agitation (1920) 248–9, 287
    auctions boycotted 33
    blocked 23–4, 29
    church support 36
    Dáil control 280–1, 284
    effects of Ranch War 103
    effects of Wyndham Act 87–8, 289–
        90
    Galway secret society aim 177–8
    IRA aim 264–8
    IRB aim 146–7
    pace of 238–9
    Sinn Féin aim 241–3, 243–4, 246,
        256–7
    Sinn Féin land courts 255–7
    statistics 1921, 286
    UIL aim 28, 30–1, 38–9, 127–8
Land Settlement Commission 255, 256,
    257
land stock, payment in 121
land valuation 6, 273
Land War 19, 58, 85, 149, 268, 280, 301,
    303
    effects of 16, 59
    historiography of 287–9
    IRB faction 146–7
    no land redistribution 25–6
    rent combinations 96
landlords 4, 9, 59, 280
    and 1881 Land Act 48, 50–2, 53, 54,
        56
    abolition sought 127
    boycotting of 141
    and graziers 15, 19–20, 52, 53
    historiography of 287–9

intimidation 289–90
IPP conciliation 294–6
IRB attacks 145
land conference (1902) 76–8, 89, 92, 96
and land purchase 27, 78, 86
and local authorities 39
and 'no-rent' campaign 62–3
payment in land stock 121
religion of 288
UIL campaign against 84; courts 129, 135–6
and Wyndham Act 69, 73, 79, 87–92, 96–8, 131
Landowners' Convention 79
Laois, county, *see* Queen's county
Lardner, Lawrence 115, 176, 182 n, 194, 199, 203, 267
Easter Rising 206, 207, 211, 214, 218
and Mellows 201
large farmers:
Craughwell factions 162–4
and IRA 259, 260(t), 261(t), 262, 263
and SF 246
and UIL 148–51, 235
Larkin, Jim 181 n
Larkin, Patrick 164
Law, Hugh 110
Leech, Mary 204, 273
Leinster 45, 46, 104, 185 n, 247 n
congested districts 92 n
labour movement 300–1
rent combinations 97
Sinn Féin activity 170–1
strikes 282
UIL councillors 62
War of Independence 258
Wyndham Act 90
Leitrim, county 10 n, 102, 112, 171, 185 n
agitation (1920) 247 n, 251
by-election (1908) 113–14
rent combinations 97–8
Leitrim Guardian 113

Letterfrack, county Galway 10, 27–8, 237
Lewin, Lt-Colonel 251
Lewin, Thomas 251
Lewis Estate 244
Liberal Party 117, 119, 120, 122, 295
Home Rule commitment 123, 189
Home Rule failure 107, 110–11, 170
Irish Council Bill 107–12
Lickerrig, county Galway 244–5
Limepark, county Galway 136, 216–18, 273
Limerick, county 138–9, 158, 159, 185 n, 216, 232 n
War of Independence 258
Limerick Leader 60 n
Lisdoonvarna, county Clare 144
Lisdurra, county Galway 244
Lismanny, county Galway 14
Lismore, county Longford 143
Literary Revival, Irish 56
local government 231, 232
Dáil control 279
nationalist influence 39–40
Sinn Féin control 167
and UIL 61–2, 236–7
Local Government, Dáil Department of 279
Local Government Board 107–8
Local Government (Ireland) Act (1898) 39
Londonderry, county 264
Londonderry, Lord 79
Longford, county 107, 112, 143, 185 n, 225 n
by-election (1917) 283 n
War of Independence 258
Longford Leader 60 n, 143
Lough Corrib 4, 252, 281
Loughnane brothers 278
Loughrea, county Galway 4, 13, 27, 148, 156, 233
agrarian agitation 64–9

Loughrea, county Galway (*cont.*):
  Easter Rising 208–9, 221
  IRB activity 147, 172
  National League court 132–3
  secret society 188, 189, 191
  Sinn Féin activity 171, 237, 242, 245
  UIL activity 135–8, 192
  Volunteers 195, 199, 202
  War of Independence 268
Loughrea and Athenry Guardian 65
Louth, county 171
Lucan, Earl of 23–4
Lundon, William 20
Lynam, James 35, 65
Lynd, Robert 249
Lyons, F. S. L. 83
Lysaght, Edward 293 n

MacBride, Major John 40, 94 n, 169 n,
    172, 174, 176–7, 186, 200
  and Kenny 187–8
McCabe, Alex 243
McCann family 283 n
McCarthy, Tim 62
McCormack, Dr Francis J., Bishop of
    Galway and Kilmacduagh 137
McCreery, Lt 274–7
McCullough, Denis 169, 186
MacDermott, Sean 176–7, 186, 192–3,
    207
McDonagh, Máirtín Mór 178–9, 206,
    234
MacDonnell, Anthony 85, 111
McDonnell, Peter 209
MacDonnell, P. S. 234
MacEvilly, Dr, Archbishop of Tuam 36
McGloin, Constable 265
machinery 27, 31
McHugh 113
McInerney, Thomas 208
McKean, J. H. 110
Macken, Peter 193 n
McKenna, Myles 114

MacNeill, Eoin 192, 193, 196, 197, 199
  Easter Rising 205, 206, 298, 299
Madden, Judge 158, 159
Maguire, Conor 255
Maguire, Tom 249
Mahon, John 151
Mahon estate 90
Mallon, John 175 n
Malone, Patrick 156, 157
Manchester Guardian 1
Manning, Constable David 210 n
Manning, Michael 198
Manorhamilton, county Leitrim 113
Manton, J. 125
Manton, Mr 135
Maree, county Galway 208, 210, 211
Martin, Harris 143
Martin, Thomas 181
Masonbrook, county Galway 242
Maume, Patrick 40
Maune, Patt 138
Mayo, county 3, 9, 10 n, 14, 15, 21, 29, 55,
    70, 90, 185 n
  agrarian agitation 62, 100 n, 102,
    283–4; (1920) 247 n, 249, 251, 253
  by-election (1899) 40
  crime levels 37
  famine (1897–8) 30
  graziers 150
  IRA activity 264
  poverty 9, 27
  redistribution blocked 23–4, 29
  Sinn Féin activity 243
  UIL activity 32, 33–5, 36, 38–9; courts
    128–9
Mayo News 23–4, 29, 34, 60 n
Meagher, Michael 110
Meath, county 12, 14, 43, 46, 101, 107,
    185 n, 247 n
Meehan, F. E. 113
Mellows, Liam 200–2, 203–4
  Easter Rising 206, 207–18
Menlough, county Galway 264

middle classes 230
Midland Tribune 60 n
migratory labour 10–11
Military History, Bureau of 7, 77–8, 173, 180, 194, 269, 272–3
Millmount farm, county Galway 136
Milroy, Sean 186
Moffett, Constable 181
Mogan, grazier 250
Molloy, Brian 182 n, 209
Molloy, Captain 212
Monaghan, Alfred 194, 200, 206–7, 215
Monatigue, county Galway 178–9, 234, 267 n
Moneylending, Departmental Committee on 22
Monivea, county Galway 188, 264
Moorfield, county Galway 250
Moorpark, county Galway 252
Morning Post 71
Morris, Mr 273
Morrissey, Gilbert 162, 172, 177–8, 194, 208, 268
Morrissey, Patrick 178
Mount Bellew, county Galway 180 n, 194, 195, 208–9
Mountjoy jail 159
Moycullen, county Galway 209
Moylan, Sean 283–4
Moylough, county Galway 180
Moyode Castle 213–16
Moyode estate 136 n, 244–5
Moyvilla, county Galway 188
Mulcahy, Dr 112
Mullagh, county Galway 171, 198, 208–9
Munster 45, 46, 90, 185 n, 286, 295
  agrarian agitation 97, 102, 104, 247 n
  congested districts 92 n
  IRA activity 264
  labour movement 282, 300–1
  Sinn Féin activity 170
  UIL activity 61, 125, 128, 131

War of Independence 258
Munster Express 60 n
Murphy, Dick 172, 176, 182 n
Murphy, J. 110
Murphy, Seamus 269–71
Murray, Martin 266
Murrisk, county Mayo 31

National Council 169–70
National Land Bank 257
National League 25, 29, 44, 65, 235
  courts 126, 132–3
National Volunteers 196–7, 198, 203, 215
nationalism 2
  agrarian agitation: Ranch War 85–123
  and agrarian agitation 3, 5, 53, 69, 286–7, 303–4
  cross-class support 254
  declining interest (1909–13) 189–92
  effects of Easter Rising 296–9
  effects of Great War 200
  Galway (1905–18) 166–225
  grazier participation 290–2
  historiography 295
  and Irish Council Bill 108–12
  social composition 231–2, 285
  and UIL 39–41, 70
  Wyndham's opinion of 70
Naughton, Bartley 158–9
Naughton, Volunteer 198
Neilan (Niland), Mattie (Martin) 207–8, 215
'New Departure' 145–6
New Inn, county Galway 148, 188, 243, 266
'New Tipperary' 62–3
Newbridge, county Galway 65
Newcastle, county Galway 211
Newell, A. C. 159 n
Newell, John 175
Newell, Martin 77–8, 157, 162, 172 n, 173, 194, 210

Newell, Martin (*cont.*):
  on Bourke murder 175–6
  Easter Rising 213, 215, 219–20
  on Kenny 186–7, 191 n
Newell, Michael 182, 212
Newell, Ned 210
Newell, Tom 212
newspapers 71, 109
  names of boycotted persons 60–1,
    65
  UIL court decisions 134–5
Nicholls, George 193, 194, 202, 203, 231
  n, 232
  Easter Rising 205, 206, 209
Niland, Thomas 181
Nolan, Joseph 110
Nowlan, Jim 188

Ó Cadhain, Máirtín 4 n
Ó Droighneáin, Mícheál 205 n, 209,
  221–2
Ó Fathaigh, Pádraig 201, 202 n, 203,
  208
Ó Gráda, Cormac 293
Ó Maille, Padraic 190
O'Brien, Dermot 144
O'Brien, William 6, 22, 25–6, 39–40,
  120, 127
  and CDB 31–2
  compulsory purchase campaign 57–
    63
  conciliation 93, 131, 148
  and IPP 42, 44
  opposes agitation 62–3, 104–5
  parliamentary campaign 129–30
  and UIL: expansion of 45, 47;
    foundation 28–30, 35, 36–7;
    funding 34
  and Wyndham Act 75, 93, 96–8
O'Byrne, Dr 272
O'Callaghan, John 119
O'Connor, Arthur 256
O'Connor, Emmet 299–300

O'Connor, Sergeant 68
O'Connor, T. P. 40
O'Dea, Dr Thomas, Bishop of Galway
  179, 181, 253
O'Dea, Louis 231 n
O'Donnell, John 22, 35, 40, 60, 110
O'Donnell, Peadar 302, 303
O'Donnell, Thomas 110, 112
O'Dowd, John 110
O'Duffy, Eoin 186
O'Farrell, Father 216
Offaly, county, *see* King's county
O'Flanagan, Father Michael 241
O'Hegarty, P. S. 190, 287, 288, 296, 297,
  298
O'Higgins, Kevin 227
O'Kelly, Conor 60
O'Leary, John 169 n
O'Loughlin, Father 152 n
O'Malley, Peter 23
O'Malley, William 110, 190, 237
O'Mara, James 110, 112
O'Meehan, Fr John William 204, 205,
  208, 256, 272, 273
O'Neill, Seán 149 n, 259, 262
O'Rahilly, The 193, 202
Orangeism 46
Oranmore, county Galway 179, 188,
  208, 210–12
O'Reilly, William 182 n
Ormsby estate 116
O'Shea, Katharine 5, 28
O'Shee, J. J. 110
O'Shiel, Kevin 246–9, 252–5, 280, 285
O'Toole, Lawrence (Lorcan) 186, 188
Oughterard, county Galway 23,
  249–50

Parliament Act (1911) 123
Parnell, Anna 114
Parnell, Charles Stewart 5, 28, 44, 59,
  73, 114, 288, 294–5
Partry, county Mayo 11

Paul-Dubois, Louis 8–9
Peace Preservation Act (1881) 59
Pearse, Patrick 193, 205 n, 206, 207, 209
Pelly, Father Joseph Alfred 14, 24
Persse, Harry 135–8
Persse, Major 213, 244
Peterswell, county Galway 188, 216
Plan of Campaign 35, 58, 62, 63, 65, 81, 85
  rent combinations 96
Plunkett, Joseph M. 240–1
policing, *see* Royal Irish Constabulary
Pollock, Alan 14
Pomfret, J. E. 287
Poor Law Unions 14–15, 30
Portumna, county Galway 19, 106
poverty 8–11, 20–1, 25–6
Power, John 134
Prendergast and others v *Hyland and Murphy* 280–1
professional classes 228(t)
  in Sinn Féin 231–2, 233
  in UIL 234
property, threat to 302
Protection of Person and Property (Ireland) Act (1881) 147, 149–50
Protestants:
  employment of 231
  as graziers 19, 290
Provisional Government 6, 282–3
Public Record Office, London 6

Queen's county (Laois) 102, 185 n, 247 n, 291
Quinn, Father 179, 180 n
Quinn, Mrs Ellen 277–8

Raffalovich, Sofie 34
Rahassane county Galway 77–8, 175
Ranch War (1904–8) 3, 99–102, 115, 185, 240, 241, 286
  aims of 85–6

assessment of 290–1
beginnings 93–5
cattle driving 101–2, 174
effects of 102–5
extent of 97–9
historiography of 289, 293, 294–6
and IPP 118, 119–20, 122–3
and nationalist politics (1904–10) 85–123
need for legislation 120–1
and Sinn Féin 117–18
ranching system 19–20
rates 160
Rathfaran, county Galway 250
Rearden, Mr 138
Rebellion, Royal Commission on the 218
Reddy, Michael 106
Redmond, John 6, 40, 70, 75, 104–5, 107, 108, 195, 288
  and 1909 Land Act 122
  agrarian policy 86–7, 116, 118, 119–20, 286, 295–6
  Birrell on 120
  compulsory purchase campaign 57–61, 106
  conciliation policy 93, 131, 294–6
  Leitrim by-election 113–14
  opposes abstention 112
  and UIL 42–3, 45
  and Volunteers 195–6, 198
  and Wyndham Act 80, 93
Redmond, Willie 60
Regan, John 279, 300
Reidy, Thomas 205
Reilly, Michael 245, 262
Reilly, Mr 273
rent combinations 86, 94–9, 100, 103, 290, 291, 293
  beginnings, 94–5
  number of 97–9
  Sinn Féin policy 240

rents 11
  agitation against 62–3
  determination of 48, 51, 52, 73, 79,
    130; land courts 54
  no-rent campaigns 76, 116, 130, 183;
    see also rent combinations
  and Ranch War 85–6
  untenanted land 90–1
  withholding tactic 93–4
Republican Labour 231 n
Resident Magistrates 74
revolution, Irish 2
  historiography of 296–304
  nature of 226–7
  social component 279–85
Ribbonmen 174, 189
roads 27, 31
Roche, John 65, 94, 148, 152
Rockfield, county Galway 199, 208, 211
  Volunteers 194–5
Rodney estate 116
Rohan, Kevin 152 n
Rooney, William 169
Roscommon, county 3, 10 n, 14, 60, 70,
    140, 185 n
  agitation (1920) 247 n, 248, 251, 252,
    253, 280, 281
  by-election (1917) 241
  cattle driving 102
  landlords attacked 145
  no-rent campaign 62
  Ranch War 93–4, 100 n, 107
  rent combinations 97–8
  Sinn Féin activity 242, 243, 255–6
  War of Independence 258
Roscommon Herald 243
Roscommon Messenger 60 n
Roscrea, county Tipperary 267
Rosmuc, county Galway 158
Ross estate 250
Rosscahill, county Galway 250
Roxborough estate, county Galway
    136 n

Royal Commissions 1, 2, 7
Royal Irish Constabulary (RIC) 6,
    46 n, 178, 205
  and agrarian agitation 95, 103, 248,
    249; barracks attacked 268 n;
    cattle driving 144, 174
  and Catholic clergy 180–1
  Craughwell 66–9, 162
  Easter Rising 206, 209–15, 215, 298–9
  on Galway secret society 175, 188–9
  on IPP 295
  IRA ambushes 264–6
  IRB statistics 146
  on Kenny 173, 186–7, 190–2
  murders of 156–60, 274–8
  police protection 104
  and Sinn Féin 171–2, 245
  and UIL 33, 37, 39–40, 71, 125–6
  and Volunteers 199
  War of Independence 270–1
  see also County Inspectors;
    Inspector General
Ruane, Tom 213
Rumpf, Erhard 258
rundale 53, 56
Russell, T. W. 47–9, 84
Ryan, Anthony 68
Ryan, Brigid 274–5
Ryan, Daniel 275, 276
Ryan, Mrs Mary 153–6, 160
Ryan, Michael 138, 156

Saunders, Agent 138
Scotland 11, 12, 19
  Sinn Féin in 170
  tenants from 15–16, 31
Scott, C. P. 1
secret societies 70, 145–6, 174–5, 181,
    224–5
Sharkey, Frank 143
Shaw-Tener, Edward 136
Shawe-Taylor, Frank 18, 19, 77, 252,
    253, 266–7

Shawe-Taylor, Captain John 76–8, 83, 84, 135–7, 138, 294
Sheehy, David 101, 102, 106, 113, 114
shop assistants 231, 232
shopkeepers 33, 232
  economic power of 21–4
  as graziers 17, 19, 20–1
  in Sinn Féin 230
  in UIL 145, 148–51, 233–4, 235, 236
Silke, Tim 152
Sinn Féin 2, 94 n, 185, 188, 272
  abstentionism 110
  agrarian policy 221, 223–4, 237, 240–6, 286–7, 298, 301–2; Connacht (1920) 249, 254–5; land courts 255–7
  convention (1917) 245–6
  courts 126, 167, 286
  cross-class support 246, 254
  decline (1909–13) 189–92
  and Easter Rising 220–5, 297–8
  elections 113–14, 166–7, 220, 227, 235–8
  expansion 114–18, 170–1, 220
  Galway 166–225, 222–4, 291, 301 n
  and Galway secret society 191
  and IRA 262
  land purchase agencies 243–4
  literature 117–18
  membership 7, 112–13, 122, 164–5, 171–2, 222–4, 298; age groups 235; social composition 227–33, 291
  policies of 168–9
  post-revolution settlement 282–3
  threat to IPP 116–19, 122–3, 223, 295
  and UIL 164–5, 166, 167–8, 291
  and Volunteers 192, 194, 199, 200, 218
  War of Independence 278
  women members 232 n
Sinn Féin 111, 112, 113, 170, 190
Sinn Féin clubs 117, 160, 170–1, 173, 241
  land purchase agencies 243–4

numbers decline 189–90
Skehana, county Galway 264–5
Slieve Aughty mountains 3
Sligo, county 10 n, 70, 90, 154, 185 n, 243
  agitation (1920) 247 n, 251
  cattle driving 174
  no-rent campaign 62
  Ranch War 100 n, 102
  rent combinations 97–8
  trials 37
Sligo, Lord 23–4, 58
Sligo Champion 60 n, 61
small farmers 27, 49, 86, 92 n, 240–1, 249, 288
  as 'breeders' 12–13
  CDB aid to 26–8, 122
  Craughwell factions 162–4
  intimidation of 33, 141
  in IRA 259, 260(t), 261(t), 262, 263
  poverty of 10–11, 25–6
  radical politics 301
  in Sinn Féin 227–30, 232
  in UIL 145–8, 153, 235, 237
Smith, James, 265, 290 n
Smith, J. V. 151–2
Smith-Barry, Arthur Hugh 62 n, 76
Smiths, the 151–2, 265, 290 n
Smyth, J. J. 242
social mobility 231
social revolution 57, 226–7
socialism 181, 215
South African war 51
Special Infantry Corps 282–3
Spectator 20
Spelman, Bernard 140–1
Spiddal, county Galway 209
Springlawn, county Galway 180
Stack, Austin 186, 241, 256, 284
Stanford, Joseph 275, 276
Staunton, Lynch 280 n
Steele, E. D. 287
Steinberger, Dr 231 n
Stenson, John and Mrs 174

Stephenson, Thomas 135
strike activity 282, 299–300
students 228(t), 231, 260(t), 261(t), 263
Sturge, Sophia 28 n
Sullivan, A. M. 159
Sullivan, Serjeant 161
Swinford, county Mayo 42, 89
Sylaun, county Galway 267
Synge, John Millington 1

t-Óglach, An 176
Tallaroe farm, Craughwell, county
    Galway 67–8
Tample, county Galway 94 n, 151, 152–3
Tannian, Micky 265
tariffs 169
Taylor's Hill, county Galway 271
Templemartin, county Galway 154,
    155–6
tenant farmers 4–5, 13, 291
    and compulsory land purchase 49–
    50
    divisions among 288, 289–92, 301
    effects of 1881 Act 54–5, 56
    and Home Rule 43–4
    in UIL 33–4, 145
tenants 121
    and 1881 Land Act 48, 53–5
    imported 15–16
    instalments 78, 79, 82
    in UIL 35–6
    and Wyndham Land Act 69, 87–8
Terry Alts 174–5
Thompson, E. P. 2, 293
Thornton, Pádraig 209
Thrashers 126, 174
threatening letters 250
Thurles, county Tipperary 115, 139
Tiaquin, county Galway 152 n
tillage, compulsory 242
tillage agitation 242
Tilly, Charles 226
Times, The 71, 76, 78, 257

Tipperary, county 3, 62 n, 70, 185 n,
    189 n
    agrarian agitation 100 n, 102, 107,
    247 n
    IRA activity 264
    Sinn Féin activity 115, 171, 190
    War of Independence 258
Tipperary Champion 60 n
Tonlagee, county Roscommon 102
Tottenham, Colonel 144
Town Tenants' League (TTL) 115–16,
    171 n, 182–3, 188, 194
Townshend, Charles 297
tradesmen 230, 232
Tralee, county Kerry 205
trials, venue of 74
Tuam, county Galway 4, 231, 251, 267
    IRA activity 259
    secret society 166, 221, 224, 245
    Sinn Féin activity 171
    UIL activity 147
    War of Independence 268
Tuam, diocese of 36
Tulla Poor Law Union 14
Tullamore, King's county 115
Tully, Father 210
Tully, H. J. 250
Tullyra, county Galway 166, 175, 208
turf-cutting rights 53
Turk, Sean 269
Turlough, county Mayo 21
Turloughmore, county Galway 147,
    179, 188
Tycooley, county Galway 164
Tynagh, county Galway 244
Tynan, P. J., 175 n
Tyrone, county 247 n
Tyrone House, Clarinbridge 175

Uí Coincheannain, Mhiceáil 217
Ulster 40, 45, 90, 185 n, 247 n
    congested districts 51, 92 n
    IRA activity 264

Ranch War 104
sectarianism 46
Sinn Féin activity 170–1
strikes 282
UIL councillors 62
War of Independence 258
Ulster Volunteer Force (UVF) 192
unionism 83–4, 123
United Estates Committee (UEC)
94 n, 183–4, 185, 188
United Irish League (UIL) 2, 3, 5, 26,
52, 53, 56, 80, 119, 134, 189, 290,
301 n
agrarian policy 106, 184–5, 238, 240,
286–7, 291; boycotting 139–43;
intimidation 74, 141–5; legitimate
targets 241; official and unofficial
96–7; Ranch War 85–123, 117;
strategies 32–3, 37–9
aims of 28, 30–1, 127–8
and Birrell Act 122
branch activity 66–9, 75, 122, 124
and CDB 239
Chamberlain on 63–4
clerical support 181
Constitution and rules 43, 127, 129
corruption in 150
courts 124–65, 131, 145, 160, 162;
Loughrea 135–8; procedures 132–
5; used by bourgeoisie 151–3
east Galway case study 64–9
Easter Rising 215
expansion 45–7, 61
funding 34, 44
and Galway secret society 184, 188,
191–2
'grazier' defined 18
and IPP 42–5, 129–30
and IRB 145–8
and Irish Council Bill 109
Land Bill campaign 74–8
land purchase policy 47–50, 57–63
local leaders 34–5

membership 7, 30(t), 33–6, 145–50;
age groups 235; Galway 291; no
women 232 n; numbers 87, 104,
113, 170, 189; shopkeepers 22–3;
social composition 227, 230,
233–7
national convention (1900) 42
National Directory 74–5, 184–5
nationalist support 39–41
'no-rent' campaigns 62–3, 130
organizers 146
parliamentarianism 235–6
political influence 39–41
Provincial Directory 127–8
rules 127–8
and Sinn Féin 112–13, 118, 164–5, 167–
8, 173, 174, 177, 222
structures 297, 298
threat to tenant farmers 55
and Volunteers 195
and Wyndham Act 80, 81, 82–4, 86–
8, 131, 294
Wyndham on 70
United Irishman 36, 110–11, 168
United Irishmen 30
United States of America (USA) 10, 45
emigration to 152, 153–4, 155, 175
escapes to 218
UIL in 110 n, 119
University College, Dublin (UCD) 192
University College, Galway (UCG) 231
untenanted land 2, 86
cattle driving 102
CDB acquisitions 121–2, 239–40
clearances 13–15
redistribution sought 127–8
eleven-months system 52, 53
extent of 10
investment in 54–5
market restrictions 19
pressure on graziers 129, 289
prices 90–1
rent combinations 100

untenanted land (*cont.*):
  rents 90–1
  sales 27, 87–8, 238–9
  Sinn Féin purchases 244
  and Wyndham Act 79, 87–8, 131
usurers 24 n

valuations 7, 9 n, 48, 273
Varley, Tony 301
Vaughan, W. E. 292
Voice of Labour, The 282

Wales 218
Walsh, Dr Thomas 231 n
Walshe, Hubert 201, 207
War of Independence 3, 285
  agrarian agitation 254–5, 301–3
  Ballyturin ambush 274–8
  casualty figures 274(t), 279
  chronology, Galway 312–15
  Galway IRA 257–79
War Office 216
Ward, Martin 154, 164
Waterford, county 139, 247 n
Waterford, Marquis of 76
Waterford News 60 n
Waterford Star 60 n
Weekly Freeman 60, 88
Western News 60 n, 65
Western People 60 n
Westmeath, county 12, 46, 107, 185 n,
  247 n, 258
Westport, county Mayo 28, 47, 59, 62,
  127
  Poor Law Union 9, 30, 128 n

Wexford, county 46, 117, 171, 190, 264
Whelan, Constable 212
White, Patrick 112
Whiteboys 126
Wills-Sandford estate 93–4
Winder, District Inspector 46
Woodenbridge, county Wicklow 196,
  199
Woodfield, county Galway 250
Woodford, county Galway 10, 19, 27,
  65, 158 n
Woodlawn, county Galway 253
Woodville, county Galway 136–8
Wyndham, George 26–7, 47, 52, 53, 54,
  55, 76
  on IRB 146
  and Irish Office 70–2
  land reform plans 69–74, 72–3, 81–2;
    and UIL 58, 59–60
  on no-rent campaign 93
  seeks improvement 56–7
Wyndham Land Act (1903) 42–84, 95,
  106 n, 116, 121–2, 136, 177, 286, 289,
  292, 303, 304
  assessment of 289–90
  Bills 72–3, 78, 79–80
  effects of 80, 86, 87–92, 119, 131, 295
  historiography of 293–4
  terms of purchase 89
  UIL reaction 74–8, 86, 131
  'zones' system 88–9

Yeats, Jack Butler 1
Young, Joe 206
Young Ireland 18, 43

Printed in the USA/Agawam, MA
May 1, 2024

865346.003